D1072030

Clarence Brown

CLARENCE
BROWN

*Hollywood's
Forgotten
Master*

Gwenda Young

Foreword by Kevin Brownlow

UNIVERSITY PRESS OF KENTUCKY

Copyright © 2018 by The University Press of Kentucky

Scholarly publisher for the Commonwealth,
serving Bellarmine University, Berea College, Centre College of Kentucky, Eastern
Kentucky University, The Filson Historical Society, Georgetown College, Kentucky
Historical Society, Kentucky State University, Morehead State University, Murray State
University, Northern Kentucky University, Transylvania University, University of
Kentucky, University of Louisville, and Western Kentucky University.
All rights reserved.

Editorial and Sales Offices: The University Press of Kentucky
663 South Limestone Street, Lexington, Kentucky 40508-4008
www.kentuckypress.com

Unless otherwise noted, photographs are from the author's collection.

Library of Congress Cataloging-in-Publication Data

Names: Young, Gwenda, author. | Brownlow, Kevin, writer of introduction.
Title: Clarence Brown : Hollywood's forgotten master / Gwenda Young ;
   foreword by Kevin Brownlow.
Description: Lexington, Kentucky : The University Press of Kentucky, [2018] |
   Series: Screen classics | Includes bibliographical references and index.
Identifiers: LCCN 2018014280| ISBN 9780813175959 (hardcover : alk. paper) |
   ISBN 9780813175966 (pdf) | ISBN 9780813175973 (epub)
Subjects: LCSH: Brown, Clarence, 1890–1987. | Motion picture producers and
   directors—United States—Biography.
Classification: LCC PN1998.3.B7599 Y68 2018 | DDC 791.43023/3092—dc23
LC record available at https://lccn.loc.gov/2018014280

This book is printed on acid-free paper meeting the requirements of the American
National Standard for Permanence in Paper for Printed Library Materials.

Manufactured in the United States of America.

Member of the Association of University Presses

To Kevin Brownlow, my esteemed mentor, adviser, and dear friend.
I hope I've done justice to your favorite director.

Contents

Illustrations follow page 208

Foreword

I was an enthusiastic film collector when young (still am). Sixty years ago my collecting had just progressed from the home-movie gauge of 9.5mm to 16mm, a semiprofessional gauge introduced in 1925. By the 1950s, hundreds of silent films had been transferred to 16mm, but the popularity of television soon led the majority of film libraries to close down.

When a film library in Coventry sent me a list of available films, I was amused by a title with a very un-Hollywood ring: *The Goose Woman* (1925). "Who would want a film with a title like that?" I thought. These lists gave little away. They sometimes mentioned the star—if it was Chaplin—but seldom the cast, let alone the director. I considered passing up *The Goose Woman* but then decided to take a risk. The price was a bit steep, but the list did mention a remarkable "all-star cast" that included Louise Dresser as the goose woman, Mary Pickford's brother Jack as her son, and Constance Bennett as his fiancée.

With ex-library prints, one was invariably heartbroken by the ripped footage and badly duped picture quality. But the moment I switched on the projector, I was overwhelmed with delight. For one thing, the print had been taken from the camera negative—the quality was almost stereoscopic—and it had been tinted and toned in the style of the original. The script had been adapted from a story by Rex Beach, a surefire source for remarkable early films such as *The Spoilers* (1914) and *Winds of Chance* (1925).

I sensed that this film would be an exception to the rules of silent-era Hollywood, and so it proved. Imagine an American release from the glamour-obsessed Golden Age that showed the squalid living conditions of a crazy old woman, a former opera star. Made in a period when mother love was sacrosanct, this mother accuses her son of ruining her voice (she insists she lost it when giving birth to him). When he retaliates by blaming her drinking, she says, via a title, "How dare you call me a drunkard?" and slaps him hard across the face.

Brilliantly acted and superbly photographed, the film was directed in a style both subtle and striking. When I'd finished watching it, there seemed no book I could turn to for information about the film or the filmmaker. I felt that if there were any more American silents as good as this one, I'd happily devote my life to finding them.

I decided to write a fan letter to Clarence Brown and sent it in care of the Screen Directors Guild in Hollywood. While this tactic had worked before, I received no reply. (One could only dream of receiving a response.)

A week later, the telephone rang; it was Thomas Quinn Curtiss, theater critic of the Paris-based *New York Herald-Tribune*. "I hear you have found *The Goose Woman*," he said. He asked me to bring it to his suite at the Savoy Hotel, which I did, and we ran it on the wall. He was most impressed and declared that Brown had just arrived in Paris on his annual visit to the Motor Show. Curtiss was obviously testing me on Brown's behalf. Having proved the film's existence, I received a date to meet the great man.

I hauled my heavy 16mm projector to Paris, only to discover, to my embarrassment, that it would not work on the French electrical system. I appealed to Henri Langlois, head of the French Cinémathèque, who agreed that we could watch the film in his theater at Trocadero the following morning. When we arrived, however, we had to wait. The theater was occupied by Roger Vadim, Brigitte Bardot's director and ex-husband. When he finally emerged, I thought Vadim would be thrilled to meet Greta Garbo's director, but he simply shook hands with Brown and departed.

There was no musical accompaniment, which was a pity because the silence led Brown to talk through his film, something I would never have encouraged, as I felt it shattered the mood. Of course, he provided fascinating information; for instance, the picture was based on the real-life Hall-Mills murder case, which had never been solved because the chief prosecution witness, a woman who looked after pigs, kept changing her story.

At one point, a long tracking shot showed the goose woman (and her pet goose) walking along a path in the open country—this was now the heart of Westwood, California, home of UCLA. Brown himself played the murder victim toward the end; he accepted walk-on parts long before Hitchcock.

When the film was over, Brown turned to me with a satisfied grin. "I didn't know I was that good," he said.

Brown may have been a remarkably sensitive director, but he came across as a typical American businessman—at first glance, you'd take him for an oil tycoon. But he was generous; he asked me to lunch at the exclusive Hotel George V, although when he saw my tape recorder, he said he didn't want me to use it. (He must have thought I was from *Confidential* magazine.) I was determined to get a proper interview—as a tribute to his achievements, it was the least I could do. So I ate with one hand while the other held the microphone beneath the tablecloth.

He was quite brusque and unemotional at first, but I realized he was protecting himself from becoming *too* emotional. He clearly loved the art of making pictures. He emphasized how indebted he was to the French émigré director Maurice Tourneur, who had given him his start—"Tourneur was my god," he said. I realized that this collaboration would have made a very poignant film all on its own.

He spoke about the films he had made with Greta Garbo, Joan Crawford, and Pauline Frederick but tended to skip over the major successes like *National Velvet* (1944). Perhaps he was trying to be helpful, for he knew I was primarily interested in the silent era. But I should have encouraged him to talk about such outstanding films as *Ah Wilderness!* (1935) and his masterpiece *Intruder in the Dust* (1949).

I kept in touch with Brown and hunted for more of his films. *The Signal Tower* (1924) had been preserved by a collector in the seaside town of Worthing in East Sussex, England, while I found *Smouldering Fires* (1925) on an ostrich farm in South Africa. Each production seemed to get more and more interesting, even though Brown frankly acknowledged he had made his share of "dogs," such as one with Lon Chaney called *The Light in the Dark* (1922).

Years later, I wanted to make a documentary about Brown. In 1980 my filmmaking partner David Gill and I had completed a television series on silent-era Hollywood that included a few minutes of Brown talking about working with Garbo. I approached an American TV executive, hoping to get the backing for a documentary. I recounted the facts much as you will read them in this book. He sat back with a satisfied sigh, "I love it," he said, to my delight. "That's a fantastic story." And after a pause, he added, with emphasis to ensure I would never bother him again: "But we would *never, ever* make a film like that."

I think they should, and when you've read Gwenda Young's marvelous book, so will you.

Kevin Brownlow
London, January 2018

Preface

"Garbo's Favorite Director" was how obituary writers chose to remember one of the last remaining directors of Hollywood's Golden Age when he died in 1987. He was the "Starmaker," the director that made Garbo "talk"; he put a violet-eyed English girl on the path to stardom, gave Joan Crawford and Mickey Rooney their greatest successes, introduced new discoveries, and revived the careers of fading stars.

He was the man who, for five decades, gave audiences nostalgic tales of life on the frontier, heartwarming slices of Americana, closely observed portraits of families and of communities; and he offered one of the most searing exposés of racial prejudice in the Deep South.

His work seemed to prove wrong the adage "Never work with children or animals."

His was a cinema of sentiment in which "the sternest of realities" were tempered by "soft poetic glimpses" (Jim Tully).

"He wanted his craftsmanship and his direction to speak for itself. And they did" (Margaret Booth).

He was Clarence Brown.

A Brown Boy

It is often said that in order to understand the man, one must look to the child. Though he lived most of his life in California and spent five decades in the film industry, Clarence Brown never forgot that he came from humble stock, a child of a southerner and an Irish immigrant. Larkin and Catherine Brown were weavers of textiles, demonstrating both technical skills and creativity, and they raised a boy who would become a weaver of another sort: of dreams. At the 1977 Directors Guild of America ceremony to honor Brown's long career, Katharine Hepburn, who had worked with him on *Song of Love* thirty years before, noted that he was a man driven by two impulses: "by nature highly romantic, by education an engineer."[1] In that short description she identified the contradictions that defined Brown: celebrated as a maker of stars who mingled in the most glamorous social circles and counted Garbo, Valentino, and Gable as close friends, he was a private man, not especially sophisticated or ostentatious in his wealth. The riches he accumulated were achieved through hard work and the shrewd business acumen acquired from his parents and from generations of their clans working in the milling industries of Ireland and America.

Even though they were raised on different sides of the Atlantic Ocean, Catherine and Larkin shared surprisingly similar backgrounds. Her family—the Gaws—originated in one of Ireland's most picturesque regions, the Ards Peninsula in County Down in the north. Flanked by the imposing Strangford Lough and dotted with pretty villages and a smattering of small islands, Ards boasts its own rich and complicated history: visited by early Christians in the sixth century and by Vikings in the ninth century, it was settled by the Anglo-Normans in the twelfth century. The seventeenth century saw a large-scale though unofficial "plantation" by Presbyterian Scots. By the nineteenth century, the population was mixed, and the once native stock of Catholics had become greatly outnumbered by Protestants (mainly Presbyterians). Like much of Ulster, communities maintained distinct identities, and instances of sectarian and political tension were not uncommon. The lough was (and still is) at the heart of life on the peninsula, and this was especially true in the years when the Gaw clan inhabited its environs, settling in towns and villages such as Portaferry, Newtownards, and Greyabbey and taking up jobs in the textile mills, maintaining smallholdings, or fishing and collecting kelp from the shores. Because the narrow roads were susceptible to tidal flooding, the lough was used to move goods to Newtownards and from there to the hub of Belfast, where its massive shipping industry opened up links to the world.

Brown's maternal grandparents, Alice and Hugh, established themselves in Greyabbey, a village dominated by the ruins of a twelfth-century Cistercian monastery and surrounded by thriving textile mills. It was at one of these mills that Hugh found work as a weaver, and in 1865 the family expanded when Alice gave birth to a daughter, Catherine.[2] The Gaws belonged to the Presbyterian majority: hardworking, taciturn men and women who despised ostentatious displays of wealth and bore a streak of nonconformism. Despite their impressive work ethic, Hugh and Alice must have struggled to maintain a good standard of living, especially as their employers faced increasing competition from the larger textile producers in Belfast. As soon as their daughter came of age, she looked to America for a more prosperous future. It is probable that the family already had some connections stateside: there existed a strong tradition of immigration by the Scots-Irish to the eastern and southern United States, especially along the Appalachians, which stretch from Alabama to Canada. Based on the 1900 census, it seems that Catherine left Belfast around 1882 and made her way to Boston. Perhaps she was met by relatives who helped her secure a job in the New England mills—at least one account suggests that before her marriage she was employed as a weaver. Because no record of that part of her life remains, one must piece it together with some degree of conjecture. Brown's papers at the University of Tennessee at Knoxville contain little about his parents' early life; there are no anecdotes about their first encounter or the courtship that led to a marriage spanning five decades. We may never know how their romance began, but there seems little doubt that when Catherine fell for Larkin Brown, he was a slightly younger, dynamic go-getter already working his way up in the textile industry.

Though he always viewed himself as a son of the South, Larkin was actually born in Pennsylvania, to a family of southerners that had been temporarily displaced by the Civil War. His grandfather (also named Larkin) was a farmer in Georgia who sired five children, including John, born in 1835. In time, John married Mary White, and the newlyweds settled in Roswell in Cobb County, Georgia, where John found work as an operator and later an

2

overseer at Roswell Mills, an important cotton-processing facility that was later burned down by Union soldiers in 1864. With the onslaught of the Civil War, John and his bride were forced to relocate to the safer environs of Delaware County in Pennsylvania. Once there, he took a position at a mill and welcomed the newest addition to his family, a son, Larkin, born in 1866. The family may have been safer in Pennsylvania (where they stayed for several years after the war ended), but John and Mary yearned for the South and eventually returned in the late 1870s, accompanied by a brood that now comprised three sons and three daughters. John became a "boss weaver" at Huguley's Mill in Chambers, Alabama, alongside his now fourteen-year-old son Larkin, and he apparently spent his remaining work life there.[3] In retirement, John and Mary moved back to Atlanta, where they rented a house first on Bartow Street (1900 census) and then on Pearl Street; whatever income they had came from taking in lodgers. Larkin, did not accompany his parents on their final move. Instead, he headed north and probably met Catherine when both were employed at mills in Massachusetts. Together or separately, Catherine and Larkin found their way to Clinton, a town in Worcester County that had a considerable Irish population (albeit mostly from the south rather than the north of Ireland). Mark Twain had visited the town in the 1860s and had been dismayed at the lodgings there: "Here I am in a hotel—the Clinton House— and a villainous one it is—shabby bed, shabby room, shabby furniture, dim lights—everything shabby and disagreeable."[4] By the end of the nineteenth century, however, Clinton had evolved into a more pleasant place, mainly due to the flourishing mills that dotted its periphery, fed by the powerful Nashua River. The largest of these was Lancaster Mills, which turned out reams of gingham and other textiles; by the 1880s, it was run as a progressive company that "looked after" its workers. Larkin took a job there and married Catherine on July 29, 1889. The couple moved into a company-owned house at 8 Grove Street, where their only child, Clarence Leon, was born on May 10, 1890.

On Clarence's birth certificate, Larkin's occupation is listed as a "loom fixer," but in the years that followed he carved out a successful career, advancing into supervisory roles at the mill. Though they never became wealthy, the family led a comfortable life in a community that was quintessentially close-knit and "small town." The Brown house was just a few minutes' walk from the school on Pleasant Street, where Clarence was taught reading and writing by Miss Celia Carlisle Ferguson. His closest friend was another Clarence, Clarence Grady, whose family lived just across the street; Grady's father was also a mill worker. The two boys developed a strong bond that endured even after the Browns left Clinton in 1897. The family's relocation was prompted by Larkin's new position as a supervisor in a mill in nearby Grafton, Massachusetts. Their new hometown was not so different from their old one: both had predominantly white populations, and both boasted historic buildings, town commons, and mills on the outskirts. Although this period of his life lasted just over a decade, growing up in small towns undoubtedly made an impression on Brown, contributing to his nostalgic and sometimes sentimental view of the American heartland. In the years that followed, he would be celebrated for his work with glamorous stars, but Brown himself regarded his more "intimate" films such as *Ah Wilderness!* (shot in Grafton in 1935), *Of Human Hearts*, and *The Human Comedy*, in which he honored the lives of ordinary families and small towns, as his best work.

A slow-paced New England childhood shaped Brown's affectionate view of small-town life, but spending his teenage years in the South introduced him to the excitement, as well as the complexities, of life in a vibrant metropolis. When the Browns moved to Knoxville, Tennessee, sometime around 1902, it was a bustling hub of industry set against a backdrop of the picturesque Great Smoky Mountains and a rich Appalachian culture that blended Scots-Irish, English, and German–eastern European influences. Knoxville was something of an oddity among southern cities, not least because it had been split in its support for both sides during the Civil War. One historian labeled it the "Great Gatsby of American cities," chiefly because of its apparent ability to continually reinvent itself.[5] In the post–Civil War era, Knoxville led the mission to modernize and create a "New South." In the space of forty years, the city became one of the most important wholesale centers, third only to New Orleans and Atlanta. Its postwar surge was attributable mainly to the nurturing of a vibrant manufacturing sector that was well served by an excellent railroad network linking North and South. With 30 percent of the city's population employed in milling and manufacturing (flour, garments and textiles, and iron), Knoxville's reputation as a booming city where an ambitious man could find new opportunities no doubt prompted Larkin to move his family there. He was hired as an assistant supervisor at Brookside Mills, which employed close to 1,200 people and supplied garments to leading stores such as Sears.[6] Founded in 1885 as a "progressive" employer committed to dispelling the bad reputation of many textile plants, Brookside Mills provided its workers with access to medical care, social clubs, and a well-run kindergarten on Le Roy Street.[7]

Knoxville prospered in the years the Browns called it home, but there were less pleasant aspects to the city as well. The heavy industries located relatively close to the downtown area ensured that smog was a constant problem.

Writing in *Fortune* magazine in 1935, novelist James Agee recalled the "sooty Gay Street" and "smudgy Union Square" of his childhood.[8] The busy district along Central Avenue, with its saloons and brothels, also saw its fair share of violent skirmishes and homicides, at least until the city went "dry" in 1907. As the population expanded to around 35,000, the sanitation system was stressed, and the need for housing resulted in an expansion of the city's boundaries—out toward Fort Sanders for middle-class residents, and the East Scott–Oklahoma Avenue district for working-class citizens. Knoxville's reputation for interracial relations was better than that of many southern cities, and it even accommodated a growing black middle class. Nevertheless, racial tensions continued to simmer (in 1919, long after Clarence had left, the city experienced serious race riots). It is difficult to say how much young Clarence was exposed to racial conflict and disreputable behavior in Knoxville, but as an adored only child guided by parents who were teetotalers and churchgoers, one can assume he led a fairly sheltered existence. He recalled his childhood in Knoxville as a time of routine and contentment punctuated by Sunday outings to the Great Smoky Mountains and visits to relatives in Georgia.

Larkin worked hard to better himself and his family's circumstances, and the houses they occupied in these early years provide clues to their improving economic status: in 1903 they were living in North Knoxville and renting houses, first at 206 East Anderson Avenue and then at nearby East Baxter Street, both in working-class neighborhoods. In 1906 the city directory lists the family as residing at 113 West Scott Avenue (a better neighborhood), and Larkin's occupation is recorded as "assistant supervisor." By the following year, the family had moved to a firmly middle-class Arts and Crafts–style house on East Scott Avenue (still known as the "Clarence Brown house"). All these changes in address indicate a certain restlessness and an aspiration to move up the social ladder, but they also reveal that the industrious Larkin stayed close to his workplace (all his residences were within ten minutes' walking distance). For Clarence, living in North Knoxville was less convenient, as it meant a half-hour walk to his school on Walnut Street in the downtown district; most likely he rode the new electric streetcar to school each day. This no doubt appealed to young Clarence, who was already showing signs of a lifelong obsession with machines and technology, including the new-fangled cars that were beginning to show up on Knoxville streets. Larkin encouraged his son's interest, often bringing him to the mill to show him the machines and give him a tour of its impressive 152-foot smokestack. Brown would later write a dissertation about the facility, outlining how modifications of certain machines could enhance efficiency and yield higher output.

At Knoxville High School his classmates remembered "Brownie" as diminutive in stature—"a regular little runt. We just babied him to death—he was just like a little mascot."[9] What he lacked in physical presence, however, he made up for in brimming self-confidence. Although they instilled in their son a respect for authority and plain labor, Larkin and Catherine also indulged all his hobbies and ventures, constantly assuring him that he was the brightest and the best. And in many ways, he was. Already adept at fixing machines, when he turned his hand to performing, he became his drama teacher's star pupil. He delivered the graduation speech for his high school class and then enrolled at the University of Tennessee at the tender age of fifteen. Before age twenty, he had earned a double degree in engineering and set up his own business. When Katharine Hepburn noted in 1977 that Brown seemed to have a dual nature—two sides that were apparently contradictory yet in perfect union—she identified the traits that often make up a natural filmmaker. Like Buster Keaton and Allan Dwan, Brown loved technology; he understood how machines worked and brought this knowledge to the set. But he also strongly identified with creativity and performing, and it was this trait that helped him coach the most sensitive and insecure of Hollywood actors.

Those who knew Brown the film director as a brusque and sometimes harsh taskmaster may have been surprised to learn that his first "career" was as a child performer under the tutelage of Miss Laura Tidd Fogelsong. Though the adult Brown was reticent, the polar opposite of flamboyant or "actorly," it seems he was sentimental enough to hold on to a few mementos from his early years as a juvenile performer. Preserved in his archive is an advertising flyer featuring elaborate script and accompanied by a photograph of a serious-looking boy dressed in a silk and velvet shirt, leggings, and boots. The brochure promotes "Master Clarence Leon Brown, Juvenile Entertainer, Dramatic Reader." Miss Fogelsong assures the reader that her pupil is a "juvenile entertainer excelled by none. . . . He is a handsome child with a most charming appearance and personality, and with culture combined with natural magnetic force he easily captivates an audience of thousands. . . . He moves his audience to tears and laughter at will." It seems that Miss Fogelsong was not the only one enraptured by Brown's skills, which won the praise of some of Knoxville's most respectable citizens, including Mr. J. R. Frazier, listed as a chaplain with the US Navy, and Pastor W. A. Atchley of Knoxville's Broadway Baptist Church. If nothing else, the flyer reveals that even as a child Brown had a sharp business mind and had already ventured further afield, including a recent appearance at Atlanta's Grand Opera House.

When Brown graduated from high school and embarked on a taxing double degree in engineering, he did not leave amateur dramatics and music behind. He joined some of the theatrical clubs at the University of Tennessee, as well as dabbling in debating as a member of the Philomathesian Literary Society. Though generally affecting a serious air, it seems that he had a mischievous side too. He revealed to Charlie Brakebill (his link at the university's alumni foundation) that he and his mother often played pranks on each other, and as a college freshman he once greased the tracks on Cumberland Avenue so the tram could not make it up the steep incline. Increasingly, however, he was too occupied with his studies to devote much time to practical jokes or amateur theatrics. Having enrolled in the university at age fifteen, he may have struggled to keep up with the intellectual and social demands of campus life. Taking an extra year to complete his degree, he graduated in 1909 after writing a dissertation, under the supervision of Professor J. A. Switzer, titled "Economy and Power Distribution Test of Plant No. 2, Brookside Mills." Research for the dissertation entailed extensive fieldwork at the mill to determine how energy-saving initiatives and efficiency models might be adopted (there is no record of whether his proposals were ever implemented). While testing and monitoring furnaces at Brookside and meticulously recording his findings in logbooks, however, Brown also found time to stoke a little romance. Screenwriter Frederica Sagor Maas, who knew Brown in the 1920s, remembered him as a shrewd businessman whose marriage to his second wife, the well-connected Ona Wilson, may have had more to do with his career ambitions than love. It seems that young Clarence fell hard for Elizabeth Ayres, his first girlfriend in Knoxville, sweeping her off her feet with recitations of poetry and eloquent letters. Intriguingly, though, the shy girl that Clarence chose to court just happened to be the daughter of the university's president, Brown Ayres.

The Master's Apprentice

Larkin Brown may have hoped his clever son would follow him into textile processing, but Clarence had his heart set on gaining a foothold in the burgeoning automobile industry. Armed with his double degree in engineering and a practical knowledge of machines, he left Knoxville to look for employment. After a stint working for the Moline Auto Company in Illinois, he took a job at the Stevens-Duryea Company in Chicopee Falls, Massachusetts. The following year, with the help of a benefactor that recognized his potential, twenty-two-year-old Brown set up his own dealership, the Brown Motor Car Company, in Birmingham, Alabama.[1] In a 1928 profile, Brown recalled that during this period he was earning a very comfortable salary of $6,500 a year, and his future looked bright.[2]

With new stability in his professional life, Brown may have thought it was time to settle down and create the kind of happy home life his parents enjoyed. Having left Elizabeth Ayres behind in Tennessee, Brown evidently thought he had met a suitable partner when he wooed Paula Herndon Pratt, a young Florida woman of Tennessee extraction, in the spring of 1913. Details of the courtship and subsequent marriage remain sketchy: in later interviews, Brown rarely referred to his first wife (the mother of his only child), and he sometimes failed to mention his first marriage when speaking with the press (usually upon the occasion of his latest marriage or divorce). Yet marry Paula he did, and an announcement was printed in the *Washington Post* on May 13, 1913. Over five decades of marriage, Larkin and Catherine weathered various tribulations and remained devoted to each other until his death in 1942. Their son, however, quickly realized that his marriage was a mistake.

It was perhaps personal frustration that prompted Brown to seek fresh challenges in his career. In a step that must have bewildered his conservative parents and his new wife, he resolved to break into the film industry, which at the time was still viewed as a somewhat disreputable and certainly precarious occupation. It was all rather surprising, because in contrast to his fellow Knoxvillian James

Agee, Brown admitted to having few memories of a childhood "lost at the movies" at the Majestic Theater on Gay Street. Only while running his car dealership in Birmingham did he come across the "shooting galleries" (cinemas) and fall "under the spell of the screen."[3] He fell hard and was particularly taken by the work of émigré filmmakers such as Maurice Tourneur, Émile Chautard, and Albert Capellani, all of whom were based in Fort Lee, New Jersey.

According to most accounts, Brown traveled north in around 1915 (presumably with Paula in tow) with the firm intention of getting hired by one of the directors he so admired. However, he may have been hatching his plan to enter the film industry for some time. Leatrice Gilbert Fountain, the daughter of John Gilbert, has offered an intriguing account of a "Brown sighting" in New Orleans in around 1913. Her mother, actress Leatrice Joy (while working under her real name, Leatrice Zeidler), had a curious encounter with someone who would later play a significant part in her life. While sitting with director René Plaissetty in an office at the NOLA studios, they were interrupted by a very enthusiastic young man. According to Fountain:

> A young man appeared and asked for a job as an actor. There was no need for one at the moment, but the boy persisted and asked if he could recite a poem. The director looked at Leatrice and she nodded, so he was told to get on with it. He began a wild recitation, arms waving, eyes rolling, about "Jacques, the Sailor," a brave lad who went through endless torments and persecution at the hands of his cruel ships' officers, defended them all against pirates and finally fell dead on the deck of his ship. At which point the boy hurled himself down on the floor and remained there in total absorption of his role. Plesetti [sic] and Leatrice waited anxiously but he never moved. Somewhat alarmed they touched him but he remained thoroughly dead. Finally they tiptoed out of the office. The next time Leatrice saw him it was a year later, he was assisting Maurice Tourneur at Fort Lee, New Jersey and his name was Clarence Brown. They never discussed his dramatic audition.[4]

This recollection may be unreliable in terms of date—1913 seems too early, given that NOLA was formed in 1915 and Plaissetty's credits date from that year—but it is plausible that Brown auditioned at the studio while he was based in Alabama. It must have seemed like a logical step for someone so determined to enter the film industry, and he might have assumed that his background as a juvenile entertainer gave him some leverage. The fact that his dramatic performance left both Joy and Plaissetty unimpressed, however, perhaps served as an epiphany of sorts, and Brown realized that if he were going to make it in the film industry, it would not be as an actor. Instead, he would gain entry in a much less showy fashion, by impressing a key figure with his knowledge of machines and his willingness to work hard for a modest wage.

Renting an apartment in Upper Manhattan (Harlem) at 515 West 122nd Street, Brown set out to make contacts in the industry in Manhattan and further afield, in Fort Lee, New Jersey. Today, "Fort Lee" doesn't have the same cachet as "Hollywood," but in the 1910s, the New Jersey town was a significant production center with a distinct Continental feel. French companies Champion and Éclair were the first to establish studios there, soon followed by Universal, Peerless, and Solax. They brought an array of foreign-born talent that would, in turn, help create the American silent film style. Fort Lee wasn't for everyone—art director Ben Carré remembered that it was still very much a rural outpost even in 1914—but those willing to put up with the poor infrastructure were rewarded with fresh locations and the freedom to shoot without fear of bumping into rival companies or members of the dreaded "Trust" (those producers intent on maintaining a monopoly over film production).[5] At Fort Lee's creative heart was Maurice Tourneur, arguably the most prestigious of all the directors working there and the man who would go on to shape Brown both professionally and personally.

In later years, Brown's account of their initial meeting varied, from a chance encounter in a Maine woods where Tourneur was shooting a film called *The Cub* to a planned appointment facilitated by mutual friends.[6] However, the version he tended to repeat most often, and the one that is likely nearest the truth, confirms Brown as an ambitious go-getter. Crossing over to New Jersey on the ferry, he overheard some men discussing Tourneur's search for a new assistant and, sensing an opportunity, sought out the director. He made a potentially unforgivable faux pas when he interrupted the master as he was shooting an exterior, but somewhat surprisingly, the notoriously short-tempered Tourneur merely banished him to the sidelines until he wrapped up the day's shoot. When given a chance to explain himself, Brown convinced Tourneur to take him on *despite* his lack of experience, arguing that if his previous assistant, who had been hired from another studio, hadn't worked out, maybe a "young, fresh brain that knows nothing about the business" would.[7] Something about Brown appealed to Tourneur, and he hired him at the modest salary of $35 a week.[8] Brown proved to be an apt pupil: within a matter of weeks, he was juggling roles as props man, title writer, editor, and second-unit director.

Tourneur's uncharacteristic patience with the rash Brown may have been attributable to his own experience working for some harsh taskmasters. The son of a jeweler with a dangerous taste for absinthe, Maurice Thomas was born in 1876 in Paris, in a district known as Épinettes.[9] After attending the Lycée Condorcet on the Rue Amsterdam, he worked as a painter, illustrator, and designer before taking up apprenticeships under sculptor Rodin and muralist Pierre Puvis de Chavannes. At the turn of the century Tourneur moved to the theater, acting in small parts and serving as stage director for legendary actress Gabrielle Réjane, with whom he toured South America in 1902. Returning to Paris, he became stage manager at the Théâtre Antoine on the Boulevard de Strasbourg, home of the Théâtre Libre movement and of its founder, André Antoine. The ambitious young manager, already quite the ladies' man, developed a passion for one of the theater's stars, Fernande Petit (who acted under the name Van Doren), and it seems the affection was mutual: the two married in February 1904 and their son, Jacques, was born the following November.

According to his biographer Christine Leteux, Maurice Tourneur initially enjoyed a close relationship with his mentor André Antoine, but they fell out over "artistic differences" in 1909. Thereafter, Tourneur drifted a little, spending some time working in theater and in a casino in the South of France before transitioning to films in 1912 and acquiring a new mentor, Émile Chautard of Éclair studios. The studio was a significant player in the flourishing French film industry of the 1910s, with a prolific and eclectic output. Tourneur would have found plenty to keep him busy, and Chautard was evidently impressed enough with his work to quickly promote him to director. Tourneur cut his teeth on a range of film genres that included comedies, crime capers, and horrors, all released just as the first signs of war appeared on the horizon. When he was offered the chance to run Peerless, a new division of Éclair studios based in Fort Lee, he seized it. Though Tourneur would later be celebrated (by himself, among others) as an artist who never "fit in" with the crass Hollywood film industry, it seems he was quite the pragmatist in these early years. He knew the war would decimate the French film industry, and he sensed that a more lucrative and artistically rewarding career might be had outside of Europe. France, however, never forgave him: when his American career floundered in the 1920s, Tourneur returned home to face accusations that he had intentionally avoided military service (technically true, but somewhat unfair, given that he had spent three years in the military during the 1890s and had moved to New York months before the assassination of Archduke Franz Ferdinand in June 1914).[10]

If Tourneur felt any guilt about avoiding wartime service, he scarcely had time to indulge it. In his first year at Fort Lee he directed *Mother*, *The Man of the Hour, The Pit* (based on a novel by Frank Norris), and *The Wishing Ring.* Of these, only *The Wishing Ring* and fragments of *The Man of the Hour* survive, but both demonstrate Tourneur's innovative handling of mise-en-scène. *The Wishing Ring,* directed a mere six months after his arrival in America, shows the confidence of a master in its delicate composition, witty treatment of plot and character, and virtuoso tracking shot to capture the final scene of a wedding breakfast. Although Brown never mentioned *The Wishing Ring* as a film that impressed him, he most likely saw it and absorbed it as an influence: Tourneur's tracking shot is a veritable template for the even showier ones used by Brown in *The Eagle* (1926) and *Anna Karenina* (1935). *The Wishing Ring* attracted considerable attention upon its release, with one critic rhapsodizing that "the whole atmosphere of the tale is light and as graceful as a minuet and colored with the nicety of a pastel."[11] The following year Tourneur wowed audiences again with his version of the Paul Armstrong drama *Alias Jimmy Valentine*, a caper about a suave thief. He had directed it on the French stage a few years before, but now he embraced the new medium's potential, using authentic locations, which included some exteriors shot at Sing Sing prison, designing an exquisitely expressive lighting scheme for interiors, and keeping the story moving with some fast-paced editing.[12] *Alias Jimmy Valentine* was shot just before Brown joined Tourneur's company, but he was certainly familiar with the film and drew from it when shooting his own directorial debut, a prison drama called *The Great Redeemer*, and again for a scene in one of the final films of his career, *When in Rome.*

The early years of his American career were Tourneur's heyday. He was happy because he enjoyed relative autonomy in an industry in which the director was still considered the boss. Unlike his apprentice, who would mainly keep a low profile and avoid lofty claims to art, Tourneur was eager to promote himself as an auteur, often regaling the press with his opinions on cinema. Writing in *Harper's Weekly* in 1916, he argued that critics should take films seriously and acknowledge their power to move audiences.[13] This emphasis on film as an art form was reiterated in numerous articles attributed to Tourneur, such as his piece in *Vanity Fair* in 1919: "The functions of the motion picture director and of the master of the ballet have much in common. Each, to tell his story, must enlist the sympathetic co-operation of human beings quickly sensitive to the emotions to be aroused and more keenly interested in being a sentient part of a perfect whole than in personal aggrandizement. Each must make his appeal to his public through their sense of beauty of grace, of line of rhythm and tempo, and each must know when harmony must be struck across with discord."[14] Clearly, Tourneur took himself very seriously, but so did the critics who wrote of his work. In one profile published in the *Brooklyn Eagle*, Tourneur is described as "a master of illusion, of atmosphere, of otherwise dreams and fantasies, and his ambition is to make the screen as expressive of the finest and subtlest thought and emotion as great music, inspired poetry and lyric prose. His successes in making picture players enter into the spirit of symbolism and evocation has made some call him the Svengali of the films."[15] So highly was Tourneur esteemed that Harrison Haskins ranked him on a par with D. W. Griffith, Thomas Ince, and Cecil B. DeMille in a 1918 article, noting that he was a "man who apparently combines the eye of a painter with something of the dramatic sense of a Reinhardt."[16]

Brown was fortunate indeed to be taken on by Tourneur just as the director's star was ascending and American filmmaking was experiencing a period of intense innovation. When he joined the company in 1915, Brown became the rookie on an extraordinarily gifted team that included Dutch-born cameraman John van den Broek and French art director Ben Carré. The trio of Carré, Tourneur, and van den Broek was already pioneering a striking and dynamic use of mise-en-scène, one that emphasized deep space composition, atmospheric lighting inspired by the Dutch masters, dark foregrounds, and mobile camera work.[17] The seven years that Brown spent with Tourneur proved crucial: he honed his skills as an editor, developed a firm understanding of the power of distinctive visual aesthetics, and grew to understand the delicacy with which actors should be handled. These lessons would hold him in good stead during his directing career, and his ability to balance artistry with commerce—arguably something that Tourneur proved unable to do—ensured that he would remain at the top for five decades.

It is interesting that Brown's first credited work with Tourneur was on *The Cub*, given that its story of romance and feuding is set in rural Virginia, not far from Brown's own eastern Tennessee past. It was a star vehicle for the popular comedy actor Johnny Hines, who plays a cub reporter sent to discover the cause of a famous feud between two warring families. He soon becomes embroiled in their lives, mainly because of his romantic interest in the daughter of one of the clans, and much of the humor arises from his character's "fish out of water" experiences in the rough-and-ready world of the Virginia hillbillies. The comedy is broad in style but rather endearing; however, the film's aesthetics are perhaps of most interest. From the sidelines, Brown would have observed how Tourneur and van den Broek poured their energies into creating a striking look, using silhouettes and dark foregrounds, soft lighting to create the effect of sun-dappled landscapes, and even a startling point-of-view shot from the barrel of a gun. *The Cub* was released in July 1915 to positive reviews that praised Hines's performance and the "truly thrilling" climax of the film.[18] By that time, Tourneur had moved on to his next production, and as a mark of trust in his protégé, he promoted Brown to assistant director and editor on it.[19]

In an interview in 1969, Brown remembered that he "cut his teeth" on *Trilby*.[20] An adaptation of the George du Maurier novel and successful play from the 1890s, *Trilby* was the pet project of Lewis Selznick (father of David), who was intent on advancing the career of Clara Kimball Young, whom he had just lured from rival studio Vitagraph. The story of the mesmerist and the model was set in Paris's Left Bank, a district Tourneur knew very well and set about re-creating in Fort Lee. Designer Ben Carré modeled the sets on real ateliers and added authentic atmosphere by hiring students from a New York art school as extras.[21] Even though the stage origins are evident in the theatrical performance delivered by Wilton Lackaye as Svengali and in the preponderance of interiors and rather static camera work, there are glimpses of the low-key lighting and dark foregrounds that were rapidly becoming the director's trademark. Of interest, too, is Clara Kimball Young, who was already a significant star at the time and shows considerable charm in her performance as a bohemian cross-dressing muse. Noting the film's similarities with Young's real life as a woman torn between an obsessed mentor (Selznick) and a jealous husband (James Young), Tourneur even went so far as to include a wry in-joke: a close-up of Svengali's calling card reveals his middle name to be "Belznick." Brown, the novice assistant, took it all in—the jockeying for power, the cossetting of the stars, the balancing of commercial appeal and artistic creativity—and when the shoot wrapped he went all out to impress his mentor with his self-taught editing skills. To judge the right tempo, he drew on his engineering background and happily discovered that he "took to cutting like a duck to water; timing meant a great deal to me, having been an engineer. . . . Tempo is one of the most elusive things, but when you get it right there's nothing greater."[22]

Brown was kept busy: the American Film Institute catalog lists him as the assistant director and editor on seven Tourneur films released in the space of just twelve months: *The Ivory Snuff Box*, *A Butterfly on the Wheel*, *The Closed Road*, *The Hand of Peril*, *The Rail Rider*, *The Velvet Claw*, and the George Beban vehicle *The Pawn of Fate*. Regrettably, with the exception of a fragment of *The Closed Road*, these films have apparently been lost. The rapid pace of production continued into 1917, with Tourneur relying more and more on Brown to fulfill a number of duties. Of all their film projects during this period, one of the more enjoyable was *A Girl's Folly*, an early satire on the movie industry that was shot at Fort Lee and starred Doris Kenyon and Robert Warwick, with cameos by Tourneur, his old boss Émile Chautard, and rising starlet Leatrice Joy. Perhaps not surprisingly, given Tourneur's reputation for cynicism, the script he cowrote with Frances Marion (who would go on to work with Brown on *Anna Christie*) made some sharp observations about the fickleness of fame and the superficiality of the industry. The film also introduced Brown to Robert Warwick, who was a leading man at the time but would eventually settle in to a comfortable niche as a character actor, appearing in Brown's *Anna Karenina* in 1935. Working with the good-humored and pragmatic Warwick was a pleasant experience, and Brown retained fond memories of him and, indeed, of all the character actors he had directed over the decades. His apprenticeship also exposed him to the challenges of handling major stars and dealing with a range of behaviors that included tantrums and tears, preening and delusions, volatility and indifference, and shrewd manipulation. Because Tourneur could be impatient and cutting with his actors, Brown often had to play the role of mediator between the director and whatever frustrated or distraught player was in his firing line.

Brown may have helped calm relations between his boss and one of the most important stars he ever worked with: Mary Pickford. Tourneur had signed on to direct two vehicles for her in 1916, *The Pride of the Clan* and *Poor Little Rich Girl*, both significant films that contributed to the fine-tuning of her star persona. It should be noted that there are conflicting accounts of Brown's involvement in these productions: in historian Anthony Slide's overview of American silent films, he lists M. N. Litson, not Brown, as Tourneur's assistant;[23] however, cameraman Charles van Enger clearly recalled that Brown was present on both sets. In fact, *Pride of the Clan* was van Enger's first experience on a film set (he had previously worked in the Paragon studio lab), and he claimed he owed it all to Brown: "I did an awful lot of work for him, I helped him out, and finally I was getting $100 a week and I asked him if he could get me a job as an assistant cameraman for $20—twenty a week, with Maurice Tourneur and John van den Broek, and that's where I started on *The Pride of the Clan*."[24]

The film features Pickford as Marget MacTavish, a feisty Scottish lass who is the life force of her small fishing community. After her father drowns, she takes charge of the village and becomes the chieftain of her clan. She also finds time to develop a romance with a fisherman named Jamie (played by Matt Moore, Pickford's real-life brother-in-law), who, it turns out, is the son of an aristocrat. Fort Lee was used for the interiors, but some of the exteriors were shot by John van den Broek and Lucien Andriot at Marblehead, Massachusetts, in November 1916. Poor weather conditions, as well as the powerful airplane engines used to simulate a dramatic storm, nearly cost the production its set and its star, when a boat carrying Pickford capsized.[25] Despite the difficult shoot and some disappointing reviews, *Pride of the Clan* is a film of some beauty, showcasing Pickford's talents and Tourneur's trademark dark foregrounds, deep space, and atmospheric lighting that recalls Rembrandt and anticipates Murnau's evocation of rural life in *Sunrise*, made a decade later.

More successful, but even more volatile, was the Tourneur-Pickford collaboration on *Poor Little Rich Girl*. Based on Eleanor Gates's popular play, it is about a girl who is rich in material possessions but poor in parental love. A good corset and an impish air helped the twenty-four-year-old Pickford play an eleven-year-old, and Carré's innovative sets did the rest. The ever-inventive van den Broek contributed to the realization of this child's world, creating a surreal dream sequence in which a feverish Gwendolyn imagines the adults of her conscious life as manifestations of their vices: her social-climber mother is pictured with a real "bee in her bonnet"; a duplicitous housekeeper is shown with a revolving head that has two faces; another servant is transformed into a weird snake-woman creature, living up to her reputation as a "snake in the grass"; and so on.

Artistically, *Poor Little Rich Girl* was a rewarding experience for Brown, but it also opened his eyes to the power wielded by major stars like Pickford. Though never regarded as "difficult," she was acutely conscious of her image and of her audience's expectations, and this led to a number of clashes with her director over the interpretation of Gwendolyn. Eleanor Gates's creation was an ethereal, saccharine character, but Pickford knew her devoted fans expected her to play the typical "hoyden," so she asked screenwriter Marion to come up with an extra scene in which Gwendolyn enthusiastically participates in a mud fight. It was intended to show the poor little rich girl as a down-to-earth American kid, but for the refined Tourneur, it was too much; it converted the scene into "une horreur."[26] In her autobiography, Marion gleefully recalled that the females "ganged up on poor serious Mr. Tourneur and either sweet-talked or fast-talked him into letting us include some wild comedy scenes which were not in the play or the script. These could have been called spontaneous combustions, and Mr. Tourneur went home many a night with an aching head."[27] Perhaps. According to Gary Carey, however, Brown told him a different story about the clash of egos between star and director, which may have expressed an unrealized attraction between them: "while Mary and Tourneur had their differences on the set, they were friendly after hours, too much so for Zukor [her boss] and Charlotte's [her mother's] liking. To put an end to the friendship, they exiled Mary to California."[28] Whatever the truth, Mary won the power struggle on the set and was vindicated in her belief that audiences wanted broad comedy: those were the scenes that won over audiences and critics when the film was released in March 1917.

The clash between Tourneur and Pickford was actually more significant than a routine dispute on a soon-to-be-wrapped film: hers was an overt challenge to the director's authority and a demonstration that she made the decisions on content. As such, it was symptomatic of a changing power dynamic creeping through the industry. For Tourneur, the director commanded complete respect on set, with the actors contributing to his overall vision, as he elaborated in a profile credited to him shortly after *Poor Little Rich Girl* was released: "I mean that I have certain elements to work with—actors, sets, furniture. I move them around as I need them. I am very impulsive. I speak abruptly, often impatiently . . . I may speak to a star as severely as I do to an electrician, or impersonally as I push back a chair, or move a vase. Not because I do not respect the artist, but simply because he is the only one of the elements with which I can get the effects."[29]

Being treated as if she were a piece of the furniture would not have been appreciated by Pickford, and her reaction would have been noted by Brown, who adopted a very different approach when he directed major stars such as Garbo, Crawford, and Gable. During his long career, Brown generally "played the game" when dealing with demanding actors, preferring to express his irritation in private. In contrast, Tourneur made little effort to hide his impatience and even went so far as to attack stars' egos—and specifically Pickford's—in the press. He put his name to an article for the highbrow journal *Shadowland* in which he sneered at the types of characters he had to accommodate in his creative vision: "[the] cute, curly-headed, sun-bonneted, smiling and pouting ingénue . . . [who] runs thru beautiful gardens (always with the same nice back-lighting effects). . . . Torn between the sheer idiocy of the hero and the inexplicable hate of the heavy, is it any wonder that her sole communion is with the dear dumb animals, pigs, cows, ducks, goats—anything so long as it can't talk." Pickford's reaction, if any, was not recorded.[30]

The pressure to please Tourneur, to continually prove himself, resulted in moments of both elation and misery for Brown, and it gradually took a toll on his private life. His marriage to Paula was already shaky, and the arrival of their daughter, Adrienne, on January 23, 1917, did little to cement the relationship. Perhaps running away from his new responsibilities as a father,

Brown immersed himself in work, preparing for an extended trip to Florida to assist Tourneur on three Olga Petrova vehicles: *The Undying Flame, Exile,* and *The Law of the Land.* By the time the company departed for Florida in March, Brown had apparently concluded that he and Paula had reached the end of the road. When their divorce was finalized in 1920, the papers filed by her lawyers revealed that Brown had ended the relationship when he announced he was "tired of being married." Even making allowances for legal-speak, it seems like a cold way to cut off a loyal wife, and perhaps Brown harbored some remorse: when he alluded to the marriage in a conversation with Charles Brakebill in the 1960s, he admitted he "hadn't given it time to work out."[31]

Reminiscing to Kevin Brownlow about this period of his life, however, Brown recalled that the major trauma was a falling out with his boss. The cause of the dispute was apparently some confusion over the parameters of his role as an assistant. As they prepared to leave for Florida, Tourneur discovered that they were missing a cast of supporting actors, which he assumed Brown had organized. When he learned that he hadn't, the director blasted his assistant in a fit of a temper; this was followed by a glacial front that lasted for the two months of shooting and continued even after they returned to New York. Brown remembered "dying" and being made to feel "two inches high" by his mentor.[32] It was their first significant dispute and reminded Brown that no matter how much responsibility Tourneur gave him, he was still merely the assistant, the underling who must show appropriate deference to the maestro. It was a lesson well learned, and this episode may have helped establish the complex dynamics of the close relationship the two men shared until Tourneur's death in 1961.

Tourneur employed a number of assistants over the years, but his connection with Brown was something deeper, a quasi-paternal relationship that was probably more significant than either man's blood bonds. They shared many character traits: both could be emotionally distant, demanding, and volatile; both tended to prioritize work over relationships, at least until their later years. Their relationships with their offspring, too, were not dissimilar. Although Tourneur helped his son establish a career in the 1920s, Jacques frequently felt that Brown, not he, was Maurice's golden-haired boy.[33] Similarly, Brown's paternal attentions were hit-and-miss; in the early years of his daughter's life he was mainly absent, preferring to pour his energy into his work. Adrienne was raised largely by Paula, who remarried and settled in Washington, DC, and had another child, Lea, with her second husband, William Williams. According to her son, his mother rarely spoke about her first marriage, and the age gap between the half-siblings was such that they did not develop an especially close relationship.[34] Whatever contact remained between Brown and Paula most likely centered on Adrienne's needs. Although father and daughter were by no means estranged, Brown later admitted that he had kept his distance following the divorce, in the belief that a "fresh start" would be in his daughter's best interests.[35]

Despite his personal and professional setbacks, Brown was nothing if not pragmatic. At the end of 1917 he approached William Brady, the head of World Pictures, to inquire whether he might be interested in hiring him. Brown was delighted when he was offered a three-year contract at $150 a week (much more than Tourneur had been paying him). It was an impressive deal after a mere two years in the industry, and Brown must have gloated a little when he tendered his resignation. However, he was astonished by the reaction of the usually frosty Tourneur, who pleaded with him to stay. Faced with a choice between money and loyalty, Brown chose loyalty—but only after negotiating a modest pay raise.

Tourneur was glad to have Brown back, as he was about to embark on two complex and artistically adventurous productions. The first was a version of *The Blue Bird*, based on the Maurice Maeterlinck story. According to Jacques Tourneur, this film was his father's personal favorite.[36] This is hardly surprising. In its evocation of a fairy-tale world of good and evil in which the most mundane elements of everyday life are transformed and given a new appreciation, the film remains a delight. *The Blue Bird*'s extraordinary sets (by Carré) and its balancing of light and dark, both thematically and aesthetically, anticipate another film about a child lost in a strange fantasy: Fleming's *The Wizard of Oz*, made two decades later. Importantly for Tourneur, *The Blue Bird* allowed him to explore the parameters of the narrative film, taking it in new directions that were inspired by his knowledge of modernist and experimental artistic practice and by his own background as an apprentice to nineteenth-century artists such as Puvis de Chavannes. As historian Richard Koszarski points out, *The Blue Bird* exhibits a deliberate, "almost Brechtian insistence" on foregrounding artifice and forces us to reconsider received historiographies that identify German expressionist cinema as the pioneer in such experiments.[37] It must be noted that Tourneur was not the sole innovator in this respect. As Kristian Moen has recently explored, *The Blue Bird* can be placed within the wider context of an American cinema that was testing just how far fantasy could be pushed in films made for both children and adults.[38] Perhaps paralleling the divided views on what direction American cinema should take in the 1910s, *The Blue Bird* received a mixed response; for every critic who commended its "exquisite loveliness," there were others who dismissed it as pretentious or boring.[39]

Tourneur pressed on with his experiments in a version of *Prunella*, the Symbolist play by Harley Granville-Barker and Laurence Housman. It was shot in early 1918 by van den Broek, again using startling sets to conjure up a fantasy world. The film now exists only in fragments, making it impossible to judge how successful these innovations were; however, the critical response was mixed, and the film underperformed at the box office. The extent of Brown's involvement in this production and in *The Blue Bird* was unexpectedly minimal: he had been drafted for military service in mid-1917, and unable to postpone it any longer, he left his close-knit company in the winter of that year. As he later remembered, John van den Broek became rather emotional as they said their good-byes, fearing they would never see each other again. He was proved right, but not as he imagined it. In June 1918, as van den Broek was shooting exteriors off the Maine coast for Tourneur's production of *Woman*, he drowned when a freak wave swept him off a rock he had perched on to capture some atmospheric shots of the wild sea.[40] His death was a personal blow for everyone in the company, and the film industry lost one of its most promising cinematographers. In a piece in *Moving Picture World*, Tourneur seemed genuinely distraught as he mourned the loss of "more than a cameraman. He was a lovely, sensitive, delicate artist—little more than a boy."[41]

3

Brown Goes to War …
and Returns to Tourneur

Brown received his draft notice in June 1917, but it wasn't until January of the following year that he appeared in army records as a private first class cadet. The army, it seems, wasn't for him, and he requested a transfer to the air service in May 1918. After a brief period stationed in Missouri, he took up a post as a second lieutenant at Scott Field in Belleville, Illinois, in July and stayed there through December (when he was discharged due to demobilization). In the 1960s Brown admitted to Kevin Brownlow that at age twenty-seven he was considered "too old for a fighter pilot," so he spent most of his time training cadets. His discharge records confirm that he was involved in no skirmishes and received no medals. However, according to *The Scott Field Army Book of 1918*, he was injured in a minor crash during a training exercise: "The Tennessee mechanical expert had a very narrow escape in what seemed at first a very serious accident in which he did suffer painful injuries, but to the great satisfaction of his many friends, not permanent. By his cool-headed judgment and quick action he succeeded in making a very creditable landing under the circumstances." Apart from this, Brown's months with the air service were both useful and pleasurable, and it might be said that they served him more than he served the United States. Right into his sixties he remained a committed aviator, a proud member of "The Quiet Birdmen," a fraternity for fliers, and a significant investor in aircraft (when he became rich enough, he bought a ranch in Calabasas, installed an airstrip, and often flew his own plane to work or to various locations).[1]

After his discharge from the military, Brown headed back to service of a more familiar kind. Catching the Golden State Limited from Chicago to Los Angeles in December, he met up with Tourneur and his unit as they were busy shooting a Drury Lane melodrama called *White Heather*. Just recently Tourneur had permanently shifted his operations to California, bringing with him

Charles van Enger, Ben Carré, and John Gilbert, an ambitious writer, actor, and would-be director. Brown joined them for what turned out to be his final eighteen months of collaboration, during which time he took on a heavier directing load. Van Enger later recalled that the line between boss and assistant had blurred: "There was no set procedure. . . . Tourneur would tell Brown what he wanted and the work would get done." As a consequence, it is somewhat difficult to construct a definitive list of the films on which Brown performed significant directorial duties. This had been the case even in the months before he was drafted—he told Brownlow he had directed major sections of the 1916 film *The Whip* but hadn't been given credit. But certainly when he returned from the military he officially took on responsibility for most of the second-unit work. On some productions, such as *County Fair*, *Victory*, and *Deep Waters*, he claimed he directed key scenes (and according to van Enger, Brown directed a substantial portion of another film, *Treasure Island* starring Shirley Mason).[2]

Of these, *Victory* may be the most interesting. Based on Joseph Conrad's novel and adapted for the screen by Jules Furthman (writing under the pseudonym Stephen Fox), it starred Jack Holt, Wallace Beery, and Lon Chaney, with Seena Owen as the romantic interest. Despite its South Seas setting, it was shot on location in an Indian village in Palm Springs in July 1919. According to Brown's account, he directed at least half of it, although Tourneur came up with some intriguing flourishes, such as kitting out actor Ben Deeley with a pair of dark glasses to make his chilly character, Mr. Jones, appear more menacing. Though not exactly faithful to the Conrad novel, it was a tightly paced, impressively atmospheric slice of exotica. More routine, but not without its charms, was *County Fair*, which Brown claimed he directed; he even remembered soliciting advice from jockey Tod Sloan to get the horse-racing scenes right. If he did direct the film, it fit nicely into his oeuvre: its whimsical story of a spinster aunt and her niece who enter their horse "Cold Molasses" in the county fair brings to mind *National Velvet*, while its evocation of small-town life and "simple folk" anticipates his finest work in Americana. In one contemporary profile, however, van Enger stated that he had collaborated with Edmund Mortimer on *County Fair*, who directed it under Tourneur's supervision.[3]

As the decade came to a close, Brown was chafing against the limitations of a career as an assistant director. Tourneur was supportive of his ambitions, and the two began a search for a suitable property to launch Brown's directing career. Brown thought one likely candidate was Clarence "Tod" Robbins's 1917 novel *The Unholy Three*, a truly bizarre tale of three carnival performers who pass themselves off as a family—an adult midget plays the baby—so they can prey on wealthy Park Avenue society. He secured the rights to the story for $1,500, but Tourneur put a dampener on his enthusiasm, arguing that such a perverse tale was neither suitable nor prestigious enough. Brown reluctantly let the idea go, but he held on to the story rights and later sold them for a considerable profit to Irving Thalberg. *The Unholy Three*, directed by horror maestro Tod Browning and starring Lon Chaney, Harry Earles, and Victor McLaglen, was released by MGM in 1925.[4]

Tourneur may have believed that the world of carnivals was not the right milieu for his protégé's debut, but evidently prisons were just fine. When Brown came across a magazine article by H. H. van Loan that fictionalized an allegedly true story of a prisoner's spiritual epiphany during his incarceration at a San Bernardino jail, Tourneur bought the rights for him. In *The Great Redeemer*, a cowboy artist played by House Peters paints a mural of Christ on the wall of his prison cell. Through a trick of the light, the mural apparently "comes to life," and another prisoner (Joseph Singleton) undergoes redemption and confesses his crimes. Brown freely admitted it was pure "hokum," but he called it "surefire stuff for audiences of the time." In his career as a director, Brown rarely contributed to the writing of scripts, but on this occasion he apparently collaborated with experienced screenwriter Jules Furthman and John Gilbert. Gilbert and Brown had first met when they were both working at Fort Lee, and their friendship continued through the rise (and in Gilbert's case, fall) of their respective careers. When Brown relocated to Los Angeles in 1919, he became Gilbert's temporary housemate in an apartment at the Garden Court complex, a fashionable enclave on Hollywood Boulevard that attracted a movie crowd. From there, the two worked furiously on the script for *The Great Redeemer*: "We worked around the clock arguing and yelling at each other, living mostly on coffee and doughnuts, but we got it done."[5]

Script in place, Brown assembled a young crew drawn mainly from the Tourneur company: Charles van Enger was behind the camera, Floyd Mueller served as art director, and Freddie Carpenter was chief electrician. Now that he was a full-fledged director, Brown got to hire his own assistant, Charles Dorian, who would stay with him for many years. Despite the presence of familiar faces, Brown felt the weight of his responsibilities, and his nerves became increasingly jangled as the time approached to reveal the finished film to his mentor. He later recalled that the preview screening seemed to be a disaster, as Tourneur maintained an inscrutable expression and an ominous silence. When the lights went up, Gilbert turned on Brown, berating him for botching the script and producing "the worst thing I've ever seen in my life."

Distraught, Brown ran from the projection room and vomited, then sank into misery at the thought of his ruined career. However, in an ending worthy of a Hollywood movie, Tourneur followed him out and, placing a comforting hand on his shoulder, proclaimed *The Great Redeemer* to be a "wonderful picture."[6]

Audiences evidently agreed, and the film was a hit when it screened on Broadway. It was later released nationwide, including in his hometown of Knoxville, where his proud parents attended a well-received showing (for seven decades, Brown kept the congratulatory telegram they sent him). If its promotional campaign and reviews are any measure, *The Great Redeemer* was regarded as a commendable debut, albeit one produced under the close supervision and influence of Tourneur. The *New York Times* was a little guarded in its praise, noting that in many respects it was an "exceptional picture," but it was "weakened by surrounding melodrama." *Screenland*'s Clarke Irvine was more generous, calling Brown a "1920 directorial phenomenon" whose "make-up is that of the thinker . . . his work shows every necessary quality of a director." Brown must have been encouraged by the generally warm response, and he was especially touched by the letters he received from a number of prisoners, including one Sing Sing inmate who commended him for an affecting film that brought "reality in to a picture of criminal life." Regrettably, *The Great Redeemer* survives today only in the form of exquisite stills kept by Brown and other collectors. These show how much he absorbed from Tourneur's lessons on visual composition: proscenium-style dark foregrounds, silhouettes, and extensive play with light and shadow abound.[7]

A close attention to detail took center stage when Brown returned to the fold to help his boss shoot *The Last of the Mohicans*, based on the James Fenimore Cooper novel and produced by the newly established Associated Producers, a company formed by Tourneur and other major directors such as Allan Dwan, Marshall Neilan, and Thomas Ince. Shooting took place around the Big Bear and Lake Arrowhead areas of Northern California, a location Tourneur had used a year before on *The Broken Butterfly* and one that had become popular since Cecil B. DeMille filmed *The Squaw Man* there in 1913. Tourneur drew from the work of artists such as Frederic Remington, Edwin Curtis, and Charles Russell to come up with a visual design that served as an effective realization of Cooper's tale of wilderness and man. Lake Arrowhead proved to be a revelation for Brown, too: he was stunned and inspired by its glittering lakes, thick forests, and majestic mountains and by a sense that this place might hold the remnants of America's disappearing frontier.

Although *The Great Redeemer* was his directorial debut, in some regards

The Last of the Mohicans emerged as a more significant film for Brown's career. It was the first on which he received official credit as codirector, and it called on all his problem-solving skills and his engineering background. In planning the film, Tourneur had been inspired by the locale's natural wonders but he seemed less inclined to be immersed in them: he was absent for the majority of location work because of injury or illness. When Brown later discussed the film, he took credit for directing a significant bulk of it, a claim disputed by art director Floyd Mueller (who maintained Brown did only second-unit work) and by Tourneur's son Jacques (who estimated Brown's contribution amounted to one-third of the footage). Van Enger, who was on the set throughout, had no recollection of Tourneur being incapacitated, but he confirmed that the bulk of the work *was* passed over to Brown, with the boss directing only a few interiors himself.[8] It is impossible to determine who directed what and how much; however, there is little doubt that Brown executed significant portions of the film, working from Tourneur's precise instructions. *The Last of the Mohicans* brought Tourneur's decade-long experiment in aesthetics to fruition: it is a film of overwhelming beauty, saturated in lush contrasts of velvety blacks and ghostly whites, silhouettes, and dynamic camera work.

It was liberating for Brown to be away from Tourneur's influence, negotiating the unexpected challenges presented by location work. Of course, this was not the first time Brown had worked on location in difficult terrain—the Florida films with Olga Petrova had been a baptism of fire—but the shoot for *The Last of the Mohicans* confirmed to Brown that location work could be immensely rewarding. In this respect, his views differed from those of Tourneur, who was gradually retreating to the studio as his interest in creating controllable, self-contained worlds that brought to life his aesthetic experiments took precedence. As Brown's career took off in the 1920s, he relied on real locations to place his somewhat improbable plots and the heightened human behavior of his characters within recognizable and "authentic" worlds. Likewise, in the 1930s and 1940s it would be the films he made away from the confines of the "dream factory" of Culver City soundstages that afforded him the greatest satisfaction and the most critical acclaim.

The Last of the Mohicans gave Brown free rein to experiment with how to achieve the visual effects Tourneur's design demanded. In an interview with Brownlow, he vividly remembered the artifice it took to show nature's beauty onscreen: smoke pots were used to "create the suggestion of sunrays striking through woodland mist. The rainstorm in the forest was simply a fire engine and a hose. We got clouds because we waited for them, and used filters." His engineering background came in handy when he wanted to shoot one action sequence: "When the girls are escaping from the Indian ambush, I put the camera on a perambulator. We built it from a Ford axle, with Ford wheels, a platform, and a handle to pull it down the road. We follow the girls running away; suddenly, two Indians block their path. The camera stops—the perambulator stops—and this accentuates the girls' surprise."[9] Sometimes, though, his enthusiasm for adventurous camera work was too much for cameraman van Enger:

> We went up to Yosemite . . . well, they've got a thing called
> "Over-Hanging Rock," and it's a big rock that sticks way the hell and
> gone out and it's straight down 3500 feet. So, Brown and I used to
> kid around a lot and he walked out and he said, "I want the camera
> right here." Now, here's the cliff and he says, "I want the camera right
> here." So I said, "All right." So I took my camera and I backed out
> and I got my feet right at the edge. Now it was 3500 feet right
> straight down there and I set the camera up and I said, "Now, you
> look at the camera and check it." And he wouldn't do it, and I
> wouldn't shoot the scene."

It was challenges like this that made it a "tough picture" but also an exhilarating one for Brown and the crew.[10]

Brown's confidence grew as he successfully negotiated logistical hurdles. Directing the cast, however, produced a degree of frustration that may have given him a greater understanding of Tourneur's famously curt treatment of actors. Ironically, the cause of Brown's headaches was largely of his boss's making. Appearing as Cora, the white settler who has a romance with Indian warrior Uncas, was nineteen-year-old Barbara Bedford. According to both Brown and Jacques Tourneur, the elder Tourneur had embarked on a relationship with Bedford when he directed her in *Deep Waters* some months before, and despite his stated disdain for the star system, he was determined to be her mentor as well as her lover. *The Last of the Mohicans* was supposed to be the vehicle that transformed her into a star, but as it turned out, the results were decidedly mixed.[11] Although her performance has its admirers—including critic Andrew Sarris, who has applauded it as "expressively perverse"—it took all the energy Tourneur and Brown could muster to coax it out of her.[12] If, as is generally assumed, Tourneur directed the interiors, his efforts were less effective than his protégé's. For example, Tourneur probably directed the early scene that introduces the character of Cora, as she plays a harp with a listlessness that borders on the catatonic. Perhaps he thought the claustrophobic framing and Bedford's energyless performance would effectively convey her character's entrapment within the oppressive yet fragile world of white settlers on the eighteenth-century frontier, but it made for dreary cinema.

In contrast, both the pacing and Bedford's performance are more vibrant in the scenes where she interacts with the virtuous Uncas (played by Al Roscoe) and the villainous Magua (played by Wallace Beery). Almost certainly these were directed by Brown, and he sometimes employed some unorthodox methods. In his MGM career in the 1930s, Brown would be heralded as the "starmaker," the sympathetic director who could handle the most sensitive of actors, but on location in Big Bear, brutal action took precedence over patient nurturing. He later admitted being so frustrated with Bedford that he broke down and tossed a bucket of water over her when she "threw a faint on me." He probably wouldn't have pulled such a stunt on a major star like Mary Pickford (or, even more improbably, Greta Garbo), but it seemingly had the desired effect on Bedford: she found a new interest in the production (and indeed, in her costar Al Roscoe, whom she later married) and began to deliver a sparkier performance. Evidently, she didn't hold a grudge, happily reuniting with Brown a couple of years later for *The Acquittal*.[13]

The treatment of Bedford is perhaps the earliest indication that, for all his stated empathy with actors, Brown wasn't above resorting to a spot of bullying. This confirms the accounts of some of actors who worked with him in later years, who remembered that his perfectionism on the set could lead to the occasional loss of control, especially with supporting cast or crew. If Brown was tempted to play up this side of himself on *The Last of the Mohicans*, he quickly realized that he was outranked by one of his stars. The rather flabby Wallace Beery had been improbably cast as the vicious Magua, and Brown soon learned that when dealing with Beery, he would be well advised to employ a light touch. Famously mean-tempered, Beery resisted all attempts to shift his views on how a role should be played. Although reviewers would criticize the Grand Guignol theatrics of his Magua—a villain so bad that, like Erich von Stroheim's "Horrible Hun" of *Heart of Humanity*, he hurls babies in the air and dashes their brains out—there is something perversely compelling about his performance. It goes without saying that the grotesque "red-face" makeup and exaggerated melodramatics depict an offensive caricature rather than a respectful or nuanced characterization, but that was entirely in keeping with the conception of both American Indians and masculinity in this version of Cooper's novel. As Jan-Christopher Horak has explored, the "excessive" figure of Magua expresses a wider fear of "the other" and, specifically, of miscegenation, which was quite common in both American cinema and American culture of the 1920s (and beyond). This film version of the Cooper novel, the first of two made that year, remains stark in its depiction of the brutality that underpinned life on the frontier and defined the relationship between whites and Indians. Even the reassurance offered by the introduction of the "good" Indian, the "noble savage" Uncas, who delivers nuggets of Rousseauesque poeticism as he dreamily gazes out over the awe-inspiring landscape, pales in the face of graphic violence and Beery's ferocity.[14]

When *The Last of the Mohicans* was released in December 1920, it was acclaimed for its faithfulness to its source, its exciting action sequences, and, above all, its stunning beauty. *Photoplay's* Burns Mantle commended Tourneur for achieving "great beauty of background without sacrifice of story value," while *Life* noted, "Here is a photoplay that combines magnificent pictorial quality with real dramatic power—and that can hold the spectator's attention without insulting his intelligence."[15] *The Last of the Mohicans* is almost universally regarded as one of Tourneur's greatest achievements, as well as evidence that it sometimes takes a foreign-born director to realize the potential of an American literary classic. Brown's role is scarcely mentioned. There is no denying that the finished product owes much to Tourneur's guidance and aesthetic vision, with Brown proving just how apt a pupil he was. But the sidelining of his contribution must have confirmed to Brown that if he ever wanted to receive the credit he was due, he would need to break away.

Even as he planned a future without Tourneur, Brown collaborated with him on a final production, *Foolish Matrons*, starring Hobart Bosworth, Doris May, and Mildred Manning. The film was intended to cash in on the vogue for marital stories sparked by DeMille and von Stroheim, a genre that would find further expression in the work of Ernst Lubitsch. Again, Brown was called on to direct many of the exterior scenes as well as the few action scenes, which, as he told Brownlow, were shot in several New York locations and in an automobile repair shop owned by a friend. One particular scene fired him up: to capture the car crash scene, he set up a camera inside the repair shop and filmed through an "O" in the shop's "automobile" sign. It was gimmicky, to be sure, but the authentic New York setting and the spontaneous reactions of passersby, who were unaware they were caught up in a movie, helped inject a degree of realism into what was otherwise an artificial concoction.[16] Despite all his innovations, when *Foolish Matrons* was released in June 1921, reviewers generally attributed its best qualities to Tourneur's input. Grace Kingsley of the *Los Angeles Times* led the field, identifying the master's touch in "the use of small, but significant and intimate events, which makes one have the feeling of peeping through a window at real happenings."[17]

Foolish Matrons assumed significance for Brown insofar as it marked the end of his apprenticeship. His seven years with Tourneur had been crucial in opening up a world of aesthetic sophistication to the sheltered kid from Knoxville, but it was inevitable that one day he would want to strike out on his own. When the time came, it was not unexpected, as Jacques Tourneur observed: "My father appreciated his [Brown's] dedication to films . . . [but] . . . felt instinctively that Brown would leave him and become a director." If Tourneur viewed the departure of his protégé with both nostalgia and pride, Brown's feelings were more complex. He was saddened that as his own career began to flourish, he witnessed the decline of Tourneur's. In the changing landscape of American filmmaking in the 1920s, how one played the game was more important than the game itself, and Brown proved adept at striking a balance between commercial viability and artistic creativity. Tourneur, in contrast, could not envisage a career in which he played second fiddle to producers or stars. Like many of his peers, most notably that other great pictorialist of the cinema Rex Ingram, Tourneur resisted producers' efforts to supervise his set or standardize his work.

However, the decline of Tourneur's American career cannot be read simply as a clash between artist and studio. He had demonstrated both ruthlessness and pragmatism in his early career, and he would do so again in France and Germany between the world wars. Brown identified a number of factors that precipitated the slow demise of Tourneur's Hollywood career. In an interview with Brownlow, he expressed his unstinting admiration for his mentor and for the films he made but suggested that, for all their beauty and sophistication, they lacked a key element that was especially important to American audiences: heartfelt sentiment. Brown recalled that Tourneur was not blind to his own inadequacies: "Sometimes he [Tourneur] would ask me to retake a scene. 'What is the matter with it?' I'd ask. 'It looks all right to me.' 'That's the way I wanted it,' he'd say. 'But it's no good. You do it.'" Brown would then "get the actors in the corner of the set and we'd talk and kid around awhile. Then we'd take the scene again, the same way as he had taken it. But now it had a little something that it didn't have before—warmth."[18]

Some of the emotion lacking in Tourneur's films was also evident, rather damagingly, in the director's relations with his cast and crew. Jacques Tourneur recalled that his father was "cold, hard, exacting" on set, and his actors "either hated or admired [him]. . . . I don't think he was ever loved." Brown, who seemingly had a warmer relationship with Maurice, confirmed this but excused it to some extent: "Tourneur shouted at you, he'd blow up and scare everybody off the set . . . [but] that was his temperament. He wasn't malicious but he did use sarcasm."[19] Many directors behave harshly on set, and it need not have disastrous results, but in Brown's opinion, it was Tourneur's reluctance to negotiate—with actors intent on finding their own way in a performance or with producers trying to balance their books—that constituted his most serious flaw.

For his own part, Brown was not immune to displays of cruelty or anger on set, but he seemed to make a greater effort to keep his emotions in check and to call on his reserves of warmth and tenderness to nurture the more delicate talent. As he emerged from the shadow of Tourneur, Brown began to carve out a niche as a director who was especially attuned to the needs of actresses and children. This, too, distinguished him from his mentor, who had openly expressed his exasperation with (mainly) female stars and his bewilderment with children: "[I] cannot work so well with children. They are disturbing . . . they cannot be regulated."[20] Occasionally, Brown intimidated both the adults and the children he worked with, but he was better than Tourneur at judging how an individual player should be handled: he knew when a firm hand was needed, perhaps to deal with an experienced professional who was delivering a lazy or hammy performance or an unschooled novice who needed precise instructions to create an apparently "natural performance"; equally, he understood when standing back and giving the actor free rein would be the more effective strategy.

Perhaps the greatest trait Brown developed during his apprenticeship was pragmatism—knowing when to concede defeat and when to go to war. In contrast to Tourneur, he was willing to accept that American movies were largely motivated by commercial concerns, not artistic imperatives. He recognized that directors were obliged to fulfill the assignments handed to them not only to establish their worth but also to earn the brownie points that could then be leveraged for more personal projects. It was this accommodation to the system that helped ensure Brown's longevity, even if it sometimes had a negative effect on the quality of his work.

As Brown embarked on his first solo production, he discovered that he would have to call on those reserves of pragmatism and stoicism much sooner than he had imagined.

4

Striking Out

The Light in the Dark and
Don't Marry for Money

In late 1921 Brown signed up with the colorful Jules Brulatour, a Louisiana-born Creole who was a leading producer in the Fort Lee film industry. Brula-tour had formed an alliance with Tourneur around 1914, but the two had a volatile relationship that deteriorated when they clashed over a woman, Texas-born Hope Hampton. The married Brulatour had met Hampton on the set of Tourneur's *Woman* in 1918, and similar to William Randolph Hearst's cham-pioning of Marion Davies (indeed, Hampton served as one of Herman Mankiewicz's inspirations for Susan Alexander in *Citizen Kane*), he pledged to make her a star. There was a significant difference between Hearst's campaign and Brulatour's, however: while Davies was a gifted comedienne hampered by Hearst's ill-judged choices of roles for her, Hampton was pretty—but pretty hopeless as an actress. Undeterred, he pushed to have her cast in major parts, including a lead in Tourneur's 1921 film *The Bait* (which was directed largely by John Gilbert). After that experience, Tourneur balked at another collabora-tion, allegedly declaring that he would not "direct that whore anymore," and it was up to Brown to step into the breach.[1]

Charles van Enger remembered that he, not Brown, finalized the deal: "Brown and I were having lunch and I asked him if he would like to go to New York [and work] for Brulatour and he agreed. I borrowed two dollars and sent a wire to J.B. He answered in the affirmative. We got the expenses money from J.B.'s office." It was a promising opportunity, but one that Brown approached with trepidation: van Enger recalled that he had to virtually force him on to the train. Brown's fears may have been prompted in part by the prospect of working with Hampton, but he was also worried about how Tourneur would respond to the news that he was heading off, having secured "more artistic freedom and also more money," to serve a man who was now his mentor's sworn enemy.[2]

In his own account, Brown admitted that he overcame his reservations because the production he had signed up for, titled *The Light in the Dark*, contained "an idea that intrigued me." It intertwines a medieval story of the Holy Grail with a modern one about Bessie, a young working-class girl (played by Hampton) who falls for a rich man, J. Warburton Ashe (E. K. Lincoln), but is secretly loved by Tony Pantelli, a disreputable thief played by Lon Chaney. In the convoluted tale that follows, she is abandoned by Ashe when he decamps to England and unearths what appears to be the Holy Grail (which is where the medieval story comes in). Back in New York and pining away for her upper-crust lover, Bessie falls gravely ill and is tended by her devoted admirer. When Ashe returns, Pantelli steals the "grail" and gives it to Bessie for safekeeping, and she is miraculously "cured." Initially, her recovery is assumed to be due to her spiritual faith, symbolized by the Grail, but it is later revealed that a vial of radium hidden in the chalice has effected the cure.[3]

The story was determinedly daft, the brainchild of one of America's great crackpots, William Dudley Pelley. He was an enthusiastic supporter of right-wing ideology and messianic religious belief, claiming that God and Jesus had visited him and entrusted him with a mission to lead America in a radical transformation (as well as bestowing on him the power to levitate). Later, as his screenwriting career dried up, Pelley developed a passion for fascism, founding the Silver Legion in 1933 and even making an unsuccessful bid for the presidency in 1936. Although it is unclear how closely the two worked together, in later interviews Brown was contemptuous of Pelley, dismissing him as a "a Nazi—a Blackshirt." It wasn't Pelley's politics or even the story that attracted Brown to *The Light in the Dark*. What intrigued him most about the project was the chance to test out some new technology.[4]

As part of his campaign to convince the public of Hampton's talents and showcase her beauty, Brulatour invested in a new two-color process called Kodachrome, developed by John Capstaff. Kodachrome had already been trialed in some experimental tests and shorts, but Brown was one of the first directors to adopt it for a full-length feature film. He started off by making some test shots of Hampton dressed in a medieval costume and a blonde wig (not used in the completed film) at Fort Lee. These were screened in February 1922 and attracted considerable interest and acclaim. Even so, Brown decided against using the novel process for the entire film, opting instead to use it only for the medieval scenes. The bulk of *The Light in the Dark* was shot using the lush black-and-white palette he had developed under Tourneur's influence, executed here in collaboration with van Enger. To achieve the right blend of luminosity and halftones in the interiors (shot at Fort Lee), director and cameraman lined the set "with glazed cardboard paper, white to reflect light. On one side was a bank of incandescent lights. With the light coming from one point, the reflected light gave us the half tones." They took to the streets of Manhattan to shoot some of the exteriors in the summer of 1922. For one sequence that featured Chaney jumping onto a bus, Brown used a hidden camera and achieved such realistic effects that bystanders reacted in shock at the apparent sight of a criminal making his escape.[5]

It was just as well that Brown was excited by the technical challenges of the film and the possibilities of color, because handling Hampton was no easy task. According to press agent Lloyd Lewis, Brown had to stand behind the camera and pull faces in the hope of provoking the appropriate emotions from her— exactly the kind of "acting out the scene" directing style he despised and would later criticize Ernst Lubitsch for using. Hampton's limitations and Brown's frustrations led to frequent tension on the set, as Ben Carré recalled: "Clarence was rehearsing a scene with her when she suddenly interrupted him to discuss her costumes. Clarence became very angry and told her 'If you don't want to pay attention to what I am saying, there is no use going on.'" His rebuke prompted Hampton to walk out, and although a truce was eventually reached, a "glacial atmosphere" remained. Looking back in the 1960s, Brown dryly remembered that Hampton "was no actress," but she "made a beautiful color subject" and, if nothing else, directing her was part of an often taxing learning curve. The challenges presented by working with an actress of such limited abilities, as well as the pressure exerted by Brulatour, influenced Brown's approach to filming her: a preponderance of close-ups serves to display her beauty but also to disguise her awkwardness in scenes with the more experienced Chaney.[6]

According to the American Film Institute catalog, when the film was released it ran for six to eight reels (5,600 to 7,500 feet), of which approximately 1,000 feet were in color. Until it was recently restored and reconstructed by George Eastman House to a length of 5,933 feet, *The Light in the Dark* existed only in a truncated version, cut down in the 1930s by a religious group and re-released as *The Light of Faith*. This distributed version, which contrasts the modern story with inserts about the medieval Holy Grail, leaves out the detailed plot exposition and the prosaic explanation of the chalice's strange light. Consequently, the public-domain prints in circulation have confused viewers for decades, but in truth, reviewers who saw the film in its entirety in 1922 were pretty baffled, too. *Variety*'s reviewer commended the "real and rare beauty" of the color photography but declared himself exasperated by Brown's direction (which "lacked coherence") and the hodgepodge plot: "starting with the time-worn Cinderella motif . . . [the film] turns abruptly into crook stuff and then suddenly launches into the highly spiritual depiction of the story of the Holy Grail." He wasn't the only one to be baffled; audiences at the premiere were reportedly "plainly bewildered." Predictably, the trade press was more deferential, but even *Motion Picture News*'s acclaim for Hampton's "best role to date" was slyly undermined by the insinuation that this wasn't much of a compliment. Possibly in a bid to placate the influential Brulatour, *Variety* did a follow-up to its September 1 review, but the writer could do little to disguise the sarcasm behind his hyperbolic praise of Hampton's "usual effective work" in a role that required "a dozen or more negligees."[7]

Viewed today, *The Light in the Dark* is a puzzling oddity, with its mishmash of medieval and modern story and its naïve pseudoreligious didacticism. Brown knew it was a mess at the time, and he never really changed his opinion. Interviewed by Brownlow in the 1960s, he could barely bring himself to discuss this "dog. It was awful." Admittedly, there was plenty to criticize, but in his rush to exorcise the experience, he may have overlooked some of the finer qualities of *The Light in the Dark*. The silly story is lifted out of utter banality by some impressive lighting techniques, especially in interiors, where Brown employs Tourneuresque dark foregrounds, and there is an imaginative use of windows, doorways, arches, and bars for symbolic effect. Brown's experience as an editor ensures that the action scenes in which Chaney negotiates the alleyways and clotheslines of tenement New York as he makes his escape are tautly paced (they bring to mind a similar sequence in Raoul Walsh's influential gangster film *Regeneration*, made in 1915). *The Light in the Dark* also introduces elements that would become part of Brown's visual style, such as an expressive shadow to depict an approaching gunman (in this case, a policeman, but later used to portray murderers in *The Goose Woman* and *The Eagle*) and a three-shot of the film's key players that visually suggests their emotional connections (used frequently in Brown's work). Alongside these visually engaging sequences, there is the pleasure of watching one of the silent screen's greatest stars, Lon Chaney, develop his character from a seemingly amoral brute to a sympathetic and morally complex hero (who still doesn't get the girl). Many viewers warmed to his Tony Pantelli character. Chaney received "dozens of letters from convicts . . . and they all say the same thing: that they appreciate my characters because no matter how evil they are, there is always some redeeming spot of good in them."[8]

For his part, Brown was relieved when the film was over, and he swiftly distanced himself from Hampton, Brulatour, and, rather harshly, van Enger, who observed, "I do not know what happened but Brown would never give me a job after that." Brown later explained to Leatrice Gilbert Fountain that he dealt with the failure of this film—the first made entirely separate from his mentor—by chalking it up to experience. "Anyone can make a bad movie," he said, and he pragmatically moved on to his next assignment. In contrast, his old pal John Gilbert wasn't so stoic: hired by Brulatour to direct Hampton in *Love's Penalty*, he produced a commercial and critical flop and responded by dramatically walking out of his contract, never to direct again.[9]

In the days before the studio system firmly embedded itself in Los Angeles and established its assembly-line production mode, many directors worked for small independent producers, picking up one-off projects. Doing just that, Brown signed with a short-lived independent company, Weber and North, for a marital drama titled *Don't Marry for Money*, written by the husband-and-wife team of Louis Lighton and Hope Loring (who were also behind some of the biggest hits of the 1920s, such as *Little Annie Rooney* [1925], *It*, and *Wings* [both 1927]). *Don't Marry for Money* was shot by cameraman Silvano Balboni in April 1923 and was designed to cash in on the vogue for risqué marital dramas, along the lines of another recent release, von Stroheim's *Foolish Matrons*. Its plot centers on the character of Marion (Rubye de Remer), who marries a millionaire, Peter (House Peters), but begins a flirtation with the gold-digging Crane Martin (Cyril Chadwick). Through a series of convolutions, it is revealed that Crane is a blackmailer; his trickery is exposed by Peter, who eventually reunites with his (wiser) wife. On this shoot, Brown apparently had a better experience with his lead actress, the former Ziegfeld girl Rubye de Remer. Although there are no reports that the two had a romance, they developed a warm friendship that endured for decades, meeting up socially and even working together one more time on *The Gorgeous Hussy* (1936).

After several months of waiting, Preferred Pictures released *Don't Marry for Money* as a six-reeler in August 1923. Disappointingly, it received lukewarm reviews, with many commenting on its hackneyed plot and the typical movie ploy of peddling a moral lesson while providing ample visual evidence of the rewards of immoral behavior. Whitney Williams of the *Los Angeles Times*, reviewing the film some months later, acknowledged that it was formulaic but pointed out that its director was a man worth watching: "it is directed by Clarence Brown which is a certain recommendation all its own." Others commented on the lush production and the fetching costumes worn by de Remer. We can't judge for ourselves how formulaic the film was, as *Don't*

Marry for Money is now considered lost, but it is clear that Brown was beginning to earn a reputation as someone who could deliver on time and on budget. Evidently, someone at Universal was taking note, and even before *Don't Marry for Money* hit the cinemas, Brown was already shooting one movie and planning another in a five-picture deal with the studio, which netted him $12,500 per film. It was a contract that would truly launch his career and secure his place in the pantheon of the silent screen's most talented directors.[10]

5

Early Years at Universal

By 1922 Brown was carving out an independent career and a social profile in the Hollywood community. The latter was enhanced when, in October, he married a former Ziegfeld Follies girl who was five years his senior. During the 1910s, Ona Wilson had been a dancer and the rumored mistress of one of the Vanderbilts, but by 1920 she had settled in Los Angeles. One member of her circle was screenwriter Frederica Sagor, who worked on two films with Brown and formed her own opinions about what drove him and what prompted him to marry for a second time:

> Pretty Ona ditched Vanderbilt and his millions forthwith for the young
> man who was aspiring to become a great director. Ona married for
> love, but Clarence Brown, cold, calculating hombre that he was,
> married Ona for other reasons: Ona was aggressive, fearless, and could
> open doors to make way for his future—none of which he could do
> himself. He was innately shy and did not know how to sell himself. I
> would hazard a guess that Ona Brown manipulated every man of
> importance (and some who were not important) on the Universal lot to
> further her husband's ambition.[1]

Sagor's account, written decades later, was probably colored by Ona's own assessment of Brown and her bitterness after their marriage failed. Speaking to the press in 1927, as their divorce was being granted and Brown's dalliance with a starlet was an open secret, Ona maintained that he had been just a "second rate assistant director" when they met, and she had catapulted him onto the A-list. While it is difficult to imagine that Ona possessed the charm or the clout to engineer a whole career—Brown was, after all, already making a name for himself before they met—there is no denying that she played a part in nudging it along. In a 1925 piece in the Los Angeles Times she is described as a "delightful hostess [who] . . . is always press-agenting her husband."[2]

It may have been her confidence and her ease in social situations that attracted him, but Ona was also Brown's preferred "type." Similar to his third and fourth wives and a host of girlfriends in between, she was a statuesque brunette with dark eyes—a woman more striking than beautiful. Whether their union was motivated by love or ambition or both, they made a handsome couple, and during their short-lived marriage they enjoyed a luxurious lifestyle that included parties and premieres.

Having a "fearless" partner by his side must have been reassuring, because working at Universal was certainly daunting for Brown. It was a huge facility with some impressive resources and talented directors and actors, but the management system was, by turns, ineffectual and overbearing. This was the studio where Erich von Stroheim had clashed with newly appointed general manager Irving Thalberg over the costs of *Foolish Wives* in 1921—a dispute that signaled the beginning of the end of the director-led industry. When Brown arrived at Universal in 1923, it was still in a state of uncertainty, especially after Thalberg defected to Louis B. Mayer's company later that year. The lot was dominated by the superproduction *The Hunchback of Notre Dame*, which would go on to win both critical praise and massive box-office returns, but it wasn't especially representative of Universal's output. Quantity, rather than quality, seemed to be the studio's governing ethos, and despite the presence of notable directors such as Tourneur, Rex Ingram, and John Ford on the payroll, there was a sense that the most talented simply passed through on their way to something better (or, occasionally, something worse).

For the novice Brown, however, a contract with a major studio was a step up, and he was excited about his first assignment. *The Acquittal*, a courtroom drama by Rita Weiman, had enjoyed a successful run on Broadway in 1920, and the studio considered it promising enough to be made as a prestigious "Universal Jewel." The strong cast, which included Norman Kerry (fresh from *Hunchback*) and Claire Windsor, and Jules Furthman, was tasked with crafting a screenplay that would open out the action by introducing multiple flashbacks. All that remains today of *The Acquittal* is a truncated, forty-seven-minute-long print lodged in the Library of Congress (in comparison to the original seventy-two minutes), but in the original script (among Brown's papers at the University of Tennessee) the twists and turns of the plot are revealed. In the extant opening scene, which takes place in a courtroom, Kenneth Winthrop (Richard Travers) is being tried for the murder of his adoptive father Andrew Prentice (Charles Wellesley). The script indicates that a series of flashbacks was used to map out the convoluted events leading to the murder charge (some of which remain in the print). Family tensions have been stirred up by the patriarch's announcement of his engagement to his much-younger secretary, Edith (played by Barbara Bedford), and his son Robert (played by Kerry) has been cast out of the family for voicing his disapproval. Shortly thereafter, Andrew is found dead, and suspicion falls on his adopted son Kenneth, who has recently married Madeline (played by Windsor). With all circumstantial evidence pointing to Kenneth's involvement, the action opens as he and Madeline attempt to prove his innocence. Furthman's script furnishes a complete timeline of the events leading up to the murder, as well as the details of Madeline's ingenuity in unearthing clues, all of which appear to exonerate her husband. Soon after his acquittal, however, there is a dramatic twist in the tale: a letter arrives that has been recovered from a mailbag stolen weeks before. Written by Andrew to Robert, it details his discovery that Kenneth and Edith are having an affair and outlines his suspicion that they are trying to murder him by substituting poison for his antacid tablets. Following a showdown, the evil duo's crime is revealed. Edith abandons her lover, and Kenneth breaks down and admits to staging events to ensure his acquittal. In an ending that allows the two stars (Kerry and Windsor) to claim a romantic future, Kenneth does the "decent thing" and consumes poison. With her husband now dispatched, Madeline can look to a future as the wife of Robert, the rightful heir to Andrew's fortune.[3]

Though far-fetched, the story made for some gripping drama, and the extant sequences indicate that Brown handled it with assurance. Working with cameraman Silvano Balboni, he made extensive use of dark foregrounds and illuminated backgrounds, framing his characters against impressive sets for symbolic effect. In one striking shot he sets the vulnerable Madeline against a backdrop of huge French windows that seem to overwhelm her, while in another the guilty Edith is driven to hysteria by the sight of a door with "mesh-like" decorative bars. Brown's penchant for symbolism, cultivated during his apprenticeship with Tourneur (but a relatively common feature in many silent films of this period), is further expressed in a shot of a pristine rose intercut with a close-up of a worm emerging from its center, as Andrew realizes that his relationship with Edith is based on a lie. Instances of such intricate and admittedly showy camera work abound, suggesting that Brown was keen to use *The Acquittal* to establish himself as a director with a distinctive visual aesthetic.

Clearly, he immersed himself in the film's visual design, but not at the expense of the actors. Looking back in the 1930s, Brown recalled the cast (most definitely with the help of his publicist) as "a gay crowd. Claire [Windsor] was rated one of the screen's most beautiful women. Barbara [Bedford] was just approaching stardom. [Norman] Kerry, a former steel salesman who was lured into pictures by Art Accord, had just reached stardom; a happy, exuberant boy." This was a sanitized profile of Kerry, a hell-raiser whose wild nights often landed him in compromising situations and quite possibly led to an injury he sustained during *The Acquittal*. As Brown recalled, Kerry arrived on the set with his hand "bandaged, because of . . . [an] infection," and the explanation supplied—that he had been bitten by his pet wolf—stretched belief. Brown didn't really care how the injury had happened; he was just impressed that the actor battled on, concealing the injured hand "either under a desk or behind him" (the contrived shots are plainly visible in the film). This kind of cooperation made life easier for Brown, as did the presence of some familiar faces. Ben Deeley, with whom he had worked on *Victory*, was cast in the role of the Prentice family butler. It was one of the actor's last films: Deeley died the following September, at age forty-six, of drug-related pneumonia. Another old acquaintance—or perhaps nemesis—was Barbara Bedford, who tackled the role of Edith with relish and managed to deliver a surprisingly compelling performance. Brown even cast himself in a small cameo (the first of several in his career). The *Los Angeles Times* solemnly recorded that he took his role as court reporter so seriously that he enrolled in a short course in law.[4]

When *The Acquittal* was released in November 1923, it won respect from *Photoplay*'s reviewer, who commended the "subtle and unusual" direction from this "Tourneur pupil." *Variety*'s "Skig" was more guarded, noting that even though Brown excelled at the visuals, he hadn't quite established the right tone, resulting in a plethora of "overly stressed dramatic sub-titles . . . [that] give the film a decided lurid atmosphere." The reviewer also found fault with Brown's direction of the actors, complaining that he allowed the cast to "exaggerate the action to the point of heroics." Such comments may have tarnished Brown's first "jewel," but they didn't dent his confidence or dampen his ambition: by the time the film was released, he was already immersed in his next production.[5]

In 1920 a short story appeared in *Metropolitan Magazine*, a sophisticated New York publication that printed new fiction alongside the work of established writers such as George Bernard Shaw and H. G. Wells. "The Signal Tower" by Wadsworth Camp was a tension-filled tale of a signalman stationed in a remote location who must choose between fulfilling his duties (and preventing a likely collision) and defending his wife and child against a violent assailant. Brown loved the story so much that he purchased the rights, but other commitments prevented him from putting it to use immediately. As soon as *The Acquittal* wrapped, however, he returned to his pet project and enlisted writer James Spearing to flesh out Camp's story and introduce characters and symbolic oppositions that would gradually build an atmosphere of slow-burning tension.[6]

Perhaps for the first time in his early career, Brown was genuinely fired up by the prospect of working with a beautiful cast—in this case, of both the human and the locomotive variety. Growing up close to the railroad in Knoxville, Brown had a nostalgic affection for trains, while the engineer in him appreciated their efficiency and the sleekness and majesty of their design. Making a railroad film was a smart move, as the genre tended to enjoy box-office success, as the Lumières and Griffith had learned; it also seemed to invite technical innovations, as Abel Gance's *La Roue* and John Ford's *The Iron Horse* would soon demonstrate. As he readied *The Acquittal* for release, his head was filled with plans for *The Signal Tower:* where to shoot it, what trains to use, how to depict the operations of a signal tower, and so on.

Over the course of his long career as a studio director, Brown remained firmly convinced that the benefits of shooting on location far outweighed the potential risks, both financial and logistical. The studios that employed him weren't always so keen, but in Brown's case, the superior quality of these films attested to the validity of his convictions. Ironically, it was Tourneur, who viewed location work as something of a chore, who had sparked Brown's passion and introduced him to the wonders of Lake Arrowhead and its surrounds. As he set out to bring Camp's rather thin story to the screen, Brown became convinced that only with a backdrop of awe-inspiring nature could this tale of human vulnerability in the face of overwhelming forces be properly realized. After bringing *The Acquittal* in on time and on schedule, he had some bargaining power, and luckily, he found that Carl "Junior" Laemmle was quite receptive. It was Laemmle who sanctioned the expense of shooting on location at Fort Bragg in Mendocino County and at a railroad yard in San Francisco, as well as giving the go-ahead for the construction of a railroad spur on the Universal lot. According to one source, the main location was "the Noyo River Tavern—21 miles east of Fort Bragg near Northspur," where the "railroad lines of the Skunk Train" were used. Brown, together with cinematographer Ben Reynolds (fresh from von Stroheim's *Greed*), "worked among the big trees for six weeks," convening early in the morning to commence shooting "the locomotive climbing the gradient, with the sun coming up and the steam mingling with the trees." Most of the exteriors and the action scenes that featured trains were shot at these locations, but somewhat unusually for the time, Universal also sanctioned the building of a rustic cabin and a signal tower (with windows glazed in a specially commissioned amber glass) on-site, which were then used for both exterior and interior scenes.[7]

When he chose Mendocino County in Northern California, Brown secured a location of spectacular natural beauty, one that provided the perfect backdrop for shots of trains tunneling through towering redwood forests and traversing dramatic ravines. There was a particularly American look and feel to the setting, allowing an elaboration of the themes he and Tourneur had introduced in *The Last of the Mohicans*. Chief among these were the majesty of nature and its impact on man, and the continuance of America's pioneer spirit. As his own directorial career unfolded, Brown would return to these themes and to the portrayal of the "folk" he viewed as the essence of the nation—whether '98ers on the Klondike, families eking out an existence in rural Florida, nineteenth-century homesteaders in Ohio, or ex-slaves battling the odds in rural Mississippi. When he finally bowed out after five decades in the business, it was with a film that celebrated the founders of Plymouth Rock.

While shooting *The Signal Tower*, Brown didn't have much time to map out the themes he would focus on throughout his career; he was too busy coming up with inventive ways to film this particular story of human tensions and the relationship between man and machines. Naturally, his engineering background meant that he was drawn to all things mechanical, seeing beauty where others perceived only metal held together with nuts and bolts. In the case of steam trains, few could dispute their grandeur, and Brown's cinema offers some exquisite portrayals of them (here, and later in *Flesh and the Devil*, *Anna Karenina*, and *The Human Comedy*). At this stage of his career, Brown was eager to push the boundaries of film technology, even though in interviews he was quick to downplay any artistic or intellectual pretensions. He thought deeply about his craft and viewed the offerings of his Hollywood peers, as well as the output of directors working outside the system, with keen interest. While he never specifically cited the astonishing cinema coming out of Soviet Russia or Europe in the 1920s as influences, his depiction of the power and elegance of machines in both *The Signal Tower* and *Flesh and the Devil* shares many similarities with the vigorous machines in Sergei Eisenstein's *Strike* and Gance's *La Roue*. Indisputably, *The Signal Tower* also fits into an established railroad "genre" wherein trains are portrayed in a rather anthropomorphic fashion, be it Ford's *The Iron Horse*, Jean Renoir's *La Bête Humaine* (1938), Fritz Lang's *Human Desire* (1954), or Sergio Leone's *Once upon a Time in the West* (1968).

Location work yielded great results for Brown, but also it brought some risks and discomfort. Charles Dorian, the assistant who had worked with him since *The Great Redeemer*, was "nearly cut in two" as he tried to couple a pair of flatcars, and the company found the accommodations—primitive cottages with windows covered only in muslin—less than ideal, especially during the chilly November nights. Luckily, the cast of Rockliffe Fellowes (as David Taylor), Virginia Valli (as his wife, Sally), and Frankie Darro (as their son, "Sonny") were good-humored about it all, and Brown and Valli formed a friendship that lasted into retirement. However, Wallace Beery, playing the villainous Joe Standish, was his usual cantankerous self, doing little to disguise the disdain he felt for his fellow cast members, especially Darro. Those who knew Beery remembered him as a bad-tempered man: even Louis B. Mayer, called upon to defend him, admitted that he was "a son of a bitch," before adding that at least he was "our son of a bitch." Perhaps there was a method to Beery's meanness: by maintaining an air of menace, he was able to generate fear and dislike in both Darro and Valli, which proved useful in the scenes in which he had to convincingly terrorize them. Beery was an underrated actor, and here he shapes a compelling performance as the malevolent Joe. The character's roguish humor, which initially wins over Sonny (and us), is gradually revealed to be a strategy by which he ingratiates himself into the family.[8]

There is no doubt that *The Signal Tower* adheres to the familiar plot of the woman in peril, but the "triangle" at the heart of the story—David, Sally, and Joe—underpins a rather complex examination of human dynamics and one that anticipates Brown's later work such as *Butterfly*, *Smouldering Fires*, *Flesh and the Devil*, and *Anna Karenina*. Brown would often win acclaim for his nuanced approach to depicting human emotions and relationships, as well as for the sensitivity with which he directed child actors and nonprofessionals. *The Signal Tower* is the first of Brown's many films in which a young actor, in this case Frankie Darro, delivers a natural and affecting performance as a child trying to find his path in the adult world. In many ways, this theme—the clash between innocence and experience, between naïveté and cynical world-weariness—is at the heart of Brown's work and is given early expression here.

The film's careful pacing and the attention to detail in its mise-en-scène build up a slow-burning tension (largely absent from Camp's original) and reveal the shifting emotions at play. Whereas Camp's story furnished impressionistic one-line descriptions of the Taylor home as "cheerless" and the lives of David and Sally as ones of "stagnant loneliness . . . [and] perpetual drudgery," the film offers evocative visual detail. Brown needs only one shot of the interior of the Taylors' cabin, an intimate space crammed full of rustic furniture and knickknacks and lit by the warm glow of oil lamps, to convey the sense that Sally has devoted her life to creating a comforting "nest" for her family. It is a space both "real" and loaded with symbolic significance, making Joe's subsequent invasion of it all the more traumatic and affecting. Exteriors of the family's fairy-tale cottage, nestled in a hollow and accessible only by a rickety bridge, also give the impression that the Taylors have created their own Edenic world, apart from the forces of modernity (including the railroad that brings Joe into their lives). Through visual detail alone, Brown suggests innocence under threat from a cruel world, a theme he returns to in his masterworks *Of Human Hearts, The Human Comedy,* and especially *The Yearling.* As in these later films, he introduces notes of doubt, clues to existing tension in the relationship between husband and wife, and, more importantly, hints about the hidden depths and conflicted emotions that drive the character of Sally.

The Signal Tower is perhaps the first film directed by Brown in which a complicated woman is put center stage, and his sensitive handling of Valli allowed her to transform the paper-thin character of Camp's story into a rounded protagonist that views Joe with both fear and desire. The cat-and-mouse game that slowly unfolds also gives Beery space to add layers of warmth, humor, and disturbing undertones to Camp's more unambiguous villain. In early scenes he spends most of his time with Sonny, charming him with magic tricks and winning him over with friendly attention, but even then, the audience has niggling doubts as to his motives. And it soon becomes clear that this is part of Joe's campaign to possess everything David holds dear: his wife, his son, and his identity as the family patriarch.

This theme of a family under threat, of a patriarch who is less than effective (or in some way compromised), is something that intrigued Brown, himself a man devoted to two father figures (Maurice Tourneur and Larkin Brown), albeit in a somewhat complicated fashion. A number of critical assessments of Brown's work have categorized him as a conservative director, one whose films endorse the traditional values of family, fatherhood, duty, and nationhood. Yet a closer examination of his oeuvre, starting with this film, reveals that his endorsement of traditional values is rarely unambiguous. Nowhere is this more evident than in *The Signal Tower.* After an exciting "race-against-time" climax that results in Joe being shot and the threat to the family removed, Brown offers a final shot of the restorative embrace among husband, wife, and child, but he obscures our view by placing a hulking train in the foreground. It was a mark of Brown's succinctness that he could encapsulate the film's core theme of human (and familial) vulnerability in the face of the inescapable encroachment of modernity using just one shot. When Brown's boss Carl Laemmle Sr. viewed the film, he was reportedly baffled by this scene, regarding it as a deliberate (and perverse) attempt to obscure, symbolically and visually, the "view" of the restored family. Interestingly, his son Junior instantly understood what Brown was trying to achieve, and on his insistence, the shot was retained.[9]

The Signal Tower was released in August 1924 and found an approving audience among railroad enthusiasts, who were invited to special screenings. Critics, too, were impressed: Kenneth Taylor, writing in the *Los Angeles Times*, noted that the film was a showcase for Brown to display "a technique and ability that raise him above the common group of directors." Taylor was particularly taken with the imaginative filming of trains and landscape: "There is something intriguing about giant iron monsters faithfully creeping over vast spaces . . . they are seen winding up mountain grades, the cool morning sunlight gleaming through tall trees and giving the prosaic trains a breath of life."[10]

In the absence of prints of *The Great Redeemer* and *Don't Marry for Money*, it is probably safe to assume that, like *The Lodger* was for Alfred Hitchcock, *The Signal Tower* was the first of Brown's more personal films. And just as Hitchcock was apt to do, Brown elected to step in front of the camera, appearing onscreen as the ineffectual switchman who fails to stop the runaway train (he also "appears" as the unseen "Conductor Brown," the addressee of a telegram). There is a little intentional irony here, as Brown, eminently in control on the set and deftly achieving a balance between personal themes and crowd-pleasing fare, takes the onscreen role of the incompetent employee who cannot do his job. For his final two films for Universal, Brown had even more opportunity to prove that artistry and efficiency are not mutually exclusive.

6

Brown and the Universal Women

In his short study of Brown, Allen Estrin locates him among a group of film-makers that excel at directing women: "Brown might be considered Cukor's predecessor as the premier 'woman's director' in Hollywood, not only because he was renowned for his handling of female stars, but because his early films also deal with the problems of the heroine rather than the hero." His collabo-rations with Greta Garbo are well known, but before he even met her, Brown was establishing himself as the "screen authority on womanhood." In his years at Universal, he would secure that reputation with a trio of productions fea-turing female protagonists, films that touched on the burning debate in 1920s America over women's roles and the pressure to retain beauty and youth.[1]

The first of these was *Butterfly*, adapted by Olga Printzlau from a 1923 novel by Kathleen Norris (sister of Frank Norris of *McTeague* fame). The story focuses on the lives of two sisters: Hilary, a demure secretary, and Dora ("But-terfly"), a spoiled violin prodigy to whom Hilary devotes her life. Both novel and film follow the tangled web created when Dora, casting off the chrysalis of her straitlaced upbringing, transforms into a social butterfly and marries the object of Hilary's affection, the spineless but very rich Craig, only to quickly tire of him. The story culminates with Hilary finally standing up to her selfish sister, fighting her for the attentions of a new love interest, Kronski, and forcing her to accept her future as a discontented wife and mother-to-be.[2]

Brown shot *Butterfly* in the spring of 1924, with Ben Reynolds behind the camera and on impressive sets designed by E. E. Sheeley. It had been expected that Virginia Valli would play Hilary, but instead Ruth Clifford—an effective but journeywoman actress who later became a favorite of John Ford—was cast. The part of the mercurial Butterfly was given to up-and-coming actress Laura La Plante, who developed a warm friendship with her director (in the years that followed, the two occasionally holidayed together, joined by their

46

respective spouses). For the male leads, rumors had circulated that heavy-weight champion of the world Jack Dempsey might be involved, but instead the more underwhelming Kenneth Harlan and Norman Kerry were selected. Brown had already worked with Kerry on *The Acquittal,* and the two had a good dynamic, but it proved to be a different story with Harlan. In Brown's view, Harlan was utterly unconvincing as a romantic lead, and the actor's lim-ited abilities so frustrated the director that tensions exploded. Brown later admitted, somewhat inaccurately, that Harlan was "the only fellow I ever had to slug."[3]

If Harlan irritated Brown, working with Clifford and La Plante turned out to be more rewarding. Clifford confessed that she initially had some doubts, especially when she arrived on the set and was greeted by an obviously indif-ferent director (Brown had wanted Irene Rich for the role). She also worried that she was not mature enough for the role, as she later told Sue McConachy: "When you're young and you haven't had experience in life, you require a good director—and an inspiration like that. You can't just go ahead and do it ... you can't have the depth." After Brown thawed out, she found him to be that "good director": sensitive, open to her ideas, and sage in his advice. He suggested that when she had to convey deep emotion, the scenes might work better, and win over the audience, if she played them in a stoic, reactive man-ner. For one scene in which her character must renounce romantic love in favor of sisterly devotion, he advised her to "swallow hard, keep a stone in your throat, [but] don't shed a tear." It was advice that, in time, he would also offer to Garbo, Joan Crawford, and Jane Wyman, and it was based on a careful consideration of how the creative process works: "I want everything an actor knows. If it's a woman, she'll know more about playing a woman than I know. I want to get her angle on the picture. So I always rehearse without giving a word of direction. I follow them around, and watch, and listen, and I get their interpretation first. If their interpretation doesn't agree with the one I have in mind, then we begin to talk. A little shading here, a little shading there, a few quiet directions."[4]

Brown's responsiveness to the woman's perspective brought out the best in both Clifford and La Plante and ensured that the film's Jazz Age themes were handled effectively. Although not as well known as others in the "flap-per" genre such as *It, The Plastic Age* (a film that Brown was set to direct at one point), or *Our Dancing Daughters, Butterfly* offers a fascinating portrait of America during the Roaring Twenties. In particular, it reveals the challenges faced by young women presented with new (sexual, social, economic) oppor-tunities, yet expected to adhere to traditional moral codes. Just as in his previ-

47

ous films for Universal, Brown creates a rich and inventive mise-en-scène that facilitates the sketching out of these contrasting values. As the film traces Dora's path from sheltered child prodigy to frivolous socialite, Brown vividly evokes those worlds. It is interesting that the great novel of the Jazz Age, *The Great Gatsby*, was published within months of *Butterfly*'s release, as some scenes in the film wouldn't be out of place in Fitzgerald's work. Like him, Brown reveals the brittle superficiality of the world of the wealthy: endlessly frenetic, endlessly frivolous, and endlessly empty.

In exposing the lives of the rich—ironically, the class he had recently joined—Brown's conservatism emerges. Certainly, his sincere admiration for the middle-class world of Hilary, defined by a respect for the work ethic and for familial values, suggests his continued reverence for the worldview passed down to him by his parents. The self-effacing Hilary, played with such subtlety by Clifford, might be seen as one of the "pure souls" that surface again and again in Brown's films. Yet the endorsement of her world is somewhat muted: when the set for the sisters' cottage was being prepared, Brown stipulated that its walls be painted a somber gray, hinting, perhaps, at the claustrophobic drabness that often defines simple lives. Similarly, and in keeping with a number of his later films, *Butterfly* contemplates the status of women in a changing society, but it ultimately refuses to offer clear-cut resolutions or outright condemnations. Dora is spoiled, obnoxious, and narcissistic, but she is nothing more than the product of her society, one in which youth, beauty, and self-indulgence are prized. After all, 1920s America celebrated boyish men (Douglas Fairbanks), girlish or androgynous women (Mary Pickford, Louise Brooks), and even man-babies (Harry Langdon). Dora's "helplessness," a trait nurtured in her by Hilary, is also what first attracts Craig (he finds it charming). It is hardly surprising, the film suggests, that this pettish child-woman who is scarcely equipped for adult life cannot handle marriage or motherhood. Like a baby fixated on her own desires—and anticipating the selfish boy-man Jason in Brown's later *Of Human Hearts*—Dora is a victim of a consumer-driven culture that has "sold" her a false dream.[5]

There is a certain fascinating irony that, just as he was "breaking in" to Hollywood and becoming part of a studio system that generally sold audiences fairy-tale romances and neat resolutions, Brown chose to present this rather sobering message about the dangers of romantic fantasies. Unlike Borzage, to whom he has often been compared, in Brown's world, romantic love rarely conquers all, and marriage usually disappoints. The naïve superficiality of the courtship between Dora and Craig is conveyed in distinctive and revealing visuals: it begins in the pastoral setting of the sisters' garden where, like children, they innocently flirt while swinging on a kitschy garden seat. Diffused lighting and inane dialogue further underline their romanticized understanding of human relations and, more particularly, of marriage. Rapidly, Dora discovers that marriage entails a banal existence with a man she barely knows; it is little wonder she soon succumbs to the omnipresent temptations.

Just as Brown used symbolism-laden sets in *The Acquittal,* here he uses props such as mirrors and photographs to mark not just Dora's deepening self-absorption but also the crisis in her marriage. The first hint that she has broken her marriage vows comes when she commissions two miniature portraits of herself—one for her husband and one for her lover. Later, Brown frames her in a mirror, her face smeared with cold cream, as she coolly attempts to deny her adultery. It is an intriguing scene, offering a succinct allusion to America's (and Hollywood's) fixation on beauty and transformation: the mask of the cold cream "reveals" her duplicity while visually referencing the "industry" behind beauty (a theme that Brown's next two films explore in some depth).

Despite a certain iteration of the "reap what you sow" morality in *Butterfly,* Brown and La Plante shape Dora into an antiheroine that possesses some depth and is treated with a degree of sympathy. The film's ending, which sees Dora rejected by Kronski and forced to return to her marriage, continues the pattern of ambivalent final shots that Brown introduced in *The Signal Tower:* though the married couple is reunited and restored, the camera frames La Plante's face as she registers not joy and contentment but dismay and uncertainty as she contemplates imminent motherhood. The butterfly, once so alluring and mercurial, has been captured and pinned.

The muted tone of the film was echoed in the reviews it attracted upon its release in the summer of 1924. Edwin Schallert of the *Los Angeles Times* conceded that *Butterfly* was "human and interesting ... [with] decided merit" but complained that it was too long and that Brown sometimes drew the oppositions too crudely: "a lot of the early shots are just about as far-fetched with their depicting of a jazz party. . . . It does not seem to me necessary to overdraw artificiality to the point of burlesque just to make simplicity seem like a good thing." *Photoplay's* reviewer was not entirely convinced by the cast: "Clarence Brown has done considerable in humanizing the characters, but somehow the whole thing savors of the Cooper-Hewitts, the cast seems very actory, although Ruth Clifford does the best work of her career here." Reviewers may have found aspects of the film to dislike, but Brown and his cast were satisfied. Clifford remembered that at a party at the Cocoanut Grove to celebrate the premiere, the hitherto aloof Brown dropped his reserve and whispered to her while they were dancing, "Ruth, you were lovely and I appreciate it." She thanked him and thereafter had only praise for him as "a lovely man and a marvelous director . . . he was wonderful."[6]

Brown didn't get another chance to work with Clifford, but he was reunited with La Plante for his next assignment, *Smouldering Fires*. Veteran stage and screen actress Pauline Frederick took the lead in that film. Although she was barely into her forties, Frederick was considered something of an "elderly" actress by Hollywood standards, having appeared on Broadway in the 1910s and in films since 1915. She was now taking on more mature roles, mainly in melodramas such as *Madame X* (directed by Frank Lloyd) and *Three Women* (Ernst Lubitsch). Despite all her experience, Frederick was insecure and arrived on the set suffering from an acute case of nerves. Brown recalled, "the first two days on this one I thought she was going to give up." Her troubles may have been related to the turbulence in her personal life—she was on her third husband and would go on to have two more—or she may have been nervous because she hadn't had a hit film in a while. In any case, Brown responded with patience, reassuring her by "telling her how good she was." Her nerves steadied, shooting commenced in August 1924.[7]

Brown was assisted once again by Charles Dorian (who appeared in the film in a photograph) and by veteran cinematographer Jackson Rose. Everyone realized that this production was something special: Universal had already upgraded it from a "Jewel" to a "Super Jewel," which meant a larger budget, more extensive promotion, and a specially tinted release print. The expanded budget allowed Brown to head to Yosemite National Park to film some of the key sequences, giving the company time to bond and Frederick an opportunity to prove that she still possessed ample charms. For one scene, Brown wanted to frame his actors as they perched on a ledge with a spectacular ravine in the background. It was a variation of a shot he had used in *The Last of the Mohicans*, but this time his perfect frame was obscured by a lone tree. A request to the park ranger to have it cut down met with a firm refusal, but Frederick proved quite the team player when she offered to intervene. As Brown remembered: "She liked great big strong men—and he [the ranger] was sure that. So I suggested that [she] take him off for a couple of hours. She knew what we meant. So he got what he wanted, and we cut down the tree and dropped it to the bottom of the valley."[8]

Frederick's romantic success off camera was in contrast to her character's entanglements in the film. Based on a story by Sada Cowan and Howard Higgin, the production went through a variety of working titles, including *Clinging Fingers* and *Married Hypocrites*, before finally settling on *Smouldering Fires*. Behind all these title changes was a desire to cash in on the popularity of sophisticated dramas of the DeMille–Lubitsch–von Stroheim variety (to which Cowan had previously contributed) and to exploit Frederick's past successes, which included a 1917 hit, *Sleeping Fires*. In a departure from the cynical, flippant characters that populate those films, however, the plot centers on the more nuanced Jane Vale (Frederick), a ruthless businesswoman who has built up her empire by an impressive force of will and an adherence to her father's dictum: "Let no man be necessary to you." Brown uses a witty montage to introduce us to Jane: a shot of a rigid back, followed by a close-up of a foot tapping impatiently, and then a fist being thumped on a conference table. This raises expectations that the imposing figure onscreen is the kind of male go-getter to whom America was devoted in the 1920s. It comes as a surprise, then, when Frederick turns to the camera, revealing a "mannish" woman clad in a sober business suit and sporting a severe haircut.

This is the first of many scenes in which Brown toys with the audience, allowing them to form assumptions, only to have them undermined or entirely reversed. With inventive camera work and dynamic editing, as well as an affecting performance by Frederick, Brown teases out the gender-defined double standards that characterized the corporate world and, implicitly, 1920s America. The 1920s saw a significant increase in the number of women working in white-collar industries, but the assumption persisted that these jobs were little more than a temporary prelude to a woman's "real" vocation: marriage and motherhood. In such a world, nothing was more pathetic than a woman who couldn't "fulfill" her natural destiny and attract a man. The traits of efficiency and ruthlessness, which would inspire admiration if found in a male leader, are taken as evidence of Jane's overbearing nature and her "failure" as a woman. Nowhere is this clearer than in a scene depicting a staff meeting: while Jane sets out her plans for more efficient management, one of her male employees is engrossed in sketching a cartoon of her kicking a figure of Cupid. The disdain she inspires extends even to her closest female colleagues: her own secretary mocks the loveless and pathetic existence her boss endures because she has "mistakenly" focused on her career.

When Jane falls for Bobby (Malcolm MacGregor), a go-getter who is the first man who dares to challenge her authority, she breaks another unspoken rule. Although May-December romances are ubiquitous in American movies, these are nearly always of the younger woman–older man variety, and they generally work out because, it is implied, the man understands the game and accepts that the woman is a commodity, available at the right price. In *Smouldering Fires* Jane excels at playing the corporate game, but she is hopelessly adrift in the game of sex and romance, and her attraction to Bobby is viewed as inappropriate, pathetic, and creepy (the last attempt of an aging vampire to cling to a source of youth). For this woman to whom no man has ever been "necessary," the rather unimpressive Bobby becomes vital, the proof that she is a "real" woman after all. When, out of a sense of gentlemanly duty, he proposes marriage, Jane eagerly accepts and embarks on a new quest to transform both her appearance and her behavior.

As in *Butterfly*, Brown reveals the poignant and depressing fact that, despite the social changes occurring in the 1920s, women will always be judged first on their physical appearance and their ability to retain a youthful façade that confirms their reproductive potential. Of course, there is a deep irony in the fact that explorations of beauty and aging, and specifically their effect on women, are scattered throughout Brown's career, which itself was built on the showcasing of stars and the selling of images of consumption and luxury. Yet it was seemingly a topic that interested him, and in *Smouldering Fires* he gives Frederick the space to deliver a nuanced performance that challenges and affects the audience and largely discourages comic potential. As the confident businesswoman becomes something of a tragic clown in her efforts to conform to the ideals of feminine appearance and behavior, both Jane and the viewer can only conclude that individual empowerment and the freedom to choose one's destiny amount to nothing when set against the juggernaut of societal forces. In this regard, *Smouldering Fires* very much anticipates several films Brown made with Garbo in the 1930s and, in another variation, those in which he navigates the differing worlds of children and adults.

Interestingly, both Universal and several reviewers found that *Smouldering Fires'* exposition of Americans' fear of aging cut too close to the bone. In one scene, shot with unflinching realism, Brown depicts Jane's efforts to keep up her youthful façade. As the scene opens, she rises early in the morning and applies an assortment of antiwrinkle creams, all while framed against the backdrop of the deepening shadows of her dimly lit bedroom. The subtle and evocative symbolism here—the light of youth slowly extinguishing—is characteristic of Brown's best work, but the realism was apparently thought to be too much for American audiences: the scene was excised from prints released in the United States.

Visual inventiveness of this kind runs through much of the film. Brown was lucky to be working with Jackson Rose, who was so esteemed that he even wrote a manual for the American Society of Cinematographers. With Rose,

Brown came up with some evocative touches that worked in tandem with the impressive performances by Frederick, La Plante, and character actor Tully Marshall (who plays Jane's loyal adviser, Scotty). Unlike her character in *Butterfly*, here La Plante plays the loyal sister, Dorothy. She is tortured by guilt because she is attracted to Bobby (the feeling is mutual), and she tries desperately not to succumb to temptation. Brown encouraged both actresses to underplay their parts and allow his mise-en-scène to suggest their emotional turmoil. This is nicely realized in an intimate scene in which Jane, anxious to get to the root of her sister's unhappiness, tries to uncover the identity of her secret lover. As she playfully lists the names of the young men who attended a party they just hosted, she pauses, distracted by the sight of Bobby outside the window. As she calls out his name, she notices Dorothy's startled reaction, captured in a reflection on the window, and discovers the identity of her secret crush. In an act of self-sacrifice that is a hallmark of many Brown heroines—Hilary in *Butterfly*, Diana in *A Woman of Affairs*, Anna in *Anna Karenina*, and Ma in both *National Velvet* and *Of Human Hearts*—she resolves to sabotage her own happiness to ensure that Dorothy and Bobby can be together.

In the film's most poignant scene—one that Brown later singled out as among the most effective in his work—Jane hosts a twenty-first birthday party for Dorothy, hoping to engineer a situation that will nudge her closer to Bobby. She sends the two of them upstairs, on the pretense of retrieving a gift from her dressing table, where they glimpse Jane's array of cosmetics and other paraphernalia used in her futile attempt to stay young. As they return, Jane stages a "confidential" conversation with Scotty—knowing they will overhear it—and confesses that she never loved Bobby and wants to be free. It is a moment of supreme sacrifice, one typical of melodrama, and it facilitates the restoration of the "natural order" of youth coupling with youth. Brown ends with another of his beloved three-shots: we see Jane, costumed in a Pagliacci-style clown outfit, framed by the oblivious Dorothy and the dreary Bobby (one more in a line of plodding males that populate Brown's films). Closure is achieved and "true love" conquers, but only at a terrible—and terribly cruel—cost for the film's heroine.

This final shot is a familiar one in Brown's work, but in fact, it was a case of making the best of an ending he had not chosen. Interviewed by Kathleen Lipke soon after the film's release, he revealed that he had intended to end with a kind of epilogue in which Jane triumphantly returns to work and to professional success. It was an intriguing addition that attempted to alleviate Jane's tragedy and reassert her resilience, while perhaps making the point that romantic love fades and women can't expect to "have it all." However, while

Brown was on a short trip to New York, the studio decided to remove the epilogue and close the film with the uneasy three-shot of the leads. Brown admitted he was disappointed, noting that his ending had emphasized the story's cyclical nature and would have encouraged the audience to admire Jane's phoenix-like return to glory: "A very human drama and tragedy had happened in the meantime [between the film's first and last scenes], but life, being life, went merrily on, and her life had to go on. By ending the picture at the moment of renunciation, the impression of finality is given, but by showing her again taking up the threads of business, the challenging quality of life, which will not be downed, is given, ending the picture triumphant."[9]

The imposition of a new ending may have reminded him that no matter how efficiently he handled his assignments, the producer had the final word, but it also made *Smouldering Fires* more ambivalent, more poignant, and more of a "Brown film." Sophisticated, visually complex, and emotionally affecting, his newest release was recognized as one of the high points of his career thus far. The reviewer for the *Los Angeles Times* may have disliked the "abominable title," but he lavished praise on the film's "sheer force," concluding that it was a "distinct triumph for the director who made it." In the same publication, Edwin Schallert noted that the film was convincing evidence "that its director is destined, with opportunity, to be one of the ruling forces in film-making, even as he is now showing extraordinary promise and even attainment." Among the raves, however, there were notes of disquiet at the way the May-December romance was depicted. Brown friend and supporter Alma Whitaker, writing in the *Los Angeles Times*, viewed Bobby's dilemma as implausible: "Any woman seeing that picture knows jolly well that in real life Pauline Frederick would be infinitely more fascinating and attractive to a young man of 27 or thereabouts than a fluffy headed little blondie." Perhaps. But the film was released the same year that Anita Loos published *Gentlemen Prefer Blondes*—all about the fickle foibles of the American male—so the story by Cowan and Higgin wasn't far off the mark. Whichever writer came up with the bones of the plot, Whitaker blamed Cowan, the more experienced of the two and a woman who had apparently expressed her dislike for women: "No one but a woman who doesn't like women and doesn't understand women, could have written that story." Brown, according to Whitaker, was probably blinded by his own romantic preferences: "He is so bright that I can only hope some chic young woman of 30 holds him an enthralled slave. I kind of believe one does. And he probably thinks her a superflapper."[10]

As it happens, Brown *was* still in thrall to his former Follies girl Ona Wilson. Cracks were already beginning to emerge in the union, however, and this may have colored the rather weary view of marriage expressed here. Whatever the case, *Smouldering Fires* opened up new opportunities for Brown, especially when producer John Considine saw the film one afternoon and was captivated by its visual sophistication and risqué themes. Considine had missed the opening credits and assumed he was watching a film by Lubitsch—a comparison that would have made Brown swoon—and he was genuinely surprised when he discovered it had been directed by homegrown talent. Considine had a keen eye for talent and told his boss at United Artists, Joseph Schenck, about his new "discovery." Schenck quickly offered Brown a two-picture deal at $3,000 per week, an improvement on the $12,500 per picture deal he had at Universal, and one that he was eager to accept. Before he could say good-bye to the Laemmles, however, his contract committed him to make one last film for them.

In her autobiography, published at age ninety-nine, screenwriter Frederica Sagor Maas discloses that, on her recommendation, Universal paid $20,000 for the rights to Rex Beach's short story *The Goose Woman*; she then persuaded the studio to assign the property to Brown. In writing his story, Beach had drawn from the sensational Hall-Mills case of 1922, in which a love triangle involving a New Jersey Episcopal preacher, his wife, and a female member of the church choir had ended in a grisly double murder. Part of the prosecution's case had hinged on an account given by a local woman (a reclusive pig farmer), who claimed she had witnessed significant events leading up to the murders. The real-life case ended in the 1926 acquittal of Mrs. Hall and her two brothers, and the murders remained unsolved. Beach opted to model his story along the lines of a whodunit, with the guilty party eventually exposed.[11]

It seems that Universal expected Pauline Frederick to take the lead role of Mary Holmes, the goose woman, but she was unavailable owing to stage commitments. Another veteran of the theater, Louise Dresser, was drafted and received a contract that gave her $350 a week. The role of Holmes's son went to Jack Pickford (brother of Mary), and Constance Bennett was lined up to play Hazel Woods, his love interest. Filming began in February 1925 on Universal's back lot, but Brown also had the opportunity to shoot on what is now UCLA's Westwood campus. The location work proved crucial in opening up the story and injecting some much-needed realism into a rather conventional whodunit. Brown was committed to getting the small details right, and this involved significant expenditures. For the ramshackle home of the goose woman, he wanted that lived-in look, and he found it in a dilapidated cabin in the San Fernando Valley. He asked the studio to buy it and transport it back to the Universal lot intact. Once there, the studio designers went to work, kitting out the interior with tattered curtains, peeling wallpaper, and a decrepit kitchen—a fittingly revolting environment for the slovenly character. For one of the first times in his career, Brown had to deal with a considerable animal cast, as the studio sourced hundreds of geese in California and New Mexico. When the birds arrived, they proved to be quite a challenge for Universal's animal wranglers, who were more accustomed to handling dogs and horses. After the initial chaos, and much honking and pecking, a few birds were selected to be featured players. The surprisingly patient Dresser worked closely with them, and in time, a couple of them became so friendly they would follow her around the set. The actress was scrupulously professional and cooperative with the human cast and crew, too. She immersed herself in the role, seldom objecting as makeup and costume teams prepared her to face a "cruel and unrelenting camera without an atom of make-up."[12]

The determination to imbue the film with a gritty look influenced Brown to abandon his original plan of using color footage for the scenes showing the goose woman's glamorous past life as an opera star. Instead, a murky black-and-white palette was adopted. The film's grimy tone is signaled with an opening shot of the crumbling backwoods cabin where the reclusive Mary Holmes lives with her geese, her gin, and her memories. She spends her evenings drinking, listening to old records, and bitterly flicking through photograph albums detailing her past life as the great opera star Marie de Nardi (real photos of Dresser in stage roles were used). Her lonely evenings are interrupted only by occasional visits from her son, Gerald, whom she blames for ending her career. She claims his birth changed her voice "from that of a nightingale to that of a frog." Her spick-and-span son is appalled by the squalor in which his mother lives, and Brown certainly doesn't hold back in showing her disgusting environment and shocking personal hygiene. For audiences raised on a constant diet of advertisements linking cleanliness with American values, the close-ups of Dresser's worn, smudged face, her ratty hair, and the clods of dirt beneath her fingernails must have been repulsive—and probably made some of them wonder whether they were watching a von Stroheim film.[13]

At the center of Brown's exposition of human flaws are scenes depicting Mary's alcoholism (her drink of choice is gin, but hair tonic will do in a pinch) and the shocking exchanges in which she spits venom at her loving son. As his career unfolded, Brown would be closely associated with glamorous star vehicles and sentimental celebrations of family values, and *The Goose Woman* might seem like something of an anomaly in that oeuvre. Yet his striving for authenticity and his use of location work, as well as his exploration of the themes of aging, beauty, and individual identity in the face of oppressive societal forces, recall and anticipate a number of his films. And although Mary's alcoholism is sometimes played for laughs—for instance, she hides her gin bottle in a coffee pot, only to later discover that its contents have evaporated on the hot stove—for the most part, Brown and Dresser portray it as a disease that degrades its sufferer. Brown was a lifelong teetotaler and a former juvenile performer for the temperance movement, but he was compassionate when it came to alcoholics (including his third wife) and offered several sensitive representations of them (*Anna Christie, Ah Wilderness!, Sadie McKee, The Human Comedy*).

The Goose Woman's theme of the maternal bond and all its complications appears in much of Brown's work, be it the self-sacrifice of mothers (or their substitutes) in *Butterfly, Smouldering Fires, Anna Karenina, Of Human Hearts*, and *The Human Comedy* or the troubled relations between mother and child in, among others, *Possessed* and *The Yearling*. There is no better expression of the duality of that bond than the depiction of Mary Holmes's relationship with her son. Though their initial scenes are marked by bitterness and resentment (by her) and sadness and repulsion (by him), the twists and turns of the whodunit plot facilitate a deepening of their connection and the emergence of the "true" mother that years of alcoholism and self-abasement have masked. When a local roué, Amos Etheridge (played by Marc McDermott), is murdered by an unknown assailant close to her farm, the press and the police swarm the area, and Mary becomes infuriated when she is mocked and dismissed as a "drunken goose woman." In an effort to reclaim the spotlight as a person of importance, she fabricates a story: she claims she witnessed the murder and even furnishes alleged details about the murderer's car (she says it had a defective headlight). Unfortunately for Gerald, his car happens to have a broken headlight, and suspicions deepen when it emerges that Amos was a rival for the affections of Hazel. Eager to prosecute the case, the district attorney exploits Mary's vanity, lavishing attention on her and transforming her into the model of an imposing *grand dame* and a convincing witness. She must then make a choice: continue the lie and retain the respect it has brought her, or sacrifice everything to save her son. Rather predictably—this is, after all, a Brown film, not a von Stroheim one—she chooses altruism over selfishness and confesses that she concocted her account of events. The film ends as the true murderer is conveniently revealed to be a man (played by Griffith veteran Spottiswoode Aitken) who is creepily obsessed with saving Hazel from the clutches of the caddish Amos. The final shot of the film is a Brown trademark: a three-shot of mother, son, and future daughter-in-law.

Shooting on *The Goose Woman* was challenging at times, especially when Jack Pickford developed "kliegl eyes," resulting in a six-week delay. But overall, the collaboration between Brown and Dresser proved to be a rewarding one. She impressed him with her fearlessness and her lack of vanity, and her commitment inspired him to go all out to inject the film with a striking visual flair. Expressive lighting and camera work, visual symbolism, and little bits of business that convey characters' emotions without the need for intertitles all indicate Brown's eagerness to show off his ability to make a subtle and challenging film out of formulaic fare. He was keen, too, to ensure that sharp-eyed viewers might spot a few in-jokes, such as his role as the "murderer" in the (false) flashbacks, a visual reference to his recently released film in a background poster outside a theater ("Married Hypocrites," one of the working titles for *Smouldering Fires*), and a gag revealing that Gerald's faulty car had been bought from the "Brownell" Motor Company.[14]

Given such personal engagement by Brown and his cast and crew, they must have been heartened by the rave reviews when the film was released in August 1925. Mordaunt Hall singled him out as a director of "marked ability" who has a "genuine desire to tell the tale in a modulated but effective tone," while critic Frances Peck (writing as "Mae Tinee") awarded it the top spot on a list of the twelve best films: "*The Goose Woman* is to me a 'best picture' because of the remarkable characterisation of Louise Dresser, who portrayed a gin-sodden wreck of a woman in an unforgettable way. Her blear-eyed, sloppy-fat, sodden-mouthed, grizzled-witch-haired, filthy hag of a Mary Holmes was a triumph of make up and intelligence." In later years, Brown would cite *The Goose Woman* as one of the films he was most proud of, and he continued to be touched whenever he heard that it still impressed viewers. One unexpected admirer was critic and filmmaker Paul Rotha, who tended to favor European directors but was astonished by some of the realism in this American's work. In his influential study *The Film Till Now*, he praised the director's "clever handling" of the early scenes and *The Goose Woman*'s gritty realism. Later, after watching *Intruder in the Dust*, Rotha was so moved that he wrote to Brown to commend him. In a similar vein, historian William Everson viewed *The Goose Woman* as something of a revelation because it didn't seem to "fit" Brown's profile: "In many ways it is a most curious film, romantic and emotional about a theme that one envisions rather better as a hard-bitten 30's film by Le Roy or Wellman."[15]

Despite the admiration it earned upon its release and subsequently, *The*

Goose Woman enjoyed only moderate success at the box office. However, the appeal of the story was such that, within a decade, it was remade by RKO as *The Past of Mary Holmes*, with Helen MacKellar in the role of the goose woman and Eric Linden playing her son. In retirement, Dresser, who had always been ambivalent about her film career, admitted that *The Goose Woman* was her highlight, and for this she credited Brown: "[we] worked together beautifully—he will always be one of the great directors in my book."[16]

7

Brown at United Artists

The three years he spent at Universal gave Brown valuable experience handling actors and fine-tuning his technical skills. As he began working for Schenck at United Artists, he certainly had a keener appreciation of the delicate balance between commerce and art. For every unconventional film like *The Goose Woman*, there would be formulaic ones like *The Acquittal*; the challenge was to get one's personal projects made and to make something personal out of standard fare. The two films he made for Schenck undoubtedly served specific masters—namely, two major stars—but for Brown, they solidified his place in the Hollywood system.

First up was a comedy-drama set in Imperial Russia, a high-stakes project on a grander scale than any production Brown had previously helmed. *The Eagle* was a vehicle for one of the major stars of the early 1920s, Rudolph Valentino. Although he had appeared in films since the 1910s, the actor's "overnight" success came only after he landed the lead in Rex Ingram's *The Four Horsemen of the Apocalypse*, followed by George Melford's exotic romp *The Sheik* (both 1921). Valentino was probably the first male star to be filmed in a manner that eroticized him; audiences were encouraged to enjoy his body, his mesmerizing eyes (in reality, myopia accounted for the intense stare), and the unabashed sexual interest he took in women. This presentation, and Valentino's promotion in movie magazines, led to a mainly female fan base; male viewers and commentators tended to regard him with some disdain. In a society where gender roles were under discussion, some feared that the popularity of a man like Valentino, who willingly colluded in his own construction as spectacle, might have a pernicious impact on the red-blooded American male. Added to this was a xenophobic, anti-intellectual group that regarded him as inappropriately "beautiful," dangerously "foreign," and pretentiously "arty" (especially when they saw some of the films he made with dancer-wife Natacha Rambova). This hostility increased when Valentino took the role of a foppish (faux) aristocrat in *Monsieur Beaucaire*, laying himself open to insinuations that he and the "powder puff" character he played were of the same ilk.[1]

When he was introduced to Brown, Valentino had just returned from a hiatus and was at something of a crossroads in both his career and his personal life. His marriage was crumbling, and he despaired at the recent barrage of slights in the press. He wanted to leave behind the "lounge lizard" persona and reinvent himself as a lighthearted action hero that would appeal to male audiences. It was a little surprising, then, that Considine and Schenck selected Brown, a director most recently associated with somber "women's pictures," to direct this comedy starring the manly Valentino. However, it seems that both the producer and his boss believed that Brown was versatile enough to take on this new challenge. The trade papers and wider press played ball, building up excitement at the impending reinvention and giving Brown—or, more likely, Schenck's publicist—opportunities to air his views on how Valentino might advance his career. In one piece in the trades, Brown advised that Valentino should take on a "virile story . . . something that will attract the men to him and overcome their prejudice against him as a 'sheik' and 'woman tamer.' He must enact a role where he faces great odds and overcomes them with difficulty in a natural, everyday manner, and not with great flourishes and hullabaloo of romantic exaggeration."[2]

It was reported that Valentino was honing his comedy and action skills for a film version of John Frederick's *The Bronze Collar*, a story set in California during colonial days. Instead, an unfinished Pushkin novel, *Dubrovsky*, was selected, and Schenck hired Ernst Lubitsch's favorite writer, Hans Kraly, to adapt it. Kraly was an inspired choice because his scripts were famous for their dry wit and sophisticated "light touch." The title changed several times—from *The Untamed* to *The Black Eagle* to *The Lone Eagle*—before *The Eagle* was finally chosen. The changes probably reflected Schenck's desire to put some distance between this new project and the actor's other films: *The Untamed* sounded too much like an exotic romp, and *The Black Eagle* and *The Lone Eagle* wrongly implied a rather dark content (and were a little too similar to Fairbanks's recently released *The Black Pirate*).[3] Kraly supplied only the slightest of plots: Valentino plays Dubrovsky, an army lieutenant who saves the life of Catherine the Great but later falls from favor and becomes an outlaw. Over the course of the film he learns that his father has been killed and his lands seized by an evil nobleman, Kyrilla (James Marcus). Plotting revenge, Dubrovsky disguises himself as a French tutor and infiltrates Kyrilla's household, but he soon falls for Mascha (Vilma Banky), the daughter of his enemy. He must decide between vengeance and love;

eventually, he chooses the latter, and the film ends as the couple leaves for France.

Shooting commenced in the summer of 1925, and with so much riding on the production, Brown arrived on the set with a degree of trepidation, but his nerves soon steadied at the sight of some friendly faces. Spottiswoode Aitken and Gustav von Seyffertitz, both of whom had appeared in *The Goose Woman*, were playing minor characters. They were joined by Louise Dresser playing Catherine the Great—and looking a lot more glamorous than in her last outing for Brown. The director had been assigned a top-notch crew that included cinematographer George Barnes, in the industry since 1918 and soon to become Gregg Toland's mentor, and acclaimed set designer William Cameron Menzies, later of *Gone with the Wind* and *War of the Worlds* fame. Here, Menzies was responsible for the fanciful fusion of Imperial Russian Gothic with *Thief of Bagdad* "Oriental style." Even though Brown could be a demanding boss and was sometimes disliked by his crew, he respected talent and was drawn to Barnes, who shared his interest in developing a "pure" cinema in which the exposition of plot and delineation of theme were achieved mainly through the dynamic use of mise-en-scène and editing, with intertitles kept to a minimum. Brown was inspired by the experiments of European directors such as Murnau (who had *almost* achieved titleless cinema with *The Last Laugh*), and together with Barnes, he came up with an elaborate style that included showy tracking shots, expressive lighting, witty and symbolic use of props, and editing that incorporated rapid montage-style cutting. The distinctive style enhanced Brown's growing reputation as an intensely *visual* director, but it also worked well in terms of presenting the film's stars, Valentino and Vilma Banky, in a lively and appealing fashion.

Tourneur's influence still held sway over Brown, and it is evident here in his extensive use of dark foregrounds and atmospheric lighting. In a scene that takes place in a prison, velvety shadows and luminous soft lighting envelop Dubrovsky and Mascha as they enter into a secret marriage. In another, silhouettes and deep expressionistic shadows build up ambiguity and tension as Dubrovsky sneaks into Kyrilla's bedroom, apparently with murderous intent (audience expectations are proved wrong, however). As he did in *Smouldering Fires*, Brown toys with the audience, leading them to expect one outcome only to reveal something entirely different (for instance, in one scene, Mascha rushes in to save her father, who is apparently being strangled by Dubrovsky, only to discover that he is receiving a particularly vigorous neck massage). Brown also makes witty use of props and unusual faces in the character roles, lending the proceedings a light, Lubitsch-style feel. Typical is our glimpse of Mascha's grossly overweight aunt (played by Carrie Clark Ward), who carries a small doppelgänger in the form of her obese, squashed-face Pekingese dog.

When F. W. Murnau came to Hollywood in 1926, Brown was one of the first to request access to the *Sunrise* set, and he marveled at the German's bold experimentation. It was clear that, like many American directors, Brown was keeping an eye on European cinema, and there is a rather Murnau–Lupu Pick–"unchained camera" feel to the extraordinarily mobile camera work employed by Brown and Barnes here. It makes *The Eagle* a visual delight, even if it involved significant complications for the director and his cinematographer. Brown was up for the challenge—after all, his training as an engineer meant that he was wired to solve problems—and the results are moments of brilliance. In an early sequence that sets the dynamic tone of the whole film, Dubrovsky displays agility of both mind and body as he rescues Mascha from a runaway carriage. A camera placed on a truck follows the action as Valentino mounts his horse and gives chase. Cutting between shots from the truck and shots from inside the carriage, Brown and Barnes capture the star as he performs the impressive stunt of jumping from his horse onto the carriage's team of horses, bringing them under control. If ever there was a scene devised to prove Valentino's macho credentials, this was it.

Perhaps even more striking, and influential, is the banquet scene. Brown wanted to emphasize the decadence and excess of Imperial Russia, and he ordered the table piled high with a gross amount of food and wine. Discarding the more conventional way of filming (using a side view), he and Barnes designed a special platform so the camera could glide down the table's center, skimming over the food and the crockery. In an interview with Brownlow, Brown explained the setup of this astounding scene:

> The camera started with a character (James Marcus) eating at one end. Then it traveled along the middle of the table, past all the other occupants, right the full length of the table—which must have been sixty feet long. To get the camera in that position was very difficult; no equipment existed to do it. So we made two perambulators. We put one on each side of the table and we constructed a bridge, with stressbeams so that it was rigid. Then we dropped a crosspiece and fastened the camera from the top, so that the bottom of the camera could travel along the top of the table. Of course, nothing could obstruct the movement of the camera, so we had prop boys putting candelabra in place just before the camera picked them up.[4]

This kind of ingenuity inspired not only Brown (who cribbed from himself and used a variation of this shot in *Anna Karenina*) but others as well. Josef von Sternberg uses a strikingly similar camera movement in *The Scarlet Empress* (1934), another film about Catherine the Great that features Louise Dresser. Von Sternberg never credited Brown, but it seems impossible that he had not seen *The Eagle*, given both the link with Dresser and his own loose friendship with Brown, whom he knew from their Fort Lee days. Influential critic Andrew Sarris thus seems mistaken when he dismisses Brown's self-homage in *Anna Karenina* as "pseudo-Sternbergian"; it is more accurate to label the shot in *The Scarlet Empress* "pseudo-Brownian." Even if von Sternberg didn't acknowledge Brown as an influence, Delmer Daves at least paid him homage in *Never Let Me Go* (which Brown produced in 1953).[5]

Executing the intricate camera work and lighting took up much of Brown's time, but he also ensured that his actors were content. He had worked with stars before, of course, but perhaps none so important as Valentino. Happily, the two men got along very well, bonding over a passion for luxury cars, and the press reported their visits to local dealerships to test-drive Franklin coupes (in later years, Brown was more of a Mercedes man). The two men were close in age, but they possessed very different temperaments, with the conservative and cautious Brown providing a steadying influence on the impulsive and insecure Valentino. Yet the actor was no pampered diva; he proved eager to please and was anxious to perform some of his own stunts. These didn't always go according to plan: one stunt that involved Valentino and a bolting horse ended in significant bruising and dented dignity for the star. He may not have been the greatest horseman, but Valentino's participation in action sequences and he-man wrestling matches—with a (tame) bear, no less—made for great press and played a part in his rebranding. There were moments, however, when the actor's derring-do caused headaches for Brown and generated less positive publicity. During a break from shooting, he was arrested for speeding and arrived in court wearing his Cossack costume. His defense, that his foreign-made car's speedometer confused him, was rejected.[6]

Apart from these distractions, Valentino confined his exploits to the set and focused on a fruitful collaboration with Brown, the first top-notch director he had worked with since the Rex Ingram films. Brown's decisiveness, but also his willingness to give actors room to work out their own performances, was especially appealing to an actor who desperately wanted to be taken seriously. Valentino gushed that Brown "knows what he wants and goes right after it. He knows the scenes so well that he never uses a script," and he compared Brown to the "leader of an orchestra" who directs "not so much by words as by tone." Valentino's enthusiasm was transmitted to others in the cast, who vied with him to come up with the most scene-stealing performance (and in the case of Dresser, she was successful). Vilma Banky entered into the campy spirit with a delightful performance as Mascha, though reports of a passionate affair between the "fiery" Hungarian and the "temperamental" Valentino were far off the mark (she was in love with actor Rod La Rocque, whom she soon married).[7]

Filming for *The Eagle* wrapped up in late summer, and Brown readied it for a much-anticipated release in November 1925. As befitted a major Valentino vehicle, there were glitzy premieres in Los Angeles and London, and audiences at the Strand Theater in New York were treated to an orchestra playing Tchaikovsky's *1812 Overture*, live performances of Russian dances, and gifts of brass coins bearing an imprint of Valentino and an eagle. Amidst all the ballyhoo, however, there was a dark cloud: Alexander Ikonnikov, who claimed to be a former army general under Czar Nicholas II, initiated a lawsuit against United Artists, alleging that the film presented an inaccurate picture of life in the imperial army. The lawsuit was most likely a publicity stunt initiated by an eager publicist at United Artists or by Ikonnikov himself, and it was evidently dropped rather quickly. Ikonnikov had his (limited) reward: he resurfaced in a bit part in von Sternberg's *The Last Command* (1928).[8]

The Eagle is now regarded as one of Valentino's most appealing films, but critics in 1925 were surprisingly grudging in their praise. The same commentators who had endlessly mocked his passionate posturing in *The Sheik* were now dismissive of his efforts to poke fun at that persona and reinvent himself. Norbert Lusk, writing for the *New York Telegraph*, complained that the film "is far less intelligent than I looked for . . . [and Valentino's] best qualities as an actor are discarded in favor of trivialities." In Lusk's view, the film would have been a great deal better if Brown had emphasized the "tempo of dark, romantic drama instead of capering comedy." Mordaunt Hall attributed the film's best qualities to Brown's influence, which, he noted, "demonstrated no little skill and imagination," but this was in spite of Valentino (whom he compared to Douglas Fairbanks and found wanting) and the star's "will of his own." Interestingly, in light of Brown's later reputation as a "starmaker," Hall mused that the presence of Valentino actually put a dampener on Brown's creativity. Contemporary critics may have been a little mealymouthed, but historian Jeanine Basinger cites Valentino's performance in *The Eagle* as one of his finest: "[it] puts on full display many of those characteristics of Valentino's that are seldom associated with him; it's a textbook display of how he has been misunderstood and underappreciated." Valentino also listed *The Eagle* as one of his favorites and was enthusiastic about the prospect of collaborating again with Brown. The latter would have liked nothing better, but it was not to be: less than a year after *The Eagle*'s release, its thirty-one-year-old star was dead from peritonitis.[9]

The Eagle secured Brown's growing reputation as a director who was both efficient and innovative. His personal profile, too, was on the rise, with a rash of complimentary profiles that quoted his views on directing, on working with stars, and on his hopes for the industry. In *Motion Picture Classic* Harry Carr included him on a list of exciting directors, alongside King Vidor, Mal St. Clair, and Ernst Lubitsch. In Carr's view, Brown "promises to be the best director since the great days of Griffith," mainly because his "great asset is a sense of balance and logic." A little surprisingly, given the innovations of *The Eagle*, Carr qualified his praise by adding, "I wouldn't say that he has a great camera eye like von Stroheim, but he has a fine sense of drama, and an extraordinary instinct for character drawing." A profile by Grace Kingsley provided insight into Brown's methods of handling actors: "He never gets in and plays a scene for an actor. He wants each actor to do the scene in his own way, providing he gets the meaning and feeling of it." This noninterventionist approach, which was in significant contrast to the methods used by Lubitsch, for instance, was one that Brown maintained throughout his career, and it is cited in almost all major profiles of him. It was hardly a maverick method, however; Vidor also favored a hands-off style.[10]

As Brown's professional methods attracted attention, so did his private affairs. His daughter Adrienne, now eight years old, made a high-profile visit to the set of *The Eagle*, where she posed for photos with Valentino and her father. The press carried several reports that Brown's skills as a "maker of stars" would soon be called into play to transform this "wistful, childishly serious" girl into a professional actress (as soon as her private schooling had been completed), but he seemed noncommittal, telling journalists he would leave it "up to her." Nothing came of Adrienne's acting career, and she returned to Washington, DC, to live a private life with her mother; she was rarely mentioned in the press again. Brown may have been uncomfortable when his private life became the subject of public interest, but Ona had no such qualms. She was determined to maintain a high profile and be a constant feature in the gossip columns and social diaries of the Los Angeles newspapers. These accounts often detailed the lavish parties she attended or threw or her profligate spending, but a common thread was the enthusiasm with which promoted her husband: she was, one profile noted, a "courageous and tireless champion of anything and everything that will tend to enhance and forward the cause of her husband."[11]

Brown didn't really need Ona's help, as Schenck was already sold—so much so that he entrusted his wife to him. Mrs. Joseph Schenck was film star Norma Talmadge, who had been a successful actress for almost a decade. She inspired slavish devotion from her fans, and as one of her favorite directors, Sidney Franklin, observed: "You could take 1,000 feet of Norma Talmadge in a chair, and her fans would flock to see it." Her star image was associated mainly with tragic roles, but by the mid-1920s, she was eager to branch out into comedy. "Daddy"—as she referred to her husband—duly lined up what he viewed as a suitable property, an André Picard–written, David Belasco–produced play called *Kiki* that had been a smash hit on Broadway in 1921 with Lenore Ulric in the title role. The choice was definitely a bold one, given that the main character normally would have been played by an established comedienne with a flair for slapstick, such as Mabel Normand or Mary Pickford (who later remade it and recycled some of the original film's footage). Even Norma's bubbly sister Constance seemed a better fit, but Schenck was adamant and spent $75,000 to secure the rights. His enthusiasm wasn't simply an old man foolishly pandering to his wife: Schenck was a very shrewd judge of talent (he was an early admirer of Buster Keaton), and he was generally regarded as a mogul whose head overruled his heart.[12]

He poured money into hiring the best writer (Hans Kraly); a distinguished crew that included prolific cinematographer Oliver Marsh, set designer William Cameron Menzies, and a Frenchman, Jean Bertin, as a technical assistant; and a cast selected to support rather than overshadow Talmadge. Ronald Colman, then at the start of a distinguished career playing suave gent roles, was lined up to play Kiki's love interest, Renal; Marc McDermott (late of *The Goose Woman*) played his rival, Baron Rapp; and child actor Frankie Darro took a small role as an urchin. Presiding over all of them was Brown. In just five years, he had come a long way.

The film went into production in December 1925 and was still being shot in early March. According to press reports, Brown filmed a number of sequences in color, but these were later excised, apparently on Talmadge's instructions. It is a measure of her star power that she could make such a decision, although it undoubtedly followed consultation with Schenck. The reasons are not entirely clear, but columnist Grace Kingsley cattily implied that it was because Talmadge was unhappy with how she looked, especially in comparison to costar Gertrude Astor. Astor was "mourning just a bit because Clarence Brown had decided to cut all the color photography out of 'Kiki' and they do say she looked simply gorgeous in it." Maurice Tourneur had been offended when Pickford used her star power on the set of *Poor Little Rich Girl*, and Brown would later confess that he was irritated by Talmadge wielding power as the boss's wife, but relations remained amicable on the set of *Kiki*. Granted, Brown was still finding his way in his directorial career and was anxious not to make any significant enemies, but he seemed to have genuine affection for Talmadge and certainly admired her work ethic: "give . . . [her] one hint . . . and you just get enchanted with what she's doing you forget to holler cut . . . oh she was marvelous, nobody could touch her." In truth, their collaboration didn't make Hollywood history, but Brown remained steadfast in his belief in her talents: "Norma was the greatest pantomimist that ever drew breath. She was a natural-born comic; you could turn on a scene with her and she'd go on for five minutes without stopping or repeating herself."[13]

There is no doubt that *Kiki* was all about Talmadge. Its plot—a street gamine falls for a theater owner and sets about proving her charms—is utterly formulaic, and Brown adopted a conservative style to film it. Although the energetic camera work in the opening shot of a line of chorus girls promises a lively pace, it is not sustained. As in several of his vehicles with Garbo, Brown apparently made a conscious decision to eschew any "showy" camera work or brisk cutting, for fear that it might distract viewers from the star's performance. *Kiki* features little character exposition and not much in the way of intricate plot, so its appeal lies almost entirely with the viewer's response to Talmadge. Certainly she delivers a performance of some charm and plenty of technique—her playing of a person in a cataleptic state is a veritable master class—but one gets a niggling sense that it's all *too* contrived, *too* efficient, rather than spontaneous or deeply felt. It would be difficult to dispute that in comparison to the hoyden roles played by Mary Pickford or Mabel Normand (or even Dorothy Gish), Talmadge trails behind.

As Brown recalled, even Schenck, the star's most loyal admirer, had reservations about the film. When the producer watched a rough cut, he turned on Brown and accused him of mishandling the story and, more importantly, presenting Talmadge in an unflattering light. "What do you mean lighting Norma like that? Do you realize we're going to have to re-shoot half the film?" Shell-shocked, but also exhibiting his customary pragmatism, Brown planned his exit strategy from United Artists before news leaked out. He approached Paramount boss B. P. Schulberg, who was more than happy to offer him a contract, but before he could sign on the dotted line, *Kiki* received a delighted response from a preview audience. Once again, Brown was the golden-haired boy, and now he was looking for a better deal. Schenck's efforts to win Brown back fell on deaf ears, so he approached his friend Louis B. Mayer and asked him to persuade Schulberg to drop Brown. Mayer duly obliged, and Schulberg withdrew his offer, but even the wily Schenck was no match for the Lion of Hollywood: Mayer swooped in and offered Brown an even more lucrative contract at MGM. Soon Brown was gathering his belongings and moving into an office in Culver City, where he made his home for more than thirty years.[14]

Kiki was released to respectful reviews in April 1926, with most commentators noting the departure for its star: "Norma Talmadge is a comedienne now. And a comedienne of such charm and whimsicality that you are going to love her even more than you did in 'Smilin' Through' and other lachrymose dramas. She is funny and sad and gawky and gay all in one." In the *New York Times*, Mordaunt Hall acknowledged that the character of Kiki was an "exaggerated one," but he praised the actress's skill in shaping her into a "resourceful, sympathetic little creature." French critics, too, were entranced by this little gamine, with one reviewer noting in *Cinémagazine* that Talmadge had proved herself talented and charming in her first comic role. Yet if reviewers in Paris and New York were warm, there were some dissenters on the West Coast. Grace Kingsley, who had been providing her readers with updates throughout the production, watched the film with Mabel Normand (who would have walked away with the part) and offered only faint praise: "[Talmadge's] comedy methods and mannerisms are not particularly original." *Variety*'s "Sisk" was blunt, pointing out that Talmadge was "not a comedienne and never has been . . . [but] she gives a creditable and amusing performance which, if it isn't as subtle as it might have been, is about as effective as possible in its slapstick way."[15]

The mixed reviews may have caused Talmadge to reconsider her reinvention as a comic actress, and the last few successes of her career were mainly in dramatic roles. But as it happens, time was running out for Norma as well as for her two sisters, Constance and Natalie. They may have moved in high society, but none of them lost the strong New Jersey accents of their childhood. When sound movies arrived just a few years later, Norma listened to Connie's advice to "Quit pressing your luck, baby. The critics can't knock those trust funds Mama set up for us." She retired gracefully at the ripe old age of thirty-six.[16]

8

Brown Meets Garbo

Flesh and the Devil

When Brown left Schenck and went to work for Mayer, he was elevated to the ranks of Hollywood's top directors. Ironically, his ascent coincided with the decline in fortunes of his mentor, Maurice Tourneur, who was also employed by MGM. Tourneur had recently had a dispute with Irving Thalberg over the production of a now-lost South Seas film, *Never the Twain Shall Meet,* and ill feeling rumbled on. When Brown arrived on the lot he got caught up in their latest quarrel, over an adaptation of Jules Verne's *The Mysterious Island* and over Tourneur's decision to eject producer Hunt Stromberg from the set. When Tourneur was informed that on-set producer supervision was now the policy at MGM, he walked out of his contract, and as it turned out, his Hollywood career. In an example of the studio system's pragmatism, if crassness, Brown was asked to step in, but he refused, and the production was assigned to Danish import Benjamin Christensen. Christensen, too, experienced difficulties, and when the film was eventually released in 1928, writer Lucien Hubbard was credited as director. The departure of Tourneur marked a sad end to an important American career, but his friendship with the loyal Brown remained intact.[1]

The curtailing of the master's career imparted an important lesson to Brown. Over his long tenure at MGM, he would encounter production difficulties and engage in clashes with producers (including Thalberg), and he sometimes came close to quitting. Ultimately, he stuck it out, adopting the rather stoic, long-view philosophy that if storms could be weathered, more stable (and productive) conditions might soon prevail. Perhaps the challenges he encountered were worth it, because MGM was *the* prestige studio, in a league above both Universal and United Artists. The studio was not yet two years old but was already accumulating a bank of talent that would garner it the tagline "more stars than there are in the heavens themselves." Brown joined an impressive roster of directors that included European émigrés Viktor Sjöström and Mauritz Stiller, as well as American-grown talent Marshall Neilan and King Vidor. MGM's generous salaries and world-class technical departments attracted some of the best, but it wasn't always the most comfortable work environment: the practice of deferring to the producer and fervently relying on the audience preview system (earning the studio the nickname "retake valley") was anathema to directors accustomed to greater creative control.

Even though MGM never came to be regarded as a "directors' studio" in the way Paramount under Lubitsch in the 1930s would be, it facilitated filmmakers' creativity; the trick was to juggle the run-of-the-mill assignments with more personal ones. In his study of the Hollywood studio system, Thomas Schatz observes that directors such as Brown and Vidor did just that: "[they] learned their craft in the teens and distinguished themselves as silent filmmakers, but then adjusted to—and in many ways helped to shape—MGM's increasingly complex production system." According to Schatz, Brown was the "consummate Company Man," able to accommodate himself to the demands of the system, even if it meant stifling his own creative impulses. Underlying this characterization is a certain assumption that Brown invariably and passively toed the line, yet this wasn't always the case during his prolific career at the studio. Those who worked with him, such as Gene Reynolds, Claude Jarman Jr., and Marvin Kaplan, could attest to the fact that he was not above displays of temper, and Brown had a reputation for being impatient and demanding, especially in dealings with the casting and technical departments. Correspondence with various producers also confirms that once Brown was on the set, his word was law, and he rarely countenanced challenges to his authority by interfering producers (which is why working with David O. Selznick so exasperated him). True, he took on his fair share of mediocre assignments, as did most studio directors of that era, but when he fought for a project, he fought hard. It was perhaps his appreciation of studio politics—knowing when to push personal projects and when to acquiesce to the corporation's wishes—that accounted for this "Company Man" profile more than any unquestioning acceptance of his lot.[2]

Brown's confidence and determination were revealed in a 1927 profile by visiting English journalist Alice Williamson. She noted he was "a born director because of his own strong personality and his power to bring out—to *wring* out if necessary—the personality of others. Yes, he was *born* to be a

71

director, though he and his people had very different ideas in his boyhood of what a young man's career should be. He studied engineering . . . [and] . . . it implanted ideas of constructiveness and showed him his own talent as an organizer. Perhaps, also, it gave him something of his famous 'flair' for 'spotting' successes. Clarence Brown seems to know by instinct what will succeed and what will not." Williamson's profile may be gushing, but it offers some interesting insight into the qualities that would earn Brown respect in the industry. There is no denying, too, that his position at MGM was greatly enhanced by his immediate and close friendship with his boss, Louis B. Mayer. Mayer has often been caricatured as a vulgar philistine, but even his worst enemies had to concede that he was "a consummate tactician and psychologist, well known for his ability to cultivate and control MGM's top talent." Mayer was a strong leader who appreciated talent, but he inevitably favored those directors who kept an eye on the bottom line. Some may have regarded Brown's friendship with his boss as purely tactical, but there is no doubt it was genuine; in fact, it deepened after Mayer was ousted from power in the 1950s. The two men had different backgrounds and religions, but they shared similar outlooks on politics (conservative), business dealings (ruthless and canny), and family (a sentimental attachment to traditional values, even though they didn't adhere to them in their private behavior). When interviewed by Gary Carey in the 1970s, Brown identified Mayer's combined pragmatism and creativity as the trait he most admired: "he [Mayer] still had his weak spots and he got the right people to fill them in. Like Hearst and Henry Ford, he was an executive genius."[3]

Relations between Brown and second-in-command Irving Thalberg, the former "boy wonder" of Universal, were less hearty. They had encountered each other earlier, when Brown had negotiated a hefty price for the rights to *The Unholy Three*. According to Brown, Thalberg still nursed a grudge, but business came first. In the decade that followed, Brown and Thalberg developed a working relationship that was cordial but not exactly warm. In truth, Thalberg was not the kind of man who encouraged his staff to treat him like a pal, and although his tight circle of confidants considered him a creative genius and regarded him with awe, he was every bit the hard-nosed businessman. Compared with Mayer, Thalberg exercised his authority in a subtler but no less tyrannical fashion. As studio manager and fixer Eddie Mannix once observed: "Irving was a sweet guy but he could piss ice water." Brown had fewer dealings with Thalberg than with Mayer, but Thalberg had masterminded the system of producer supervision, and Brown was obliged to adhere to it.[4]

It goes without saying that diplomatic skills were crucial to survival at MGM. When Brown first reported to the lot, it was with the understanding that his debut assignment would be an epic of the Gold Rush, *The Trail of '98*, based on a long poem by Robert Service. However, he soon found that plans could change if the box office dictated. With the studio basking in the astonishing success of *The Big Parade*, everyone was eager to rush out a new film starring the now-hot John Gilbert, and Brown was lined up to direct. The property chosen was *The Undying Past*, an 1893 novel by Hermann Sudermann set in nineteenth-century Prussia; it related the tale of a love triangle involving two best friends, Ulrich (a sickly intellectual) and Leo (a robust he-man), and the alluring but heartless Felicitas. Sudermann's overwrought (and overwritten) melodramas are now largely forgotten, but Hollywood was having a bit of a love affair with them in the 1920s: several of his works were adapted to the screen, including his story "Die Reise Nach Tilsit," which served as the basis for Murnau's *Sunrise*.[5]

The Undying Past had been floating around since 1922, and it was generally accepted that extensive cutting would be required to shape it into a viable script. Records show that a host of top writers tried to come up with a treatment, including Mary Alice Scully, Frederica Sagor (with Max Marcin), and Benjamin Glazer. All concentrated on slashing the 400-page novel, eliminating some of the superfluous secondary characters and subplots, and transforming it into a blunt exploration of the dynamics of male-male and male-female relationships. The drafts by Scully and Sagor retained the basics of Sudermann's novel (for example, Felicitas's child) but added some bizarre details, such as a description of Felicitas as having "the face of an angel, but the temper of a sow," and an ending in which Felicitas elopes with a sea captain, only to end up as his skivvy. A happy ending in which the newly meek Felicitas reunites with Leo was also tested (but ultimately not retained). Most treatments concentrated on building up the character of Leo: Sagor's correspondence with collaborator Marcin outlines her attempt to imbue the character with "as much of a romantic flair as possible" and to elevate the heavy Sudermann mood and turn it into "a lighter, more entertaining story." New comedy scenes were added in the hope of winning over the audience and enhancing the theme of male solidarity: in one scene, soldier Ulrich tries to cover for an absent Leo during an early-morning drill exercise, and a subsequent one details their punishment (shoveling manure). Both were retained in the shooting script that was eventually used.[6]

As the screenwriters toiled, the studio tried to win over a reluctant Gilbert. He viewed the Sudermann story as a potboiler, the character of Leo as a foolish cliché, and the whole project as unworthy of his talents. He may have been swayed, just a little, when Brown was assigned to direct, but the deciding factor appears to have been the promise that the most intriguing actress on the lot, Greta Garbo, would be cast as Felicitas. Mayer had signed Garbo during a visit to Berlin in the spring of 1925, and she had arrived in Hollywood with her mentor, the great Finnish director Mauritz Stiller. Garbo's expectations that she and Stiller would be allowed to continue their collaboration were immediately dashed when MGM assigned Monta Bell to direct her in *The Torrent*. Stiller was put in charge of her second film, *The Temptress*, but he was fired within weeks, and the more amenable Fred Niblo took over. As Garbo was struggling to adjust to life in America and to speaking English, she became increasingly dismayed at the kind of roles she was being asked to play, both on camera and off. In one of the few interviews she gave before famously clamming up, she complained about being assigned femme fatale roles that required little of her apart from "getting dressed up" and "tempting men." She sank further into depression when the studio informed her that her third assignment would be more of the same: another melodrama, another temptress, and no Stiller. Despite her strenuous objections, and with no sympathy for the personal difficulties she was coping with (including the recent death of her sister), MGM pressed ahead, threatening to sue her for breach of contract if she didn't acquiesce.[7]

It was a defeated and hostile Garbo who showed up for her first day of shooting on August 17, 1926, at Lake Arrowhead. Brown did his best to thaw her out by showing tact, sympathizing on the loss of her sister, and encouraging her to "find" her way in the role of Felicitas. Gilbert was eager to help, not least because he was smitten and hoped to become more than just her costar. An attractive man, Gilbert was used to getting what he wanted, but on this occasion, his ardent advances were coolly rebuffed by the seemingly self-assured twenty-one-year old. Resistance made her all the more desirable, and he persisted. Within weeks she had capitulated, and the two were living together at his Tower Road mansion and enjoying an intense affair. Theirs was no slow-burn romance that unfolded in quiet moments between takes; it was ignited by the rolling of the camera, flaring bright but extinguishing almost as soon as it began. Brown witnessed it all, as he later told Gilbert's daughter: "Nobody else was even there. Those two were alone in a world of their own. It seemed like an intrusion to yell 'cut.' I just used to motion the crew over to another part of the set and let them finish what they were doing. It was embarrassing." Whatever it was—true love, true lust—it certainly did Brown's picture no harm.[8]

Eager to exploit the romance, MGM drafted screenwriter Frances Marion to rewrite some of the love scenes, making them even more provocative and giving full expression to the stars' undeniable chemistry. It was this, rather than the overheated plot, that provided some of the film's more memorable scenes, both for Brown and his crew and for audiences. Among them was what Brown called the screen's first "horizontal love scene." Shot in an opulent boudoir, it depicts the lovers luxuriating in postcoital bliss, with Felicitas taking on the traditional "masculine" position of the active lover, positively devouring her prone prey, the passive Leo. Actually, such staging was hardly unknown in Hollywood movies—in some of her "vamp" roles of the 1910s, Theda Bara strikes a similar pose—but in this case, what could have been high camp became sensuous and sensational, inevitably raising the hackles of the censors.[9]

The success of the boudoir scene was undoubtedly dependent on the performances of Gilbert and Garbo, but the exquisite cinematography—deep shadows enveloping Cedric Gibbons's opulent set and light sparking off the rich, luminescent material of Garbo's dress—played a part too. Brown had collaborated with his fair share of excellent cinematographers, including Milton Moore on *The Goose Woman,* van den Broek and van Enger on various Tourneur projects, and George Barnes on *The Eagle,* but something truly "clicked" when Brown and William Daniels met on the set of *Flesh and the Devil.* Their subsequent creative collaborations were intense, rewarding, and career-defining for both. It is not difficult to see why the two worked well together: both were methodical and businesslike on the set and committed to their studio, and both had personalities that were more retiring than gregarious. Daniels exhibited great self-assurance when handling the thorniest of problems, be they temperamental stars or demanding directors (he had worked with von Stroheim, after all), and Brown respected the way he combined that practicality with the sensitivity of an artist. Daniels admired Brown's "thoroughness" and his grasp of both the creative and the technical components of camera work, which, in his view, made Brown "a great technician and a fine director." The two came up with a complex and ambitious visual schema for *Flesh and the Devil* that included mattes, montage editing, chiaroscuro lighting, and silhouettes. Naturally, the design was all about showcasing the most important commodities in the film—the stars—but it also effectively underlined the sensuous mood and the various symbolic associations Brown was interested in exploring, such as the links between female sexuality and death and between desire and corruption. When Daniels was interviewed in the 1960s, he listed several scenes from Brown films as career highlights. One was the scene in which Felicitas seduces Leo, luring him away from a formal party and guiding him to a densely foliaged arbor bathed in nocturnal shadows, where they have their first kiss. As Brown and Daniels tried to figure out how to retain the shadows but illuminate the stars' faces, they hit on the idea of giving "Jack Gilbert two tiny pencil carbons to hold. When they kissed, the carbons lit up. His hand shielded the mechanism from the lens." This simple, if highly contrived, solution was a stroke of genius: few scenes can match the intensity and the combination of intimacy and danger on display here.[10]

They took an even more startlingly adventurous approach in the duel scene, which ends in the death of Felicitas's cuckolded husband (played by Marc McDermott) at the hands of Leo. As Brown explained, the decision to shoot the scene in such a highly stylized manner was intended not simply to show how arty he and Daniels could be but also to cleverly tackle a potential problem: "We had a case where the audience's sympathy was with Gilbert, of course, while a sense of justice gave sympathy also for McDermott. His character was not so well known, but he was the injured party. Now to show him actually killed would rob Gilbert of sympathy—and still the needs of Sudermann's story had to be met." According to Daniels, the answer came to Brown early one morning as he drove down La Cienega Boulevard and noticed "the stark trees against the white buildings." Excited and inspired, he described the effect to Daniels, and the two got to work: "We had to build a platform for the camera way, way back from the scene: it was almost like building a bridge. The difficulty was to maintain a proper level to ensure the silhouette worked." With the scene now framed in a long shot and the actors merely silhouettes, the potentially visceral action became more abstract but no less dramatic. As Brown noted: "we made this phase a sort of impersonal narration—the artificial aspect of the silhouettes removed the effect of the men's personalities still making their identities clear."[11]

Even before filming had wrapped, the buzz surrounding *Flesh and the Devil* was gathering pace, ramping up the pressure on Brown to pull it all together. There was a lot at stake: records indicate that MGM spent around $373,000, which included the costs of building a reproduction of the interior of Berlin's train station and a prewar Lutheran church. Brown paid attention to expenditures, worked out the technical challenges, and did his best to keep his patience when dealing with his two high-strung stars. Barbara Kent, who played Ulrich's little sister, Hertha (but was not a Brown "discovery," as inaccurately claimed elsewhere), remembered the director as having a "style that allowed us to rehearse and to find our own characters." He was, she recalled, "a very quiet man, and would talk to us in the softest voice." She witnessed the initial encounters between Brown and Garbo, and she marveled at how acutely he could sense the star's mood and adjust his technique accordingly: "He was especially careful with Garbo and would almost whisper his instructions to her."[12]

If Kent remembered an instant connection between director and star, Brown's recollection was a little different. He later admitted to Brownlow that he felt disappointed when he met her, especially when she made it clear that she resented the assignment. His heart sank at the prospect of spending weeks working with this enigmatic young woman who "never seemed to be doing anything" and, "when I'd ask her for a bit more . . . wasn't terribly responsive." His creeping sense of dismay was tempered, however, by his hunch that Garbo had *something*. Any reservations were swept aside when he viewed the dailies and realized he was dealing with a rare commodity: an actress truly *made* for films, one whose greatest lover was the camera. "It was all there," he recalled. "She had this remarkable ability to register thoughts and emotion without doing much of anything." Brown's oft-quoted assessment of what made Garbo such a formidable film actress also casts light on the universal qualities essential to acting for the camera: "Garbo had something behind the eyes that you couldn't see until you photographed it in close-up. You could see thought." In a host of interviews he gave in the 1960s, Brown confirmed that he adopted a special technique for directing Garbo, one defined by a willingness to let her go with her instincts in "finding" her character. Understandably, some who observed the interactions between Brown and Garbo assumed that she was a self-directed actress, but the considerable leeway Brown accorded her was based on an understanding that she would retreat or shut down if forced to perform a role in a certain fashion. According to at least one of Garbo's many biographers, Brown exercised an important influence over her American career because he was the "first director since Stiller to see the distinctly cinematic possibilities in her technique, the first who was sensitive enough to elicit a subtle performance from her, and the first who was capable of creating something more than a diverting melodrama."[13]

The technical and human demands of *Flesh and the Devil* were taxing, and adding to Brown's woes was the fact that the film lacked an ending even as it was being shot. In the novel, Leo and Ulrich are torn apart by their love for the destructive femme fatale, but they are finally reconciled when Felicitas conveniently drifts away and goes to live in Berlin. Hollywood, however, was much less inclined to let moral transgressions go unchecked, even in an age of apparent female emancipation and gender equality. As an adulterer and, more important, as the woman who comes between two men, Felicitas had to be punished, and in American movies, this usually involved death or, occasionally, jail or madness. It was an attitude shaped by larger forces—commercial, cultural, and industrial—as well as by pressure from the censors, which, though not as proactive as they would become in the post-1934 period, wielded considerable power. A variety of endings were toyed with, involving Felicitas's transformation from wanton and destructive she-devil to meek hausfrau, but all were deemed insufficiently harsh. Benjamin Glazer eventually concocted a climax that swiftly and nastily dispatched the hot-yet-chilly Felicitas: she falls through the ice and drowns as Ulrich and Leo, apparently oblivious to her flailing arms, gear up for a tender reconciliation. It was a rather campy way to end a film that admittedly often teetered on the brink, and Brown was concerned that it would be greeted with howls of laughter. To offset this campiness, and presumably to reassure audiences that the male characters were committed heterosexuals, MGM ordered an "epilogue" featuring a marriage between Leo and Hertha. Brown had mixed feelings about it, but he was also fearful that audiences might interpret the final fade-out on Leo and Ulrich as evidence that the two were "a couple of fairies." Company man that he was, he acquiesced to MGM's request and shot the ending, even though "it killed me," he admitted. Audiences were thus spared the specter of a homoerotic finale; whether they believed in the uniting of the heterosexual couple is another matter.[14]

When Brown commenced final editing in late 1926, he was confident he had a sensational film on his hands. He and Daniels had used striking visuals to immerse the audience in a lush, sensual world; now he collaborated with ace editor Lloyd "Ben Hur" Nosler to shape sequences to reflect the emotional mood and retain the viewer's interest. Varying the pace between languid and energetic, Brown called on all the skills he had acquired during his Tourneur apprenticeship, and after weeks of work he declared that he was satisfied. He was particularly proud of one sequence that depicts Leo making his way back across continents, using all modes of transport, to be reunited with Felicitas. It was shot on land that later became the Los Angeles airport, and he assembled it using montage-style cutting to emphasize the internal rhythm of the sequence: "I synchronized the beat of the hoofs with the name of the girl . . . Fe-li-ci-tas . . . superimposed . . . from the hoofs hitting the sod, we went to a steamer, and pistons seemed to be saying 'Fe-li-ci-tas.' . . . Each cut was faster as the method of transportation became faster."[15]

Viewed today, *Flesh and the Devil* seems to encapsulate the apex of silent cinema: innovative cinematography and editing, as well as intense performances, convey the story without the need for dialogue. Screenwriter John

Howard Lawson, however, has offered an intriguing anecdote that suggests the studio was worried that audiences might not be sufficiently hooked. According to Lawson, Thalberg asked him to write a sound sequence for the film, and although he was skeptical that "Gilbert and Garbo were not ready to undertake the ordeal of speech . . . [and] . . . that words would annihilate the pictorial magic," Lawson claims that he came up with "a fantastic dream sequence for *Flesh and the Devil*, with sounds and voices coming from a void." He recalls that the sequence was presented to Brown, who read it and "tossed it aside," but Thalberg was more appreciative, even though he ultimately decided not to use it. It is certainly a fascinating snippet, one that might force historians to rethink the backstory of this important film, but it simply doesn't add up: shooting ended on *Flesh and the Devil* in the fall of 1926, a year before Warner released *The Jazz Singer*. However, it is possible that Lawson's memory was generally accurate but he was mistaken about the title of the production: Mark Vieira quotes the same anecdote, but in relation to the later Brown-Garbo-Gilbert production *A Woman of Affairs*.[16] Neither film has any sound sequences.

After a preview for critics in December 1926, MGM officially launched *Flesh and the Devil* at glitzy premieres in New York's Capitol Theater and the Forum in Los Angeles in January 1927. In a romantic dress of pink chiffon (so unlike the androgynous attire she later favored), Garbo attended the Los Angeles premiere on the arm of Gilbert and greeted the crowds with a smile. Once inside, the audience was treated to stunning cinematography, the ardent embraces of the beautiful lovers, and risqué material that thrilled and titillated, all to the strains of a full orchestra. Afterward, Brown and Ona hosted a party for cast and crew and the cream of Hollywood society at the Montmartre Café.

In the days that followed, the buzz around *Flesh and the Devil* intensified, sparked by the public's interest in the stars' real-life love affair, but also by the largely enthusiastic reviews that were trickling in. Writing in the *New York Times*, Mordaunt Hall praised Brown's blending of "hard and fast realism with soft and poetic glimpses" and cited some stand-out scenes, such as the lovers' first encounter, the couple's first dance, the duel scene, and the church scene in which Felicitas scandalously makes her desire apparent. "Mae Tinee" was titillated by MGM's "hot drama" and praised it as "magnificently produced and beautifully photographed." Such "hot drama" raised concerns among those inclined to censor such shenanigans, with trade journalist Herbert Moulton predicting that the love affair between Leo and Felicitas was so "superheated" it would lead to "censorial objections." He noted that "some souls are likely to squirm because of a realism in certain scenes that leaves very little even to a poor imagination." Years later, Garbo's performance still had the power to enrapture even the most intellectual of men. Theorist Rudolf Arnheim recalled a frisson of delight when he witnessed her entrance in *Flesh and the Devil* and speculated that most of the audience had experienced the same: "On quiet cat's feet, her coat pulled tightly about her and her hands folded in her lap, Greta Garbo passes censorship. And every evening in the theater, three hundred men are unfaithful to their wives."[17]

Flesh and the Devil also attracted considerable attention for its director, with *Variety* citing the film as proof that American directors could hold their own against the recent invasion of European émigrés: "Clarence Brown ranks with the best of the imported directors when it comes to handling sophisticated stuff. Brown is the first of our own directors to show something that carries the conviction that he knows what it is all about when he decides to adopt the German technique in the making of pictures." Raves about Hollywood directors were hardly rare in the pages of *Variety*, but even those who viewed American movies with some skepticism were entranced by Brown's film. Writing in the highbrow journal *Film Spectator*, Welford Beaton praised this "director's picture," noting that Brown, "more than any other American director . . . invests a picture with the proper atmosphere to match the mood of the story" and, in doing so, creates a film "extraordinary for the beauty of its scenes and businesslike connection between the scenes and action" (which Beaton attributed to Brown's engineering background). Beaton was impressed by the versatility of a director who, after making the "drab and sordid" *The Goose Woman*, could move on to make such a "colorful and elaborate" film and "elevate a program picture to one of the greatest works of art ever produced." The notion that *Flesh and the Devil* was a "director's film" seems to be borne out by the significant attention and admiration it earned among Brown's peers: Ernst Lubitsch acknowledged it as an influence on his own *The Student Prince in Old Heidelberg*; screenwriter Philip Dunne, who worked with Brown in the 1930s, remembered *Flesh and the Devil* being screened by his Harvard professor during a lecture on film as art; and Jean Renoir was so impressed by the film (and by Brown generally) that he reportedly hoped to direct a remake of it in the 1950s.[18]

Amidst all the acclaim, however, there were some notes of disquiet. Back in Sweden, Garbo's mother complained that her daughter and Gilbert "didn't need to kiss so much," while the star herself expressed indifference to the role: "I am just the bad woman. In the end I fall through the ice so the play can go on." But Garbo's quote became just another way to sell the film, an illustration of her growing reputation for churlishness in the face of stardom. A more damaging appraisal appeared in the *New York Times*. Commenting on a scene in which Leo realizes Felicitas's true nature, John Cohen mocked Gilbert's delivery and expressed approval of the audience's less than respectful response: "[he] gives her a look of utter contempt, mingled with pain and disgust—in other words, a dirty look—and at that tense moment the audience . . . fairly howled with laughter. . . . Healthy American lads like Mr. Gilbert can't get away with such tactics." It was a shrewd if mean-spirited assessment of Gilbert's inadequacies as an actor, and it wouldn't be the last. Similar to Valentino, Gilbert's acting and his star persona had a tendency to alienate male audiences, as acquaintance Louise Brooks noted: "He was a kind of disgrace to their sex—feminine, not homo, but wildly emotional." It was Gilbert's overly emotive but increasingly dated technique, combined with a reckless approach to personal matters, more than any feud with Mayer, that led to the actor's sad, final fade-out in the early 1930s.[19]

If Gilbert seemed to be on borrowed time, Brown was riding high, bringing in a salary of $2,500 per week (on a par with King Vidor) and accompanying Ona to Hollywood soirées, nights at the Cocoanut Grove, lunches at the Brown Derby, and endless charity events. As was expected of major Hollywood players, the Browns purchased a luxurious house at 1022 Tower Road in Beverly Hills, with Gilbert and Vidor as neighbors, and Ona presided over ambitious remodeling and decorating projects. Brown also engaged in the profitable sideline of real estate investment, which he had initiated upon his arrival in Los Angeles in the early 1920s, and he proved to be a canny investor, amassing a largely blue-chip portfolio (it included part ownership of the Beverly Hills Hotel and extensive holdings in the developing tourist mecca of Lake Arrowhead).[20]

Yet in spite of his wealth and success, Brown was increasingly unhappy in his marriage to Ona. The couple seemed to have it all, but they were living separate lives, and rumors of marital discord became impossible to quash when it was reported that Ona had holidayed alone in Honolulu in December 1926. Hasty efforts were made to reassure the public that all was well, and a "lonely" Brown, accompanied by a photographer, rushed to the railroad station to welcome her home, but it was only a matter of time before the official announcement of divorce was issued. In February 1927, as he left for Denver to begin location work on his next assignment, Ona served him with divorce papers, accusing him of being "cold and indifferent" and conveying the "public indication that she bored him." More damaging were statements she made in a mournful interview soon after the divorce was granted. She claimed she had sacrificed her own independence to help him advance his career and had been rewarded with a stripping away of her dignity: "[this marriage] cost me my home, for he got to thinking so well of himself he attempted to boss the house. He went nearly a year without even speaking to me."[21]

It was an acrimonious split, and the two remained bitter even after they both remarried. Yet for all her alleged self-sacrifice, Ona Brown didn't do too badly in the marriage. As the wife of a Hollywood director, she could spend money freely and excessively, without even a hint of self-scrutiny. In a 1926 profile she claimed to "live for others, never for myself . . . I am always nice to poor people . . . I often take boxes of candy down and hand them around on my husband's lot." But as the writer dryly noted, she made these statements while wearing at least "$50,000 worth of jewels." When they divorced, Ona accused her husband of indifference, and he claimed that she was profligate, but it was Ona, not Clarence, who garnered most of the sympathy in Hollywood: the sin of being a spendthrift was apparently a lot less serious than that of being a cold fish. Seventy years after the Browns' divorce, screenwriter Frederica Sagor (now Frederica Sagor Maas) still carried a grudge about how the "cold hombre" had treated his wife, yet the sad portrait she paints of the forlorn Ona who fell in love, gave up everything, and was cast aside was less than accurate. Even Sagor Maas had to admit that Brown gave Ona "a generous legal settlement" when he "retired her to the desert sands of Palm Springs . . . in obscurity . . . far from the limelight of Hollywood that she had loved so very much." But what she didn't reveal was how swiftly Ona bounced back. Within a year, she had announced her engagement to Harvey Barnes Jr., a "member of a wealthy and prominent Pittsburgh family." The couple settled in Palm Springs, and the marriage was apparently still going strong in March 1937 when the *Los Angeles Times* carried a short piece on Ona.[22]

Perhaps the prospect of an uncertain future pushed Ona into a hasty remarriage, but Brown was under no such pressure. He walked away from his failed second marriage and enthusiastically embarked on what he would later call "tom cat" behavior with his pals John Gilbert, King Vidor, and serial womanizer Howard Hughes. He soon discovered that there was no lack of eager, commitment-phobic starlets to play with, including the vivacious Sally O'Neill, who helped distract him from the pressures of work and post-divorce stress; a brief but apparently serious flirtation with actress Dorothy Burgess; and an affair with Argentinean star Mona Maris that almost brought him to the altar for a third time. And while he later maintained that he was one of the few directors to steer clear of on-set romances, he bent his own rules when he met the sparky ex-lover of Buster Keaton on the set of *A Woman of Affairs*.

Dorothy Sebastian was unlike the poised, rather aloof women to whom he was typically drawn, and she apparently so beguiled him that he proposed to her. If there was any truth to reports that the often morose Brown treated his wives with coldness, it seems fitting that the mischievous, free-spirited Sebastian gave him the runaround for several months before dumping him after the film was released.

But all that was still in the future. Before the shocking Miss Sebastian could turn his world upside down, Brown's next project for MGM, *The Trail of '98*, was on the horizon. It turned into the most challenging production of his career thus far, a film that ended up costing the studio a fortune and several stuntmen their lives. It also brought Brown to the brink of collapse.

9

On the *Trail of '98*

Even as he was putting the final touches to *Flesh and the Devil*, speculation was rife about what was next for Brown. He had been tapped to direct Lillian Gish in an adaptation of *The Wind*, Dorothy Scarborough's novel about life on the harsh West Texas frontier, and he had even done some location scouting in the San Joaquin Valley and at Yosemite in October 1926. At the end of the year, however, he bowed out of the project, later confessing that he couldn't face a grueling shoot for a film that might flop at the box office ("People just don't like wind!" he claimed). *The Wind* was reassigned to his friend Viktor Sjöström, who directed it under his Americanized name Seastrom and endured unbearable conditions while filming in the Mojave Desert. The result was one of the last masterpieces of the silent era, but Brown's prediction was borne out when the film scarcely recouped its costs.[1]

It is ironic that the prospect of a taxing production discouraged Brown from directing *The Wind*, because the project he replaced it with developed into a veritable nightmare. In December 1926 it was announced that Brown would commence production on the film he had originally been set to direct when he first signed with MGM. Robert Service's *The Trail of '98* was an epic account of the Klondike Gold Rush, detailing the lives of the '98ers and the turbulent romance of one prospecting couple, Berna and Athol. It had first been considered by the Goldwyn studio as early as 1921—when a reader's report warned that the novel's controversial elements of rape and illegitimacy would need to be "toned down." B. P. Schulberg bought the story for $5,000 in 1922; he sold it to director Frank Lloyd, who in turn passed it on to MGM for $18,000. Presumably, the studio hoped the prestige of the Service name, along with the story's ambitious sweep, would capture audiences' hearts and wallets in the same way *The Big Parade* had. Former journalist, sometime director, and now producer Hunt Stromberg was assigned to make it happen. It was something of an industry joke that Stromberg was fixated on producing movies with democratic appeal that could speak to even a "dumb Scranton miner."

Certainly, his correspondence with the writers, Benjamin Glazer and Walde-mar Young—a former journalist who had been working in San Francisco when gold fever struck in the Klondike—was littered with demands that they incorporate heartwarming content into the script. In one memo he reminded the writers that at the core of the story was "a beautiful, delicate soul, the soul of a woman, [who] is being sacrificed on the altar of . . . Gold! Klondike! Gold!" Stromberg had lofty expectations that *The Trail of '98* would be a sen-sitively realized story of love against the odds, set against a spectacularly shot re-creation of a historical moment. However, in an effort to hedge his bets, he also instructed the writers to include a few comic scenes featuring perennial buffoon Karl Dane.[2]

With script preparations ongoing, Brown's assistant Charles Dorian, along with MGM's research department, trawled the archives of the *San Francisco Chronicle* and interviewed some of the remaining "sourdoughs" who had made the trip up north. No expense was spared to buy memorabilia, letters, and diaries of the day, as well as photographs of Gold Rush towns and miners' camps. Hundreds of photographs of San Francisco (where the prospectors departed from) and of the infamous trek up the Chilkoot Pass were also acquired, along with some substantial props from the period, including a ferry that had transported prospectors out of San Francisco. Because this was relatively recent history, a few veterans were still sharp enough to be hired as consultants: Frank Smith, a former employee of the Alaska Commercial Com-pany, was taken on as "chief technical adviser," aided by old-timers "Slim" Morgan and "Cherokee Ed" Scott Turner.[3]

Brown's confidence that his epic would have the success (and scale) of King Vidor's *The Big Parade* took a dent even before the cameras started to roll. Despite all the resources MGM had assigned to the project, a crucial problem arose when the studio was unable to cast a star in either of the lead roles. Brown had hoped for John Gilbert, but Gilbert and the studio couldn't agree on terms, and the actor moved on to another production (*Twelve Miles Out*). MGM made the decision to hire a second-string actor, Ralph Forbes, in his place. Forbes was barely known and lacked the charisma of a leading man. There was no enthralling leading lady, either. Rumors that Pauline Starke or Joan Crawford (then relatively new to the studio) would be cast proved to be untrue, and MGM selected Dolores del Rio to take the lead. Although Brown knew del Rio socially and liked her, he had reservations about her suitability: she had more star power than Forbes, but whether she could carry a film was another matter. Brown could at least take consolation that the supporting cast featured some of the cream of Hollywood character actors, such as Tully Marshall, Cesare Gravina, and future western star Harry Carey, as well as a very young Lou Costello (who appeared as an extra). As a favor to Maurice Tourneur, his son Jacques was given a small role, and the latter retained some vivid memories of what turned out to be a punishing shoot. Perhaps in anticipation of things to come, Brown seemed more enthusiastic about (and admiring of) his nonhuman cast of hundreds of husky and malamute sled dogs, goats, and horses than he was about his human stars.[4]

Trail required a significant amount of location work, and as Brown prepared to depart for Colorado in March 1927, he had a buoyant air. Yet even as he assured journalists that the epic sweep of the film would not "overshadow his story" of "real men and women," his doubts were intensifying. His enthusiasm had suffered another blow when he read the Glazer-Young script and found it to be mediocre, filled with thinly drawn characters battling through a storm of clichés about gold fever and the limits of human endurance. It was the kind of script that would have challenged even the most accomplished actors, and regrettably, neither Forbes nor del Rio could be regarded as such. Although Jacques Tourneur recalled witnessing some warm moments between Brown and Forbes on the set (especially when the two celebrated the news of Charles Lindbergh's crossing of the Atlantic), Brown apparently retained no such fond memories. At the time, Forbes praised his director as the kind who "listens to what people say," but Brown was less than complimentary, later ranking Forbes as "the lousiest leading man that ever lived" and sneering that the makeup department had to glue hair on his chest to make him "look like a man." Brown's glacial front no doubt affected Forbes, who delivered a pretty unconvincing performance, but Brown didn't get much out of del Rio, either. In fact, apart from the much-admired sled dogs, it seems that the only actor Brown warmed to was Harry Carey, playing the villain Jack Locasto. The two collaborated affably and stayed in contact, but not, as it turned out, because of any pride in their mutual endeavor: Carey thereafter referred to *Trail* as "The Smell of the Yukon."[5]

One has a sense that the methodical engineer in Brown overwhelmed the dynamic storyteller, despite his best efforts to bring the thin narrative to life. Working closely with John Seitz, the famed cinematographer for most of Rex Ingram's films, Brown made ample use of innovative camera work, and there was certainly no shortage of logistical problems to solve on the set. Many of these were of Brown's own making, given his insistence that this complicated production be shot on location. The obvious choice would have been the historical site of the Gold Rush—in the Yukon (Canada) and along the border with Alaska (for the Chilkoot Pass scenes)—locations that studio scout Al

Rehbeck had checked out in the summer of 1926. However, it was ultimately decided to situate the main unit a little closer to California. Colorado was identified as the most suitable location for the majority of exteriors; interiors, including replicas of Dawson City's business district, a saloon, and a dance hall, would be shot back in Culver City. According to some sources, "location work" was also faked on the studio back lot, though neither MGM nor Brown was keen to admit it. In addition, the studio sent several second units to Alaska, under the supervision of Harry Schenck, to film some of the action sequences and capture authentic backdrops.[6]

Brown later rated *The Trail of '98* as "the hardest picture I ever made," ranking it alongside the miserable experience of shooting *The Yearling*. The earlier-than-usual thaw that had been predicted never materialized, and even in March temperatures dipped well below zero at night. Brown and his unit endured a "constant battle against the elements," which included cold, wind, snowstorms, and high altitude. The main unit settled into a replica of a small mining camp that had been built at the Continental Divide, close to the Gold Rush ghost town of Corona, and an on-site Pullman train, equipped with a radio car and sleeping bunks, served as their makeshift accommodations. It was a difficult adjustment for actors who were accustomed to the luxuries of MGM dressing rooms and back-lot bungalows, and even comedienne Polly Moran's attempts to lift everyone's spirits with nightly camp broadcasts rapidly wore thin. For members of the cast and crew involved in filming the trek up the Chilkoot Pass, conditions were even more abysmal. The move into the high Rockies resulted in an intensification of altitude sickness and a plummeting of living standards. As Brown remembered: "The first night we spent in the snowsheds, I nearly went out of my head. I woke up in the middle of the night, almost suffocated by fumes from the engine and the smoke pouring in from other trains passing through. I tried to get some air, but I couldn't find a way out. I'll never forget that experience."[7]

Originally, Brown and Seitz had planned to use aerial photography to depict the prospectors' ascent through the daunting pass, but poor weather and a desire for "authenticity"—close-ups of the strained faces of the men as they laboriously trudged along—had convinced them that the sequence must be shot from the ground. With the terrible conditions affecting everyone's health, Brown was weighed down by a sense of responsibility to his cast and crew, as well as by the practical problems of filming in such difficult terrain. He had a reputation for driving his crew hard and was often not well liked, but those who worked with him remembered Brown as the kind of director who never went for the easy option; he preferred to be in the thick of things, working to come up with solutions to technical challenges. To capture the ascent of the '98ers, once again Brown called on his engineering background: "We built a track parallel to their route and built a sled for our cameras. We lashed three cameras to the sled, with three different lenses. At the top was a power windlass, which could be controlled by signals from the camera, so that we were able to follow people up, stop, go back, and take close-ups of the incidents that happened on the way up."[8]

Brown's immersion in the technical side came at a cost for some of the less important members of the cast: the scores of extras MGM had brought in to fill the background or depict the '98ers. In the days before the Screen Actors Guild or the Screen Extras Guild, studios could pay as little as they pleased, and shooting on location often meant even less regulation. For the Chilkoot Pass sequence, indigents were scooped up from the streets of downtown Denver with the promise of food and a day's wage; they were transported up to the high Rockies before dawn, spent the day trekking up the trail, and were then deposited back on the Denver streets as night fell.[9]

The weeks spent in Colorado were undeniably grueling for Brown and his company, but they didn't compare to what the second unit lived through. Their location near Skagway, Alaska, was about as harsh as it could get: difficult to access, unrelentingly cold, and with only the most primitive facilities on-site. The second unit was responsible for shooting many of the most demanding and dangerous live-action sequences. Interviewed for the television series *Hollywood,* two of the stuntmen recalled the lengths to which they went to capture one sequence depicting prospectors traversing the dangerous White Horse Rapids—and the tragic events that ensued. Hollywood stuntmen in the 1920s were the toughest of the tough and fairly phlegmatic about the risks associated with their profession. Even so, Bob Rose and Paul Malvern admitted that this particular sequence made everyone unusually nervous, and they had requested special safety measures (iron hoops fitted to the safety ropes to ensure a firmer grip). As a camera mounted on a Ford chassis shot from shore, the men boarded makeshift canoes and rafts and began their trip down a river that had more water "pouring through" it than "the Mississippi at its highest tide." Malvern recalled how quickly his canoe gathered speed, eventually hurtling along at thirty-five miles an hour in the face of ten-foot walls of water. It was undeniably a spectacular sequence, but it was achieved at an appalling and unforgiveable cost: while attempting to pull themselves out of the water, several men were dragged down by the current, and their efforts to grip the rope failed as they discovered that the promised safety hoops had never been installed. This carelessness resulted in several deaths and a hasty effort by MGM to hush up the remaining crew. It is unclear how many men died during the filming of this sequence and how many others died during production. Malvern recorded that four men drowned, but only two bodies were recovered. Brown believed the total was three dead in Alaska, along with another "two or three" fatalities in an avalanche in Denver. In addition to the human loss, scores of animals succumbed to accidents and pneumonia.[10]

Location shooting for all units finally finished up in July, but Brown still faced weeks of interiors and some retakes, albeit in the warmer climes of Culver City. He was left with reams of footage that had to be fashioned into a reasonably coherent film. It was a difficult and time-consuming task that required all the skills of Brown, editor George Hively, and the MGM editing department, presided over by the legendary Margaret Booth. She recalled that a team was still working on it, frantically splicing in titles, even as they were on board the studio's special train, headed for the preview at San Bernardino. Despite their best efforts, little could be done to make the film hang together.[11]

Perhaps in the hope that ballyhoo publicity and bold exhibition strategies would divert attention from the content, MGM hosted a lavish premiere at the newly opened Grauman's Chinese Theater on May 7, 1928. It was a fitting venue, given that its owner had traveled to the Klondike as a teenager and spent two years there gambling, staging revues for miners, and selling newspapers. Grauman himself helped devise a special prologue, featuring an Alaskan dance-hall set, that preceded the screening. The live-action segment was in keeping with the spirit of an "event" screening, which had become quite common for big-budget extravaganzas. In the case of *Trail*, it introduced audiences to a new gimmick: the "Fantom screen." Edwin Schallert described the spectacle: "The Alaskan dance-hall set on which the prologue was staged was arranged in two movable sections, and at the finale these were separated giving a gradually enlarging view of the motion picture screen in the background. As the two movable platforms were carried off, one to the right and one to the left, respectively, the words 'the Trail of '98' began to appear on the screen with the aurora-borealis lighting effects. Then by degrees the screen itself was moved forward to its normal position in relation to the audience."[12]

The prologue may have been imposing, but neither audiences nor critics were sucked in. The latter commented on the film's weak narrative and poorly drawn characters, noting that these flaws distracted from the elements of the film that *did* work, such as the live-action sequences and scenes of life on the trail. Mordaunt Hall concluded that the film was a mixed bag: it had too much of what he regarded as Brown's weakness—a certain "penchant" for symbolism—but sufficient action sequences that could "compensate for any overacting, lack of true psychology or other minor shortcomings." Norbert Lusk's review was more positive, but interestingly, he reported that audiences responded most warmly to the slapstick scenes featuring Karl Dane.[13]

As it turned out, the harshest critic of *The Trail of '98* was Brown himself: "[It] wasn't too hot. Storywise, directionwise, and actingwise I was never too happy with it. It was just one of those conglomerates." If nothing else, *Trail* served as a lesson about the perils of big-budget productions: because there was so much at stake, everyone got a say, and everything—comedy, drama, romance—was added to the mix in the hope that something would stick. The need for extensive location work, and the complications that ensued, meant that for the first time in his career, Brown lost control over the production, and once the footage came in from the various units, he couldn't meld it together. Brown's damning judgment of *Trail* was undoubtedly colored by his frustration, his hurt pride, and his disappointment, because it overlooked some of the film's finer qualities. There is no shortage of memorable moments and the flashes of inventiveness that define Brown's best work, and some sequences work very well, including an opening montage showing San Francisco in the grip of gold fever and a motley crew of eager prospectors departing on a train. To capture the embarkation, Brown uses the kind of fluid tracking shot he later employs in *Possessed* (a 1931 film in which Joan Crawford plays a prospector of another kind). The symbolism that Mordaunt Hall disliked is effective and visually striking in several scenes, including one in which the destitute Berna, now fallen on hard times and working as a "saloon girl," becomes the victim of the villainous Jack Locasto. Cribbing from his own *Flesh and the Devil,* and inspired by similar rape scenes in Griffith and von Stroheim films, Brown places the camera behind del Rio's head as she lies in bed, and as the door opens and Locasto enters, the screen is filled with a close-up of her hands, splayed and grasping as she realizes her fate. With a nod to the censor and to the strictures of good taste, Brown tactfully ends the scene with a cut to black.

With *Trail of '98* rapidly sinking at the box office, Brown rushed to preserve his critical reputation, and the fan magazines were happy to help. In a profile by Dorothy Manners, he was commended for his steadiness, his lack of temperament—a trait that distinguished him from European directors—and his canny commercial sense: "Brown goes along in his quiet way, never getting himself involved in a front-office rebellion, never squandering his company's money unnecessarily, never pulling any of the other fancy tricks of showmanship. . . . In meeting and talking with him you get none of that artistic sensitiveness that characterizes his pictures. He is like Jim Cruze and King Vidor in that. Off the set, these men seem to regard their work as a practicality. Only in their finished work do you sense the guidance of an artist behind it." Although his artistic vision in *Trail* had been a little blurred, Brown continued to be highly regarded by his peers, not least because most of them had endured similar disappointments and flops. The failure of *Trail* was a bitter pill to swallow, but swallow it he did, and in some ways, it helped make him into the studio director he became. It would be a decade before he tackled another mammoth production—again with mixed results—but in the meantime, he continued to develop a pragmatic approach underlined by the philosophy that filmmaking was a job: one might aspire to high art, but more often than not, the studio director had to be content (and indeed, proud) when he came up with a well-crafted piece of entertainment.[14]

Evidently, MGM still trusted Brown, and shortly after he finished *Trail*, he was asked to salvage the troubled production of George Hill's *The Cossacks*, starring John Gilbert. It, too, had been plagued with script problems and challenging location work, as well as Hill's erratic behavior. Brown shot some new scenes and oversaw the editing, but it only amounted to a patch-up job: "It was difficult to edit, the story did not hang together well, and the production costs were enormous. Whoever was to blame, it wasn't the fault of the actors." When the film was released, Brown left his name off the credits, which was just as well: reviewers were only lukewarm, and the film did weak business at the box office. After the debacle of *Trail* and the frustrations of *The Cossacks*, Brown must have experienced some creeping anxiety about the direction his career was taking. It would take a reunion with Garbo to put him back on track.[15]

10

An "Uplifting" Film

Adapting *The Green Hat*

Since last working with Brown, Greta Garbo had experienced something of a meteoric rise with *Love*, which reunited her with John Gilbert, and Sjöström's *The Divine Woman*. Even though the quality of the films was decidedly varied, it seemed that nothing could dampen audiences' enthusiasm for the enigmatic star who refused to play the publicity game. As she basked in the public's adoration and negotiated better contracts, the fortunes of her former costar and ex-lover proved less rosy. Critical disappointments such as *Man, Woman and Sin* and *The Cossacks* weren't quite death knells for Gilbert's career, but they didn't help his already precarious position at MGM. Thus, another collaboration with Garbo would be both desirable and expedient.

For their previous outings, MGM had turned to highbrow art (Tolstoy) and a potboiler (Sudermann); for their third pairing, the studio lined up one of the most sensational novels of the 1920s. With daring plotlines that included promiscuity, unwanted pregnancy, and syphilis and a cast of jaded sophisticates, Michael Arlen's *The Green Hat* had been eagerly consumed by an American public still grappling with new attitudes about sexuality. Soon after it was published in 1924, it was adapted for the stage in a Chicago run that featured Katharine Cornell; it then moved to Broadway and smashed box-office records, even as it left critics cold. Unsurprisingly, several Hollywood producers vied for the rights before Fox secured them (in 1926), but as the studio soon discovered, what played on page and stage didn't necessarily transfer to the American screen. Presented with a seemingly impossible dilemma—retain the risqué elements central to its commercial appeal and risk offending the censor, or sanitize it so completely that audiences were turned off—Fox let its option lapse, opening the way for Irving Thalberg to swoop in and buy it for $50,000 in June 1928.[1]

Thalberg's interest had been piqued even before Fox acquired the rights. Now he approached censors in the Hays office to determine how MGM could allay their concerns and assure them that the studio's proposed treatment (by Bess Meredyth) would be "practically a new story, taking all that is fine and worthwhile in the book . . . [and] . . . building it on a new clean foundation." He promised that MGM would cleanse the grubby novel and impart some moral lessons to the audience: "basic effect of the picture as a whole will have an uplifting quality . . . as a picture it will be a story of fine people fighting for fine ideals." In private, though, Thalberg was already grumbling about the Hays office's allegedly preferential treatment of rival studio Paramount and about the likelihood that the bulk of Arlen's titillating material might end up in the trash can even before the cameras rolled.[2]

Thalberg was a pragmatist, however, and he was also protective of MGM's reputation for releasing "clean pictures." He was therefore fully aware that Arlen's novel could never be filmed without amendments. Garbo, too, understood the need to tread carefully when it came to choosing roles, even if she privately admired the controversial work of playwrights such as Ibsen (whose *Ghosts* also dealt with the taboo topic of venereal disease). While visual suggestion could be used to allude to Arlen's more provocative elements, and a new ending could be introduced to ensure that all transgressions were punished, playing the bride of a syphilitic husband was simply too much for Garbo. After casting around for alternative "diseases," Meredyth eventually came up with the crime of embezzlement to explain David's guilt that drives him to suicide on his wedding night.[3]

As amendments were made to Arlen's plot, there was still the thorny issue of that infamous title. The Hays office was adamant that the studio change it, if only to create some distance (albeit superficial) from the Arlen novel. MGM toyed with various alternatives, including *The Outcast Lady*, before coming up with *A Woman of Affairs*. Meredyth also changed the heroine's name from Iris March to Diana Merrick, signaling a shift away from Arlen's nihilistic, promiscuous antiheroine whose name carried mythological associations with death to a more tragic, brave, Garboesque heroine whose only sin is to love and pander to a host of weak and unworthy men. The Hays office confirmed its approval of the new script, which had "removed from the situation the objectionable details," and shooting was set to commence in late July.[4]

The protracted negotiations were certainly frustrating for Thalberg, but at least they ensured that Brown, the studio's favored director, had time to finish

The Cossacks before reporting to the new production. After his experience on *Trail*, Brown may have been quietly relieved that there were no plans for extensive location work, other than short trips to nearby Franklin Canyon and to Busch Gardens in Pasadena, and he was certainly happy that he would once again be assisted by Charles Dorian and cinematographer Bill Daniels. The production also reunited Brown with Hobart Bosworth, with whom he had worked on *Foolish Matrons*. Here, Bosworth would be playing the role of the meddling father who destroys the lives of both his son (played by Gilbert) and Diana.

Initially, there was optimism that the success of *Flesh and the Devil* could be replicated with *A Woman of Affairs*, but Brown soon discovered that the power relations on the set were radically different. The end of Gilbert and Garbo's love affair had led to mutual bitterness, and the hot chemistry between them had been replaced with a coolness that colored their performances and played a part in neutralizing Arlen's novel. As the world-weary Diana, Garbo seemed older than her years, and Brown recognized a new confidence in the actress, tinged with wariness and moments of intransigence. Previously, whatever resistance he had encountered from Garbo had taken the form of emotional withdrawal and, from time to time, a seeming reluctance (albeit respectful) to "deliver" the kind of performance he wanted from her. By the time they reunited on *A Woman of Affairs*, the director and star were more in tune with each other both personally (they occasionally saw each other socially) and professionally (he now understood that she flourished when he stepped back and gave minimal direction).

Theirs was a generally amiable relationship, but there were occasional moments of strain. Photographer Edward Steichen recalls arriving on the set of *A Woman of Affairs* to take some stills, only to discover that tension was brewing. Garbo was the kind of actress who could deliver in one or two takes, and she tended to become increasingly stale with each new take. Brown was unhappy with her performance in the crucial wedding night sequence where, as she waits in bed, her husband paces the room and then suddenly hurls himself out the window. In Garbo's view, it had been good enough, but Brown refused to let it go. A stalemate was reached, and a short break was called. Steichen, who was both admiring and disapproving of Brown's doggedness, realized that now would be the perfect time to capture Garbo's authentic mood. Seating her on a chair, he suggested that she give vent to her emotions. Pushing back her carefully styled hair and staring moodily into the lens, she radiated frustration and melancholia—resulting in one of the most memorable portraits ever taken of her. The session evidently had a therapeutic effect on Garbo, too. As they finished up, she hugged Steichen and whispered, "Oh you, you should be a motion-picture director. You understand." She returned to the set, submitted to one more take, and resumed a cordial relationship with Brown.[5]

Minor skirmishes aside, Brown was quick to commend Garbo, marveling at her ability to inhabit a role and convey the inner life of even the most thinly drawn character. Indeed, the combination of Garbo's skill and Brown's directorial style produced a performance that easily ranks as one of her best. Her Diana Merrick is a master class in filmic acting: understated, reactive, natural, and startlingly *modern*. Actress Françoise Rosay, who was friendly with Garbo at the time and whose husband Jacques Feyder later directed her in *The Kiss*, her final silent film, offered an appraisal:

> She has in addition a quality of beauty that the camera favors; and sensitivity, a transparency, which provide her with a deep sense of the characters she has to perform. She doesn't play, she doesn't have any tricks of the trade or visible experience, she always seems to be performing in a documentary about herself, and without affectation. She seems to have been surprised by a skilful cameraman, and finally nothing that happens inside herself is enclosed and everything that crosses her mind goes through the spectator. She constitutes with her body, her voice and her face and her walk the whole atmosphere that surrounds her, a set of intelligible signs, and a living language that doesn't need commentary or translator.[6]

This evocation of inner life dominates Garbo's entire performance in *A Woman of Affairs*, but it is most striking in two scenes that also reveal Brown's visual inventiveness. Having endured years of mistreatment at the hands of her weak lover Neville, who has dropped her and married the more respectable Constance (played by Dorothy Sebastian), Diana succumbs to his advances one last time. Faced with the challenge of shooting a sex scene without showing the act itself, Brown uses visual symbolism to impressive effect. As the lovers recline on a chaise longue, the camera pans down to Garbo's hand as it clenches in passion and then relaxes in (assumed) surrender to Neville's attentions. The climax is naughtily conveyed with a close-up of her finger as her ring slides off, reminding the viewer of her previous observation that the ring, like her, is "apt to fall." It is a moment designed to exasperate the censors while titillating the audience, and one that illustrates how sophisticated and witty Brown could be. Brown later cited it as one of the scenes he was most proud of because it "summarizes my idea of sex." He may have had four wives and many lovers, but he was of the opinion that sex and romance were private activities that should not be tawdrily depicted onscreen.[7]

This kind of subtlety is also evident in his and Garbo's handling of one of the more controversial sequences in the film. As is so often the case in American movies of the time, Diana's moment of passion leads to devastating consequences: an unplanned pregnancy that ends in a stillbirth. Meredyth has peppered the scene with allusions and elisions that amount to a standard shorthand: pregnancy thus becomes an "illness," a "confinement" that takes around nine months to "cure." Brown opted to film the scene in a generally unobtrusive style that facilitates the tense unfolding of the action and allows Garbo's performance to slowly build. As Diana emerges from her hospital room, she comes across a bouquet of flowers left for her by Neville. She takes it in her arms and cradles it, as if it were her lost child. It is an extraordinarily intimate moment, filled with a sense of raw honesty and loss, and it still has the power to move. In the muddled belief that Neville has come back to her, Diana confesses her love, only to discover that his new wife is also in the room. Brown's camera alternates between reaction shots from Neville, Dr. Trevelyan (Lewis Stone), and the hospital staff and two-shots as Diana and Constance communicate their understanding of and sympathy for each other's plight. Although some directorial flourishes are in evidence—a fast track-in to Garbo's reaction as she realizes that Neville is lost to her, and a close-up of her hand clenching in anguish as her ring slips once more—Brown graciously lets this scene be about the two women, allowing the two actresses to convey their inner emotions so eloquently. As one Garbo biographer put it, the scene facilitates "one of the most majestic transformations in the cinema: from acting to being."[8]

With *A Woman of Affairs,* Garbo confirmed her assuredness as a silent film actress and reiterated her star persona as a melancholic outsider. For John Gilbert, however, the film proved less career defining. To his credit, he accepted the unsympathetic role of Neville Holderness, even though it was unlikely to enhance his fading reputation as a romantic lead. Gilbert's willingness to play such a weak character was a rather bold move, perhaps revealing his desire to prove that he could be a versatile actor (and not just a star). Brown had been skeptical about Gilbert's taking the part, but the actor had been adamant, even refusing offers of a rewrite to transform Neville into a more active and engaging character. Gilbert explained, "[I'd] rather you didn't touch my part a bit, Clarence. . . . My character *is* a weak character and he's got to be handled in that way." It is tempting to speculate that, after being rejected and humiliated by Garbo, Gilbert almost relished the prospect of playing a petulant, emotionally stunted character who causes the misery and eventual suicide of her Diana Merrick. Undoubtedly, and in anticipation of his final screen performance with her in *Queen Christina* (1933), Gilbert drew from his own reserves of regret and loss, adoration and passion to shape his performance.[9]

For all his bravery, though, it was clear to Brown that Gilbert was losing his nerve as an actor. With the advent of sound films and new styles of acting, Gilbert seemed self-conscious, as Brown remembered: "[He] kept enlarging on his performance with those extravagant stage gestures as if he were playing to a peanut gallery." Brown later speculated that Gilbert's failure to come to grips with the role and adjust his acting style was related to a larger personal crisis following the public disintegration of his romance with Garbo and ongoing squabbles with MGM and particularly with Mayer. Also lurking in the background was the stark reality that his films were not making the money they once had, and his luster seemed to be fading. Gilbert's drinking, which had once been manageable, became excessive, and he often arrived on set suffering the consequences of a binge. Gilbert's problems became Brown's, and a production that had promised to be relaxed and convivial became rather fraught. In the face of unreasonable behavior from his star, however, Brown remained loyal; above all, Gilbert was his friend, the man who had lent a sympathetic ear when Tourneur had bawled him out and the collaborator who had helped him make his directorial debut. Brown could be a tough character, and he was often regarded as a consummate tactician, but that was only one side of his complex character. Time and again, Brown showed sympathy for the underdog (offscreen and on), compassion and patience for those in a vulnerable state, and an abiding sense of loyalty, even at the expense of his own career. The teetotaler in Brown must have been disgusted by Gilbert's drinking, but he refused to turn his back on him. He even offered to help wean Gilbert off alcohol and to serve as a mediator in his dealings with Mayer. Despite his intervention, however, there was no stopping the actor's self-destructive decline.[10]

With so much of his time taken up negotiating with Garbo and tending to Gilbert, it is surprising that Brown had any energy left for the rest of the cast. Veterans like Bosworth and Stone scarcely needed much guidance, but the film also featured relative novices Douglas Fairbanks Jr. and Dorothy Sebastian. Fairbanks was struggling to carve out a career in the shadow of his father's overpowering stardom, and he later admitted that in those early years he had been both deeply insecure and brashly arrogant. Here, he was playing the unusual role of Diana's younger brother Jeffry, whose suppressed homosexuality leads to bouts of hysteria, rage, and uncontrolled drinking. It is unclear whether Brown approved of this casting choice or whether he regarded

Fairbanks Jr. as just another Hollywood brat who got the job through nepotism. Nevertheless, he maintained a professional front and, as Fairbanks recalled, was "very easygoing, soft spoken. . . . He directed by the subtlest of suggestions. He never demanded, he just kept going until we got it right." Only once did Brown lose his temper, during the shooting of Jeffry's death scene, The scene required Fairbanks to remain slumped in a chair, catatonic from an alcoholic binge, while being lectured by Dr. Trevelyan, but Fairbanks repeatedly broke character. He dissolved into fits of nervous laughter when his costar, who suffered from Parkinson's disease, was unable to control the involuntary nods and shakes that were part of his illness. After numerous ruined takes, Brown, "normally the soul of quiet, gum-chewing patience," called a halt. He bawled out Fairbanks and, suitably chastised, the actor finally got it together and completed the scene.[11]

With no end of actorly drama and directorial challenges on the set, it is little wonder that Brown sought distraction. Uncharacteristically—given his vow never to mix business with pleasure—he took up with Dorothy Sebastian, affectionately known as "Slam" owing to her tendency to slam into furniture when drunk. The pairing took many by surprise because the aloof Brown and the warm Sebastian were polar opposites. Nor was Sebastian the kind of girl Brown could bring home to his strict parents: she may have been southern (from Alabama), but her free-and-easy attitude toward drinking and sex would have offended their values. Brown remained devoted to his mother and later admitted to screenwriter Lenore Coffee that he had "never tasted liquor," but he couldn't resist the beautiful and sexy Sebastian. In truth, she was not unlike some of his former lovers: similar to Ona, Sebastian was a former showgirl who had started her career as a George White Scandals girl, before ascending the showbiz ladder by force of will, talent, and connections (some influential boyfriends). Yet Brown found in Sebastian a spontaneity that was markedly different from Ona's ambitious social climbing and his own cautious nature.[12]

Photoplay reported that their love was sealed when she accompanied him to a steak dinner after the Dempsey-Sharkey boxing match. Sebastian wasn't intent on snaring a husband, and she apparently had few qualms about moving in with him, but Brown was enough of a traditionalist to want to marry her. *Photoplay* was impressed, noting that he had given her the "largest engagement ring in Southern California."[13] Western star Tim McCoy, who was friendly with Sebastian around the time of the romance, doubted that she was truly in love with the dour Brown:

I remember the day Dorothy Sebastian arrived on the set wearing a ring in which was set a diamond seemingly only slightly smaller than a goose egg. "He asked me to marry him," Dorothy explained before any questions could be posed. "Will you?" I asked. "Hell, no!" she laughed and then recounted how her beau had given it to her the previous evening, pressing his case and adding rather gratuitously that even if Dorothy rejected him she need not return the ring. Gazing appreciatively at the glittering stone, she murmured warmly, "You can bet your sweet ass I won't."[14]

Although McCoy doesn't name Brown as Sebastian's "beau," news of their engagement coincided with her appearance in one of McCoy's westerns.

Ultimately, whether Sebastian saw Brown as a soul mate or a sugar daddy is a moot point: shortly after the release of *A Woman of Affairs*, it all fizzled out. Sebastian rekindled her relationship with Buster Keaton, and Brown moved on to starlet Sally Blane. If nothing else, his affair with Sebastian confirmed what Louise Brooks later observed about Brown: he was a complicated man who "detested lesbians . . . [but] adored Garbo; who hated whores and adored Dorothy Sebastian; who abominated drunkards and adored his [third] wife, Alice Joyce."[15]

A Woman of Affairs wrapped on September 11, 1928, and Brown spent the remainder of the fall preparing it for a December release. As expected, when it debuted, reviewers seemed fixated on the changes made to Arlen's novel. *Variety*'s critic appreciated Brown's direction but noted that the influence of the Hays office had resulted in a "vague and sterilized" film. Filmmaker Pare Lorentz, then a critic for *Judge*, filed a more considered review but admitted that he was baffled by the film's none-too-convincing elision of Arlen's risqué themes: "for some strange reason, instead of using the word 'purity' (the boy died for purity, according to Iris March) they substituted the oft-repeated word 'decency.' To anyone who can show me why 'purity' is a more immoral word than 'decency,' I'll gladly send an eighty-five cent Paramount ticket." Lorentz also offered his opinion of the film's strengths, which he attributed mainly to its star: "For the first time I respected the performance of Greta Garbo. She shuffled through the long, melancholy and sometimes beautiful scenes with more grace and sincerity than I have ever before observed, and the fact that she rode down and practically eliminated John Gilbert's goggling is in itself grounds for recommendation." Garbo also impressed Mordaunt Hall: "She compels attention, either by her languid eyes, her imperiousness or her marvelous understanding in registering before the camera just the right expression, never exaggerating, always true to the mood of this intense young woman." He offered praise, too, for Brown, citing his handling of "this production imaginatively and resourcefully," although he regretted the director's continued "penchant for flashes of symbolism." Others were more sniffy: Norbert Lusk, in a review that suggests he had some trouble separating Garbo from her character, noted that she played "a neurotic heroine modernized and excused by being termed a 'gallant lady' while there is really no excuse for her wayward promiscuity at all." With this lesson imparted to Garbo, he then offered some pithy advice to her costar, warning Gilbert that with roles like Neville, he was "sacrificing himself . . . to advance the fame of Miss Garbo."[16]

In spite of muted reviews and the inevitable competition from sound films, *A Woman of Affairs* performed relatively well at the box office, reaping a healthy profit of $417,000 and ensuring that MGM would recycle its basic plot in a later sound version called *Outcast Lady*, directed rather stodgily by Robert Z. Leonard. While it wasn't the smash hit that *Flesh and the Devil* had been, *A Woman of Affairs* certainly enhanced the reputations of both its female star and its director. It proved to be the perfect showcase for both Garbo's evolving acting style and Brown's blend of understatement and flamboyance. To circumvent the censors, he was allowed to let his creative imagination run free, using roving cameras, fast track-ins, intricate visual symbolism, and expressive lighting to suggest everything the Hays office had ordered expunged. Surprisingly naughty is the scene that suggests Diana's eagerness to consummate her marriage to David: reclining on the marital bed, she impatiently tugs on the light pull in an increasingly frenzied fashion, but when the climax comes, it's wholly unexpected as the groom jumps out the window. Equally striking is the scene in which Diana discovers her abandonment by Neville. Brown uses an elaborate tracking shot to capture her utter desolation as she walks away, along an overgrown pathway obscured by the dense early-morning mist. Of course, Brown had used elaborate tracking shots before, but this one seemed especially indebted to Murnau's *Sunrise*, and Brown implied as much in an interview with Dorothy Manners when he revealed how thunderstruck he had been by that film's brilliance.[17]

Brown's experiments didn't go unnoticed. An unnamed reviewer for the *Washington Post* expressed admiration for his bold choices: "instead of making a number of separate scenes of a particular sequence, for example, Brown employed the perambulator, or moving camera platform, and followed his characters throughout the action smoothly and without breaking up the action by close-ups, medium shots and long shots. He permitted, in this way, his characters to act naturally." The studio was also happy with his efforts and, signaling its confidence in his ability to handle new technology, assigned him to direct one of MGM's first part-sound films.[18]

11

Transition to Sound

Wonder of Women and *Navy Blues*

When Warner unveiled *The Jazz Singer* in October 1927, few could have predicted how rapidly the landscape of films would change. Over the coming months, most studios embraced the new technology, but MGM adopted a cautious wait-and-see policy, finally releasing its own sound debut, *The Broadway Melody*, in 1929. In the interim, studio bosses dangled the threat of sound over their personnel, using it as "an opportunity to put all us arrogant, overpaid sons of bitches out of their way." Hollywood watched as theater directors and actors were imported from Broadway, and although some of his peers decided it was time to retire, Brown remained unfazed. He adopted the phlegmatic attitude that the shortcomings of the new pretenders would soon be exposed, and he was proved correct. Only a select group that included George Cukor and Rouben Mamoulian (both admired by Brown) made the grade, while the grizzled veterans "learned their business in three weeks."[1]

The pragmatist in Brown welcomed the new technology, believing it could only provide new horizons for him to explore, but his more romantic side viewed the passing of the silent era with regret. In a 1929 interview he urged directors not to abandon the techniques that distinguished filmmaking from other arts, and he advised them to be selective in the use of sound: "It is easy to plant the plot with pictures, and it is highly effective to emphasize the climaxes with spoken words." In the years that followed, Brown certainly mastered sound, but he never quite got over everything that had been lost: "talkies have dialogue, and dialogue belongs to the stage. Too many people let the dialogue do their thinking for them, do the plot expression for them. . . . Silents were . . . subtler, I guess." Brown's observations about the unique and subtle qualities of silent films are revealing of his own strengths as a director. His sound career lasted longer than his silent one, but he remained very much a craftsman shaped by his apprenticeship with Tourneur and by his work in the 1920s. Even in his sound films, the most effective moments are those in which the visual image takes precedence over spoken dialogue or music. Even though he directed a very showy and verbose Lionel Barrymore to Oscar success in *A Free Soul*, Brown always preferred actors who adopted an interior style (like Garbo) or an intuitive one (like a number of nonprofessionals he directed). Indeed, directing actors proved to be the greatest challenge for him in the early sound era. Referring to the theater actors the studios hired (because they had "voices"), an exasperated Brown recalled: "They used to come on the set, those stage actors, and throw their voices up to the gallery. Whenever I had to direct a New York stage actor, I did an imitation of him. 'This is how you're playing it,' I would say. 'Is this how a human being behaves? You're talking to me when you make a scene. It's intimate. The camera is there, and I'm here, right beside it.'"[2]

Whether Brown's problems with overemoting actors surfaced in his sound debut cannot be determined because *Wonder of Women* is generally considered a "lost film," existing only in script form and a set of Vitaphone sound disks. Based on another Hermann Sudermann novel, *Die Frau des Steffen Tromholt*, its plot concerns a weak man torn between love for his unsophisticated country wife and desire for a sensuous city vamp. Thalberg assigned several writers to work on the adaptation, including Dorothy Farnum, Bess Meredyth, Endre Bohem (later of *Rawhide* fame), and Robert Harris (who suggested that the "other woman" be an opera singer). In their correspondence with Thalberg, Farnum and Meredyth both noted that sound effects might enhance the film's box-office appeal, but the latter came up with the neat gimmick of transforming the main character from a painter to a composer. Some of the actors considered for the film included Nils Asther as Stephen Tromholt, Janet Gaynor as the devoted wife Brigitte, and Dutch import Jetta Goudal as femme fatale Karen, but none of them were hired. A few of Sudermann's more controversial topics, such as abortion and attempted suicide, were considered for inclusion, but they were quickly rejected to avoid months of wrangling with the Hays office. Thalberg approved Meredyth's final shooting script (for which she later won an Oscar) in January 1929, and Brown was assigned to direct.[3]

If press stories are to be believed, Brown was all fired up about being given the "opportunity to handle human problems on the screen." *Wonder of Women* was adult fare that required the cream of acting talent, and he was hoping to make a new discovery for the lead, ideally a cross between "[Emil] Jannings and [John] Barrymore." Brown told the press that such a man could only be found outside of Hollywood, and he played along with studio publicity as MGM sought to market the production as highbrow material. With much ballyhoo, journalists saw Brown off as he departed for New York—piloting his own plane—on a mission to trawl Broadway for new talent. Embarrassingly, his mission was aborted due to bad weather, and Brown had to settle for seasoned yet dull Lewis Stone for the lead role. Brown had worked with Stone a number of times and apparently respected him, but the fifty-year-old actor wasn't the right choice for the charismatic, temperamental Stephen. It is likely that Stone was cast only because he was reliable and available. Nor did Brown get an actress with much box-office draw: instead of Gaynor and Goudal, he had to make do with Peggy Woods and Leila Hyams.[4]

Shooting began in February 1929 on Cedric Gibbons–designed Art Deco sets that depicted the glittering world of early-twentieth-century Berlin and, for contrast, simple yet stylized sets to represent the cozy domestic world threatened by Stephen's transgressions. In the absence of an extant print of *Wonder of Women*, one must rely on the shooting script, kept by Brown among his papers. Clearly, he was working with a rather hackneyed plot: composer Stephen Tromholt earns fame for his song "Liebeslied" but finds himself torn between his love for an innocent, "pure" country woman and the temptations available in decadent Berlin. A chance encounter between Stephen and the childlike but widowed Brigitte leads to marriage and his "inheritance" of her young children. After a short period of contentment, Stephen begins to get restless and abandons Brigitte to take up with sexy opera singer Karen because—as the script tells us—"there is a certain primitive something between these two, as though they were physically mated." Predictably, punishment must follow such transgressions, and in this case, it is the tragic death of his favorite stepchild "Wulle-Wulle" (Wally Albright), who falls from a window. The remainder of the story concerns Stephen's frustration as his career declines and his resentment of his domestic responsibilities deepens. He finally has enough and walks out on his wife a second time, into the waiting arms of Karen. This time, Brigitte is the self-sacrificing reminder of his conscience: when she becomes gravely ill, he rushes to her deathbed, admits his profound guilt, and promises to take care of her children. Brigitte's death finally redeems Stephen and conveniently serves as the inspiration for him to start composing again.[5]

Based on what can be gleaned from the script, the film was a ludicrous yet somehow predictable melodrama. But there are indications that Brown attempted to inject a little humor, à la Lubitsch, in the early scenes depicting the flirtation between Stephen and Brigitte. These may have fallen flat in execution, because neither Brown nor Stone were noted for their light comic touch, and critics failed to mention much comedy when they reviewed the film. Perhaps what interested Brown more than the plot was the potential to experiment with sound and dialogue. These elements were on the minds of the scriptwriters, too: the MGM files were filled with ideas for sound effects—a train steaming into the station, musicians tuning their instruments, church bells ringing, and people chattering.[6]

Wonder of Women was not an all-talkie. The decision to incorporate sound effects, music, and speaking voices in a few of the reels (reels 7–11) was finalized only in February. As was common at the time, sound was introduced in a rather contrived manner, such as a scene in which Karen must "test" her voice by singing into a phonograph. Speaking voices were apparently used only sporadically in the film, and it is possible that some recordings never made it into the released print: the cutting continuity, dated July 3, 1929, indicates that ten of the eleven reels were silent. However, musical interludes and sound effects were used, because the *Los Angeles Times* commented on one of the major sound sequences—a performance of Wagner's *Siegfried* set in a German opera house. It also noted that MGM had commissioned a song by Martin Broones, featuring lyrics by Dorothy Parker, for Hyams to sing. For Brown, the introduction of sound was not without its problems: the actor cast as Stephen's friend Bruno had a strong "dem and dose" Brooklyn accent that was ill suited to his role as a sophisticated, highbrow critic. As Brown later recalled, another actor had to be drafted to dub the lines.[7]

The technical complexities meant a slowdown in production, and editing did not commence until June. The film was released, in both silent and part-sound prints, the following month. Some reviewers expressed their appreciation of the film's attempt to tackle adult themes, such as adultery, and its presentation of a flawed central protagonist, but predictably, most focused on the use of sound. In a generally positive piece that commended the "unusual story," the *New York Times* warned readers that this was mostly a silent feature with only occasional uses of sound, such as the short scene in which Brigitte's children sing "Silent Night" in "faltering voices." As far as the unnamed reviewer was concerned, *Wonder of Women* "might better have been either all silent or all talking." *Variety*'s initial review was especially critical of the casting of Stone in a role that seemed more suited to Adolphe Menjou, and although the reviewer warmed to the domestic scenes involving Brigitte and the children, he observed that her death scene was weakened by "dialoging nearly all that had been related in the sub-titles and the action." *Wonder of Women* was, he concluded, "a rambling mess that gets audiences squirming in seats."[8]

The flaws of *Wonder of Women* had more to do with the hodgepodge nature of early sound production than with any deficiency in Brown's directorial skills. MGM regarded him as a "safe pair of hands," and he was soon called on to salvage yet another troubled production. *The Gob* had started life as a silent vehicle for popular comedy actor Billy Haines and his frequent costar Anita Page, under the direction of Edward Sedgwick. Shooting had commenced at the studio and on location in San Diego during the early weeks of 1929, but MGM shut it down in March. Brown took over four months later and retained most of the cast, but everyone was informed that they were now making a talkie. Brown shot for thirty-one days in the back lot and on locations in San Diego, Franklin Canyon, Ocean Park, and Cawston Ostrich Farm in Pasadena. What had promised to be a quickie assignment turned out to be more time-consuming because several cast members were nervous about their future in the brave new world of sound. Haines, the star around whom the thin film was built, apparently found the shoot exhausting but manageable, but his costar struggled to cope. In an interview with historian Michael Ankerich, Page later confessed that she "didn't like working with him [Brown] because he was worried too much about little effects," and she "wasn't very enthusiastic" about the finished film. Page wasn't the only one. Brown left the project on August 13, before its completion, and thereafter regarded the film with contempt. He was probably right in his view that the film was "a dog," and certainly its full potential was never realized. The rather risqué plot concerns a fleeting romance between Alice and a womanizing sailor, Kelly. When the two are parted, Alice is abandoned by her family (they assume she has flouted moral conventions), and she ends up penniless, living in a squalid flat and earning her keep by "dancing" at seedy clubs. Perhaps if Brown had been involved from the start and had been working with an actress he liked and respected, such as Garbo or Joan Crawford, he might have made more of the material. However, there was little time to delve any deeper, and perhaps Brown had no interest in doing so. The formula had to be adhered to, and that meant a happy ending: a reunion between the lovers and a détente between Alice and her stern father Mr. Brown (played rather well by writer-actor J. C. Nugent).[9]

The film was finished by a third director and released in December 1929 with the new title *Navy Blues*, to underwhelming reviews. For Kenneth Porter, writing in the *Los Angeles Examiner*, it was all so uninspired, with only J. C.

Nugent's "stellar performance" as Mr. Brown worth watching. The most intriguing part of Porter's review was the suggestion that Haines's homosexuality was an open secret: about his character he wrote, "that boy sure knows the sailor's delight, whether or not he is seagoing." Edwin Schallert of the *Los Angeles Times* contributed a more thoughtful review that criticized Brown's clumsy handling of a scene in which Kelly brings Alice to a rooming house after she has been thrown out of her family's home: "a scene which, to all intents and purposes, should have been a brief masterpiece of poignant humor . . . succeeds only in being tedious, banal and a little unpleasant to boot." *Navy Blues* hardly seems worthy of deep analysis, but Schallert's comments do identify the film's key problems: a director bored with his assignment and a performance by Haines that only his most ardent fans could admire.[10] It is doubtful that Brown gave *Navy Blues* much thought at all. By the time it was released, he was already deep into one of the most important projects of his career and a production that all of Hollywood was eagerly anticipating: the sound debut of Garbo.

12

A Year with Garbo

By 1929, most major studios had taken their first steps into sound, but MGM was still mulling over possible debut vehicles for its most prized asset: Greta Garbo. Among the contenders were Shaw's *Saint Joan* and a remake of Dreyer's *Passion of Jeanne d'Arc* (to be directed by him), but to some surprise, it was announced that Eugene O'Neill's Pulitzer Prize–winning *Anna Christie* had been selected. To research the lives of indigents, prostitutes, and sailors on New York's waterfront, O'Neill had lodged in a dive called Jimmy the Priest's and then built his play around the character of Chris Christopherson, the captain of a sea barge. By the time it came to Broadway in 1921, the focus had shifted to Chris's estranged daughter, Anna, whose childhood abandonment by her father has led to a life of misery and prostitution. First National Pictures released a critically acclaimed version in 1923, directed by John Griffith Wray and starring Blanche Sweet and George Marion. According to writer-producer Sam Marx, it was Paul Bern, one of Thalberg's favorite producers, who suggested that it might be revived for Garbo. MGM approached O'Neill with an offer of $75,000 for the rights to the dialogue, which the writer accepted (a decision he later came to regret).[1]

There was no doubt the play had drawing power, but it was hardly the most orthodox project for the studio, given O'Neill's frank depiction of alcoholism and prostitution. A flurry of memos between MGM and "Colonel" Jason Joy of the Studio Relations Committee (the Hays office) during March and April 1929 reveals that office's disquiet about references to Anna's past life and the studio's wish to retain some of O'Neill's pessimism and melancholia. Achieving a delicate balance would require the most accomplished of scripts, so Thalberg entrusted the project to one of the studio's most respected writers: Frances Marion. She later recalled adhering as "closely as possible to the text," except for "necessary changes which had to be made to give the picture movement." There was no decision yet on who might direct it, but the consensus seemed to be that Garbo worked best with Viktor Sjöström. The problem was that he had taken a break and was visiting Sweden. Anxious not to delay her sound debut any longer, MGM moved on to its second choice: Brown. He was already familiar with *Anna Christie,* having seen the play on Broadway, but he told the press he had never seen the Wray film and wouldn't do so now, for fear it might unduly influence him.[2]

Brown started work on preproduction even as he was finishing up *Wonder of Women* and salvaging *Navy Blues,* and Marion submitted the script to Colonel Joy for consideration in September. In contrast to more hard-line censors such as Joseph Breen in the 1930s, Joy maintained an amicable relationship with the studios, allowing them a degree of self-regulation and adopting a surprisingly placatory tone in much of his correspondence. The studios regarded him as somewhat ineffectual, as evidenced by MGM's election to ignore most of his suggestions for the *Anna Christie* script. In a memo dated September 18, he requested that off-color words such as "damn," "bum" (meaning tramp), and "house" (referring to a brothel) be eliminated. The studio assured him they would be, but "house" certainly made it into the film.[3]

With so much at stake, Brown insisted on extra time for rehearsals, and Garbo was unusually cooperative, arriving on the set and announcing: "I have learned my lines, Mr. Brown. I am ready to rehearse." The time undoubtedly helped the cast adjust to their roles and the new technology, but when shooting commenced on October 14, Garbo remained nervous about her first speaking part. As her friend Wilhelm Sörensen recalled: "Suddenly it occurred to me that she must have stage fright, though she didn't betray herself with a word. . . . Then I heard a voice from underneath the rug beside me in the car. Instead of a rich, deep timbre, I heard the moving plaint of a little girl: 'Oh, Soren, I feel, like an unborn child just now.'" Garbo may have delivered her best performance in front of the cast and crew that first day, because to them, she seemed "lighthearted about the whole thing." Only later did she admit to being pleasantly surprised: "It wasn't really so bad, though I became a little scared when I heard my own voice." She even noted the reactions of others as her husky delivery was captured by the recording equipment: her assistant made "a dramatic gesture with her hand towards her forehead and appeal[ed] to the Lord," her makeup artist got "hysterics" and bolted from the set, and even some of the seasoned crew were overcome with emotion and began "clearing their throats." The overwrought response by the crew amused Garbo, but she must have been secretly relieved when Brown pronounced the take "wonderful" and sound engineer Douglas Shearer delivered the judgment everyone wanted to hear: "OK for sound."[4]

There was no doubt that Garbo was the main attraction in *Anna Christie*, but she had some stiff competition from the supporting cast: George Marion as Chris, Charles Bickford as Matt (the love interest), and Marie Dressler as Marthy (a down-at-the-heels barfly). Marion had played Chris on Broadway and in the Wray film, so he essentially repeated his interpretation for this new version. It was a different story for Bickford. He was just starting out in his career but had already caused quite a stir with his performance in Cecil B. DeMille's *Dynamite*. Though he seemed a natural for the part—brusque physicality mixed with a certain boyish charm—Bickford wasn't too enthusiastic about playing Matt; he considered the role a supporting one and feared he would inevitably be overshadowed by Garbo. Thalberg worked to convince him that appearing in *the* film of the year could only help his career, and Bickford was finally swayed, but he was grumpy and unforthcoming when he arrived on the set. His prickly behavior continued for the duration of the shoot, and although he apparently courted Brown (whom he later recalled as "an amiable gent") and was delighted to be working with Dressler ("an old pro"), he was less impressed by Garbo. Hollywood columnist Sidney Skolsky remembered that whenever the subject of *Anna Christie* came up, Bickford was quick to dismiss the star, and he barely mentioned her in his autobiography (actor John Loder alleged that Bickford was sour because Garbo had snubbed him at a party).[5]

Bickford may have sniped and grumbled, but Marie Dressler, cast as Chris's aging, alcoholic girlfriend, was thrilled to be a part of the production. She was a true Hollywood veteran who had started off in 1900s vaudeville and was a staple of silent comedies, including some early Chaplin. Recently, she had suffered from poor health and a decline in her career following the disastrous reception of *The Callahans and the Murphys* in 1927, which had caused outrage among Irish Americans. Dressler confided in Frances Marion that she was desperate to get her career back on track and reclaim the affection of the public. Resolving to write the perfect role for her old friend, Marion came up with a new take on O'Neill's Marthy, one that capitalized on Dressler's unique talent for physical comedy tinged with poignancy. The next challenge was to persuade the studio and Brown to cast the "has-been" actress. Brown was skeptical, fearing that Dressler's brand of broad humor might "spoil the picture," but when he ran a test of the actress, he couldn't help but be charmed. When it came to directing her, however, she was the first to admit that he needed a firm hand to rein in her excesses and ensure that she didn't "play horse with Old Marthy." His approach worked, because it was Dressler, rather than Garbo, who won over the American public and MGM (the studio gave her a new contract, and she starred in a string of films that ended up being box-office gold).[6]

Dressler was a charm both onscreen and off, but Garbo's relationship with Brown evolved in its usual complex way. It was already a complicated production, and the director was grappling with the new sound technology, nervous performers, and delays when the sets, costumes, and makeup failed to satisfy his high expectations. More serious was a dispute with Garbo over her interpretation of Anna. According to one of her biographers, Garbo was insulted when Brown suggested that she adopt a clichéd Swedish twang to deliver her lines; she was also worried that playing the part of a "low down Swede" might offend people in her homeland. The director later offered a slightly different version to the press, candidly admitting that he was exasperated because Garbo's command of English was still shaky and her pronunciation of specific words was inconsistent. Their difficulties probably arose from a combination of factors, but it was up to her agent Harry Edington—husband of Barbara Kent and also Brown's agent before they had a falling out—to break the impasse and broker a meeting where the actress and director discussed the character of Anna and agreed to reshoot a few scenes.[7]

Despite their differences of opinion, in public, Brown remained unwavering in his admiration of Garbo. In an interview with Stuart Jackson published shortly after Brown completed his fifth film with her, he dismissed any comparisons between Garbo and emerging rival Marlene Dietrich and confirmed that his contribution to her success had been a modest one: "Anybody who knows them both would not mention Dietrich in the same breath with Garbo. . . . Garbo gets her effects from herself. All the director has to do is lead her gently along and she will do the rest. But Dietrich is all director. Her work conveys the impression of a man with a gun—standing over her, forcing her through every action, all the time." Observing from the sidelines of the *Anna Christie* set, Frances Marion was fascinated by Garbo's "economy of gesture" and the "constant changing of moods revealed by her luminous eyes that never played the little physical tricks used by so many actresses." Only her costar Marie Dressler analyzed the consequences of such immersion: Garbo was, she observed, a "lonely" figure, one who seemed to come alive only when she played a film role.[8]

After five intense weeks, filming finally wrapped and a team of editors took over, working frantically to finish the film in time for a sneak preview in San Bernardino on December 11. Audiences were expecting a screening of Garbo's most recent film, Jacques Feyder's (silent) *The Kiss*, so there was "a gasp of utmost surprise" when the credits came up and *Anna Christie* was announced. Their reaction was certainly more positive than that of Jason Joy and his assistant W. F. Willis. When they finally saw the film—*after* the preview audience—they were irritated that MGM had ignored their requests to take extreme care when depicting Marthy's alcoholism. Both of them found Dressler too convincing in her role of a drunk, although Willis grudgingly admitted that she delivered the best performance in the ensemble. Interestingly, one of Willis's criticisms touched on the issue over which Brown and Garbo had clashed. Willis had no special fondness for Garbo (or for O'Neill, whom he dismissed as a "dramatic charlatan whose vogue will pass"), but he was scathing about the actress's delivery of her lines: "we get the English of the drawing room as it would be spoken by a Swedish lady accustomed to associating with stage people." Stilted delivery was not uncommon in early sound films, but the reference to a certain theatrical quality suggests that Garbo had been pressured—by whom is not clear—to enunciate her words carefully. This may have helped with audial clarity, but it did little to enhance the naturalism of an already stagey film.[9]

Joy may have been disgruntled, but he granted the film his seal of approval, and MGM organized a lavish Los Angeles premiere in January. Frances Marion and Marie Dressler were in attendance, and the screenwriter later remembered how nervous they were as they waited for the audience to respond to Garbo's onscreen entrance and the utterance of her first laconic, and now iconic, line: "Gimme a whiskey, ginger ale on the side, and don't be stingy, baby." Their fears were soon allayed, as "no pyrotechnical display ever drew more oh's and ah's than when Garbo talked." It was not an entirely spontaneous reaction, however. MGM's head of publicity, Frank Whitbeck, had been tantalizing the public for weeks with a simple yet effective ad campaign that proclaimed, "Garbo Talks," so expectations were at a fever pitch. As fans flocked to grab tickets, the woman of the hour kept a low profile and did not attend a screening until several weeks later. As her companion recalled, she "seemed to be suffering in silence" as they watched the film. "Perhaps an occasional intonation did not sound quite right to her, and she would have liked to change it. But when we sneaked out just before the end, I got the impression that she felt fairly pleased." Garbo was always her own harshest critic, and she seemed to derive little pleasure from her career (other than the paycheck). Brown remembered that the only time she ever smiled at her work was when she asked him to run the rushes backward, rendering her words comically garbled ("yakabloom-yakabloom").[10]

Critics reviewing *Anna Christie* were certainly preoccupied with Garbo's voice. Several commented on its "masculine" quality, and Creighton Peet went so far as to quip, "When she says 'I love you, I love you,' it is necessary to look twice at the screen to know whether it is she or Charles Bickford who is talking." Mordaunt Hall also commented on her "masculine voice," but he was respectful, if not very enthusiastic about the film as a whole. Others were less diplomatic: Alexander Bakshy, writing in *Nation*, criticized Garbo's performance, claiming she failed "pitifully in the big scene at the end," and he was dismissive of Brown's direction because it didn't "maintain dramatic unity and suspense." Even in his generally appreciative study of Garbo published in the 1970s, Richard Corliss concedes that while there was a "nutty intensity" to her portrayal of Anna, it was ultimately a misfire: "It's that Garbo's acting is pitched at the wrong level. Her Anna is a travesty of despair, and the gestures of our primal ballerina are often jerkily grandiose . . . to appreciate Garbo in her first talking scenes, you need to close either your eyes or your ears."[11]

Perhaps screenwriter John Howard Lawson offered the pithiest appraisal of *Anna Christie*. Noting that "the inadequacies of the film were its straddling of two cinemas (silent and sound)," he commended only one sequence, a silent one, in which the "camera moves impressively, as in the view of the East River showing the bridge and tilting down to the river traffic below." Ironically, the shot Lawson identified may have emerged from an uncertainty about the capabilities of sound technology. In an interview with Charles Higham, William Daniels explained that they filmed the scene in one long track because they were unsure how to edit the sound. That Daniels and Brown were still more comfortable in the realm of silence seems indisputable but surprising, given how technologically focused both men were. Perhaps they were intimidated by the knowledge that so much was at stake, compelling them to use the camera as a recording device to capture the main attraction—the voice. Still, it is disappointing that Brown didn't instantly grasp the new medium's potential, that he didn't have the vision to exploit sound (voice and effects) in the way William Wellman did in *The Public Enemy* just a few months later. Instead, as would often be the case in his work on *prestigious* productions, Brown maintained a respectful distance, taking few chances. Consequently, despite Garbo's compelling performance and Dressler's undeniably affecting portrait of a human wreck, *Anna Christie* feels inordinately slow to the modern viewer. Only a couple of scenes demonstrate Brown's skill at evoking atmosphere and attending to visual detail: the opening scene (which Lawson praised), with its prowling camera, expressionist lighting, and mournful foghorn, and the closing shot of the sea, which John Baxter has described as "an image of Melvillian drama and the powerful end to a mixed, occasionally brilliant film."[12]

In a film dominated by slow, dialogue-heavy sequences, it is somewhat ironic that a scene added for purely commercial reasons—to make Garbo appear more appealingly "American"—brings some much-needed vitality to the proceedings. In the scene, Anna and Matt escape to the amusement park (shot at Venice Beach), where they experience some brief happiness: a roller-coaster ride in which the camera captures not a talking Garbo but a *laughing* Garbo, and a "test your strength" game filmed from overhead. Lawson dismissed the interlude as a "cinematic cliché" that "dilutes the mood and interferes with the psychological progression," but the "escape to the funfair" scene was de rigueur in Hollywood romances of both the silent and the early sound eras—*It* (1927), *The Crowd* (1928), *Manhattan Melodrama* (1934), and *Shopworn Angel* (1938) spring to mind—and Brown had no problem offending O'Neill purists, especially if it meant winning over the American public. And win them over it did. Perhaps *Anna Christie*'s general air of hopelessness gave Americans an outlet for their pessimism in the wake of the recent Wall Street crash, while its (muted) happy ending offered a glimmer of hope. Although a new breed of gutsy or irreverent stars—Joan Crawford, Jean Harlow, Carole Lombard, and even Marie Dressler—would gradually supplant Garbo in the affections of the public, and audiences would turn to brutal crime dramas or lighthearted comedies to escape their woes, in early 1930 Garbo was still queen of the box office, and MGM had a hit on its hands.[13]

Unsurprisingly, the studio rushed Garbo into several new productions. First up was a German-language version of *Anna Christie* for the overseas market, which Brown was set to direct but Jacques Feyder took over. He was joined by Bill Daniels and playwright-actress Salka Viertel in the role of Marthy, and they completed a film that was generally considered grittier than Brown's and one that Garbo evidently preferred. Despite her positive collaboration with Feyder, MGM didn't team them up again; instead, the studio announced that Garbo and Brown would reunite on an adaptation of an old warhorse of a play, Edward Sheldon's *Romance*—the tale of an Italian opera singer whose beauty enchants the men she encounters. Sheldon had written it in 1913 as a vehicle for his then-fiancée Doris Keane; it proved to be quite the gift, because the actress subsequently built her whole career on it. Both Keane and the story captured the attention of filmmakers: D. W. Griffith paid more than $150,000 to secure Keane for the film version, in a deal that also promised her a share of profits. He ultimately turned the direction over to Chet Withey, who produced a film that flopped at the box office. Even so, Hollywood remained interested, and MGM picked up an option on the story in late December 1926.[14]

Over the next couple of years, Thalberg assigned an array of writers that included Alice Duer Miller, F. Hugh Herbert, and Edwin Justus Mayer. *Romance* was lined up as a Garbo vehicle as early as July 1928, but the project was delayed as the studio grappled with the switch-over to sound. In 1929 the script was passed to Bess Meredyth, who ruthlessly excised material from the previous drafts (such as Paul Bern's suggestion to focus on *all* the love affairs of Rita Cavallini, including one with a Venetian gondolier). Brown was assigned to direct and seemed eager to make a few suggestions of his own, including setting the main action at "Millefleurs," a villa at Lake Como, and shifting the focus away from Rita and her lovers and toward a "love conflict between the two men—between Tom Armstrong and Cornelius van Tuyl." Brown's ideas were disregarded, and the emphasis remained resolutely on Garbo's character and her affair with a young clergyman.[15]

Garbo reportedly came to regret her involvement in *Romance*, dismissing it as an insignificant and poorly executed production and another example of MGM's persistent lack of imagination when it came to using her talent. However, Garbo exercised considerable influence over the production and had the final say over the choice of Brown as director and the casting of costars Lewis Stone and Gavin Gordon (as the young clergyman who falls for her). She had worked with the reliable but dull Stone in the past, but the choice of Gordon was a little surprising and probably a last-minute compromise. Evidently, Garbo had hoped MGM would borrow Gary Cooper from Paramount, but instead the studio selected an actor who posed no threat to her screen appeal. This confirmed an emerging pattern in her career: she was invariably teamed with male costars who—with the exception of John Gilbert and *Ninotchka*'s Melvyn Douglas—seemed to wilt in her presence.[16]

Shooting commenced on March 13, and it was expected to take less than four weeks. Almost immediately, however, Brown encountered difficulties: he rejected costumes and sets that didn't meet his approval and struggled to retain his patience when the usually punctual Garbo consistently arrived late to the set. Even more alarmingly, Gavin Gordon was involved in a car crash on the first day of shooting and sustained a cracked collarbone. He told no one about the accident, fearing that he would be replaced, and the truth was revealed only when he collapsed on the set. Brown had to use a stand-in and some judicious rearranging of the schedule until the actor could resume. When he did, it soon became obvious that a broken collarbone was the least of Gordon's worries: he was floundering in the part, delivering his lines in a flat monotone and bumping into the furniture. Fixated on developing her own performance, Garbo was less than generous with him, and neither actor was helped by a lame script that included such howlers as, "Oh, I forgot you were a clergyman . . . and I forgot you were a golden nightingale."[17]

Straining to coax a credible performance from Gordon and to deal with an obviously bored Garbo, Brown seems to have given up on the production. The difficulties he and Daniels had adjusting to sound, and their resentment of the ever-present supervision by technicians from Western Electric, led to a prevailing atmosphere of discontent on the set. One report noted that the director and cameraman were left standing around while the sound technicians decided how scenes should be set up and where the boom should be placed. Faced with such stultifying constraints, the two veterans focused on getting the assignment in the can and fulfilling their commitment to MGM. By now, too, there was no doubt that all were in service to Garbo, and it was clear that the power balance in her relationship with Brown had irrevocably shifted. She was firmly resistant to many of his suggestions and increasingly fixated on maintaining her privacy. Brown was patient, going along with her request that flats be erected to shield her from prying eyes. He also accepted the practice of giving her direction off camera: "We would go to the side of the stage and discuss the scene in whispers. . . . When Garbo is actually doing a scene, it is well understood by everybody on the set that they must avoid meeting her eyes, or she will stumble and stammer. . . . This is no kind of affectation. She cannot help it." Privately, he must have been exasperated, but publicly, he supported her: "I was very sympathetic over her fears . . . she responds very easily to directions, although she will not hesitate to put up a strong argument if she feels differently to her director concerning the way in which she should play a particular scene."[18]

Brown may have presented a stoic front, but there was evidence that Garbo's demands, on set and off, were viewed with irritation and impatience. Profiles in the press and in fan magazines were becoming less complimentary as she refused to "play the game" and give fluffy interviews or pose for "cheesecake" shots. Some of her peers expressed dismay that she was allowed so much leeway—she didn't have to accept direction or even well-intentioned advice. In a 1933 interview with the fan magazine *Screenland*, English actor Leslie Howard suggested that the star had only herself to blame for the weak films that had become the norm in her career: "It is her own fault that she has been handicapped by inadequate direction, for she has scared everyone so they don't dare to supervise her, to advise her when she is mistaken." While it seems unlikely that Brown was afraid of Garbo, there is no doubt that he was acutely aware of how valuable—in terms of prestige even more than monetarily—she was to the studio. Her air of indifference to Hollywood caused many to worry that she might follow through on her oft-quoted threat to "go home." In reality, Garbo needed MGM more than she let on: her investments had taken a huge dent following the Wall Street crash, and she was eager to rebuild her nest egg.[19]

Keeping his star happy became one of Brown's main functions while directing films such as *Romance* and even more so *Inspiration*, but generous paychecks couldn't entirely compensate for the emasculation and the bruising of his ego. Garbo biographer Mark Vieira recounts an incident when Brown's manager and a journalist unexpectedly dropped by the set of *Romance*, only to be shunted into the crowd of extras by the "tense" director. And on the set of *Conquest*, Garbo blocked a visit by the young daughter of her former lover John Gilbert, much to Brown's hurt and embarrassment. On occasion, Garbo's peevishness reached ludicrous levels. Director Henry Hathaway, a good friend of Brown's and a no-nonsense kind of guy, recounted an anecdote (perhaps relayed to him by Brown himself) from the set of an unnamed movie: "She [Garbo] was getting ready to do her scene and was working herself up. Very emotional. She gets herself almost sick to her stomach for this scene, and she turns around and looks up and said to Clarence, 'Does he have to be here?' And it was the cameraman."[20]

The filming of *Romance* staggered on into late April, and when Thalberg viewed the results, he was dismayed: the "romance" between the two leads was totally lacking in chemistry, and Brown's direction was indifferent, his pacing lethargic. In a memo to his boss Jason Joy, Lamar Trotti revealed that Thalberg was so dissatisfied that he took the extraordinary step of being on the set for reshoots on May 24 and 25: "They 're-shot' the thing any number of times with Thalberg himself finally directing it, and Thalberg is positive that he has gotten out of that particular actor [Gordon] all that he had to give." Thalberg's personal intervention showed just how concerned the studio was (and how quickly Brown's authority could be usurped). The scene in question, in which Garbo's character gives up her lover, also attracted the attention of the censors. As Joy pointed out, its references to Rita's past life as a mistress ensured that MGM would be unable "to avoid censorship difficulties." The crucial line "I was his mistress" was removed from the reshot scene, but Joy reported that Thalberg could do little with Gordon, who was still unable "to express himself properly."[21]

After ten days of reshoots, *Romance* finally shut down production on May 26, but even the patch job couldn't disguise the inadequacies created by a perfect storm of miscasting, a weak script, and an indifferent director. With a backlog of films already scheduled for release, *Romance* didn't make it into theaters until August, and the reviews were muted at best. Mordaunt Hall tactfully confessed that he found "Miss Garbo's intonation not a little disappointing," but he assured readers that her "appearance and grace are bound to elicit admiration." Monroe Lathrop of the *Los Angeles Evening Express* was blunter, complaining that the film "had none of the tang of *Anna Christie* and affords no such opportunity for sharp characterization"; furthermore, the star had not been accorded enough scope to "give her talents a loose rein." In his appraisal of Garbo's career, Corliss attributes the film's failure to a mishandling of almost every scene by Brown: "Brown consistently used long shots when medium shots are called for, and medium shots when he should use closeups. It's as if Clarence Brown, the admirable technician, had died with the coming of sound." It's a harsh assessment, but not without some truth: in contrast to peers such as Lewis Milestone or William Wellman—neither of whom had an engineering background, but neither of whom directed Garbo—Brown's adjustment to sound was generally less accomplished, at least in the early 1930s.[22]

For Garbo fans, weak material did little to diminish her in their eyes, and *Romance* performed reasonably well at the box office. To satisfy those fans, MGM squeezed in a fourth production to round out the year.

Perhaps he was a glutton for punishment, or more likely he was appreciative of a hefty paycheck, but Brown went from one unhappy experience with Garbo straight into another. There were rumors that he would direct her in a racy spy film, *Mata Hari,* but that production was delayed for a year; by that time, he had finally had enough of the actress, and George Fitzmaurice was drafted to replace him. The film Brown shot in October 1930 was equally racy, yet another example of Hollywood's flouting of the Hays code. *Inspiration* was based on Alphonse Daudet's 1884 novel *Sapho,* and a team of MGM screenwriters that included Gene Markey, Edith Fitzgerald, and James Forbes worked on a script even as Brown was shooting *Romance.* What they came up with was standard Garbo fare: she played Yvonne, an artist's model who is the toast of the Parisian crowd until she falls for André and sacrifices everything for him. It was formulaic, but this time the studio made an effort to match her with a more convincing male lead—Robert Montgomery, who had recently scored a critical success with his performance in George Hill's gritty *The Big House.* Veterans Marjorie Rambeau and Lewis Stone (perhaps Garbo's most frequent costar) took on supporting roles, and for the part of Liane, a fragile young woman who is part of Yvonne's circle, MGM turned to Karen Morley, a relative novice. Sam Marx maintains that Jean Harlow was considered for the role, but Paul Bern felt she wasn't the right fit. In a 1932 interview Brown claimed to have "discovered" Karen Morley among a group of extras, but the actress had just completed Howard Hawks's *Scarface,* so it's not credible that she was already back in the extras pool. More likely, Morley got the role because she was on MGM's books and she was available and amenable. As the actress herself recalled: "I mostly did what they gave me. I was glad to have the work."[23]

Even before *Inspiration* went before the cameras, the censors were sounding alarm bells. Joy had received Markey's script and was appalled by its content. His distaste couldn't have come as a surprise to Thalberg, especially given Markey's association with risqué material—he had written *Baby Face* (1931) and would go on to write the notorious *Midnight Mary* (1933)—the script's setting in the bohemian quarter of Paris, and a cast of thoroughly amoral characters. Joy was especially vexed by Garbo's character and complained to MGM, "The situation wherein main character was shown very definitely as having been the mistress of a number of men . . . [must] . . . be toned down and made vague as possible." He also worried about the frankness of her seduction of the much younger André (played by the older Montgomery), and Markey's flippant solution—increasing the character's age from twenty-one to twenty-four—did little to win him over. The protracted wrangling over *Inspiration* is one of the starkest illustrations of the ineffectiveness of censorship in this period, because the released film retained almost all the elements Joy found offensive: the cynical portrayal of the power imbalance between men and women, references to the world's "oldest trade," and a frank depiction of a jaded world in which women are commodities to be used up and discarded by rich men.[24]

Inspiration seemingly offered both director and star the opportunity to outdo the raciness of *Flesh and the Devil* and *A Woman of Affairs,* but it turned out to be quite an anticlimax. Presuming that the Garbo name would be sufficient to attract audiences, MGM approved a script that was laden with clichés and filled with one-dimensional characters. It would have required all of Garbo's commitment and passion to pull it off, but she had little of either left. This was her fourth production in less than ten months, and it became an open secret that she "resented the story, was so bored with the humdrum routine that she could hardly bring herself to finish the work." There had been moments of conflict between her and Brown in the past, but this time, MGM couldn't (or wouldn't) keep the details of their rift out of the press. It was reported that she wouldn't agree to rehearsal time and refused to take direction from Brown. Perhaps it was a symptom of her exhaustion or her frustration at always playing the same formulaic roles, but she was indulging in increasingly diva-like behavior. Her anxieties about people watching her reached such extremes that even her costar Morley was instructed not to look at her in their scenes together. On several occasions, a humiliated Brown was reduced to directing her through gaps in the flats erected around the set. If there hadn't been so much invested in the project, it would have been comical, but Brown was far from amused. Relations deteriorated to the point that MGM took the extraordinary step of temporarily shutting down the production, amid rumors that the two were no longer willing to work together.[25]

A short break at the end of November allowed for a cooling of tempers, and the production finally wrapped up on December 10. However, the discord had been so widely publicized that it threatened to overshadow the film's release, as well as any future relationship between Garbo and her "favorite" director. It is possible that MGM fed stories to the press about Garbo's alleged "bad behavior" in an effort to put her in her place, and journalists took the bait. Firmly on Brown's side was Katherine Albert (his friend since the 1920s), who explained, "Neither Garbo nor Brown was entirely satisfied with it [the script] but there was nothing to do but experiment on the set." However, Brown's "calm" and "diplomatic" efforts were allegedly no match for "heavy Swedish sulking" from "a most unpleasant" Garbo. Obviously, Albert harbored little affection for the star, and she was not alone. The majority of female writers expressed disapproval of what they perceived as Garbo's ungrateful behavior. More sympathetic was Ted Le Berthon of the *Los Angeles Review*, who commended her "courage" in refusing to "utter a lot of banal clap-trap which Clarence Brown, the director, ordered her to speak for the dialogue of *Inspiration*." Le Berthon didn't exactly blame Brown ("poor fellow") but predicted that he was "through" as Garbo's director. In fact, Brown wasn't quite through with her, but they both seemed to welcome a break from each other— one that lasted five years—although they still socialized. Brown began the process of rapprochement when he sang her praises in a 1932 interview and reassured the Depression-era public that the star was, above all, "a business woman. . . . She is in the film business, like the rest of us, for what she can get out of it."[26]

Inspiration had not inspired Garbo, but ironically, the estrangement between Brown and his star had the positive effect of waking him up from his technical stupor. When confronted with a poor script or an uncooperative star, Brown would often divert his energies into thinking up innovative ways to film otherwise mundane action. For *Inspiration,* he used his engineering background to devise a method of craning up the impressive staircase set with the aid of a hydraulic lift and a theatrical floor. The sweeping shot certainly pushed the boundaries of mobile camera work in early sound films, but perhaps more interestingly, it invested the staircase with a kind of symbolism that recalls Borzage's *Seventh Heaven* and anticipates later melodramas such as *Gone with the Wind* and Sirk's *Imitation of Life.* On their first night together, Yvonne and André return to his apartment, and a roving camera follows them as they ascend to the attic garret, where they will consummate their love. In this scene, stairs facilitate the transgression of social conventions, but in a later scene, they serve as a barrier: when Yvonne tries to visit his rooms, a desperate André, anxious to conceal her from his "respectable" parents, blocks her. Stairs also dominate the lives of the secondary characters, often with tragic results: when the caddish Delval (Stone) ends his affair with the young Liane (poignantly played by Morley), he tries to lighten the mood by joking that he will no longer have to trudge up the stairs to her apartment. He has barely left when she throws herself out the window, and upon exiting the building, he is confronted with the sight of her crumpled body on the pavement.[27]

If nothing else, Brown's mobile camera infuses the film with energy and distracts from the weak script, but even a vigorous style could do little to salvage *Inspiration.* MGM's February 1931 ad campaign gamely promised "the soul-thrill of 'Romance' in modern setting, with gorgeous Greta in silks and satins," but few were fooled. Particularly among female writers, ennui was starting to set in when it came to Garbo. Louella Parsons, usually so eager to gush over MGM films, confessed that she was a little puzzled by the character of Yvonne, "who had lived with dozens of rich men in Paris" yet donned such "shabby clothes." Writing for the trades, Elizabeth Yeaman was appalled by Garbo's "new frizzy hairdress [that] rather accentuates the hollowness of her cheeks, [and] her extreme and clinging attire gives her a wraith-like appearance." She noted that the script and characters were so bland and one-dimensional that there was little chance the film would "stir an emotional reaction in the audience." Others, however, were still enchanted by Garbo. Mordaunt Hall offered his sympathies to the actress, noting that she had to endure "uninspired" direction by Brown and a miscast and embarrassed-looking costar: "Yvonne may be a creature of impulse, but the idea of her being madly smitten by this André Martel (Mr. Montgomery) is surprising, but never believable." *Inspiration* did attract a few admirers, especially in later years. Viewing the film in the 1970s, screenwriter and critic DeWitt Bodeen confessed to being pleasantly surprised by its "well constructed" screenplay and the "real charm and sophistication" of its dialogue. Richard Corliss, so often critical of Brown, conceded that the "stylish assurance" in the film's early sequences indicates "a top director working in top form."[28]

Inspiration marked the end of an intense period of collaboration between Brown and Garbo. Although director and star had previously shared a sympathetic dynamic, this didn't always translate into innovative or impressive films. Garbo's performances in her early sound films pale in comparison to the complexity and nuance of her silent Diana Merrick in *A Woman of Affairs*. And despite some striking moments when Brown seemed to remember how technically innovative a director he could be, none of these vehicles matches the visual inventiveness of his silent films. Brown has often been referred to as "Garbo's favorite director," but in some respects, the films he made with her in the early 1930s are among the feeblest of his sound career. For John Baxter, who has written perceptively about Brown's strengths and weaknesses, only when he had broken away from "the tyranny of Garbo's talent and the restrained style her stiff, intense acting imposed on him" did he flourish. Corliss, too, offers an astute appraisal of the difficulties a creative director could encounter at a studio like MGM, using Brown as an example: "by receding beneath the MGM patina of Good Taste, he surrendered the reins of visual authorship to Daniels and Gibbons." Perhaps Brown did better work without Garbo, at least in the early sound period, and in the opinion of most of her biographers, the actress flourished without him (for example, in Mamoulian's *Queen Christina* in 1933). When the two teamed up again for *Anna Karenina* (1935), Garbo's performance returned to the high standards of their earlier collaboration on *A Woman of Affairs*. When interviewed about his contribution to Garbo's career, Brown remained modest, and like many who have assessed it, he ranked her performance in George Cukor's *Camille* (1936) as "the finest thing she's ever done."[29]

It had been a bumpy year for Brown, and he let off steam by carrying on an active social life that included romances with some very glamorous women, actresses Sally O'Neill and Sally Blane among them. His most serious relationship during this time seems to have been with the sophisticated Argentinean actress Mona Maris. Born Maria Rosa Cap De Vielle, Maris had led a cosmopolitan life as the daughter of a wealthy businessman, and she spoke several languages. With her dark hair, expressive eyes, and elegant poise, she was just Brown's type, and the two carried on an affair for much of 1931. It was reported that Brown proposed that Christmas, but the affair ended rather abruptly the following month. Years later, in an interview with Alfonso Pinto, Maris confessed that she had ended the relationship, even though she loved this "exceptional man," because she had her "own ideas of marriage then." At the time, gossip queen Louella Parsons reported, with some disapproval, that a serious bout of bronchial pneumonia had shifted Maris's perspective away from marriage and toward a concentration on her career. Whatever the reason, Brown didn't seem too heartbroken, as he was dating another career girl, actress Dorothy Burgess, within a month. Columnist Grace Kingsley speculated that this match was more suitable than his previous one with another Dorothy (Sebastian). Burgess, she noted, possessed "the brilliancy and flair to set off Mr. Brown's earnestness and depth." But despite their apparent compatibility, the relationship fizzled out.[30]

For the moment, Brown remained a bachelor—and a wealthy one. By 1935, his portfolio of real estate was valued at $1.5 million, and he revealed in an interview that although he was generally cautious by nature, he was "a plunger" when it came to property investment. He was hard-nosed and ruthless, but his most significant investment in the mid-1930s expressed a more romantic side: in 1935 he reportedly paid $500,000 for a ranch in the Santa Monica mountains near Calabasas. Shaving razor magnate King Gillette had bought the land in 1926 and constructed a sprawling Spanish Colonial–style ranch on it, and when Brown purchased it, he made substantial changes to the buildings and the interiors and built a small airstrip for his planes. He dabbled in gentleman farming and frequently used the ranch for location work. The Calabasas ranch would be his main base for seventeen years, until he sold it to a religious order in 1952 (eventually, the National Park Service acquired it).[31]

While other Americans were enduring the Great Depression, Brown (and others in Hollywood) enjoyed something of a Golden Age. The films he made in 1930 were not his best, but they all turned a profit, and he was viewed as one of MGM's key assets. Brown's status was further enhanced when Thalberg selected him to direct his wife, Norma Shearer, in a film intended to reinvigorate her career. *A Free Soul* turned out to be one of the smash hits of 1931.

13

Starmaker

A woman of tremendous drive and ambition, Montreal-born Norma Shearer clawed her way up the ladder of stardom. After appearing as "Miss Lotta Miles" in advertisements for automobile tires, she broke into Hollywood with a series of minor roles before she secured a contract at MGM and then a husband, Irving Thalberg. As Brown emerged from his challenging year with Garbo, Shearer was heading back to work, having recently provided her husband with an heir. Worryingly for her, during her time away, some of her chief rivals, such as Joan Crawford, had risen in popularity, and Shearer was determined to retrieve her crown. Even before going on maternity leave, she had been working hard to change her good-girl image, taking on sexy roles in films such as *The Divorcee* and commissioning George Hurrell to photograph her in a series of sensual portraits. Now she was searching for a screen role that would distance her from that maternal ideal. She found it in the daring heroine of Adela Rogers St. Johns's 1926 novel *A Free Soul*.

St. Johns, the daughter of flamboyant, alcoholic Earl Rogers, a prominent lawyer in San Francisco, modeled her character Jan Ashe partly on herself. Jan eschews social conventions and lives according to the philosophy of independence instilled in her by her eccentric father, Stephen. This includes the freedom to choose her own relationships, but when she falls for gangster Ace Wilfong and begins a torrid affair with him, the consequences are too disturbing for both her and her father. St. Johns had deliberately shaped her characters to fit her favorite actors, Joan Crawford and John Gilbert, and as she waited for Hollywood to call, Willard Mack adapted the novel to the stage, adding some salacious material to whet audiences' appetites. It debuted on Broadway in January 1928 in a production starring Melvyn Douglas and Kay Johnson. The play was a roaring success, and MGM snapped up the film rights for $40,000. A procession of writers worked on the script, including Dorothy Farnum, John Lynch, Irving Pichel, Stuart Paton, Lucille Newmark, Philip Dunning, Josephine Lovett, John Colton, Gladys Unger, and Eleanor Fried.

John Meehan, who had written *The Divorcee*, finally came up with the version that was ultimately used. MGM's script files indicate that several stars were considered for the leads, including Eleanor Boardman and Ricardo Cortez, but no actress stood a chance in the face of Shearer's determination.[1]

Shearer pushed for the "Garbo treatment" for her comeback role, demanding and getting Bill Daniels as cinematographer and Clarence Brown as director. The choice of Brown, now regarded as a director of family films and gentle excursions into Americana, may seem surprising. In the 1960s he certainly encouraged an association with conservative ideologies, expressing his disapproval of the new "permissiveness" of the screen. In the early 1930s, however, it was a different story: he had already toyed with censors in the silent era, and his early sound work continued that course. *A Free Soul* gave him ample opportunity to indulge his penchant for symbolic touches and to create a stylized aesthetic to convey the controversial themes and drive Colonel Joy's office, and audiences, wild.

The appeal of *A Free Soul* was enhanced when MGM revealed the actor cast in the role of Ace. Although St. Johns had written the character with Gilbert in mind, by 1931, his star was in decline; in any case, sexy charm combined with menacing physicality did not quite fit his persona. It was reported that Brown, the well-known "starmaker," had come across a bit-part actor in the MGM commissary and instantly singled him out as the perfect choice for the "dirty dog" role of Ace. This was the typical "random discovery" story the studios liked to peddle, but the truth was more mundane: Clark Gable had been a (minor) fixture in Hollywood since the early 1920s, and his selection for the part of Ace was likely orchestrated by the studio, and specifically by Thalberg, to launch his career as a hot new star. He had already created a stir with a few credited roles in *The Secret Six* and *Laughing Sinners*, and *A Free Soul* truly catapulted him into the big league. In the three decades that followed, a number of directors played a crucial role in shaping Gable's persona and guiding his career, and Brown was chief among them. The two collaborated on ten films and developed a friendship that, like Brown's relationship with Valentino, was based on a shared passion for fast cars and airplanes. Brown remembered Gable with admiration, telling one interviewer that he was "the greatest personality the screen ever produced," unique in that he "had the women 100%, and he had the men 100%."[2]

Joining Shearer and Gable were Leslie Howard as Dwight, Jan's other (very dull) love interest, and Lionel Barrymore as Stephen. Before they could begin filming, however, there remained some outstanding issues involving the script. Colonel Joy had already voiced concern when he learned that MGM intended to produce St. Johns's story, and after reading an early draft, he was dismayed that no effort had been made to disguise the "too plain and obvious" fact that Ace and Jan were engaged in a sexual affair. A barrage of correspondence with producer Bernie Hyman followed, as Joy pressed for the excision of "offensive" dialogue, including mild swear words ("goddamn," "damn," "hell"), and scenes with Jan dressed in skimpy clothes and negligees. His demands exasperated Hyman, who pointed out that the entire continuity of the script would be compromised if they were implemented. The solution was somewhat characteristic of the time: most of Joy's recommendations were disregarded, and the spicy plot, the daring dialogue, and, above all, the skimpy costumes remained.[3]

Cameras rolled on March 6, and an interesting dynamic soon developed between Brown and the cast. On previous productions, he had gravitated toward his female stars, but on *A Free Soul,* he was distant from Shearer from the start. Naturally, he played the game, raving to the press that he had never come across an actress with an ability to "project such delicate shading of drama," but privately he dismissed her "as the smoothest of opportunists." Brown had come across "boudoir politics" before, and he apparently disapproved of Shearer using her personal status to further her career. However, he didn't apply the same standards to Gable, who was just as ruthless when it came to achieving his professional goals. Shearer's performance in *A Free Soul* was every bit as accomplished as Gable's, so it is not clear why Brown disliked her. Granted, he didn't regard her as an actress of the same caliber as Garbo, Dresser, or Frederick, but his animosity most likely stemmed from what he perceived as her attempts to undermine his influence on the set and use her relationship with Thalberg to shape the material more to her liking. Brown had encountered that on the set of *Kiki,* but back then he had still been establishing himself in Hollywood and was anxious not to ruffle any star feathers. Now he was fresh off a difficult year with Garbo, and he had no intention of enduring another production in which his authority was blatantly undermined by the star.[4]

In later interviews, Brown detailed some of Shearer's manipulations and power plays. One concerned the climactic courtroom scene in which Stephen Ashe defends Dwight on a charge of murder. Brown planned to shoot it in one take of fourteen minutes, using multiple cameras that would allow Lionel Barrymore to give full rein to his uninterrupted histrionics. Shearer, however, wasn't happy that the scene was rapidly shaping up to be *the* stand-out one of the film. According to Brown:

> [She] felt that the Barrymore scene was too empthatic [sic] and took attention away from her. She prevailed on Irving—and this wasn't the

first time bedroom politics came into play—to ask me to re-shoot the scene. I didn't want to do it, I didn't want to tone it down. I felt it needed the theatricality that Lionel had given it. Irving talked me into it, and I talked Lionel into it. He was furious, sulked, and, probably wisely, gave an odd, sullen performance in the retakes. Thalberg had no choice but to use the first version, whether his wife liked it or not.[5]

Allegedly, Shearer also exerted her influence to get the writers to make the Ace character more violent, in the hope that this would alienate audiences, but on this occasion, her plan backfired. As photographer George Hurrell recalled: "female audiences all over the world reacted to his [Ace's] rough treatment . . . [and] . . . felt that she *deserved* being treated roughly."[6]

In contrast to his strained relationship with Shearer, Brown's experience working with Gable and Barrymore was more rewarding. Gable wasn't too enamored with his leading lady either, later joking that he could feign desire only by imagining her as a "juicy steak." There may have been a little wounded pride at play, though: according to one account of the production, Shearer applied an "excellently placed knee" to Gable's groin when he attempted his "usual hands-on approach" in their first scene together. Whatever the case, the actors' mutual wariness didn't transmit to the screen; in fact, it helped color their onscreen dynamic and their portrayal of passion tinged with sadomasochism.[7]

Brown and Barrymore also hit it off (the two socialized and collaborated on business dealings in the 1930s). The actor was obviously pleased that the director seemed to be pouring all his energies into making Barrymore's court-room scene *the* scene of the film, but he also appreciated Brown's foresight and concern for his welfare when it came to planning it. In his memoirs, Barry-more recalled that he approached the scene with some trepidation because the spotlight would be on him for the better part of a reel, and it was crucial that he "carried" it. He arrived on the set "in a torpor," already exhausted at the thought of what lay in front of him. However, Brown explained that he would shoot the scene using multiple cameras, thus ensuring that any flubs, hesita-tions, or poor angles could easily be eliminated. As it turned out, Barrymore delivered the scene in one flawless take, but others on the set were less profes-sional: an enthusiastic crew member shouted out "Bravo" before Brown could call "Cut," but luckily, there was ample footage to choose from, and the offend-ing interjection was excised. When Barrymore picked up the Oscar for his performance, he wryly acknowledged that "the only decent thing I could have done was to present . . . [it] . . . to Clarence Brown."[8]

Although Barrymore won the Oscar, there is no doubt that Gable stole the film. The scenes between him and Shearer were some of the most titillating of the year, and Joy was less than overjoyed when he saw a rough cut in April. He was incensed by the sight of plunging necklines and clingy negligees and by dialogue that was transparent in its insinuations (exclamations such as, "Why, you're nothing but a cheap, common, contemptible . . ."). Particularly galling to Joy was MGM's flagrant disregard of all his earlier recommendations and requests. If he had any lingering doubts about the ineffectiveness of his office, these were dispelled when *A Free Soul* was released the following month and MGM stoked the controversy with a series of lurid posters and provocative taglines. With every note of disapproval and every report of foreign censors complaining about objectionable material or requesting cuts (or totally banning the film, in the case of Ireland), more tickets were sold. Joy was no prude and probably accepted that some of the code was just plain silly, but the furor over *A Free Soul* illustrates the gap between censors (and, in some cases, reviewers) and the filmgoing public in the early 1930s. While younger audiences in particular thrilled at the sight of Ace's rough handling of Jan and Jan's shameless expression of her sexual desire, others lamented that MGM, the most prestigious of studios, had sunk to the base levels usually associated with "lesser" studios such as Warner. Reviewer Mordaunt Hall was particularly troubled not only by Shearer's tackling such a tawdry role but also by the notion that a "young woman of Miss Shearer's type would ever become enamored" of a cad like Ace. In a similar conflation of star and role, Edwin Schallert questioned how *Shearer* could embark on an affair "predicated on scarcely anything but sheer animal magnetism, the yen for a thrill, or what you will." Creighton Peet, writing in *Outlook*, wasn't offended so much by her skimpy outfits—which he described in lingering detail—but by the film's "preposterous, illogical, over-talkative" plot, which sometimes resulted in a certain "motionless" quality.[9]

Peet's criticism of the "preposterous" and "motionless" elements isn't entirely off the mark. Like many sophisticated dramas of the early sound period, *A Free Soul* has its share of artificial moments and self-conscious acting. There are several static scenes, but Brown's pacing is generally more effective than it was in *Romance*, and the film shows a new confidence in the handling of sound and image. Nowhere is this more evident than in the controversial opening sequence, in which a shot of the city skyline cuts to an interior of Stephen Ashe at breakfast. He is interrupted by a woman's voice from offscreen, and the camera follows its source, exposing a nude silhouette behind a screen. Stephen is instructed to pass her some underwear, which, befuddled but obedient, he does, all the while commenting on the skimpiness of the lacy panties and sheer bra he dangles in front of the camera. It's a deliberately provocative and naughty scene, but it becomes unsettling when it's revealed that the voice, body, and underwear belong to Stephen's daughter, Jan.

Such scenes of life in sophisticated San Francisco society are shot using a sparkling, high-key lighting that illuminates the decadence and brittleness of the milieu and its inhabitants. However, for scenes of Jan's sexual transgressions and her foray into Ace's dark underworld, Brown reverts to the Expressionistic palette he employed in his silent work and introduces some Tourneuresque touches, such as dark foregrounds and oppressive internal framing. The mixing of styles here may be illustrative of the conflicts in the film more generally: *A Free Soul* pushes the boundaries of censorship and makes some bold statements about female sexuality, but it also offers a more conservative warning about the dangers of women "running wild." Like many pre-code films, *A Free Soul* suggests that women need patriarchal guidance and protection from themselves, but they have a lot of fun before the punishment comes (represented here by a lifetime with the dreary Dwight). Interestingly, Jan's actions have less immediate impact on herself—she doesn't end up pregnant, imprisoned, or dead—than on others. The devastating consequences of her actions can be seen in the emasculation of the men who surround her: unable to "protect" her, Stephen winds up on Skid Row—depicted by Brown as a noirish hell on earth—while "decent yet dull" Dwight kills Ace to avenge her "honor" and ends up in a grim prison.

What Brown made of the film's barely veiled incestuous subtext and Jan's sexy character is difficult to gauge: though prudish, he was no stranger to showgirls and gold diggers, and he listed the works of Havelock Ellis among his reading matter. He may not have been entirely comfortable making such a sexy film—tragic romance was more his style—but once he was committed, he gave it his all. He encouraged Shearer to ramp up the brazenness of the hedonistic Jan and bring to life a character that is neither victim nor predator. In one scene, Brown may have had the seduction scene from *Flesh and the Devil* on his mind, as he shows Jan taking the dominant position in a sexual encounter with Ace. Traditional associations of women with emotions and love and men with sex and physicality are overturned as an exasperated Jan interrupts Ace's heartfelt speech about his true feelings for her by snarling, "put 'em [his arms] around me," before the two sink into a passionate embrace on a convenient chaise longue.

Brown may not have cared for Shearer, but *A Free Soul* was an important film for him and for American cinema. In its portrait of a woman "running wild," it harks back to the Jazz Age, but in its elimination of Ace and the "taming" of Jan, it anticipates the creeping puritanism that became more pronounced in the post-1934 period. During the promotional campaign, both MGM and Shearer seemed to be aware of the need to strike a delicate balance between offering fans a little bit of naughtiness and ensuring that no serious offense was taken. Posters that declared "She was born in an age of FREEDOM" were tempered by interviews in which Shearer expressed admiration for "sophisticated women . . . who have dared to do the things they wanted to do," but she went on to assure readers that personally, she preferred to be a devoted mother and wife. Mixed reviews, mixed messages, and some degree of moral outrage only enhanced *A Free Soul*'s popularity, and it became one of the box-office sensations of the year.[10]

Brown had pulled off a major hit, but within weeks he was brought back to earth. He had expected to do a fourth collaboration with Garbo, but after the experience on *Inspiration,* he may not have been pushing hard for that. Another tentative project, *Bugle Sounds,* was canceled after its proposed star, Lon Chaney, died (MGM released a Wallace Beery film of the same name a decade later). Instead, the sobering reality of the life of a contract director was brought home when he was called in to take over a troubled production, *Girls Together.* It was hardly an auspicious start to a professional relationship that was arguably as important as his collaboration with Garbo.

Based on a Mildred Cram short story published in *College Humor* in February 1931, *Girls Together* was a formulaic affair that MGM had initially lined up for Clara Bow. However, it had been rejigged to suit an actress who was fast becoming the studio's most valuable asset: Joan Crawford. Nick Grindé was assigned to direct it, and production had progressed smoothly enough, but when the film was previewed in June, it received such a savaging that the studio was forced to beat a retreat and order a substantial overhaul. Marjorie Rambeau, who had been playing Crawford's mother, was replaced with Pauline Frederick, and Brown was asked to take over as director. Although his last salvage job on *Navy Blues* had been less than satisfactory, the prospect of a reunion with Frederick may have helped persuade him. In an illustration of the fickle nature of stardom, and of Hollywood's disinterest in developing leading roles for older women, Frederick had been cast mainly because of her strong physical resemblance to Crawford. Still, *This Modern Age*—as *Girls Together* was retitled—at least heralded her return to a major studio, and Frederick found in Crawford an adoring and respectful collaborator.[11]

Katharine Hepburn has been quoted as saying that the teaming of Fred Astaire and Ginger Rogers gave him sex appeal and her class. Something similar might be said of MGM's two greatest female stars of the early 1930s: Garbo was the darling of the intellectuals and enhanced the studio's prestige, but it was Crawford, the down-to-earth Texan, who brought in the crowds and bulked up the coffers. *This Modern Age* was designed to serve the seemingly insatiable demand for Crawford's movies. Here, she plays Valentine Winters, a young woman raised in America by her puritanical father. After his death, she travels to Paris to reunite with her estranged mother, the bohemian Diane (Frederick), who is the mistress of the wealthy André (Albert Conti). At first, Diane views the reunion with trepidation, but her daughter is so besotted with her that she lowers her defenses, and the two develop a close bond. Predictably, that bond is jeopardized when Valentine begins a serious relationship with Bob Blake (Neil Hamilton), a millionaire from a conservative blue-blood family that disapproves of Diane's lifestyle. When one of the Blakes' staid dinner parties is interrupted by a group of Diane's rowdy friends, Bob orders Valentine to choose between him (and a respectable future) and her mother. She loyally chooses her mother, but (with shades of *Smouldering Fires*) Diane stages a rejection of her daughter so she will be "free" to pursue the respectable path of marriage. However, there is twist: Valentine is so devastated by her mother's actions that she drops Bob and takes up with wastrel Tony (Monroe Owsley). As she teeters on the edge of consummation, mother and ex-fiancé forge an unlikely alliance and stage an intervention. The film ends in a trademark Brown three-shot as the trio claims a future that is "clean"—but presumably a little less luxurious.

It is unclear how much of the film Brown actually directed. Contemporary press reports suggest that he "re-shot almost the whole thing," but Grindé claimed he had taken only a temporary leave of absence, during which Brown stepped in. Whoever was responsible, the direction was often heavy-handed and the pacing leaden; only the art department emerged with some grace (the Art Deco sets are a sight to behold). If Brown did direct the bulk of it, it's disappointing that he failed to make better use of interesting (and familiar) themes and a good cast. Perhaps it is too much to expect him to leave an auteur's stamp on an assignment foisted on him with little notice, and the fact that he didn't push for credit speaks volumes. MGM did its best to generate some interest in its dud of a film, and Joan Crawford and Neil Hamilton were duly promoted as an exciting romantic duo. Much was made, too, of the film's technical innovations; these included a novel use of sound that allowed audiences to simultaneously hear Crawford taking a bath as Frederick spoke on the phone (the scene is absent from prints) and a specially designed crane used to shoot the tipsy Hamilton and Crawford crawling up the stairs on their hands and knees. Few were impressed: most of the reviews were dismissive, and the mediocre profits indicate that audiences stayed away. Crawford obediently participated in the promotional campaign, but privately she dismissed *This Modern Age* as "hopelessly artificial," advising her fans to "forget" it.[12]

Their first collaboration flopped, but MGM evidently felt that the Brown-Crawford team had potential. A new vehicle was lined up that promised to be a better fit with Crawford's emerging persona of "ambitious girl on the make." Edgar Selwyn had written *The Mirage* way back in the 1910s, and it premiered at the brand-new Times Square Theater in New York in September 1920, with a cast led by Florence Reed. A film version starring Florence Vidor and Clive Brook followed in 1924, but almost a decade later, Thalberg felt the time was right to revive it. Approaching veteran scriptwriter Lenore Coffee with the frank admission that the play was "not a good one," he suggested that the basic premise be shaped to fit Crawford, who "needed a change of pace. She's outgrown all those flapper roles and needs to get her teeth into something." Though Coffee wasn't a fan of Crawford's—describing her as "not an extremely good actress"—she shared Thalberg's opinion that Crawford was "ripe and ready to move on to something with more depth."[13]

Possessed, as the film was renamed, turned out to be an assignment that Coffee remembered with mixed feelings. Allocated a tiny, stiflingly hot office on the MGM lot and instructed to get to work, she was shocked when she opened her first paycheck and discovered just $500 instead of the $800 a week she had been expecting. Incensed, and convinced that Thalberg had hoodwinked her, she protested to her agent Harry Edington. Thalberg held his ground, and the humiliated Coffee was forced to get on with the task of weaving box-office gold from straw. She immediately shifted the focus and setting of Selwyn's play—in which the central character is the mistress of an older man and the action takes place solely in New York—and sketched in a backstory of Marian the factory girl living in Erie, Pennsylvania, and being half-heartedly romanced by Al, a local boy. As the screenplay developed, new emphases began to emerge: Erie became increasingly depressing, and the character of Marian evolved into an ambitious, somewhat amoral woman who is willing to use any means to escape her predictably bleak future. By the end of April 1931, Coffee's script had become so cynical and bitter that she had to be reminded of the possibility of objections from Crawford's fans and from Joy's office. In final drafts, she duly concentrated on softening the character of

Marian and making Al so unlikable that audiences would instantly sympathize with his girlfriend's desperate need to escape a life with him.[14]

As she worked through April and into May, Coffee learned that Brown had been assigned to direct. She hadn't encountered him before, but she knew he had a reputation for being "very demanding and a bit taciturn." Not one to be easily rattled, she recalled: "[His reputation] didn't bother me. The ones I always dreaded were those described to me as, 'a perfect darling—you'll simply love working with him!' For, I knew only too well, these always turned out to be prize stinkers." She was pleasantly surprised when she met Brown, who read the first twenty or so pages of her script with "no particular change of expression except at the end, when he gave a little nod of satisfaction, and looked up, saying, 'That's a fine start. Keep it up.'" Subsequently, she found him "easy and pleasant," and his enthusiasm was "a great spur to doing the good job that I had made up my mind to do at the beginning." She revealed that although he never sought credit for his contributions to the script, he was very "hands on": "He would come over into my hot office and sit and talk, or I would go to his office where he would show me a diagram or a sketch for a set." Together they disemboweled Selwyn's play, transforming the "small-town sweetheart [into] the heavy and the rich city man [into] the lead." For the latter, Thalberg wanted Clark Gable, but the actor needed some persuading because, as Coffee remembered, he was worried that playing the sophisticated Mark Whitney was outside his range and might jar his core fan base. By appealing to his ambition and reminding him that the film would give him the chance to work with Crawford (his secret on-again, off-again lover), he was eventually won over.[15]

Joy's office was less excited: when informed of MGM's intention to adapt Selwyn's play, it advised the studio that it was not a suitable property. But the censors were so ineffective in 1931 that Thalberg responded defiantly to Joy's reservations, reminding him that MGM "had a perfect right to use the theme provided . . . [it does so] . . . with care." Subsequent negotiations between the two yielded only a few concessions, such as a commitment that the "details of the unconventional love affair [would be kept] in the background," that the setting would not be New York (considered a hotbed of immoral activity), and that the ending would stress the superiority of marriage. Crucially, Joy's repeated requests to see a final copy of the script were ignored throughout the summer, and when Brown commenced shooting on September 2, he did so without approval from Joy's office.[16]

Joining Brown and Crawford on the set were Skeets Gallagher, borrowed from Paramount to play the dissolute playboy whose chance encounter with

Marian provides the catalyst for her escape to the big city; newly signed contract player Wallace Ford as Al; and Clara "*Wizard of Oz*" Blandick as Marian's cowed mother (Gable was temporarily absent, working on retakes for *Susan Lenox*). Brown was pleased to reunite with cinematographer Oliver T. Marsh, the brother of silent star Mae Marsh and a talented cameraman he had first encountered on *Kiki*. The two collaborated on seven films, three of which were Crawford vehicles. Marsh was the closest the actress came to having a "personal" cameraman (in the style of Garbo's association with Daniels). He was a gifted craftsman who developed a unique style for filming the distinctive bone structure of Crawford's face and ensuring that her best feature, her expressive eyes, was showcased. Because of his early death (in 1941), Marsh may not be as well known as other cinematographers of the era, such as Daniels, Seitz, Lee Garmes, or Arthur Miller, but he was an important influence in shaping the glossy aesthetic of the MGM style. Brown liked and admired Marsh—a private, complicated man who struggled with alcoholism but who was passionate about his work and about technology. In contrast to Brown, Marsh had no formal training as an engineer, but he had the same natural fascination with machines (his son, noted Jazz saxophonist Warne Marsh, recalled that his father got his big break when, as a second-unit cameraman on location, he stepped in to fix a first-unit camera). Together, Brown and Marsh planned a couple of standout sequences for *Possessed* that would be shot on location in East Los Angeles, lifting the formulaic story out of the ordinary.[17]

Perhaps because of his involvement in the project from the start, Brown rediscovered the energy and visual inventiveness of his silent career. It certainly helped that Coffee's script, though generic, was compelling and gritty. And in contrast to her previous work in a Brown film, Crawford really "owns" the Marian character: in one scene she cynically declares, "All I've got is my looks and my youth and whatever it is that fellas like," and one can't help but notice Crawford's heartfelt delivery. Just like Marian, Crawford came from the wrong side of the tracks; she was bitterly aware that life can be tough for a woman with little education and few connections, and she knew that "respectable morals" don't always get you what you desire. Brown was impressed by Crawford's drive and her unstinting professionalism, even as he frowned on her sexual promiscuity and the frankness with which she (allegedly) traded sexual favors for roles. Over the years, his affection for her grew, and he came to realize that despite her pragmatic demeanor—the actress conceded that her range was limited and that her beloved MGM viewed her as the "cash cow" beside the "thoroughbred" Garbo—she was plagued by feelings of insecurity. In that respect, she reminded him of one of his favorite actresses, Pauline

Frederick. Their physical resemblance aside, both women were sexually bold in their private affairs yet suffered acute self-doubt when it came to their professional lives. Like Frederick, Crawford needed careful handling by her director. As Brown recalled: "she needed the security of knowing somebody nearby was in sympathy with what she was trying to do."[18]

The relationship that unfolded between Brown and Crawford was productive and underpinned by a very different dynamic from the one he shared with Garbo. While *that* relationship evolved to the point where the power undeniably shifted from director to star, with Crawford, their mutual respect was tinged with some obsequiousness (on her part) and a quasi-paternal solicitude (on his). Brown may be best remembered for his association with Garbo, but he worked just as extensively with Crawford (and even more so with Gable), and he was influential in shaping her early career. Crawford certainly appreciated his contribution: in the 1960s, when she was asked to single out the directors she rated most highly, he came second only to George Cukor. She recalled that, like herself, he was a tough, demanding perfectionist who reserved his harshest judgments for himself, but he was fair and helpful on the set: "Clarence Brown was very firm . . . but very gentle and very quiet; no yelling. No screaming. You see, Clarence Brown started out as an engineer, and I always said he could engineer more people together to make a good picture. But he didn't disturb us too much. He let us rehearse, find our way, and gave us a couple of suggestions. . . . He knew . . . that we had studied what we were doing, we knew our craft." Coffee, too, saw two facets of Brown's personality when she visited the *Possessed* set: the soul of a creative artist, tempered by the pragmatism of an engineer and the prudence of a businessman. She recalled, when "completed sequences would be cut and run, his assistant always said they were 'sensational.' Clarence agreed that they did look very promising but added, 'Remember, they've all got to get together and spell—MAMMY!'"[19]

Possessed gave Crawford the chance to sink her teeth into a role with which she could identify. She took an instinctual approach that was not dissimilar from Garbo's method, tapping into her childhood memories of familial dysfunction, grinding poverty, and dead-end lives, and channeling the same pragmatic spirit that had allowed the idealistic young starlet to park her moral qualms and acquiesce to the murky principles of Hollywood. Perhaps it was this pragmatism that endeared her to Brown. Although he admired Garbo and was fond of her personally, the Swede's refusal to "play the game" and participate in studio promotion exasperated him. In contrast, Crawford was a trouper, eagerly showing up for photo shoots, enthusiastically declaring her gratitude to MGM for changing her life, and never threatening to "go home" (unlikely, given how awful that home had been). Her work ethic and the genuine respect with which she treated both the crew on the set and the fans hanging around the lot were traits that Brown rated highly, given that they were the same ones ingrained in him by his parents. In the years to come, he would watch, often with kindly bemusement, as Crawford attempted to transform herself, whether to satisfy the studio or a husband—such as her efforts to reinvent herself as a "serious actor" when she was married to would-be intellectual Franchot Tone. Through it all, Brown saw and admired Crawford for what she was: a tough broad, a tenacious survivor, and a pioneering career woman.

In Crawford's best film roles—in the 1930s with Brown and in the 1940s with Michael Curtiz and Robert Aldrich—the lines between the actress and her characters are deliberately blurred. *Possessed* is the most effective of her early films in its teasing out of these associations between star and character, all the while conveying (and reinforcing) the allure of the Hollywood studio product. The opening crane shot establishes the setting of the Acme Paper Company and captures the workers pouring out of the building after the factory whistle has sounded. Among them is Marian, who breaks free from the jostling crowd of young men and women. Brown's camera follows her and Al in an elaborate tracking shot as they walk through a ramshackle neighborhood and he presses his case for marriage. Adding just the right touch of grittiness, and in an ironic foreshadowing of how their marriage might turn out, Brown includes background shots of a drunken man fighting with his haggard wife while their grubby children look on. As Marian dreams of escaping her dead-end life that already seems predestined, she is stopped in her tracks, quite literally, by a slow-moving train passing in front of her. It's not the first time Brown has used a train as a significant "character," and here it represents the intrusion of another world into the bleak Erie wasteland. Visually, it opens a vista of opportunity for Marian, who eagerly scans the compartments—framed as if they are mini-cinema screens—captivated by the little scenario acted out in each one. The scene has been much remarked upon by modern critics, and as one historian notes, it is a good example of how Hollywood movies were inclined to offer "tempting, silken glimpses of the dream city to rural and small-town audiences." While the tableaux at the front of the train depict the all too familiar workaday world—a barman mixes a drink, a waiter prepares a table, a maid does the ironing—these give way to more enthralling images—a woman in underwear strikes a provocative pose, and an elegant couple dances gracefully through the compartments. Tellingly, the world that Marian eagerly drinks in is a racially divided one: those who serve are people of color, and those they serve are white. Marian's subsequent pursuit of a life of luxury, then, is not simply a rejection of her working-class roots but also an acceptance of a racially segregated America.[20]

Marian's enchantment with the passing scenes on the train is broken only by the interruption of sound, in the form of the words spoken by a tipsy passenger, Wally (Gallagher), who is outside on the open platform of the final car. Suggesting that she should be looking *out,* not *in,* he airily inquires whether this "city slicker [could] tempt [a] country gal with liquor" and offers her a glass of champagne. As she eagerly accepts, Brown wittily cuts from the flowing champagne to the melting ice cream dished up by an impatient Al, who waits for her at home. That chance encounter with the man on the train, and the vision of a life beyond Erie, sparks Marian into rejecting Al, a "turnip" that grows in, not out. Declaring to her sullen mother that "[my] life belongs to me," Marian strikes out for the big city and encounters a startled Wally, who offers her some canny advice: "when you meet a man never look into his eyes . . . take a peek at the pocket book."

Mark Whitney (Gable) has a large pocketbook, and Marian ensnares him with her naked ambition (among other things). Soon, humble Marian is ensconced in a world of luxury, playing the role of Whitney's companion, "Mrs. Moreland," and reaping the benefits. In an amusing montage that recalls scenes in *Smouldering Fires* and *The Eagle,* as well as several of the "naughtiest" of the pre-code films, Brown shows just how lucrative the job of mistress can be: a bejeweled hand, increasingly weighed down with baubles, tears off each year on a calendar. These scenes—and indeed, the whole premise of *Possessed*—remind audiences that sex is the most useful weapon in a young woman's arsenal and that no one—certainly not the censors—can change that. Within months, MGM would push the boundaries to the limits with the Jean Harlow vehicle *Red-Headed Woman* (which gleefully highlights the benefits of being a gold digger), but for now, the studio showed its "acquiescence" to the production code (but pretty unconvincingly) by including a couple of scenes in which Marian expresses her genuine love for Mark and her sense of self-loathing (because she is, after all, a prostitute in all but name). In truth, these scenes were designed to ensure that audiences were sympathetic with her character and, crucially, with Crawford, rather than an expression of MGM's adherence to the newly formulated production code.

Possessed may be less than sincere in its attempt to convey a moral lesson, but it remains a fine example of Crawford's effectiveness as a performer. No one plays "hurt" and "noble" the way she does, and never more poignantly than in a scene in which Mark's wealthy friend brings a cheap prostitute (played by scene-stealer Marjorie White) to one of their dinner parties, explaining, "I couldn't bring my wife *here*." As she struggles to retain her poise, Marian must confront the reality that, in the eyes of conventional society, there's scant difference between her and a street prostitute. In deference to the censors, but also with shades of other "Brown women," Marian resolves to sacrifice her own happiness. Realizing that Mark's political career would be destroyed if the truth about his private life was ever revealed, she plays out a charade in which she asks for her freedom so she can return to her natural, "common" state ("I work a 24 hour shift and I'm sick and tired of it"; "it's been a strain being a lady"). Marian is visibly punished for her and Mark's mutual sin, but there is no doubt that Brown wants to direct the audience's sympathies toward her: shots of her walking and crying in the rain, her expensive jewels no longer in evidence, soon follow. The film ends with Marian intervening in one of Mark's political rallies, bringing to a halt his enemies' campaign against him, revealing her identity, and defending his honor as a "man who loved a woman, and she loved him." Graciously conceding that now he "belongs to you, all of you," she stumbles out onto the street, only to be pursued by Mark, who declares that he will marry her, to hell with the consequences ("if I win, it will be with you and if I lose, it'll still be with you").

MGM may have given Marian a respectable ending, but when the censors finally saw a rough cut of the film, they were livid at the inclusion of lines such as, "[She] will sell her virtue to the highest bidder" and "This bimbo's only a pick up. He'll give me twenty bucks and then buy his wife a bracelet." For Joy and his assistant Lamar Trotti, this was one of the most scandalous MGM releases to date, and it reminded them not only of the studio's indifference to the production code but also of how ineffectual the system of self-regulation was. Even as Brown shot the film, Trotti continued to plead with the studio to send a final script, but he did not learn the full extent of the code's flouting until he watched a rough cut in late October. His objections were greeted with what amounted to a brush-off: "Mr. [Harry] Rapf [the producer in charge] notified us that they would shoot an additional scene in which the girl would stress the importance of marriage, and face the realization that she had not been worthy of marriage." Even if MGM followed through with this promise, Trotti admitted in correspondence with Joy, "This picture worries me more than any I have seen since arrival." So grave were his concerns that Will Hays himself stepped in, writing to Nicholas Schenck (head of MGM's parent company, Loews) to protest the studio's violation of the production code and its lack of respect for protocol. In a last-ditch attempt to save face and, presumably, protect the morals of Americans, Fred Beeston, vice president of the Motion Picture Producers and Distributors of America (MPPDA), personally wrote to Thalberg and insisted that several lines, including "all they got is their brains and *bodies* and they're not afraid to use them" and "will sell her virtue to the highest bidder," be deleted. MGM made a grand display of complying, but at least one historian has suggested that the inclusion of these outrageous lines was a deliberate strategy by the studio to distract from the more subtle visual and verbal innuendos that remained. Having authorized the cuts, Thalberg made it clear that he was not open to any further discussion and that *Possessed* was ready to be released, with or without Joy's seal of approval.[21]

Later, in a letter to his successor, Joseph Breen, Joy admitted that MGM had outfoxed him on *Possessed*: "The philosophy of this one [the film] is wrong. For some reason we did not have the script and did not get in a crack before the picture was finished. This cannot happen again." He wasn't the only one who noticed. In June of the following year, Jack Warner wrote to Joy to complain about the preferential treatment accorded MGM. His studio had released its fair share of code-flouting films, but it seemed to Warner that MGM was given much more leeway, and he gave Joy a few examples (all of which were directed by Brown): "if you haven't seen *A Free Soul*, *Possessed* and *Letty Lynton* these three made by MGM show you how to avoid censorship but still put . . . in undesirable affiliations between man and woman in pictures. Could go on forever, but truthfully am tired."[22]

The controversy surrounding *Possessed* wasn't quite over. When it was released in November, several moviegoers and local censors cited it as yet another example of Hollywood's attempt to sell sex and sin to the American public. According to the representative of Atlanta's Better Films Committee, it was "tripe," and he warned that Georgians didn't "want pictures of this kind." Southerners weren't the only ones who objected. Massachusetts, Virginia, and Ohio agreed to release the film only after significant cuts. *Variety* reported that the censors in Pittsburgh had shelved the film, and "scissor boys and girls are said to be trying to marry Joan Crawford to Gable in the first reel, and can't figure out how to do it." These were minor inconveniences that had no significant impact on the US box office, but MGM faced more serious opposition further afield: *Possessed* was rejected outright by Canadians in British Columbia, Alberta, and Manitoba, and British censors accepted the film only after a year-long battle with MGM that resulted in extensive cuts to dialogue and whole scenes. Thalberg despaired that British audiences were probably viewing a totally incoherent film: "as you will observe, this practically ruins the picture as they take out every climax."[23]

No amount of cutting, however, could extinguish the undeniable sexiness of *Possessed*, conveyed through Brown's rich visual detail. Trade journalist Jimmy Starr was impressed, comparing Brown's "subtle style" to Lubitsch's and noting how "daring [he had been] in his methods of handling love scenes, often verging on the risqué," but never becoming "obnoxiously vulgar." Mordaunt Hall noted that Brown's "able direction" and Coffee's "fairly well written script" may not have made *Possessed* high art, but it was certainly "gratifying entertainment." The reviewer for the *Los Angeles Times* was under no illusions that MGM's focus was purely commercial, with its "shrewd concoction of box office ingredients." The only hint of negative (and somewhat naïve) criticism came from *Variety*'s "Bige," who was peeved by Coffee's cynical deviations from the play: "no more deliberate aim has ever been taken at a certain patronage than at the sap class through this screen version of Edgar Selwyn's once dramatic 'The Mirage.'"[24]

Apart from *Variety*'s reviewer, no one cared about the deviations from Selwyn's play or the dire warnings from conservative commentators who feared for the nation's morals. The film was enormously successful in theaters, benefiting from repeat business and boosting Crawford's career. When the actress looked back on her career in the 1960s, she singled out a scene from *Possessed* as one of her high points, praising Brown's subtle handling of it: "I think one of the sexiest scenes I ever did was with Clark Gable . . . in *Possessed*, we had a scene in which he came up behind me and undid a string of pearls I was wearing. The string of pearls dropped to the floor. Fade to black, and use your imagination." The admiration was mutual, as Coffee revealed. During a relaxed moment on the set, she chatted with Brown about his filmmaking philosophy and asked him to speculate on what made some actors stars. He replied, in his typically succinct fashion, by observing that a true star is an actor who can make a moviegoer declare: "Let's leave the dishes in the sink and go see Joan Crawford."[25]

14

Devotion and Deceit

Emma and *Letty Lynton*

As the storm around *Possessed* began to die down, Brown embarked on his fourth film of the year. *Emma* reunited him with Marie Dressler, who was returning to the screen after a lengthy sick leave. During her absence, Frances Marion had come up with a new vehicle to highlight the star's trademark comedy mixed with pathos. *Emma* tells the story of a humble housekeeper who spends her life in service to eccentric inventor Frederick (played by Jean Hersholt) and even helps raise his family when his wife dies. As the years go by and the children grow up, Emma remains devoted to her employer, until one day she realizes that life has passed her by. She decides, with some trepidation, to set off on her very first vacation, to Niagara Falls, but in a surprising turn, Frederick tags along. After confessing his loneliness to her, a courtship, marriage, and honeymoon follow.

The elderly couple's happiness is short-lived, however: Frederick hires a boat and, as he attempts to impress his new wife with his rowing skills, succumbs to a fatal heart attack. Somber scenes follow as the children learn that their father has died and, to their fury, left his fortune to his new (secret) wife. Only the youngest, Ronnie (Richard Cromwell), who was raised by Emma following his mother's death in childbirth, remains loyal, reminding his siblings how much they all owe Emma. When they refuse to see the light, Emma is so appalled by their greed that she ejects them from the house. In revenge, they accuse her of murdering their father, and she is brought to trial. She is found not guilty, but in a devastating twist, she learns that Ronnie, who was rushing back from a trip to Canada to offer his support, has been killed in an airplane crash. Renouncing the fortune that has brought her only grief, she visits Ronnie's body, and his selfish siblings begin to realize just how monstrously they have behaved. Having forgiven them, Emma walks away forever, and a final scene shows her happily ensconced in another busy household, a new baby in her arms, her employers appreciative and admiring.

Emma's convoluted plot (with shades of *King Lear*) and mix of strong sentiments offered Dressler ample opportunity to showcase her finely honed skills. Although *Emma* is undoubtedly a Dressler vehicle, MGM assigned an interesting, if underused, support cast that included Cromwell as Ronnie, a snippy Barbara Kent in the role of one of the selfish siblings, and a pre–*Thin Man* Myrna Loy playing a "spoiled snot who ill-treats" her surrogate mother. In her autobiography, Loy confessed that she had taken the role with some frustration, regarding it as a minor part that would probably do little to advance the career she had been building for eight years ("it didn't seem like progress"). She made the most of it, though, and her compensation was the pleasure of working with the "high-spirited and caring" Dressler and, for the first time, with Brown. For Kent, who was also playing a minor role, this marked her final collaboration with Brown, and she recalled that he "handled the cast very similar to the way he did on *Flesh and the Devil*, with his quiet manner."[1]

Shooting commenced in October. It was confined mainly to the back lot, with occasional location work at Lake Arrowhead, where a "small floating studio was established on improvised rafts and boats." Using four cameras mounted on a small platform in an adjacent motorboat, Brown directed the "death by rowing" scene. To film a comic scene in which Emma visits aviator Ronnie and is treated to a hair-raising plane ride, the company traveled to Los Angeles Municipal Airport. These excursions provided welcome breaks from an intense schedule that had everyone feeling the pressure. By the end of November, principal photography was complete, and only a few retakes were needed. Some of these were requested by Brown. For instance, he wanted to reshoot the scene in which Emma says good-bye to the family because he wasn't happy with its less-than-subtle tone or with Dressler's performance. He asked that it be rewritten so audiences wouldn't "realize she's going until she makes that last turn." Retakes were also commissioned for the courtroom scene (to make Emma's role central), and a new scene was added showing a flashback to the birth of youngest son Ronnie.[2]

Brown accomplished it all with efficiency and speed, no doubt aware that his star was terminally ill. *Emma* would be one of Dressler's last films, and knowledge of her illness probably influenced the warm praise heaped on what was, in truth, a fairly run-of-the-mill star vehicle. The reviewer for the *Los Angeles Times* commended the "humanness" of the story and the touching performances by Dressler and Hersholt, while Mordaunt Hall noted that Dressler "never falters in the pathos or humor of this tale." Almost all critics acknowledged the film's sentimentality and implausibility, but they did so in an apologetic manner. Critics' affection for Dressler was shared by audiences, who made this "little movie" ($350,000 budget) one of the box-office successes of the year. It also earned its star an Academy Award nomination (although she didn't win).[3]

It's not hard to see why moviegoers loved the film, with its message that family, not money, brings contentment and in its warm celebration of Emma's loyalty and stoicism. It was just the kind of optimistic fare that Mayer adored, and it offered audiences a glimmer of hope in what was already shaping up to be one of the worst years of the Depression. Today, when sentiment is distrusted and sentimentality is often disparaged, it's easy to regard *Emma* as a cynical exercise in which every line, every gesture, every close-up, every chord of affecting music is designed to maximize the audience response and sell more tickets. Even in 1932, its formulaic nature was acknowledged, and certainly the comic scenes were contrived to showcase the comedy skills that had been Dressler's forte since her vaudeville days. However, *Emma* is a more contemplative film than previous Dressler outings, and both star and director handle several scenes with great subtlety. Brown's appreciation of simple folk and their humble values comes through in an affecting scene in which Frederick visits Emma in her living quarters and we are afforded a glimpse into her private world. The camera reveals a modest room filled with pictures of the family she has raised and the little knickknacks she has accumulated over the years. The poignancy of her life, as both surrogate mother and servant, is conveyed with little explanatory dialogue and no close-ups; everything is framed in a medium shot that simply allows the viewer to *see*, to appreciate the small things that constitute human existence. It is interesting to note that the French director Jean Renoir admired Brown—regarding him as an underrated director who was too modest in his self-appraisals—because this kind of scene would not look out of place in a Renoir film (or one directed by Robert Bresson). Brown takes the same "democratic" approach to filming that Renoir favored, allowing audiences to establish a personal connection and draw their own conclusions.

Similarly effective (and affective) is a scene in which the abandoned and betrayed Emma surveys the huge, empty house that was once a home full of children who turned to her when they needed comfort and affection. The intentional parallels with *King Lear* are clear—a cast of monstrous ingrates, a foolish patriarch, and a wronged woman—but *Emma*'s broader themes of loneliness and aging are ones that Brown explored in much of his work in both the silent and sound eras. As Hollywood continued its celebration of youth and beauty, viewing marriage as the culmination of passion and romance, this film (and, indeed, Dressler's late stardom) offered a refreshing, if unusual, bucking of the trend.[4]

Hollywood remained committed to showcasing glamor and selling sex, and Brown's next assignment returned him to that world. He was teamed again with Joan Crawford in what promised to be a tantalizing foray into the seamy world of forbidden love. No one could have predicted that *Letty Lynton* would be one of the most contentious films in MGM's history.

Marie Belloc Lowndes's novel *Letty Lynton* was based on the infamous Madeleine Smith case, in which a wealthy young woman was tried for the murder of her lover in Glasgow in 1857. Lowndes was not the only writer inspired by these events; interest had been reignited with the inclusion of a case synopsis in the 1927 publication *Notable British Trials* and by Edward Sheldon and Margaret Ayer Barnes's *Dishonored Lady*, which had been a smash hit on Broadway in February 1930 in a production starring Katherine Cornell. The play's racy content, which included a heroine with an insatiable sexual appetite, a promiscuous, drug-taking mother, and a drunkard father, prompted censors to add it to their "not suitable for motion picture adaptation" list. Undeterred, MGM made a concerted effort to purchase the rights in the summer of 1931, bailing out only when Sheldon and Barnes insisted on a hefty $30,000 and Joy's office indicated that it would not be budging in its opinion of the play. Looking around for a cheaper alternative, MGM discovered Lowndes's recently published novel, which had been deemed acceptable by the censors. It seemed a stroke of good fortune when the studio secured the rights for a mere $3,500.[5]

The real Madeleine Smith was the daughter of a wealthy architect, and she was something of a rebel in the staid world of Scottish society. At age twenty she embarked on a secret affair with an apprentice gardener, Pierre Emile l'Angelier, but she ended it when a more promising suitor came along. Her attempts to retrieve the steamy letters she had written to l'Angelier failed, and her penniless ex-lover initiated a campaign of blackmail. Soon thereafter he was found dead of arsenic poisoning, and Smith was the chief suspect. Her subsequent trial was the sensation of the decade, but even more remarkable was the verdict of "not proven," despite a wealth of evidence and a very clear motive. Following her release, Smith married, had a family, and immigrated to America; she had only recently died when Sheldon and Barnes wrote their play. Lowndes had been similarly inspired by the historical facts but tweaked them to suit her retelling: Madeleine becomes Letty, the spoiled, feckless daughter of a Scottish chemicals magnate. To stave off boredom, she starts a passionate affair with a penniless Swede, Axel, whom she then dumps when she is introduced to a richer suitor who is "marriage material." Letty dispatches Axel by serving him arsenic-laced hot chocolate and then sets about reinventing herself and her past. When she is finally brought to trial, she exhibits no remorse but so charms the judge that he sets her free. Lowndes, however, metes out her own form of punishment as Letty's once-doting father coerces her into marrying one of his employees (a jealous man who vows to kill her if she ever strays).[6]

Although the censors indicated that the novel could be adapted, it was with the understanding that MGM would make appropriate amendments and cuts. The studio was in broad agreement that the portrayal of Letty as a remorseless murderer would have to be tweaked and the novel's rather sordid mood toned down: the last thing it wanted was a Crawford vehicle that alienated her fans. Hunt Stromberg assigned two of his most experienced screenwriters, Wanda Tuchock and John Meehan, to shape the story into more palatable fare. In early drafts, the duo stuck closely to the source, making just a few alterations to the characters' names (Axel became Emile) and retaining dialogue that alluded to Letty's "oversexed" nature. Stromberg wasn't happy, and he instructed them to tone down any insinuation that the relationship between Letty and Emile is a sadomasochistic one. He was being pressured by his boss, Thalberg, who in turn was being monitored by Joy. Still smarting over the *Possessed* debacle, Joy was determined that his office would have input *before* filming commenced on another Crawford film. He reminded Thalberg that extreme caution needed to be exercised in the representation of Letty and her crime. Interestingly—especially in light of subsequent events—the correspondence regarding the production reveals some confusion over which source was being adapted. In a note to Stromberg in January, Joy pointed out that "the character of the woman herself, who here, as *in the play,* is depicted as a 'nymphomaniac' is impelled by a 'sex urge' and not by love" (emphasis added).[7]

Stromberg complied with Joy's directives and commissioned a revised script that played down Letty's promiscuity, eliminated "the nymphomaniac angle," excised references to swearing on the Bible, and ensured that the poisoning scene was shot in a manner that ruled out conscious intent. By late February 1932, the writers had delivered a script that eliminated some of Lowndes's subplots and minor characters and transformed Letty into an unhappy socialite who seeks distraction from a troubled relationship with her mother by indulging in an endless round of parties, superficial affairs, and trips to exotic locales.

Later, when *Letty Lynton* became mired in legal controversy, Brown would claim that he had read only the Meehan-Tuchock script and was unaware of the Sheldon-Barnes play. It may well have been true that *Letty Lynton* was just an assignment for Brown, who concentrated his energies on shaping it into an effective Crawford vehicle and saw no reason to trace its lineage. However, even if he was not passionately and creatively invested, he would have viewed the film as a useful stepping-stone in his career, one that promised to have a high profile—little did he know how high—and a strong cast. Crawford was joined by Nils Asther and Robert Montgomery; the latter had been assigned to replace the original choice, Clark Gable (who was probably dropped when Mrs. Gable threatened to go public about her husband's affair with Crawford). Although Brown's preference would have been to incorporate location work, as far as MGM was concerned, there was nowhere in the world that couldn't be more effectively reproduced at Culver City. As the actors lounged in couture designs by Adrian and glided through Cedric Gibbons's sumptuous Art Deco sets, technicians used back projection to concoct a series of exotic locales. A visitor to the set observed some of the artifice required and wryly noted that as Crawford and Asther sank into sensual clinches, "off set two grips burn[ed] sulphur cloth and fan[ned] its acrid smoke towards the camera to thicken the atmosphere."[8]

Letty Lynton remains an excellent example of the trademark glossy MGM aesthetic (as translated here by Oliver Marsh), but some of Brown's favored techniques are featured, such as a dark, Tourneuresque foreground in the opening scene, used for compositional contrast and to infuse the proceedings with a seamy atmosphere. For the most part, though, Brown played it safe, executing the assignment in a methodical fashion. Journalist Wood Soanes visited the set and offered the following observations:

> I saw him spend an entire afternoon on the final sequence of "Letty Lynton," unable to decide how to end the picture. Everybody offered a bit of advice, everybody from stars to grips. Brown patiently tried one after another, meditating on some, actually rehearsing others. I left before he had made up his mind. But the point is that eventually he hits upon the proper method. By dint of patiently discarding one after another of the systems that do not seem right, he gets the thing he is seeking. He is frank to admit that at times the mood is so elusive that even he doesn't know what he's after, but he keeps trying.

The reporter evidently felt that Brown's "system" was a refreshingly democratic one in which persistence rather than spontaneity paid off. A less charitable view might be that it was evidence of, at best, a director with a tenuous grip on his material or, at worst, a director who was running on autopilot. Brown may have been less than enthusiastic about the assignment, but according to Soanes, even this "mild man" could "be aroused into a fine frenzy on occasion." Brown, he noted, "objects to haste in picture making. He resents interference once he is under way, he has no patience with outburst of temperament, and the hair on the back of his neck fairly bristles at the thought of official or political censorship."[9]

Letty Lynton would become notorious in the annals of Hollywood for the headaches (and financial burden) it caused MGM, but Brown had plenty of problems on the set, too. Crawford had been readying herself for another passionate excursion with Gable, but instead she got Montgomery, who regarded her with some disdain. Crawford reciprocated, and an air of mutual indifference seeped into their performances. Brown may have been exasperated as he directed them and viewed the rushes, but in a perverse way, their lack of chemistry helped convey some of the story's risqué insinuations: Montgomery plays the respectable suitor, but it is the caddish Emile (Asther) who turns Letty on. Crawford often slept with her costars, but on this occasion, she wasn't involved with either of them. Asther generally preferred men, but his friendship with Crawford meant that the two were happy to spend time together, rehearsing and discussing their roles. As a result, the sadomasochistic dynamic between their characters is convincingly portrayed, and the film's most compelling and controversial moments (especially from a censor's point of view) are those that feature their encounters. In their final scene, Letty visits Emile and tries, once again, to break from him. A fight erupts, and there is an intriguing moment when, as Letty is being manhandled, a flash of desire crosses her face. Then she watches, in eager anticipation, as Emile picks up a flute of poisoned champagne and drinks from it. Scenes like these, in which a widening of the eyes or a slight smile expresses desire and malice, ensured that *Letty Lynton* was as salacious as any of Hollywood's pre-code films.

Shooting wrapped up on March 28, and this time MGM granted the censors a sneak preview. Lamar Trotti wrote to Thalberg soon thereafter and, somewhat surprisingly, requested only minor cuts, such as the deletion of the exclamation "Lord," the cutting of a line in which Letty swears that she will always belong to her lover, and the elimination of a scene revealing that Emile has a key to Letty's bedroom. Trotti and Joy failed to notice—or chose to ignore—a line in which Letty's maid (played by Louise Closser Hale) refers to

Emile's habit of snoring. Even more astonishingly, the censors approved a film in which the heroine poisons her lover and declares, "I'm glad I did it, you dirty, filthy mongrel," exhibiting a complete absence of remorse. Also passed by the censors was the rather extraordinary conclusion that sees Letty rewarded with a "respectable" marriage after her mother, maid, and fiancé supply her with a false alibi. There is a sense that Joy's office was merely going through the motions, perhaps recognizing that an overhaul of the self-regulatory approach to movie censorship was imminent. Further confirmation that Joy's office was serving MGM's interests rather than safeguarding public morals was his intervention with hostile censors in Ontario. Justifying his actions, Joy wrote to his boss Will Hays and explained that he had interceded because the Canadians were off the mark: *Letty Lynton* was "simply a well done story of a girl whose past caught up with her and her efforts to escape the consequences of her wrong doing." Others were not convinced. British censors passed *Letty Lynton* with some reluctance because they concluded, quite rightly, that it appeared to "justify homicide without penalty." Switzerland and Italy banned it outright, and South Africa released it only after MGM removed a reference to Cape Town as a "filthy hole."[10]

It couldn't have been much of a surprise that *Letty Lynton* proved to be a magnet for controversy. When it was released in May, most reviewers seemed preoccupied with wondering how MGM had sneaked it past the censors and, more worrying for the studio, what Sheldon and Barnes thought of this version of their play. Philip Scheuer opened his review with a reference to the film's resemblance to the play before noting the changes made, such as a softening of the character of Letty and "one of the strangest finales in the history of the movies' moralistic code: the murderess goes scot-free on the testimony of her sweetheart, her mother and her maid." Scheuer also observed that the audience in the theater where he had watched the film didn't "buy" the "redemption" of Letty and had "tittered" over the unlikely ending. Despite its implausibility, Scheuer found much to like and was especially impressed by Asther's "astonishingly good" performance. His acclaim was seconded by the reviewer for the *Washington Post*, who praised Crawford's handling of an unlikable character with more nuance than usual (less of the "hands-on-hips, eyebrow agony" style of her earlier films). Whereas most of the reviewers were busy marveling at the risqué content or assessing how well Crawford looked and performed, Mordaunt Hall offered some commentary on Brown's contribution, grumbling that he paid "too much attention to his photographic effects and not enough to the necessary psychology of the characters or the plausibility of the incidents."[11]

Few who saw *Letty Lynton* in 1932 could have imagined its cultural impact or the nightmarish afterlife it would acquire. For all intents and purposes, it was just a film vehicle that had served its function of satiating Crawford's fans and boosting both her star appeal and the MGM coffers. So smitten was *Photoplay* that it placed Crawford at the top of a list of stars who were most convincing in their depictions of a new type of 1930s woman, one who "can take care of herself . . . since she combines, with her mysterious allure, many of the hard-headed attributes and even some of the physical characteristics—the tall, narrow-hipped, broad shouldered figure—of men." Crawford's films had always been a showcase for daring costumes that displayed her sleek figure—from the flapper dresses of *Our Dancing Daughters* back in 1928 to the sophisticated Deco gowns of *This Modern Age* and *Possessed. Letty Lynton* was no exception, and *Photoplay* devoted two spreads to the stunning array of dresses designed by the studio's head costumer, Adrian. An extravagant concoction of white chiffon and silk with elaborate puffed sleeves, worn by Crawford in the romantic cruise-ship scene with Montgomery, became the most desired dress of the season when a ready-to-wear copy was sold through Macy's. Several film historians have examined the significance of the "Letty Lynton dress" both within the film and in the wider culture. For Charlotte Herzog and Jane Gaines, the popularity of the Macy's copy suggests that even the beaten-down woman of the Depression era yearned for pure fancy, however impractical it might be to wear. For Sarah Berry, the dress's rather Victorian style and the cultural association of white with innocence had narrative importance. The astonishing popularity of the dress—unverified (and unlikely) reports estimate that half a million copies were sold—ensured that *Letty Lynton* would live on even as the movie disappeared from theaters.[12]

And disappear it did, but this was no simple case of a film ending its run. A month after its release, Sheldon and Barnes filed a lawsuit against MGM, charging it with plagiarism. The studio's defense maintained that the resemblance was purely coincidental, but claims of innocence were patently disingenuous. Even in early correspondence with Joy, it is clear that the play was on everyone's mind, and just a few days after the suit was lodged, J. V. Wilson of MGM wrote again to Joy to assure him that the risqué material of *Dishonored Lady* (the title of Sheldon and Barnes's play) had been watered down for the film. The case would drag on in the courts for almost a decade, yielding a series of conflicting judgments. In August 1934 Judge Woolsey acknowledged that Sheldon and Barnes had "just cause" to sue MGM, but he refused to award them costs because the Madeleine Smith case was in the public domain. Dissatisfied, the two pursued the case in the court of appeals the following

January. Appearing before Judge L. Hand, MGM defended itself, claiming it had not "use[d] the play in any way to produce the picture," and it submitted depositions from Brown, Stromberg, and Meehan, who swore they had never read the play. The plaintiffs begged to differ, pointing out that MGM had entered negotiations to buy the play and was therefore familiar with it, and it had produced a film with specific similarities. This time around, the court found in favor of the plaintiffs, noting that if "the picture was not an infringement of the play, there can be none, short of taking the dialogue." Sheldon and Barnes were awarded costs, and shortly thereafter, federal judge John Knox ordered MGM to submit its books to show the profits made on the film. In April 1936 Sheldon and Barnes went after theaters that were screening the film, seeking $21,000 in damages from one New York exhibitor; a revival of the film by New York's Capitol Theater in 1937 resulted in a hefty fine and an order to cease screenings. For a while, MGM continued to defend the film, but by 1937, two things were clear: Sheldon and Barnes had no intention of giving up, and Crawford was losing her box-office appeal. Nearly everyone at MGM just wanted to forget it and move on, but Hunt Stromberg was evidently a glutton for punishment: one of the first properties he bought when he moved to United Artists in 1942 was the Sheldon-Barnes play, which he released as *Dishonored Lady* starring Hedy Lamarr (David Lean also made a version, *Madeleine,* starring his then-wife Ann Todd in 1950).[13]

MGM's 1937 decision to permanently withdraw the film from circulation remains in effect today. Consequently, *Letty Lynton* has acquired a legendary status as the "lost" film of a major star's career. This elusive quality may have colored Crawford's own memories of the production. In an interview with Roy Newquist in the 1960s, she recalled the film as one of her greats (it wasn't)—"one hell of a story and script and character I could really come to grips with, thanks to Clarence Brown." For his part, Brown toed the MGM line, refusing to comment on the details of the legal mire in which he had briefly been entangled. He scarcely had time to dwell on it, as he was preoccupied with the demands of a busy career and a hectic social life. His thoughts, too, were shifting to his long-term future and whether that included MGM. In one report in the trade press, Elizabeth Yeaman noted that Brown was in negotiations with his old employer, Universal, to make a sound version of *The Goose Woman.* It was a tantalizing prospect, but nothing came of it—at least not for Brown. Harlan Thompson that had the honor of remaking the Rex Beach story as *The Past of Mary Holmes* (for RKO). Instead, Brown took some time off, traveling to Paris to visit Tourneur and then on to Germany, where he checked out some of the latest films from those directors who hadn't yet exiled themselves from the fascist onslaught (newspapers reported that he was impressed by G. W. Pabst's *l'Atlantide* and the Sagan-Froelich film *Mädchen in Uniform*). He also began a new romance with actress Dorothy Burgess, and rumors of an engagement soon surfaced (but again, no marriage followed).[14]

By the end of the summer, Brown's threats to decamp to another studio had evaporated, and he accepted a more lucrative contract with MGM. The studio intended to keep him busy, announcing that he would collaborate for a fourth time with Crawford on a production titled *Lost*, featuring child actor Jackie Cooper. Before he tackled that, Brown was given the chance to work with the "First Lady of American Theater," Helen Hayes, in an adaptation of a David Belasco production. It was a rather prestigious assignment, a mark of MGM's confidence in him, but the film would be one that Brown forever viewed with mortification.[15]

15

Service and Passion

As America struggled through the worst years of the Depression, Hollywood did its part by producing films that confronted the crisis head-on (Warner's *I Am a Fugitive from a Chain Gang;* Columbia's *American Madness*) or transported audiences to exotic worlds. The vogue for "Oriental pictures" in the early 1930s reflected one strand of this escapism, and the success of Capra's *The Bitter Tea of General Yen* and von Sternberg's *Shanghai Express* suggests that audiences responded with enthusiasm. Eager to cash in, MGM embarked on two "Oriental" projects of its own: the low-budget *The Mask of Fu Manchu* and a prestigious adaptation of a David Belasco–George Scarborough play from 1919, *The Son Daughter.* The latter is set in San Francisco's Chinatown and tells the tale of Lien Wha, the only child of Dr. Dong Tong. She is romantically involved with Tom Lee, but their courtship is halted when her father, under pressure to raise funds for the revolution back in China, agrees to marry her off to the highest bidder. Enter the evil Fen Sha, who buys her but double-crosses his new bride by arranging her father's murder and the retrieval of his payment. When Tom Lee tries to intervene, he too is killed, and it is left to the gentle Lien Wha to seek revenge. The final scenes show her transformation into a steely killer who gleefully murders her new husband by strangling him with his own queue.

According to *Variety*, MGM initially considered casting Chinese American star Anna May Wong in the lead. Wong was reportedly enthusiastic, but it seems the talented and beautiful actress was just "too Chinese," and she was passed over in favor of Helen Hayes. Joining the thoroughly Caucasian Hayes were New Englander Lewis Stone as her father, Mexican Ramon Novarro as Tom Lee, and Swedish-born Warner Oland (in Hollywood eyes, an "expert" at Oriental roles) as Fen Sha. The team of writers included Claudine West, John Goodrich (who had dabbled in Chinese stories with his 1927 *Shanghai Bound*), and Leon Gordon (handling dialogue). Jacques Feyder was reportedly slated to direct, but his fortuitous escape occurred when Brown's imminent collaboration with Crawford was temporarily shelved, and the studio decided to keep him busy with this new assignment.[1]

Brown was wary of the whole project, and when he arrived on the set in October, he discovered he wasn't the only one with doubts. Stone was dutifully going through the motions, Novarro was there under some duress, and the thirty-two-year-old Hayes was unnerved by the prospect of passing herself off as a Chinese teenager. MGM's makeup department couldn't reverse time, but it could offer her the standard "yellowface" palette of dark makeup, lashings of eyeliner, and some elastic bands to pull back her eyes. Hayes later remembered the film mainly because she "suffered so much"—presumably both physically and psychologically. Her unfortunate costar Louise Closser Hale endured even greater discomfort when the makeup department inserted "a rubber hose up her nose," causing concern that it might "disappear altogether." For his part, Brown immersed himself in the technical aspects of the film, collaborating with Oliver Marsh to come up with a lush and exotic aesthetic that might distract the audience from the weak script.[2]

It was a mercifully short shoot, but it didn't pass without incident. Brown was struck down with the flu in early November, and Robert Z. Leonard was brought in to cover for him; Hayes and Novarro, though professional and courteous, didn't really jell with each other. An additional headache was caused by a short-lived strike by Chinese extras, who were unimpressed by MGM catering. Brown later recalled his frustration: despite using "every trick" in his repertoire, he could do little to salvage the production. Preview audiences seemingly agreed, and the addition of a few new scenes, some retakes, and a patching up of the sound had a negligible impact. Nevertheless, MGM went through the motions and submitted the film to the censor's office in December. Somewhat surprisingly—given the lack of punishment for the heroine's murder of her husband—the response was muted, and newly appointed head James Wingate passed it without cuts, although privately he called it one "heavy handed" film.[3]

When *The Son Daughter* was released in early 1933, critics had little to say about Hollywood's habitual recourse to yellowface, focusing instead on the merits (or otherwise) of Hayes. *New York Times* reviewer "A.D.S." was generous in his praise of her "delightful performance" and the "high level of plausibility in . . . costumings and settings," although he admitted that the film was "naturally . . . handicapped . . . because the faces which have been embelished [sic] with seemingly shaved skulls, pigtails and slanted eyes belong to such familiar actors." Perhaps reflecting an East-West divide, the press on the West Coast was less enamored with Hayes. *Variety* dismissed both the actress and the film, describing the latter as "Oriental stuff washed up" and a "mistake for both principals." It seems that many cinema owners agreed. One disgruntled Illinois exhibitor complained to the *Motion Picture Herald* that MGM's latest offering was "draggy," causing many of his patrons to walk out. Another suggested that Hollywood studios take all their prints of "Chinese pictures" to "Frisco's Chinatown and leave them there." *The Son Daughter* made a paltry profit of only $6,000.[4]

It is easy to see why Brown hated the film and was mortified by it. The chief problems were an abysmal script and preposterous casting, but his lackluster direction and leaden pacing (especially in dialogue scenes) can't escape blame. Admittedly, the second half contains more involving moments, as intricate mobile camera work reveals the shadowy world of gambling dens and Lien Wha transforms from coy virgin to avenging angel, but these can't carry the entire film. Hayes and Brown made some game efforts to promote it, but they knew *The Son Daughter* was "a dog . . . a terrible picture."[5]

Brown was optimistic that his next assignment might suit him better. Adapted from a successful play by English author C. L. Anthony (the pen name of Dodie Smith of *The One Hundred and One Dalmatians* fame), and made under the imprint of William Randolph Hearst's Cosmopolitan Pictures, *Service* was a character piece with a timely theme. The film follows the fortunes of Gabriel Service (Lewis Stone), owner of a large department store in London, and his former employee, Benton (Lionel Barrymore), as they cope with an economic crisis. When a cost-cutting exercise leads to Benton's dismissal, he is jolted into entrepreneurial activity and opens a successful bakery with the help of his wife and children. In contrast, the crisis reveals the shallowness of Service's life and the indifference with which his (second) wife and children treat him. On the brink of selling his beloved store to a rival, Service has a chance encounter with Benton and is inspired to change. The story closes as he passes the reins of the business over to his now-enthusiastic children, and together they look out at a rainbow that augurs a bright future.

Working alongside veteran screenwriter Bess Meredyth, English writer H. M. Harwood (who would soon cowrite *Queen Christina*) set about adapting Anthony's play to the screen. Harwood's notes reveal that Brown was keen to have some input and that he was erring on the side of caution to ensure sufficient footage. He requested that much of the dialogue from the play be retained so that he would have greater leeway to make decisions on cutting, and he wanted the final scene between Service and his callous wife Isabel (Benita Hume) expanded to better showcase the actors' performances.

Although Harwood objected to some of Brown's suggestions—including adding in a scene in which Isabel exhibits "incredible perversity" by expressing her dislike of dogs—he went along with them. By early February, a script was in place, and shooting commenced on sets recycled from *Possessed* and *Emma*.[6]

This production was mainly smooth sailing, interrupted by one moment of (personal) drama when Brown unexpectedly eloped to Nevada on March 31. His bride was actress Alice Joyce, whom he had been quietly dating for some months. Since the collapse of his second marriage, Brown had enjoyed several high-profile romances with starlets, but this latest relationship was a union of equals. In fact, Joyce was more of a Hollywood veteran than he was: she was already carving out a successful career as a model and then actress in the Kalem and Vitagraph companies when Brown was finishing up college, and while he was serving his apprenticeship with Tourneur, she was establishing herself as a star, nicknamed the "Madonna of the Screen." By the time she met Brown, Joyce was in retirement and recovering from a tumultuous second marriage. Her third marriage offered Joyce and her teenage daughters much-needed financial and personal stability, while also ensuring a continued presence on the Hollywood social scene. Brown later revealed that he had reached a point in his life where a respectable union seemed more desirable than a series of fleeting romances: "I decided I wanted a wife to share my table, a lady."[7]

Before he could settle into married life, however, Brown had a film to finish—one that had been retitled (rather aptly) *Looking Forward*. The change was not in deference to this new chapter in Brown's personal life; rather, it was a shameless nod to newly elected President Franklin Roosevelt's book of collected writings and speeches on the Depression. It was an especially cynical move, given Thalberg's and Mayer's vehement and malicious opposition to his campaign, but promotional possibilities trumped principles, and *Looking Forward* even featured a foreword that incorporated a quote from the new president. With its themes of working together in the face of adversity, the film consciously aligned itself with some of the emerging New Deal philosophies, yet *Looking Forward* wasn't a political film—MGM rarely made them. This suited Brown, another Hoover supporter who feared what the "radical" Roosevelt might do.

For all its timeliness, however, neither audiences nor critics warmed to *Looking Forward*. Even the usually sympathetic trade press expressed disappointment at its muted tone, with *Film Daily* noting that although it was "expertly done," it was "rather slow-moving . . . [and] talk predominates over action." A few took an opposing view, expressing admiration for the leisurely pacing and for scenes in which subtle visual suggestion made the dialogue seem obsolete, but they were in the minority. Some of the reviewers' indifference was due to the film's English setting. Grace Kingsley of the *Los Angeles Times* appreciated the "charmingly human little story" but admitted to being "put off" by the English accents. American moviegoers were similarly alienated, with one Mississippi-based theater owner reporting to the *Motion Picture Herald* that his patrons complained about speeches in place of pure entertainment and females cast members who were "tiresome to look at" and had "too much of an English brogue or something."[8]

Looking Forward (aka *Service*, aka *The New Deal*) was instantly forgettable, especially when rival studios such as Warner and Columbia were releasing hard-hitting, gritty, or heartfelt films that spoke more urgently to a very uncertain American public. The film is characteristic of the cautious ethos of MGM, and Brown's workmanlike approach suggests a director delivering service rather than innovation. Perhaps he was simply not convinced by the film's New Deal message or its neat resolutions, but more likely, his mind was elsewhere. He was about to embark on a project that truly excited him, one that reignited his passion for filmmaking.

Based on Antoine de Saint-Exupéry's 1931 novel *Vol de Nuit*, *Night Flight* was the brainchild of rising producer David O. Selznick. Inspired by Saint-Exupéry's experiences as a commercial pilot flying mail routes in South America and Europe, and featuring characters based on real-life aviators, *Vol de Nuit* tells the story of Fabien, a courageous flier whose devotion to his job costs him his life. Though several critics on both sides of the Atlantic expressed reservations about the novel's fascist overtones, it was a hit with readers in France and garnered its author a host of literary prizes. MGM leased the rights the following year and selected Brown to direct. As a passionate aviator, he must have reveled in the novel's romantic prose and its sensual evocation of the exhilaration of flying, while details about the heavy burden of Fabien's job and his adherence to duty must have struck a familiar chord. Brown's excitement about the project was recorded by journalist Harrison Carroll during a visit to the set of *Looking Forward*. Carroll found Brown "keyed up to a pitch I have seldom seen," as the director told him that Saint-Exupéry was the "only man who has ever written what a pilot feels in the air." It was reported that Brown planned to shoot the film off the lot and to incorporate dynamic aerial sequences and footage filmed in the dangerous strait between Santiago, Chile, and Mendoza, Argentina.[9]

Selznick hoped *Night Flight* might surpass *Hell's Angels* as the great aviation epic and match the success of his most recent ensemble piece, *Dinner at Eight*. However, it would be a difficult job to transfer the slim, episodic novel full of philosophical musings on the nature of freedom and the inevitability of death to the screen. Saint-Exupéry's extensive use of interior monologue, the absence of empathetic characters, and the fatalistic ending were far from standard elements in the MGM formula. Selznick hired the highly experienced Oliver Garrett to write a screenplay, but after several drafts he brought in John Monk Saunders to develop the action sequences. Saunders was considered a master at aviation stories, having already contributed to *Wings*, *The Last Flight*, *Ace of Aces*, *Devil Dogs of the Air*, and *The Dawn Patrol*, but when Brown expressed dissatisfaction with Saunders's contribution, Selznick added Wells Root, a noted fixer of troublesome scripts, to the mix. With this trio on board, there was every reason to believe that the adaptation could retain the spirit of Saint-Exupéry while appealing to an audience accustomed to more conventional fare from MGM.[10]

Even in the early part of his career, Selznick was acquiring a reputation for being a hands-on producer whose presence and input threatened to undermine the position of the director. Brown was determined that this wouldn't be the case on *Night Flight*, and he maintained an active and assertive role in the lead-up to filming. In notes from an April 12 production meeting that included Brown's assistant Charles Dorian, cinematographer Oliver Marsh, aerial photographer Elmer Dyer, and stunt pilot Paul Mantz, Brown pushed for authenticity in the flight sequences, suggesting that if real footage from the Andes could not be sourced, another suitable location might be substituted. This footage—which would presumably be shot by a second unit—should "incorporate all the beauty and all the likeness to the real Andes . . . the more impressive, the better the scene will be." He also contributed detailed notes on how action within the cockpit of the plane should be filmed—"the camera should be on a saddle mount behind the pilot, including the pilot's head and shooting forward at shots of mountain peaks and cloud"—and ideas about what sound effects might be used. Brown's enthusiasm was evidently so infectious that his friend (and MGM sound supervisor) Douglas Shearer offered to pilot his own plane to record some "sputtering and roaring engine noises" that could then be incorporated.[11]

In an illustration of the essential incompatibility between the experimentalism of the source novel and the commercial imperatives that drove MGM, the studio assigned the cream of its creative talent to play Saint-Exupéry's impressionistic characters. Clark Gable was given the role of the doomed

Fabien; Robert Montgomery played another daredevil pilot (a part initially intended for Nils Asther); and the Barrymore brothers, John and Lionel, were cast as the airline's boss and employee, respectively. For the supporting roles of their wives or girlfriends, MGM assigned Helen Hayes, Myrna Loy, and Brown's old flame Dorothy Burgess. Filming commenced in late April, and because Brown had to work around the busy schedule of each star, he was forced to take a more sporadic approach to filming than he would have liked. Whereas a standard shoot might take four weeks, *Night Flight* staggered on, in fits and starts, for three months, amidst growing buzz that it was a troubled production. In May it was reported that Loews boss Nicholas Schenck had had to reassure shareholders that the studio had not made a costly mistake in hiring Selznick and green-lighting the production. Brown kept a low profile and did his best to cope with the challenges that arose on a daily basis—dealing with a crew frustrated by the slow progress, coordinating with second units to match up the footage, advising on action sequences, and navigating through a sea of correspondence from Selznick. He didn't have much time left for the cast; consequently, some of them felt adrift, while others cooperated only on their own terms. Myrna Loy later confessed that she found the experience baffling because there had been little rehearsal time and not much discussion about how the characters related to one another. She didn't even get to meet some of her fellow cast members: "I didn't see Jack [Barrymore] or Helen [Hayes] or anybody but Bill Gargan. . . . We had a very nice scene as he goes off on a fatal flight, which everybody seemed to do in that picture" (she is mistaken here, as Gargan's character is one of the few who survives). Brown's stress levels were not helped by the behavior of the Barrymores, who were not noted for their displays of brotherly love. As the perennially scratching Robineau—an eczema-plagued clerk who must enforce the petty tyranny of his boss Rivière—Lionel did his best to steal every scene from John. Brown knew how to handle the older Barrymore, but dealing with John pushed him to breaking point. A chronic alcoholic, John was often erratic, but he was going through a particularly bad bout of drinking and frequently arrived late to the set and struggled to remember his lines. Brown later recalled that the actor was "almost imbecilic" and impossible to manage, and the director tried to get him fired from the production. MGM refused, which was just as well, because in his moments of lucidity, Barrymore gave an impressive performance as Rivière, the megalomaniacal boss who displays a reckless disregard for the safety of his pilots.[12]

Away from the hoopla of the Barrymore circus, Brown's favorite actor was contributing an understated, terse performance as the doomed Fabien. In the final cut, Clark Gable has just two lines of dialogue, and his scenes take place in the claustrophobic confines of a cockpit. It was certainly an unusual use of a star, and one that prompted criticism when *Night Flight* was released, but in some ways, it was entirely in keeping with the stoic Fabien of Saint-Exupéry's novel. Authentic, too, was Brown's retention of the novel's episodic structure and Saint-Exupéry's abstract themes of duty and individualism rather than the more conventional (and audience-friendly) theme of romance. Even as they shot it, it was clear that *Night Flight* was very different from MGM's standard all-star ensemble pieces. Likewise, it was clear that Brown's interest (like Saint-Exupéry's) had been piqued by the action-aviation sequences and by the exploration of the fatalistic passion that drives aviators, rather than the love stories between the various couples.

Brown turned in a rough cut of almost two hours, and its look was very different from the workmanlike style of his most recent efforts for the studio. Instead of a self-effacing adherence to formula, the structure was loose, the characterization was impressionistic, and the experimental and inventive cinematography recalled some of his best work in the silent era. In a nod to the stark expressionism of *Flesh and the Devil*'s duel scene, Rivière charts his plans for postal domination framed against the backdrop of an enormous map, his bosses reduced to mere silhouettes. Brown borrowed from *The Goose Woman* in a shot of Rivière writing a report in his ledger, a blot of ink falling to the page and "wiping out" the name of a doomed pilot. This visual inventiveness was not merely a case of Brown turning to the past; he was also looking forward, seeking inspiration from the finest European directors of the day. Shortly before shooting *Night Flight*, Brown had been in Europe, catching up with some of the current releases in France, Germany, and the Soviet Union. The influence of a number of innovative European directors, including Pabst, Dovzhenko, Vigo, and Eisenstein, can be seen in some of *Night Flight*'s more striking shots: the airline bosses shot entirely in silhouette, the aerial views of children playing on a carousel, and the glimpses of earthy peasants living in squalid huts looking to the sky as the mail plane passes overhead.

Brown's bold experiments and the beauty of the footage impressed his boss, Louis B. Mayer, but *Night Flight* also presented problems for the studio. Everyone had known that the source novel wasn't exactly a perfect fit with the MGM formula, but they had all hoped that the team of writers, Brown, and the ensemble cast might shape it into audience-friendly fare. Instead, the studio had almost two hours of footage containing abstract musings about life and duty and some stunning aviation sequences, but little in the way of a developed story or empathetic characters. An exasperated Mayer wrote to

Brown and Selznick and offered a brutally honest dissection of the film's fundamental flaw: "What the devil are they flying for? . . . You have terrific heroics, death and sacrifice and not a thing that will justify all the suspense and danger in the minds of the audiences." His reservations were vindicated when the film was previewed in August and the press, though respectful, commented on the "strange" story and the "unfinished" ending that "didn't quite seem satisfactory." In a surprisingly thoughtful review that expressed admiration for Brown's "impressionistic" style and its debt to European cinema (most notably, Pabst), Philip Scheuer articulated his misgivings about Brown's application of a Soviet-style "typage" to the all-star cast. However, he commended the director's creative vision and his obvious passion for the real subject of the film, aviation: "himself an aviator, a birdman, he communicates to the spectator his own mystical exaltation."[13]

Unfortunately for Brown, MGM wasn't in the business of making films purely to indulge its directors' passions. The studio decided to commission a couple of new scenes to give *Night Flight* a framing story and furnish its characters with a more convincing motivation. Thus, it is explained that the mail planes are used not only to ensure the fast delivery of frivolities such as postcards but also to dispatch urgently required medical supplies to needy children. Brown duly shot the extra scenes, which feature a robust-looking Buster Phelps as a gravely ill boy and future director Irving Pichel as his anxious father, waiting for the serum that will save his life. Although these additions were quite a departure from Saint-Exupéry's cool tone, they satisfied Mayer's requirement of heartfelt motivation and a (muted) happy ending.

A pared-down version of *Night Flight* had its official premiere in October 1933, and reviewers responded with some uncertainty. Despite the addition of the framing story, it remained an unconventional film. *New York Times* reviewer Mordaunt Hall was impressed by the realism and attention to detail in this "outstanding screen contribution on aviation," but the *Washington Post* critic grumbled that it fell "short of the possibilities of the subject," despite "the wealth of melodramatic romance inherent in the events upon which the tumultuous picture is founded." For him, the lack of interaction among the cast was the main problem of this ensemble piece: "The stellar performances, instead of being closely knit . . . are rather in the nature of solo efforts." Audiences and exhibitors agreed, with one Texas theater owner complaining about "the absurdity of casting the screen's leading artists in minor and insignificant roles."[14]

For all that, and despite some vocal criticism from Saint-Exupéry, *Night Flight* managed to return a modest profit in what turned out to be a limited run. Brown was deeply affected by the lackluster response to the most personal film he had made in years, and he viewed its mediocre box-office take as evidence of "failure." In an interview he gave a year later, he was still grappling with his disappointment and trying to come up with an explanation. He admitted the love story was a little unusual: "It wasn't the story of a man or a woman. It was the story of a motor." And he concluded that it might have worked better with a cast of unknowns. His close friend and fellow aviator Merian Cooper had no doubt that neither the content nor Brown's handling was to blame; he faulted Selznick and Hollywood's producer-led system: "Brown was a flier but no director ever worked for David without David just really being everything, you know. David had to interfere with every goddamn detail for a picture." Cooper was correct that Brown found Selznick tiresome. Certainly, when the two reunited on *Anna Karenina* in 1935, Brown did little to disguise his irritation at the producer's endless stream of memos. In 1933, however, the balance of power was a little different, and Brown probably had more clout at MGM, and with Mayer, than Selznick did. Screenwriter Phillip Dunne, who developed a personal and professional relationship with Brown in the late 1930s, offered a more credible explanation of *Night Flight*'s failure: Brown was so "blinded by his private love [of aviation]" that he forgot his stars and his audience, and once the hurt wore off, he was pragmatic enough to admit that the elements that personally moved him—such as the beauty of flying and the restless individualism of the aviator—"just didn't work for the audience."[15]

It might not have captured the imagination of the general public, but there were those who appreciated *Night Flight* as the ode to flying Brown intended. Members of the Quiet Birdmen, a rather secretive club that had welcomed Brown to its ranks some years before, were fulsome in their praise. More recent critics have offered fresh appraisals of this bold and brave effort: noting Brown's skill, Leonard Maltin commended *Night Flight*'s "poetic and arty quality . . . unusual for an MGM blockbuster." Back in 1933, Brown took comfort from the admiration of his fellow aviators, dusted himself off, and accepted another assignment from MGM. It was back to the old formula.[16]

16

Back with Crawford

In the aftermath of *Night Flight*'s disappointing release, there were reports that Brown had bought the rights to "Contact," a story about a "daring aviator" written by former US marine John Hildegard, and that this would be his next project. It never came to pass, and as he waited for his next assignment from MGM, Brown took some time off, flying himself around America to visit exhibitors, check out new plays, and attend premieres. He also made his yearly trip to Europe, staying at the opulent George V Hotel in Paris and catching up with Tourneur before traveling with Alice to San Moritz for a break at Badrutt's Palace. As most Americans struggled through the Depression, the Browns spent freely on property, vacations, and luxury goods, but they weren't immune to penny-pinching. Returning from Paris in 1932, Brown was caught trying to avoid paying customs duty for some pearls he had purchased (he was fined $1,800, and the jewels were confiscated). A couple of years later he was involved in a public dispute over debts Alice had accumulated with a local dressmaker, which he refused to pay (the case went to court, and the judge sided with Brown). Such instances of negative publicity were rare because the Browns generally kept a low profile.[1]

As he grew older, Brown was less inclined to participate in the parties and other social events that were the hallmark of the Hollywood community. Instead, he was consumed with business matters and with restoring and extending the most significant property in his portfolio: his 360-acre ranch at Calabasas. Soon after Brown acquired it in 1935, a visiting journalist reported that the interior was "Spanish Renaissance in motif, spacious and beautifully paneled rooms led to a sunlit patio, where tall, graceful arches framed a picture of acres and acres of trees and lawn, rolling to a rambling lake below, while beyond were deep blue mountains." Despite his already considerable investment, Brown was keen to put his own stamp on the ranch. He hired architect Wallace Neff, famous for his pioneering "California style" (which incorporated Spanish elements into Modernist buildings), and Paul László, a refugee from Hitler's Germany who had developed a style best described as Moderne with a Surrealist touch, to oversee the work. The interior of the ranch was substantially modified to add a projection room, and the redesigned grounds included a swimming pool, tennis court, and private airstrip. The ranch would be Brown's main base for the next two decades, and he used it occasionally for location work. It was also the site of his famed Fourth of July barbecues in honor of Mayer's (fake) birthday.[2]

Such luxuries had to be funded, and after the bruising experience of *Night Flight*, Brown was eager for a box-office success. *Sadie McKee* was another "working girl makes good" story, like those that had defined Joan Crawford's early career, and he was under no illusions: "I guess . . . in my day the thinking was that, to make a picture, all you needed was to take a little shop girl and wind up with her married to the governor of the state. The true-to-life shop girl goes to see the picture and thinks, 'Maybe I can do that, too.'" Written by Viña Delmar (whose work had already been adapted to the screen), "Pretty Sadie McKee" was published in serial form in *Liberty* magazine in the summer of 1933. Sadie, a girl from the wrong side of the tracks, worships her sleazy boyfriend, would-be singer Tommy. Abandoning her mother and an inevitable future as a drudge, she travels to the city, gives up her virtue, is ditched by Tommy, and ends up as a nightclub soubrette. There, Sadie catches the eye of millionaire Jack Brennan. She marries him, cures him of alcoholism, and nets herself a fortune for her efforts. After divorcing Brennan, she marries Michael, son of the rich family that employs her mother, but she dumps him when she grows bored with his pusillanimity in the face of his domineering father. The story ends as Sadie teams up with Gilbert, Brennan's lawyer and her former nemesis.[3]

Described by one studio reader as "a mixture of ruthlessness and chivalry," the Sadie character was right up Crawford's alley, sure to appeal to those fans who had been put off by her recent performances in *Rain* and *Today We Live*. It wasn't a simple return to the style and content of *Possessed*, however: *Sadie McKee* was shaped both by the tighter restrictions on content being introduced by the Studio Relations Committee (SRC) and by MGM's belief that Crawford's career could benefit from a softening of her roles. Unlike his predecessors Joy and Wingate, the SRC's new head, Joseph Breen, was much less inclined to pander to the studios, and as *Sadie McKee* went into production, he was already taking steps to ensure that the 1930 production code would be more rigorously implemented by his office and observed by the studios. Anticipating that Delmar's frank depiction of promiscuity and of Sadie's masochistic attachment to her boyfriend would not get past Breen's shrewd appraisal, MGM took steps to sanitize the content. A team of writers that included Bess Meredyth, E. A. Woolf, Carey Wilson, John Meehan, and Vicki Baum was assigned to supply an adaptation at the heart of which was a character more sinned against than sinning. In this revised scenario, Sadie's marriage to Jack is motivated by her insecurity after being abandoned by Tommy, and her virtue is vindicated as she proves her devotion to her alcoholic husband. Her reward is typical of the ideal world depicted in MGM movies: Jack emerges from his stupor, realizes that Sadie is staying with him out of a sense of duty, and gallantly steps aside so that she can marry (the conveniently wealthy) Michael. Tommy also gets his comeuppance with a fatal case of tuberculosis.[4]

Filming for *Sadie McKee* commenced in February 1934, mainly on the back lot (contrary to early reports that Brown would shoot the entire film in San Francisco). The main attraction was Crawford, but she had the support of her newest fiancé, Franchot Tone, in the role of Michael (an amalgamation of two Delmar characters, Michael and Gilbert, originally expected to be played by Gable) and crooner Gene Raymond as Tommy. Character actor Edward Arnold, then at the start of a long career that included some especially notable performances for Frank Capra, was cast as Jack Brennan. The role easily could have descended into the cliché of a drunken millionaire who likes showgirls, giving the proceedings some comic relief. Arnold, however, delivers a layered performance, alternating scenes of sloppy physical comedy, jumbled wordplay, and frightening belligerence with subdued, reflective moments that expose the poignancy of Jack's miserable life. What emerges is one of American cinema's bleakest portrayals of a man in the grips of chronic alcoholism, every bit the equal of Ray Milland's Don Birnam in Billy Wilder's *The Lost Weekend*, made a decade later. Indisputably, it was Arnold's considerable talent that made his character such a memorable one, but the contributions by Brown and cinematographer Oliver Marsh shouldn't be overlooked. In one scene in which a drunken Jack struggles to get undressed, the camera remains unflinching, static as it records the gradual shift from comedy to something far more poignant and pathetic. Although Brown's style in *Sadie McKee* is more self-effacing than it was in *Possessed* and *Night Flight*, the instances of visual flair (noirish lighting, canted angles, and forced perspective) are reserved for those scenes that depict the messy realities of an alcoholic's existence. Brown's nuanced and compassionate treatment of the disease—and, more precisely, the sufferer—might seem surprising, coming from a teetotaler, but he had plenty of experience to draw from in both his personal life (his friend John Gilbert and, soon, his wife Alice) and his professional career (the

Barrymores and Wallace Beery, among others). Jack Brennan joins the sad parade of chronic alcoholics who populate his work, from *The Goose Woman* to *Anna Christie, A Free Soul,* and *Ah Wilderness!*[5]

As Arnold was enjoying a productive experience on the set, Esther Ralston was having a more stressful time. A significant star in the silent era— she had played Mrs. Darling in Herbert Brenon's *Peter Pan*—Ralston had been somewhat adrift since the introduction of sound. She was on a short contract with MGM but doubted it would be renewed because, she claimed, she had rejected Mayer's sexual advances. "Then," she recalled, "I heard that Clarence Brown was going to direct Joan Crawford in *Sadie McKee* and that in the picture there was a wonderful part of a nightclub singer that was right down my alley. I went into Mr. Brown's office and told him all about Mayer." According to Ralston, Brown had a forceful and rather surprising reaction: "I finished my sad tale, Mr. Brown stood up and slammed his fist down on his desk: 'God damn it,' he said. 'Nobody tells me whom to cast in my pictures. YOU are going to play the part of Dolly!'" With one obstacle overcome, there were more in Ralston's future: specifically, Crawford. Initially the two actresses got along, but when it became clear that Ralston's charming mix of witty banter, sexy Mae West–style mannerisms, and very revealing costumes threatened to steal every scene, Crawford resorted to petty means to shift the power balance. According to Ralston, Crawford initiated a bullying campaign and did "everything she could to embarrass" her. Eventually, Ralston turned to Brown, and it seems he had quite a soft spot for her: he assured her that he already knew what Crawford was up to and was taking steps to see that Ralston's performance didn't suffer. It's unclear what those steps were, but perhaps he had a quiet word with his star or, more likely, made plans to favor Ralston in the final edits.[6]

Shooting on *Sadie McKee* wrapped in April, and Howard Dietz, MGM's head of publicity, came up with a campaign that sold it as opulent, slightly salacious entertainment. Art Deco posters featuring a sleek Crawford and boasting such taglines as "I gave 10¢ worth of love for a $17,000,000 husband" encouraged audiences to forget their troubles, leave the dishes in the sink, and go to the movies. There, they could relish the sight of clotheshorse Crawford gliding through a bedroom "hung with perrywinkle [sic] blue chintz drapes and . . . furnishings . . . of the Directoire period," dropping in on her onscreen husband as he lay in a stupor in a "millionaire's bedroom . . . the last word in gentlemanly luxury [with a] bedspread . . . encrusted with copper sequins." Such emphases on the accumulation of wealth (achieved through sexual relations) seemed at odds with MGM's early assurances to Breen that Delmar's story would be sanitized; few could deny that this "softened" Sadie was still a woman on the make. Evidence that the production managed to fly just below Breen's radar includes allusions to Sadie's mercenary motives—lines such as "every girl's got her price . . . and yours should be pretty high" and "a lot of us do a whole lot more for a whole lot less"; scenes in which it is plain that Sadie and Tommy are living together as an unmarried couple; some very transparent costumes; and a reference to the nonconsummation of Sadie's marriage to Jack.[7]

Despite this risqué material, *Sadie McKee*'s reception was rather subdued when it was released in May. Mordaunt Hall was critical of Brown's "studied" direction and the many "static interludes [and] a great deal of talk, which is by no means as interesting as the producers evidently thought it to be." In a review titled "Sad Eyes, Silk and Sex," Muriel Babcock commented on the "tawdry" tone and the absence of a "fine, real story," and she noted that Ralston and Arnold had stolen the show from under the nose of its star. "Abel" in *Variety* was more balanced, acknowledging that *Sadie McKee* was "the Cinderella theme all over again," but moments of implausibility had been "shrewdly glossed over" so that "something like an authentic human document" emerged. For *Film Weekly* and its reviewer Leonard Wallace, *Sadie McKee* was further evidence that Crawford "compels attention," despite repeatedly being forced to play "subnormal modern girls . . . oversexed creatures of untutored appetites . . . [albeit] chastened with sentimental and circumstantial whitewash . . . [that robs] . . . them of any human interest."[8]

Numbed by the steady stream of Crawford vehicles coming out of MGM, critics found much in *Sadie McKee*'s formulaic elements to dislike, but in retrospect, their complaints seem a little harsh. It is a well-crafted and entertaining film, and though it lacks the cynicism of *Possessed* and the raciness of *A Free Soul*, it contains some acute observations on class differences and gender double standards. In marked contrast to the films he made with Garbo, Brown allowed supporting players such as Arnold, Ralston, Jean Dixon, Leo G. Carroll, and Akim Tamiroff to overshadow his star. Perhaps this indicates a certain weariness with his reputation as a "director of stars." In the two decades after *Sadie McKee*'s release, his most accomplished films are the ones that feature finely etched performances by character actors such as Walter Huston, Aline MacMahon, Anne Revere, and Beulah Bondi or by child actors and nonprofessionals such as Elizabeth Taylor and Claude Jarman.

The overshadowing of her performance didn't go unnoticed by Crawford, and she had mixed feelings about *Sadie McKee*. In a letter to a fan written shortly after the film's debut, she confided that she was "pretty unhappy with the way it was cut, perhaps it will make sense—but I doubt it." By the 1960s, her attitude had changed, and she told Roy Newquist that "everything about *Sadie McKee* was right." It wasn't her best film, and it was by no means her most gratifying collaboration with Brown, but in its own low-key way, it proved significant. In Robert Aldrich's *Whatever Happened to Baby Jane?* Crawford's character—washed-up movie star Blanche Hudson—seeks solace by watching flickering images of her younger self on a battered television set. The movie she's watching is *Sadie McKee.*[9]

With the box-office success of *Sadie McKee*, it was inevitable that MGM would rush Brown and Crawford into a new production. Once again, Edgar Selwyn provided the source: *Sacred and Profane Love* (no connection to Arnold Bennett), the tale of a working girl who becomes embroiled in a love triangle. Hunt Stromberg assigned John Lee Mahin to write the screenplay in the spring of 1934. Mahin had written some great material for Jean Harlow films and was a seasoned pro, but Stromberg thought it couldn't hurt to add a few more writers to the mix, so he drafted husband-and-wife team Frances Goodrich and Albert Hackett (as it turned out, their contributions were not incorporated). The results were decidedly routine: Crawford plays Diane Levering, a young go-getter who works in a shipping company and—in a nod to the stricter Breen code—is involved in a chaste relationship with her married but separated boss, Richard Field (Otto Kruger). Although he is anxious to do the right thing and formalize their relationship, his current wife (Marjorie Gateson) is unwilling to give up the perks of being married to a shipping magnate. To cool things down, Richard sends Diane on a cruise, not anticipating that she will meet an irresistible man, Mike (Clark Gable), and fall in love. However, this being a Crawford film, the course of their love doesn't run smooth. When Diane arrives home to break up with Richard, she is confronted by the news that the first Mrs. Field is now open to a divorce. Exhibiting the usual gallantry of the MGM protagonist, she agrees to marry Richard, even though she loves Mike. But her new husband is even more gallant: when Richard realizes that her affections lie elsewhere, he grants her a generous divorce. The final scenes show Diane and Mike, happily married and settled on a ranch in Argentina.

Sacred and Profane Love—or *Chained*, as it was renamed—went into production in May 1934 for a five-week shoot. Although the scenario demanded little from cast and crew, personal drama ensued with the news that Crawford's biological father, Thomas LeSueur, was keen to reconcile with her, and a well-publicized visit to the set was organized (it proved to be a short and bitter reunion). LeSueur needed Crawford (or, rather, her money) more than she needed him. If she was looking for a father figure, she could turn to Brown, whom she continued to regard with respect and affection, despite the coolness between them during the filming of *Sadie McKee*. As always, Brown was sympathetic and patient with her, waiting while she calmed her nerves and quietly issuing instructions. Crawford later joked that he was so soft-spoken that the production ended up being "a real hearing test." It was just one of many tests she faced. Her private life was extremely complicated, and she had to field constants demands for money from both her greedy parents and her wastrel brother, deal with the temperamental and petulant Franchot Tone (who wanted his new wife to develop her skills as a "serious" actress and leave the soul-destroying Hollywood behind), and try but fail to resist the charms of her lover, Gable.[10]

The last time the lovers had worked on a Brown film (*Possessed*), Mayer had taken steps to break up their affair. This time around, the studio seemed to actively facilitate their relationship, perhaps accepting that Crawford's best onscreen partner would always be Gable. Mahin and Brown were instructed to do all they could to capture the chemistry between the two, and several scenes were added to show the couple's initial frosty encounter, Mike's good-humored charm, and Diane's capitulation to that charm in a scene that takes place beside a swimming pool occupied by a very young Mickey Rooney. All the scenes of romance and comedy called for a light touch from both the actors and the director. Gable effortlessly projected a rueful, comic air, but Crawford was less comfortable, despite Brown's assurances that she was "one of the three actresses in this town who can do anything, so do it!" In reality, she faced stiff competition from contemporaries such as Jean Harlow and, even more so, Carole Lombard. Crawford was also being encouraged by Tone to develop her skills as an actress and play roles beyond her comfort zone, adding to the pressure. Consequently, her performance seemed somewhat mannered and mechanical. When *Chained* was released, the ardor of one of her most enthusiastic fans, F. Scott Fitzgerald, was dampened as he watched her resort to clichés such as the "cynical accepting smile" and "hammy gestures" to denote emotions.[11]

Critics agreed with Fitzgerald when they saw the film in September. Muriel Babcock grumbled, "It has no ring of truth, sincerity or realism and never at any moment convinces you of anything, save the moviesque charm of its principals." Mordaunt Hall seemed to yawn through his review of "just another suspenseless triangle" with a "facile performance from Crawford." *Variety* was more forgiving and more interested in speculating how Crawford's role, which "removes her from the wild type which was her lot for several years," might be received by audiences. Evidently, fans liked this new Crawford. One Kentucky exhibitor reported to *Motion Picture Herald* that the "picture went over fine" and "did best business of the week."[12]

As a glossy showcase of two attractive stars, *Chained* has its charms, but it is also an example of the strengths and weaknesses of the MGM style: it looks sophisticated and pristine, but an air of anonymity and vacuity ensures that it's instantly forgettable. For the most part, Crawford's films required adherence to a formula that sculpted both the content and its execution. Brown's collaborations with her were no different, but their best work together contained some inspired moments, when visual suggestion conveyed risqué content or when Crawford reined in her mannerisms and gave some sense of her character's inner life. Themes of ambition, love, desire, and loss, so sharply observed in *Possessed* and *Sadie McKee,* were absent from *Chained,* and Brown's static, stilted treatment suggests a director bored by his material and his star. Sensing that the partnership had—for the moment—run its course, MGM assigned "One-Take" Woody van Dyke to Crawford's next picture.

17

Reunited

Garbo, Brown, and *Anna Karenina*

After spending the better part of a year working with Crawford, Brown expected his next project to be an adaptation of Eugene O'Neill's 1933 play *Ah Wilderness!* He had persuaded MGM to acquire the rights, and the plan was to shoot it on location in Brown's birthplace of Clinton, Massachusetts, with Will Rogers in the lead role. However, he was obliged to put it aside when the studio, in the early stages of a production of *Anna Karenina*, required his services.

Garbo, influenced by her friend Salka Viertel, was pushing to take the lead in a remake of the Tolstoy novel. She had already played the role of Anna in *Love,* Edmund Goulding's 1927 version, but she had been a relative novice at the time, unwilling to oppose decisions on casting (she had appeared opposite her recent ex, John Gilbert) or content (a happy ending had been tacked on). This time around, she wanted to play an Anna who was closer to Tolstoy's tragic heroine, in an adaptation that preserved the novel's melancholic tone. Producer David Selznick was skeptical, advising her not to make the "mistake" of tackling another historical character in a "heavy Russian drama." He thought she might do better in a modern role and suggested the Brewer and Bloch play *Dark Victory.* Selznick's appeal fell on deaf ears, however, and she requested George Cukor as her director. Garbo's enthusiasm for the director was not (yet) reciprocated: Cukor had met her at a party and found her to be "completely without humor, arty and rather pretentious," and he declined to work with her on what he predicted would be a humorless adaptation of Tolstoy's novel.[1]

With Cukor out of the running, Selznick cast around for alternatives and, despite their differences on *Night Flight,* suggested Brown. Garbo was surprisingly receptive, but after his unhappy experience on *Inspiration,* Brown needed some persuading. It proved even trickier to convince Joseph Breen at the Production Code Administration (PCA; previously the Studio Relations Committee) to approve a new version of a story crammed full of taboo themes such as adultery, illegitimacy, and suicide. Selznick spent much of the winter of 1934 and into 1935 immersed in complicated negotiations. Breen made it clear that the adulterous couple must be punished and that no dialogue could refer to Anna giving birth to her lover's child. Breen also insisted that a happy ending, like that used in Goulding's version, could not be accommodated. Even though the new censorship code disapproved of any mention or visual representation of suicide, Breen was inclined to agree with Selznick that the original tragic ending should be reinstated (mainly because he regarded it as apt punishment for Anna's transgressions).

It wouldn't be easy to come up with a script that could please Garbo, placate the PCA, and appeal to the moviegoing public. Salka Viertel seemed an obvious pick, and Selznick hired Clemence Dane (aka Winifred Ashton) as her collaborator. Selznick had first encountered the eccentric Dane when he produced the film version of her *Bill of Divorcement* for RKO, and he thought she would be an ideal choice to tackle Tolstoy. She wasn't so sure, and as the two writers discussed the novel, Dane admitted being baffled by Anna's melancholia and her passion: "I have very little understanding for Anna Karenina. What *does* she want? Her husband is a perfect gentleman; she has social position, an adorable child." Anna's peculiarities, Dane concluded, must be related to the unfortunate circumstances of her birth: "the poor thing is Russian."[2]

As both writers grappled with the complexities of the Russian psyche, Selznick continued to field Breen's requests for the deletion of specific lines (Anna: "Am I ashamed of anything I've done? Wouldn't I do the same again tomorrow?") and for the excision of all scenes depicting Anna's adultery ("You will see to it that passion in these scenes is kept well within the bounds," Breen insisted). Consequently, as the months wore on, the script became more muted and bland, and it seems that everyone had an opinion: comedy writer Ted Shane even suggested that the character of Stephen (Anna's brother) be reinvented as a kind of "high society Harpo Marx." In despair, Selznick turned to script supervisor Kate Corbaley—"Mayer's Scheherazade"—for advice, and she didn't hold back. Exasperated by a draft she read in February, she pointed out its fundamental lack of drama: "[it] begins on an even key and continues on in an even key." She regretted, too, that the censor-imposed sanitizing had turned the character of Vronsky into a mere "shadow," instead of the "dashing, handsome, fascinating devil" she remembered fondly from *Love:* "We should feel about him exactly as we felt about John Gilbert in the original silent version—that here was a man any woman might count her world well lost for. He should be, first of all a soldier, before he is the lover." Although Corbaley readily conceded that the Goulding version had been "faulty," she argued that it contained "the thing this story lacks as far as the love story is concerned—power and passion." She also voiced her concerns to the newly assigned Brown, who agreed the script was flawed but hoped the problems could be ironed out once filming commenced ("Clarence feels that he can use this skeleton of a script"). Brown and Corbaley disagreed about the amount of spectacle the film should include, with Brown voicing his preference for a "sophisticated city background and the pastoral background." In a last attempt to pull the script together, Selznick drafted S. L. Behrman, who had worked on *Queen Christina* and was regarded as a dialogue specialist. Behrman had envisaged it as a quick salvage job; instead, it took "an unconscionable time, far beyond my contract time," and yielded few tangible results.[3]

Selznick's archives at the University of Texas indicate the vast resources poured into *Anna Karenina* and how closely he supervised every detail. He hired a team, headed by Russian-born Nathalie Bucknall, to advise on historical details, including the most appropriate costumes—it was decided to use fashions from the 1880s rather than the 1870s, as the former were more "picturesque" and "flattering"—the correct music, and the specific design of Russian trains in the 1870s (apparently, the doors on the carriages opened inward, not outward). Bucknall could be as meticulous and dogmatic as her boss, and on occasion she overstepped her authority and incurred Selznick's wrath. When she began to suggest script changes and offer opinions on how certain scenes might be directed, Selznick responded with sharp annotations on the notes she gave him: "none of your business," he wrote on one. By March, he was so exasperated that he told Bucknall she "should be a writer, it pays more," and "directing pays more than research too."[4]

Joining Bucknall on the team was a White Russian by the name of General Theodore Lodijensky, allegedly the model for the Emil Jannings character in von Sternberg's *The Last Command* (1928). Lodijensky often advised studios on Russian-themed films, and he was the proprietor of a number of cafés and nightclubs in Hollywood. He readily furnished anecdotes about his years as a soldier in the Imperial Army, which apparently included a lot of carousing and womanizing. Selznick also hired Andrey Tolstoy (grandson of the author) as a consultant and translator (but mainly in a bid to generate publicity). Less colorful but much more significant was another Russian, Val Lewton. A former publicity man—he had even written some copy for Garbo—Lewton found fame in the 1940s for the series of beautiful and influential horror films he produced at RKO (including three directed by Jacques Tourneur). In 1935, though, Lewton was still an assistant, and it was his job to sift through the various drafts, chiefly to ensure that MGM didn't unintentionally plagiarize any source other than the Constance Garrett translation of the novel. His memos shed light on the problems the writers encountered as they tried to whittle down Tolstoy's epic, as well as his worries that the wordy script would become a stilted, slow-paced film.[5]

There can be little doubt that Selznick was the driving force behind the production, but Brown did more than simply check in on the first day of shooting. It was Brown who suggested casting veteran actor Robert Warwick, who had worked with him on Tourneur's *A Girl's Folly*, in a small role as an Imperial Army colonel. He also pushed to secure a job for Erich von Stroheim as a "military consultant." Brown's efforts on behalf of both men exemplified one of his more appealing traits—loyalty. Over the years, he populated his sets with individuals Hollywood had neglected or rejected, whether a major director who was down on his luck (von Stroheim, and later King Baggot in *Come Live with Me*) or an old friend who would get a kick out of spending a couple of days on a Hollywood set (Rubye de Remer in *The Gorgeous Hussy*). In the case of von Stroheim, Brown was an admirer of his work and had been influenced by some aspects of his style, especially his penchant for visual symbolism. But he also regarded von Stroheim as a salutary case of a director who had self-sabotaged his career. As it turned out, von Stroheim's involvement in *Anna Karenina* proved to be another frustrating experience for him and something of a headache for Brown. Within days of taking up his position, it was clear that von Stroheim simply couldn't take a backseat, and he offered Brown and Selznick advice on all matters, from putting greater emphasis on Vronsky's military background to replacing the proposed title cards (e.g., "Moscow, 1878") with filmic montages to more vibrantly establish a sense of time and place. Once he started, he couldn't stop, and soon he was offering his thoughts on how scenes between Fredric March (as Vronsky) and Maureen O'Sullivan (as Kitty) might be played and how specific scenes should be edited. Selznick brushed aside most of these suggestions, and Brown's reaction isn't recorded. Significantly, none were incorporated in the final film.[6]

As the weeks wore on, and with filming scheduled to begin in early March, Selznick was anxious to conclude an agreement with the PCA. Days before the start of filming, Breen was still sending reminders of what he would—and more often would not—pass. When he explained that scenes of Anna and Vronsky living together or displaying "intimate physical contact" would result in a withholding of his seal of approval, Selznick had had enough.

He wrote to Breen, objecting to these "criticisms of the script . . . [that] are so much more extensive than they have been formerly" and threatening to pull the plug entirely rather than embark on a "completely vitiated and emasculated adaptation." He pointed out that "*Anna Karenina* is solely and simply a love story and an adulterous love story. To try and make it anything else is utterly impossible," although he assured Breen that Brown would handle it all with "good taste." Selznick's challenge had the desired effect: unwilling to face the inevitable wrath of the corporate heads at Loews and MGM should the project collapse, Breen retreated. He couldn't resist a few last stipulations, though, reminding Selznick to tone down the scenes of soldiers partying with gypsy girls and to replace "explicit" references to "infidelity" with a more evasive "he wronged you."[7]

With an approved script in place, shooting commenced on March 21 on an ice-rink scene that was later scrapped. It was followed by work on one of the more striking scenes in the film: Anna's arrival at the railway station. In a replay of her entrance in *Flesh and the Devil*, Brown introduces Garbo as she materializes from the dissipating smoke of a steam engine, as if conjured up by the mesmerized March. It was an iconic shot in 1927, and it played a part in establishing the visual style used to film Garbo in later productions. Brown's return to it here seems to be a conscious nod to both her enthralling stardom and his own role in creating it. There is, too, a sense that he is reminding his peers that he is more than just a studio director, that the boldly expressive style he pioneered in the silent era contributed to the formation of a certain Hollywood aesthetic. If Brown was sending a message, it worked: a number of directors paid homage to the scene in their own films, including Julien Duvivier in his 1948 version of *Anna Karenina* with Vivien Leigh, and Elia Kazan's scene of Blanche's arrival in *A Streetcar Named Desire*.[8]

Brown's handling of the lovers' first encounter may have convinced audiences that Anna and Vronsky share an instant attraction and an intense passion, but it was a different story when the cameras stopped rolling. It was generally known, and reported in the press, that Garbo rarely formed strong attachments with her leading men, and her performance tended to overshadow that of her costars. While that rankled some of them (Robert Montgomery, Charles Bickford), others were honored to simply be in her presence and in *her* film (Gavin Gordon). Fredric March, however, did not play second fiddle to anyone, especially when the project didn't really interest him. He had resisted the role of Vronsky because he knew he was not Selznick's first choice (the producer had wanted Gable), and he feared another costume role would damage his career. March tried his best to get out of this one (which required a loan from his home studio, Twentieth Century), leaking his dissatisfaction to the press and telling Selznick he was "fed up" with "costume pictures" and believed it would be "a mistake to do another." His objections fell on deaf ears, and his resentment festered as he read the various drafts of the script, each one more damning of his character (in line with Breen's requests). His discontent deepened when he arrived on the set and Garbo made it plain that she had little interest in him—he later quipped, "co-starring with Garbo hardly constituted an introduction"—and that she would be calling the shots. March still hadn't recovered from the experience when he was interviewed a year later: he recalled that she had erected a "Garbo wall," made unreasonable objections to the presence of his stand-in on the set, and expressed boredom when he treated the crew to anecdotes about his trips to exotic locales. After months of on-camera intimacy—possibly dampened by Garbo's penchant for chewing garlic—March was none the wiser about her true self.[9]

It seems that March wasn't the only man feeling emasculated on the set. Basil Rathbone, cast as Anna's cuckolded husband Karenin, was initially intrigued by the prospect of playing a character who is not innately "cruel or unkind" but merely "insensitive and possessive, and without much imagination." As he waited for the final script, however, it dawned on Rathbone that the heavy hand of the censors was whittling away the complexities of Tolstoy's creation. The actor was particularly incensed by the deletion of scenes depicting Anna's pregnancy; their absence meant there was less tangible explanation for Karenin's ongoing fury and, more particularly, for his rigid determination to keep Anna away from their son. Rathbone predicted that audiences would find it difficult to see Karenin as a tragic figure, consumed by his anger at Anna's betrayal but also a slave to his own feelings of shame and emasculation. MGM's Karenin is a petty and vindictive man, in contrast to Tolstoy's more complicated character (a man who is, at least in part, motivated by concern for his son's welfare and for the welfare of Anna's illegitimate child).[10]

It would be tricky to play such a compromised version of Karenin, but Rathbone gave it his all, and the result is a masterly study of a man who is as damaged by social strictures as his pariah wife. Like March, Rathbone was subjected to the same coldness from Garbo. The two had met previously at a party, but Garbo gave no indication that she remembered him. Rather than being offended, Rathbone was intrigued and wondered whether, despite all her riches and acclaim, Garbo was "someone in distress." He was certainly fascinated by her technique, marveling at how deeply she immersed herself in her role. This, combined with her innate shyness, probably explained her determination to keep herself apart from others on the set. But even when she emerged from character at the end of production, she remained aloof, and when Rathbone approached her for a signed photograph, she rebuffed him with a terse dismissal: "I never give picture."[11]

Garbo may not have been a jovial presence on the set—although Reginald Owen, cast as Stephen, later recalled her "almost Rabelaisian wit"—but no one could dispute her love affair with the camera. Both Rathbone and Maureen O'Sullivan later offered analyses of her performance, with Rathbone observing that she was a "thoroughly 'economical' player. Everything she does or says on the screen means something." He cited a scene in which the growing estrangement between husband and wife is conveyed during a carriage ride. Rathbone, who maintained a rigid, unyielding pose as Karenin, was a little puzzled when his costar "seemed to do nothing" in response, but just as Brown had discovered years before, Garbo's acting was so subtle that it took the camera to reveal it. When Rathbone viewed the rushes, he saw that she had "made a tiny movement . . . the slightest possible drawing away from me, so that she did not touch me as we sat. That little gesture could not have been more effective." O'Sullivan also experienced this "invisible" technique in their scenes together: "when working with her, one felt that she was doing nothing really, that she wasn't even very good." Her opinion changed when she saw the footage and realized that Garbo had stolen every scene.[12]

Garbo's tendency to seek her own path, and her personal aloofness, prompted endless fascination and some anger among her colleagues. For his part, Brown viewed her with ambivalence: being labeled "Garbo's director" had been a mixed blessing for him, and he had taken on *Anna Karenina* with some trepidation. Fortunately, he was pleasantly surprised when he arrived on the set and was greeted with affection by a much humbler Garbo who "listened respectfully, sometimes arguing quietly but never angrily. She always wanted to give the best she had." No longer was he relegated to apologetically whispering directions from behind the camera or, worse still, to hiding behind the flats as she directed herself. On *Anna Karenina*, Brown was firmly back in control, where a director ought to be. The return to professional etiquette and respectful behavior may have been influenced by Garbo's experience working with Rouben Mamoulian on *Queen Christina* (he had refused to indulge what he viewed as her neurotic demands), but more likely it was a product of a newly confident star who was secure at MGM and committed to the production she had initiated. Columnist Sidney Skolsky claimed that he sneaked on the set—bizarrely, dressed in a costume intended for child actor Freddie Bartholomew—and captured a glimpse of the dynamics between director and star. He reported what most in Hollywood already suspected: Brown and

Garbo "got along," but she is "usually in command; she is the general even if she doesn't issue orders."[13]

Even if he wasn't the general, Brown was in command of the technical side, and he was happy to be working with William Daniels again. To overcome the inevitable wordiness of the script, the two devised several scenes that were boldly expressive in their camera work and cutting. Brown took credit for pioneering an innovative shot, later reused by several directors, in which a melancholic Anna stares out the window of a train and the reflection of the moving background is captured in the glass. Even more striking, and strikingly familiar, was a repeat of *The Eagle*'s famous tracking shot up the center of a banquet table. Here, it's used to open the film and introduce us to the masculine, coarse world of Vronsky. As the camera travels up a table groaning with food and drink, we see the grossness and arrogance of a decadent society that treats women (in this case, gypsy girls) as if they are just another "consumable." The shot is a showy one, but it's also a succinct visual summation of the conflicts of gender and class that Tolstoy explored in such detail in his novel.[14]

In his study of Brown, Allen Estrin notes that his female characters often "have to struggle against social conventions in their effort to achieve happiness, conventions which prove so strong they are seldom overcome." Even the most formidable women, such as Jane in *Smouldering Fires* or Jan in *A Free Soul*, quickly discover the limited control they have over their own destinies. Brown's *Anna Karenina* fits perfectly into an oeuvre that so often portrays women as constricted, restricted, subjected to double standards, and reduced to pawns in the games men play. Anna's capitulation to passion triggers a casting out from society, followed by the ultimate punishment of death, but her fate is merely a variation on the oppressive lives of other women of her class: her sister-in-law Dolly (Phoebe Foster), who endures an unhappy marriage to a serial adulterer (who has the affront to lecture his sister on the sanctity of marriage), or the vibrant Kitty (O'Sullivan), who is gradually crushed under the weight of social expectations. This fine sketching of secondary characters adds context and poignancy to the primary focus, which is, of course, Anna. The PCA's insistence that the theme of heterosexual passion be downplayed resulted in a more tragic character than the one Tolstoy created, and the necessary shift toward an emphasis on maternal loss enhanced the probability of audience empathy. The emergence of Anna's son Sergei as an important character was only partly dictated by the PCA's influence, however. Selznick saw it as an opportunity to showcase a star *he* had helped create, Freddie Bartholomew, and he hired Clemence Dane mainly because he felt she was more adept than Viertel at writing tender scenes.[15]

Some accounts suggest that Garbo found Bartholomew a "monster" to deal with, but if so, she certainly proved herself a great actress. She delivers a convincing performance of overwhelming devotion—similar to the one she gives opposite Philippe de Lacy in Goulding's version—in her scenes with him. In one, which takes place as Anna returns from Moscow and her first encounter with Vronsky, she greets Sergei with a flurry of kisses that seem to anticipate those she bestows on Robert Taylor's man-child Armand in Cukor's *Camille* a year later. The intensity of the relationship between mother and son is further illustrated when she offers Sergei the gift of a globe, a symbol of their private world from which Karenin is resolutely excluded. The sensuality and tactility of the bond between them is conveyed not only by the actors' performances but also by the lighting schema devised by Brown and Daniels. In the scene in which Anna prepares to exit the marital home, she makes a furtive visit to Sergei's bedroom to comfort him when he is frightened by the shadows ("dancing dragons") caused by his swaying nightlight. The lush lighting, romantic music, and intense close-ups seem more appropriate for a conventional love scene, while the expressionist shadows prefigure the dark forces that will soon sweep in to separate them.[16]

Anna Karenina has its share of grandiose moments and awe-inspiring sets, but it is the quieter moment like these, and the disturbing scenes that show Anna's fear of her husband, that most impressively reveal the talents of both Brown and Garbo. His intricate composition and expressive lighting support her performance as a woman who lives in *dread* of her husband and has done so for many years. In one of the last scenes in the film, Brown makes remarkable use of depth of field and virtuoso camera work to capture the overbearing Karenin, situated at the top of the sweeping staircase, standing in judgment over Anna. The camera cranes down to follow her slow, defeated descent and her exit from her son's life. The sweep of the camera is imposing and compelling, but it is Brown's decision to hold it a little longer than strictly necessary—instead of cutting to a close-up—that gives the audience a sense of her inexorable fate. The scene captures the fatalistic mood of Tolstoy, but it also recalls the pessimistic conclusions of other Brown films such as *Butterfly* and *Smouldering Fires*.

Just as the most tender scenes between mother and son are tinged with foreboding, so too are the scenes of Anna and Vronsky's courtship. The ambivalence with which romantic love is treated can be partly attributed to the PCA's influence, but it also continues the exploration presented elsewhere in both Brown's and Garbo's work. Her characters are almost always in thrall to their emotions and abandon themselves to a passion that is more tragic and reckless than joyous or frivolous. For Brown, too, romantic love is a topic he views with some skepticism, and he presents it in a visually complex or ambivalent fashion (even his trademark three-shot suggests the uncertain dynamics of love). In *Anna Karenina,* Brown portrays the first encounter between the lovers as a kind of magical enchantment in which Vronsky's senses are "enveloped" by the vision emerging from the shadows, but the lack of visual clarity also suggests how mercurial and unreliable passion can be. Later, as Vronsky presses his attentions and Anna's defenses begin to break down, Brown frames the two against an impossibly lovely garden (common in MGM movies). The perfect composition and the perfect romance are undermined, however, by his introduction of oppressive shadows cast by the lattice of a nearby trellis.

Brown returns to a brooding, Expressionist-influenced aesthetic in the final scenes in which an abandoned and forlorn Anna returns to the train station where it all began. Underlining the circularity of Anna's narrative and the inescapable sense that she has always been living on borrowed time, Brown frames Garbo in front of the hulk of a "breathing" train (shades of *The Signal Tower*). In our very first glimpse of her, the steam disperses to reveal her, but here it is used to obscure her, as if her very existence is being wiped out. This play with light and dark continues as her crumpled form is illuminated by the swaying lantern of the engineer, referencing an earlier scene in which Anna was gravely disturbed when she witnessed the accidental death of a railroad worker. More subtly, however, the evocative lamplight recalls those moments when she comforted Sergei and warded off the "dancing dragons."

It had been a long time in the making, but *Anna Karenina* was finally previewed in June 1935 at a screening in Riverside attended by Brown, Garbo, Selznick, Salka and Pieter Viertel, and S. L. Behrman. Behrman recalled that everyone expressed their admiration for Garbo's performance of "delicacy and distinction," but the actress herself seemed disappointed: "if once, only once, I could see a preview and come home feeling satisfied." All agreed that the film had many fine points and looked sumptuous, but there were also some elements that simply did not work. This merely confirmed Brown's long-standing doubts; in several memos to Selznick he had voiced his concerns about a script he regarded as overly stagey ("too many entrances and exits") and too reliant on dialogue. Preview audiences evidently agreed with him, and MGM brought the film back for retakes and a tighter edit by Robert Kern, supervised by Brown. As those two worked, Selznick concerned himself with the details of the promotional campaign. He was keen to highlight Bartholomew, who would "sell many more tickets than will March." He was also intent on emphasizing the production's literary credentials, and he commissioned a special study guide to be distributed to educational groups and women's clubs. It promised a film of integrity that, "in spite of handicaps rooted in the restrictions of censorship," would appeal to "critics of cinema craftsmanship and students of photoplay appreciation" and, especially, to women.[17]

As final edits concluded, a dispute arose between Brown and Selznick over the presentation of the credits. Through his agent, Brown requested that his name be given 75 percent type (Garbo's was at 100 percent), but Selznick was irked by the stipulation, writing to Howard Dietz: "I consider [the] Clarence Brown obligation one of the most ridiculous I have ever seen in any contract and urge you [to] have Bob Rubin [MGM's attorney] telephone Clarence about it unless you think you can do better with him yourself." Neither Dietz nor Rubin had much luck, and MGM eventually capitulated to Brown's demand and included his name twice in the credits ("Clarence Brown's production of . . ." and "Directed by Clarence Brown"). Brown's request illustrates his determination that his role in the production would not be overlooked, as so often happened when directors worked with Selznick. Once the studio acquiesced, he readily pitched in to promote the film. An article titled "Secrets of Garbo's New Film" recorded Brown's views on the process of adapting a novel to the screen, as well as his thoughts on how his version of Tolstoy's novel measured up against Goulding's (he regarded his film as the more faithful adaptation). When asked to weigh March against Gilbert, Brown was more guarded, offering only the diplomatic observation that it was "terribly difficult" to "find a leading man for Garbo. Only a man with an amazingly vibrant personality can be considered for such a position." More intriguing were his opinions about child actors: "Freddie [Bartholomew] has upset all my notions about screen children. I didn't really like them. I wouldn't say they had no place on the screen, but I did and do say that, once having hit the screen, they seemed generally to have no place anywhere else. . . . The first screen appearance of the average child has turned out to be, in some way, sensational. That, in my opinion, was because the child behaved naturally. Once the child got wise to the fact that it was an actor, all sincerity, simplicity and spontaneity, on which the child's charm depends, disappeared." Brown concluded the interview with some thoughts on the new censorship code, which he confessed he found restrictive, but he had to admit that it served the public demand for movies that adhered to simple formulas and reassured viewers that moral transgressions would not go unpunished ("That's the way films should be . . . the Wages of Sin is death").[18]

When *Anna Karenina* was released in the fall of 1935, few were offended by its content—even the scissors-happy Quebec censors passed it—but many commented on the obvious impact of censorship. *Variety* noted the subdued tone but commended Brown for his "dignified, strong direction. Pictorial effects he has achieved are excellent and his understanding of the handling of Garbo is mainly responsible for her good performance." In his review for the *New York Times*, Andre Sennwald focused on the actors' performances and the faithfulness of the adaptation (both of which he found effective). He was moved by Garbo's ability to suggest "the inevitability of her doom from the beginning, streaking her first happiness with undertones of anguish, later trying futilely to mend the broken pieces, and at last standing regally alone as she approaches the end." He also praised Rathbone's "excellent" performance in an unsympathetic role, but he thought Bartholomew as Sergei possessed a certain "terrifying and assured maturity," which he viewed as typical of Hollywood child actors.[19]

On the other side of the Atlantic, *Anna Karenina* attracted the attention of critics and world leaders alike. Alastair Cooke, then at the start of his long career as a reviewer, gushed over Garbo, calling her a "tolerant goddess . . . [who] . . . wraps everybody in the film round in a protective tenderness. She sees not only her own life, but everybody else's before it has been lived." Cooke wasn't the only one enthralled by the film. The jury at the 1936 Venice Film Festival awarded it the prestigious Mussolini Cup. Brown was on hand to accept the prize and to discuss potential projects, including a state-sponsored film about Leonardo da Vinci and a managerial role in the Italian film industry. Given his importance at MGM and his extensive business interests in California, Brown was unlikely to be decamping to fascist Italy anytime soon, but he was flattered by the attention and impressed by Mussolini's state. He wasn't the only Hollywood figure who initially viewed Mussolini as an inspirational leader—Walt Disney, Hal Roach, and Harry Cohn were also fans. Although unfolding events would prompt him to reconsider his admiration, Brown never entirely abandoned it. In later years he was quick to point out that Mussolini was not of the same ilk as Hitler: "I never supported Hitler . . . Mussolini—now that's a different case. If he hadn't gone over to the wrong side he'd have been OK." And he offered a naïve assessment of Mussolini's achievements: "He did more for the Italians—restored their self-respect, and trains running on time—than anyone."[20]

Anna Karenina may have had international admirers, but audiences outside the major cities were less enthusiastic. As was the case for most of her films, small-town and rural moviegoers couldn't warm up to Garbo. As one Oklahoma exhibitor bluntly put it: "Garbo is through here." Even if audiences in the rural heartland had had enough of her, MGM still regarded her as a blue-chip asset and rushed her into a new production. To direct it, the studio turned not to Brown but to George Cukor, despite his previous reluctance to collaborate with her. In all likelihood, Brown never expected to direct *Camille*—he was acutely aware that he had been Garbo's second choice for *Anna Karenina*. It was probably with some relief that he returned to the project that had fired up his passion back in 1933. *Ah Wilderness!* would be one of his most accomplished works.[21]

18

Going Home

Ah Wilderness!

A rather sunny entry in the usually gloomy universe of Eugene O'Neill, *Ah Wilderness!* was written during a burst of creativity shortly after the playwright completed *Mourning Becomes Electra*. The play sketches episodes from the lives of the Miller family and focuses on the middle son, Richard, as he transitions from adolescence to manhood. O'Neill's stated intention was to "write a play true to the spirit of the American large small-town at the turn of the century. Its quality depended on atmosphere, sentiment, an exact evocation of the mood of a dead past." *Ah Wilderness!* premiered on Broadway in October 1933, with legendary George M. Cohan in the role of patriarch Nat Miller, and it proved to be one of O'Neill's most popular and critically acclaimed efforts. A West Coast production starring humorist Will Rogers soon followed.[1]

Brown's interest had been sparked even before he attended the Broadway production. He felt sure that the play's themes of community and family, along with its gentle humor and sentiment, would be a perfect fit for MGM. In comparison to other O'Neill work, the content was relatively innocuous, and censor James Wingate was supportive when, at Brown's urging, MGM approached him in October 1933. Wingate noted that only a few scenes, such as the father's attempt to explain the facts of life to his son and the son's (innocent) encounter with a prostitute, would need "careful treatment." It was with some confidence, then, that the studio bought the rights and began discussions about script and casting. A few months later, progress was stalled when Joseph Breen took over and adopted a more hard-line approach in his office's dealings with studios. Surveying MGM's upcoming productions, he identified several scenes in *Ah Wilderness!* that caused concern, and in March 1934 he wrote to Mayer and recommended that one of them, the prostitute scene, "be modified so as to avoid any indication that the place is a house of assignation." He also advised the studio to amend the dialogue and excise any reference to "Belle's attempt to entice the boy upstairs . . . [and] . . . any shots showing money."[2]

As negotiations continued into the summer of 1934, Brown finished up a hectic schedule of productions. Interviewed on the set of *Chained,* he said he was enthusiastic about tackling a project that would return him to the world of his childhood and allow him to work with Will Rogers. The plan was to commence filming *Ah Wilderness!* in late 1934, but that was delayed when Brown was assigned to direct *Anna Karenina.* With Brown occupied, much of the supervisory responsibility fell to Hunt Stromberg. Among his tasks was monitoring the screenwriting duo of Frances Goodrich and Albert Hackett. He consulted with the writers through the last months of 1934 as they tried to come up with a script that would negate the anticipated criticism that "over-zealous studio writers" had "spoiled O'Neill's masterpiece." The two found that Stromberg wasn't shy when it came to expressing his opinions, but despite his blustering air, he was often perceptive and helpful. Commenting on one draft, he expressed some dissatisfaction with how they were shaping the character of Sid: "Sid is missing to me. I don't know whether it's because I am visualizing [W. C.] Fields playing the part, with the more complete and bombastic dialogue which his type of performance needs—or whether it's because I haven't been made to be definitely *concerned* with his presence and what it means, one way or the other, to anybody in the story." He was fearful, too, that their latest draft had diluted one of the more appealing elements of the play—the thwarted romance between the aging Lily and Sid: "[It is] too casual now. Too thrown away. Too scattered and thinly sketched to make much of a dent on the emotions." For Stromberg, this relationship—not the budding one between the youngsters—was the most affecting part of O'Neill's play: "it's a very deep and serious thing with her [Lily]. . . . Let's make something of it for both *humor* and *drama.*"[3]

Uppermost in Stromberg's mind was the need to satisfy the demands of Breen and the PCA while also meeting the studio's imperative to produce a film that was credible and, with any luck, profitable. His correspondence with Goodrich and Hackett reminded them of the importance of sketching a family "environment strong enough and secure enough and tender enough to safeguard the pilgrimage of this young kid through the wilderness of an adolescent period" and of conveying the sense that the impetuous Richard, an adolescent "on the threshold of manhood," would soon develop a maturity and integrity "molded by his father." And, as he was apt to do, Stromberg reminded the writers that the script should have broad appeal: "If we don't get the *feeling* here that this family represents *millions* of families of the good, reliable stock, we will miss one of the purposes behind the story. What we must really do is to Mirror a representative family of representative Americans in a representative town. The father in Oshkosh and the mother in Joliet must see themselves on screen. For we are treating of simple, unsophisticated people— not the sophisticated brand, nor the breed of pretense, nor false superficiality. Everything is *real* in this story." After consulting with Brown, he encouraged the writers to create a slow-paced slice of Americana—the kind of film Brown loved to make—but one that was not *too* leisurely or fey: "I don't know whether it's because we're trying to show too much—or too little. I just don't seem to feel a *running drive* throughout the story—and I don't seem to feel any suspense." Whether a nostalgic play was really the best vehicle for suspense and action was a question both the screenwriters and the critics would ask when the film was released.[4]

By June 1935, *Anna Karenina* was coming to a close, and Brown was able to fully commit to *Ah Wilderness!* The script exceeded all his expectations, but the months spent writing it had given Breen time to brood. With the new code implemented that very month, he now seemed to regard the play as "exceedingly dangerous" and felt the script hadn't neutralized the terrible threat it posed. Negotiations continued, and Breen was especially irked by a scene showing an encounter between Richard and Belle. Even though the dialogue had been sanitized to remove any references to prostitutes or brothels, he thought audiences would draw their own conclusions about what kind of "house" it was and what Belle did for a living. It was a scene that offended Breen on many levels, not least in its depiction of Richard getting drunk. He pressed the studio to do more to alter the "whole flavor" of it, and he even wondered whether the euphemistic phrase "a "certain class of women" might be dropped. Other scenes captured his attention as well. He reminded MGM that the prudish British censor would find a shot of a marital bed objectionable and that the political content was also likely to offend. Stromberg and Brown were so anxious to start filming that they gave only cursory attention to Breen's recommendations: a shot of a double bed made it into the released film, and only some of the controversial dialogue was eliminated (with the rest delivered as throwaway lines in the hope that audiences wouldn't notice). The objection to political content was more easily accommodated: a brief cutaway to a page of Richard's anticapitalist speech is all that remains of the zealous tirade written by O'Neill.[5]

With the script now ready, final decisions had to be made on casting. By July, most of the roles had been filled with MGM stalwarts such as Spring Byington (as the eccentric mother) and Mickey Rooney (as the youngest son) and with relative newcomers such as Eric Linden (as Richard) and Cecilia Parker (as his would-be girlfriend Muriel). MGM borrowed Aline MacMahon from Warner to play the perpetually disappointed spinster aunt Lily. Two crucial roles remained unfilled, and the clock was ticking. Rumors had abounded for months that W. C. Fields would play the disreputable Uncle Sid and that Will Rogers would take the Nat Miller role, and indeed, the script had been tailored to suit these two. However, negotiations with Fields throughout the spring and summer of 1935 went nowhere, and by July, MGM decided to look elsewhere. The studio briefly considered humorist Robert Benchley, but apparently his price was too high. In the end, MGM called on the services of its resident "son of a bitch," Wallace Beery. It seemed like a choice dictated by pure expediency, but in fact, it was a shrewd business decision: the actor drew in the crowds, and he could play Uncle Sid in his sleep. The promise of working with the uncouth Beery may have filled some of the cast with dread, but Brown was unfazed. He had directed Beery before and knew he could make the necessary small talk to maintain a cordial relationship (mainly, they talked about aviation, their mutual passion). Most importantly, Brown understood that Beery was at his most cooperative when he believed he was directing himself. Even if Goodrich and Hackett disliked how Beery "hijacked" their character and turned it into "Sid Beery," audiences couldn't get enough of his ad-libbing and his shambolic shtick, and several exhibitors reported patrons' enthusiastic reaction when Beery came onscreen.[6]

Brown was relatively content to substitute the irascible Fields with the boorish Beery, but he was genuinely disappointed when Rogers opted not to sign up. Brown had admired Rogers's performance in the San Francisco production and was also friendly with him socially (Rogers was another keen aviator). Brown regarded Rogers's brand of dry humor and his folksy, unpretentious air as the perfect fit for the sentimental yet gently humorous world of *Ah Wilderness!* but evidently Rogers wasn't so sure. He spent much of the summer of 1935 dithering, perhaps holding out for more money. But he also sincerely believed that a film with a few "off-color" scenes might damage his family-friendly reputation. According to Goodrich, Rogers felt so strongly that he wrote to MGM to protest that the studio was "trying to force him to be a party to an obscene, sensational picture." Whatever the case, by late summer, MGM had had enough and pulled the plug. The studio told the press that it had been "willing to abide by all Rogers's decisions" and even reedit the film should he find any "cause for objection on moral grounds," but Rogers had remained noncommittal. With Rogers out, MGM briefly considered J. C. Nugent before settling on Lionel Barrymore. Any hope that Rogers might have a last-minute change of heart was dashed when, on August 15, news came that he had been killed in a plane crash in Alaska.[7]

A production that had begun with such optimism for Brown became unavoidably tinged with sadness. There was scarcely time to ponder the randomness of life or the danger of aviation, as Brown headed straight from Rogers's funeral to his principal location in Massachusetts. The choice of New England was in keeping with the O'Neill play, but it also marked a personal return to Brown's roots. It probably couldn't have come at a better time, as the director was worn out from his seemingly endless formulaic assignments. He had always favored location shooting, despite some mixed experiences (most notably on *Trail of '98*), and this time he was determined that the setting would serve the film and not vice versa. MGM made the most of his personal interest, publicizing *Ah Wilderness!* as a "return home" to the life of "unchanging placidity" that had shaped Brown—now a highly paid and cosmopolitan A-lister. MGM promised scenes shot "under the trees where he [Brown] played childhood games" and locals filling minor roles, but the expertly woven publicity soon needed some tweaking when—inconveniently for both the studio and the townsfolk—a fire damaged Clinton High School and the company was forced to decamp to nearby Grafton. It was a close match in all respects: Brown had lived there briefly, and the town had the same nineteenth-century architecture, pastoral town square, and tree-lined streets as Clinton.[8]

Brown got down to business, shooting exteriors on the streets, in the parks, and at the school, using almost 200 locals as extras. MGM reportedly funded the construction of new bandstand for the town, but Brown's plans to populate it with (nonunion) musicians from the North Grafton Band were dashed when unionized musicians intervened. Many locals had hoped the Hollywood production would bring jobs to the town, and while there was certainly work for extras and something of a mini-boom for a few businesses, MGM brought its own carpenters and electricians. This was the norm, but it outraged Jack Hauser, head of the Worcester branch of the stagehands' union, who appealed to Brown, with little tangible result. Brown may have been the son of mill workers, but he was a bit of a skeptic when it came to unions, and he was irritated by the delays caused by Hauser's intervention. A production that had promised to be a fulfilling immersion in a gentler way of life was already starting to get more complicated.[9]

In his few leisure hours, Brown reconnected with some of the townsfolk in Clinton and Grafton he had known decades earlier. This included his best friend from childhood, Clarence Grady, who had become Clinton's much-loved family doctor. They quickly reestablished a warm rapport, and when Brown had time off, he accompanied Grady on some sentimental trips to revisit their childhood haunts. Grady helped Brown track down what turned out to be an important photograph of his elementary school classmates, as well as his birth certificate. In turn, Brown facilitated a screening of *Ah Wilderness!* at the local Strand Theater to benefit the Clinton High School Athletic Council, and he later sent Grady scrapbooks and memorabilia for an exhibition as part of the town's centennial celebration in May 1950.[10]

Whereas O'Neill's upbringing had been largely dysfunctional—*Ah Wilderness!* might best be described as an imagining of the childhood he *wished* he had—Brown had enjoyed a stable life as the only child of devoted parents. His personal memories of growing up in New England and later in the small city of Knoxville had drawn him to the play in the first place, and they profoundly shaped his handling of the Goodrich-Hackett script. He, too, remembered Fourth of July community picnics; walks along shaded streets with names like Grove, Walnut, and Chestnut; first kisses; and a high school graduation that was both a poignant end to childhood and a beckoning to adulthood. The fictional Millers were not a million miles away from the real-life Browns: neither family was rich, and home was a place where love and discipline were meted out in equal measure, where children were taught to respect their elders and to value the notion of personal integrity. Given how closely he identified with the play, it is no surprise that the scenes Brown handled with noticeable tenderness or energy were centered on the family home, such as the (contentious) "facts of life" scene and a dinner scene in which Nat's patriarchal authority is gently undermined when it's revealed that he has been eating "blue fish"—a fish with a "peculiar odor" that he always said "poisons him"—for many years. In an interview with David Weissman conducted a few years after the film's release, Brown cited this dinner scene as one of the most personal in all his work because it was "subconsciously visualized . . . from my own experience, and in working with the writers I didn't realize I was permitting my own life to enter the picture . . . I found myself visually fascinated. I saw myself in that boy [Richard]—I saw myself surrounded by my own family—I was witnessing a chapter from my own life."[11]

Subconscious memories influenced his direction of the dinner scene, but conscious ones informed his handling of the high school graduation scene. It was an addition to the O'Neill play, beautifully written by Goodrich and Hackett, that allowed Brown to give full rein to his imagination. He used a photograph of his own high school graduation to design the scene's distinctive look, had the cast sing the same song he had sung with his classmates ("Away to the Woods"), and sought to capture the same mixed emotions—awkwardness, sweetness, humor, tedium—he had experienced. Long takes filmed by a fairly static camera allow the scene to unfold in a slow-burn fashion, giving the actors the opportunity to inhabit their roles and convincingly portray the small nuances of human behavior and sentiment that make the scene ring true. As one of the film's most beautifully realized moments, the graduation scenes encapsulate its chief merit: in its quiet, gentle way, *Ah Wilderness!* offers glimpses of timeless human emotions.[12]

Filming was completed by early September, and Brown personally oversaw the editing. The film was previewed in November and released the same month. Breen had been vocal about its content earlier, and now others were lining up to have their say: the censor in Massachusetts, mindful of the power of the Irish American lobby, requested the excision of a line in which a character is referred to as a "thick Mick"; Virginia objected to a shot of Belle putting money in her stocking; and the zealous censors in Quebec wanted nothing to do with the film. As Breen had predicted, the British censors frowned on some aspects, including the "facts of life" scene, the encounter between Richard and Belle, and one troubling stunt that involved tying fireworks to a dog's tail (American movies were not yet monitored by the American Humane Association). Japanese censors were outraged by the use of slang, in particular a line that warned, "Don't you start to spoon or I'll call a cop."[13]

On the whole, though, critics and audiences embraced Brown's adaptation of O'Neill's play. The trade publication *Hollywood Spectator* declared it a "director's picture" with "no big climaxes to build to, no villains to make us gasp and comedians to make us laugh—nothing but human beings and their wholly unimportant doings." Andre Sennwald of the *New York Times* complimented MGM on getting it right: "As an American comedy of manners and as a portrait of an American family, 'Ah, Wilderness!' explores a vein of bittersweet nostalgia without losing its sense of humor," although he found Beery's "comic horseplay . . . at odds with the quiet and rueful mood of the work." More recent historians and critics still appreciate its subtle and appealing qualities. Allen Estrin ranks it as one of Brown's best among several "gentle and understanding portraits of the passage from adolescence to young adulthood." O'Neill biographer John Orlandello, though critical of the film's softening of the play, and especially the character of Richard, commends the execution as "visually imaginative and effective" and "masterful in the recreation of the milieu and physical characteristics of the period." Even Barry Gillam, perhaps Brown's harshest critic, has singled out this film as worthy of praise, noting Brown's dexterity in handling the graduation scene and describing it as a "brilliantly orchestrated set piece of personal worlds careering haphazardly within the formal structure of the ceremony."[14]

With such excellent notices and genuine affection from many industry peers, MGM marketed *Ah Wilderness!* as one of its prestige films, evidence of the studio's literary credentials and its willingness to green-light more personal, scaled-down productions. The studio initiated an aggressive campaign to win Academy Award nominations, but *Ah Wilderness!* was passed over at the 1936 ceremony. It wasn't the first time Brown had been overlooked, and it wouldn't be the last: Brown is tied with Alfred Hitchcock as the director who received the most Academy Award nominations but never won. Nevertheless, he was proud of *Ah Wilderness!* In an interview with Harry Haun in the 1960s, Brown explained that his best films, in their modest way, continued an American tradition of storytelling that illuminated the "American people, American spirit, and the great American dream." Others, too, felt that *Ah Wilderness!* was something special: Goodrich and Hackett went on to giddy heights with their *Thin Man* series, but they retained an affection for this "really wonderful" assignment that allowed them to work with "a sensitive, dedicated perfectionist with a respect for the written word." It may not have won an Oscar, but *Ah Wilderness!* was the kind of film Mayer could be proud of. As Mickey Rooney recalled: "[it] helped Mr. Mayer cast a spell on America, on its values and attitudes and images . . . [and] . . . made some money on the way." Mayer liked it so much that he kept making variations of it, often with Rooney and sometimes with Brown (*The Human Comedy*); he even commissioned a remake of it in 1948 (*Summer Holiday*). But none had the delicacy and heartfelt sincerity of Brown's original.[15]

19

Back to the Formula

Wife vs. Secretary, The Gorgeous Hussy, and Love on the Run

When Brown left Grafton, Massachusetts, in the fall of 1935, it was with a sense of satisfaction at a job well done. The warm reception that greeted *Ah Wilderness!* among both studio bosses and critics seemed to prove that personal films could be successful. But Brown's hopes that he would be allowed to continue in this vein for his next assignments were dashed when he was drafted to direct a "sex comedy" featuring MGM's top stars.

The very idea of a sex comedy produced during the mid-1930s, with the production code fully in effect, may seem like an impossibility, but a deft director could insinuate risqué content, and talented performers could convey desire, perversity, and naughtiness (the twinkle in Charles Laughton's eye in *The Barretts of Wimpole Street* being a case in point). In the case of Jean Harlow, however, her sexy appearance was enough to concern the censors, and it was becoming clear to MGM that both her movies and her wardrobe would need some revisions. The "new" Harlow was showcased in *Wife vs. Secretary*, in which she plays Whitey, a serious and ambitious secretary whose natural good looks attract catty comments from women and cause the boss's wife to doubt her husband's faithfulness. The film's unique selling point was the reversal of roles: there would be no need for Harlow to arch her famous eyebrows as she delivered sardonic lines, because she had none, and her trademark platinum blonde hair was dyed a mousey brown to complement her dowdy costumes. Playing the "sexy" (or sexier) role of Linda, the wife, was Myrna Loy (who was returning to MGM after a suspension). Linda spends her time lounging around in a succession of sophisticated outfits, waiting for her husband to return from the office. The role was not far from the part of Nora in *The Thin Man,* and in a further nod to the W. S. van Dyke film, MGM planned to cast William Powell as the husband. When scheduling conflicts made that impossible, Clark Gable was assigned. He was joined by a young James Stewart as Harlow's ardent but unglamorous boyfriend, Dave.

Studios often presented the Breen office with scripts that included deliberately provocative content, hoping to distract from the subtler innuendos, but in the case of *Wife vs. Secretary,* a trio of writers—Norman Krasna, John Lee Mahin, and Alice Duer Miller—came up with a script that contained little to provoke Breen. Nevertheless, he and his staff combed through it, attempting to identify anything that might have a sexual meaning or any implication that Whitey provided her boss with more than secretarial services. He found nothing and offered only preemptive warnings that a bathroom scene should not include a glimpse of the toilet, and there should be no repeat of the Gable "torso shot" in Columbia's *It Happened One Night,* which had caused such a furor a few months before (Breen directed: "put an undershirt on him [Gable]").[1]

Brown was assigned to the project in November, and "assigned" was an apt description: this was nothing more than a formulaic production for him, and one he executed in an efficient but uninspired fashion. Interviewed a few years later, he made the surprisingly frank admission that he "hated the story and argued over it every inch of the way"; he revealed that Gable, too, wanted to "get through it as quickly as possible." Brown's negative comments about the production are in stark contrast to the fond memories Myrna Loy retained. In her autobiography she admitted to having some initial reservations, but these had more to do with her personal embarrassment at the thought of working with Gable, who had once made a clumsy and unsuccessful pass at her. Luckily, she discovered that the confident and self-deprecating Gable wasn't the type to hold a grudge, and she soon bonded with her costar, describing him as "very sweet, very warm." Like Gable, she was under no illusions about the script and saw it for the *Thin Man*–lite production it was (Goodrich and Hackett were even brought in to do a final polish). Nonetheless, there were moments that charmed her, including one in which "Clark stands outside my bedroom door and we banter, nothing more, but there's no question about what they've done the night before. Clarence Brown, our director, made it all so subtle, yet, oh so wonderfully suggestive." She was less thrilled with a scene in which Van (Gable) hides a diamond bracelet in a trout, much to the delight of Linda. Loy complained, "[it] didn't seem chic or funny to me—merely messy, typical of Hollywood's misguided notion of upper-class sophistication." It seems the writers knew their audience better than Loy: when *Wife vs. Secretary* was released, it was the trout scene that was most warmly received.[2]

For Brown, the only memorable aspects of the production involved his collaboration with the actors. He always enjoyed working with Gable, and he ranked Loy highly and often brought out the best in her (especially in their next collaboration, *The Rains Came*). This was the first and only time he had the chance to direct MGM's resident bombshell, Jean Harlow. Brown knew her socially and, like most people who met her, found her to be charming and sweet. That unpretentious attitude didn't change when she arrived on the set, and Brown delighted in her unique and completely natural mix of earthy sexiness and touching innocence. What impressed him most, however, was how pragmatic she was about her status as a commodity and the requirements of the job. There were no displays of diva behavior, and she was (unnecessarily) modest, telling Brown, "I'm not an actress, but you tell me what to do and I'll do it." In truth, the script didn't give her much opportunity to showcase her considerable comedic skills, but the role did bring out an appealing vulnerability in her. Through it all, Brown offered her sympathetic support, and the two seemed to develop a platonic friendship that was quasi-paternal on his side (he later served as one of the pallbearers at her funeral).[3]

Newcomer Stewart was equally smitten, but his feelings for Harlow were more romantic than paternal, as he ruefully admitted: "The lines weren't much, and neither of us paid much attention to them, but in the first rehearsal, she [Harlow] took charge of the kissing. It was then I knew that I'd never really been kissed before. There were six rehearsals. The kissing gained each time in interest and enthusiasm. By the time we actually shot the scene, my psychology was all wrinkled. . . . Shooting that scene made quite a night." Harlow may have showed him the importance of a kiss, but it was Brown who showed Stewart "the importance of a look, the importance of a movement—a visual saying of a line." *Wife vs. Secretary* was the first of their three collaborations, and even though it wasn't going to set the world alight, Stewart regarded it as a "wonderful beginning and groundwork . . . I learned from watching Clarence and I watched him all day long."[4]

In spite of the best efforts of all involved, there was little they could do with a script that, though it might have offered some insights into the dynamics between women and men, was severely compromised before a single frame was shot. Perhaps a director with a flair for comedy, such as Mitchell Leisen or Ernst Lubitsch, would have used the visuals to introduce titillating innuendos or ambiguities, but Brown was either uncomfortable doing so or just plain indifferent. Nor was his characteristic "leisurely" pacing well suited to a genre in which fast cutting and rapid-fire delivery dominated (both before and after the code). Only the scenes of Dave's touching devotion to Whitey are handled with obvious ease by Brown, but given that sincerity and heartfelt emotion are usually traits to be satirized in sex comedies, these seem to be an awkward fit.

The uneven tone and insipid script were much criticized when *Wife vs. Secretary* was released the following February. Frank Nugent, writing for the *New York Times*, found it infuriating that an actress of Loy's talents had been saddled with a "cloying, colorless and stupid" role, and he laid the blame chiefly at the door of the hard-pressed screenwriters: "If the battle between the wife and the secretary is to be convincing at all, we must have two evenly matched contestants. Here Miss Loy enters the ring with glazed eyes, a crutch and one hand strapped behind her back—metaphorically of course. . . . The competition for the Gable Trophy sounds like a sham battle all the way." For Philip Scheuer, *Wife vs. Secretary* was an unsuccessful mix of two conflicting tones. He expressed admiration for those moments when it became "a naturalistic study in dialogue, quietly, almost gently turned out," but "the same methods of restraint that served him so well in directing *Ah Wilderness!*" didn't fit a comedy that desperately needed "a little, just a little, in the line of old-fashioned histrionics" to spice things up.[5]

Ironically, given Brown's dislike and the critics' indifference, *Wife vs. Secretary* was one of the director's top performing films of the 1930s, clearing a profit of $2,015,588 between the domestic and international box offices. He was astounded, stating, "I know it was the worst picture I ever made. In New York the critics panned it so hard and it did so badly, it was taken off a week earlier than had been arranged." The secret of its commercial success lay in the vast American heartland, where exhibitors reported enthusiastic crowds and repeat business. If nothing else, *Wife vs. Secretary* illustrates the simple fact that in the 1930s stars were the chief draw, regardless of the weakness of the film's content or the director's indifference.[6]

Brown's next project called for a return to his roots, of a sort. *The Gorgeous Hussy* was based on Samuel Hopkins Adams's 1934 play about Peggy O'Neal, a rather scandalous figure who allegedly influenced President Andrew Jackson in the 1820s. The film was originally earmarked for Katharine Hepburn, then at RKO, but when that studio's option lapsed, MGM picked it up as a (rather unlikely) vehicle for Jean Harlow. For reasons none too clear, producer Joseph Mankiewicz thought the studio's other "modern girl," Joan Crawford, would be a better fit, and he approached her. Despite David O. Selznick's advice to stick to her usual formula, Crawford was persuaded that the part could help her "prove" her acting credentials and topple Norma Shearer's pre-eminence at the studio. Influenced by Mankiewicz and still (somewhat) eager to impress her husband Franchot Tone, she accepted the part.[7]

Playing a nineteenth-century heroine was risky, even at the level of costumes. The crinolines and frills of 1820s fashions, and the girlish ringlets then in vogue, would do the sleek, angular Crawford few favors. Peggy O'Neal certainly *looked* different from the usual Crawford heroine, but her attitude and her dealings with men were not too dissimilar. Depending on which historical account one believes, O'Neal was a smart girl who used her feminine wiles and her intelligence to influence a succession of powerful men; a shrewd career woman living in the wrong era; or "pot house Peg," a few steps away from a simple prostitute. The daughter of an innkeeper in Washington, DC, she was married several times and sustained a close relationship with President Andrew Jackson (most assumed the two were lovers, and she was certainly vilified for using her position to influence political policy). Adams's play was largely sympathetic, even as it acknowledged some of the unsavory details of her life. These set the alarm bells ringing at the PCA, and as soon as Breen heard that MGM was lining it up as a project, he expressed his concerns to Mayer. He didn't like the provocative title, and he warned that he would withhold the seal of approval if a former president was depicted as morally dubious or if Adams's humorous scenes of drunkenness were retained. From the outset, both sides understood that there could be no suggestion of a sexual relationship between Peg and Jackson. However, Breen nixed any hint of sexual activity among the other characters too: he requested cuts to a scene in which the teenage O'Neal and her friends, seeking shelter from a storm, are "bundled" together on the only available bed by the hard-pressed innkeeper. Scenes set in the presidential bedroom and those set in the O'Neal inn were also cause for concern. And Breen advised MGM to exercise caution when it came to any allusion to slavery. Notes from the script conferences attended by writers Ainsworth Morgan and Stephen Morehouse Avery, Brown, and Mankiewicz reveal how studiously they worked within the imposed strictures and implemented most of Breen's recommendations: a proposed scene set in the "House of Fortune" (evidently a brothel) was discussed but quickly dropped, drinking scenes were toned down, and care was taken to emphasize (perhaps none too convincingly) the innocence of potentially risqué encounters. MGM also cut the word "nigger," but this was prompted less by enlightened thinking on race relations than by an awareness that middle-class audiences viewed it as "trashy." MGM continued to collude in the industry-wide practice of hiring black actors for demeaning roles, as evidenced by the decision to cast Sam McDaniel (Hattie's brother) as a dim-witted servant.[8]

Filming commenced in May, and as befitted an A-budget film, MGM filled the supporting roles with its best talent. Sporting elaborate makeup and a bouffant hairstyle, Lionel Barrymore was cast as Andrew Jackson, with Beulah Bondi as his pipe-smoking wife, Rachel. Peg was flattered by the attentions of a string of love interests, including Robert Taylor (as her first husband, Bow Timberlake), Melvyn Douglas (as John Randolph, in a role rumored to be intended for Basil Rathbone), and James Stewart (as an ardent but unsuccessful suitor). Brown had some personal input into the casting of some of the minor roles, so Rubye de Reymer appears as a local gossip alongside another veteran of the silent screen, Betty Blythe. Crawford also demanded a role for Tone, who plays Peg's second husband, Secretary of War John Eaton.

The Gorgeous Hussy turned out to be a costly and difficult production—one contemporary estimate places the daily cost at $8,000. Brown spent much of the shoot nursing a broken arm (suffered either when he fell from a beam on the set or intervened to break up a dogfight at his Calabasas ranch). Despite his personal discomfort and the escalating tensions among the cast, he diligently kept to the schedule, and both Beulah Bondi and cinematographer George Folsey later marveled at his calm in the midst of a storm. Most of the tension was caused by the increasingly fractious relationship between Tone and Crawford, which was spilling over into their professional lives. Having his wife secure him a role in her movie evidently made Tone feel emasculated, and he expressed it by turning up late to the set, not bothering to learn his lines, and needling Crawford (who was already struggling with the role). Tone was not one of Brown's favorite people, but he had tolerated him on *Sadie McKee* because the actor had behaved professionally. This time around, Brown was less inclined to humor him; it was clear that Tone's career was going nowhere and that he was entirely replaceable (both in the film and as Crawford's husband). Tone's actorly pretensions and the supercilious attitude he affected when it came to the grubby business of moviemaking irritated Brown, who always viewed displays of intellectualism with some suspicion. However, it wasn't just Tone's bad attitude that annoyed Brown on the set of *The Gorgeous Hussy*; it was also his alleged physical abuse of Crawford. Years later, Brown revealed that Tone had almost pushed him to physical violence on one occasion when Crawford arrived on the set covered in bruises. His first instinct had been to "beat the son of a bitch up," but he resisted the temptation. After one more collaboration with Tone on the salvage job *Love on the Run*, Brown revealed his true feelings. In a 1937 interview he damned the actor, dismissing his mediocre film career and declaring that he had "gone as far as he ever will principally because his public seems to feel that he has a superiority complex." Brown reiterated his disdain in an interview the following year, gleefully noting that "if Tone was going to be a star, he'd be one by now . . . but he's got a kind of smirk people just won't take to."[9]

Dealing with Tone was vexing enough, but Crawford was also being "difficult." She was caught up in the personal drama of yet another marriage on the rocks, but Brown was more worried about the professional crisis of confidence she seemed to be undergoing. As it dawned on her that she had been badly miscast, Crawford became increasingly sensitive to the judgments of her costars. On this occasion, she was probably right to suspect that some of them were mocking her. Certainly the laconic Melvyn Douglas thought she was ridiculous in the role and on the set. In his autobiography he recalled that they never hit it off: "I went on to the set where Miss Crawford, whom I scarcely knew, made a grand entrance . . . she greeted me in a gracious and distinctly Southern manner, less as if I was a fellow player than a guest in her home. This atmosphere continued throughout the making of the picture." It rankled him that the crew pandered to her at the expense of the rest of the cast, and he was especially amused by Brown's treatment of her. The director would order silence on the set to help Crawford concentrate and prepare for an emotional scene. When silence didn't do the trick, a record player was brought out to play "None but the Lonely Heart." Brown "would then step forward, and taking Joan by the hand, stand with his head close to hers and wait dreamily until she had achieved whatever emotional pitch she was seeking, after which he would signal for the cameras to begin. The record player's work and Mr. Brown's handling may have been my first exposure to 'method' preparation. At any rate it was effective. Joan would start the scene with tears streaming down her face and, with no mechanical assistance other than the record, would be able to produce the same intensity over and over again." Having been on the receiving end of Crawford's "not exactly sanitary" swearing, Douglas wasn't fooled by her "delicate comportment"; he thought she was about as "real" as the MGM set of "a perfect Hollywood facsimile of a New England house. The edifice was complete with picket fence, grass mats and a steeply sloping roof, the latter built presumably to withstand the weight of whatever northeastern snows might accumulate inside the studio." In an effort to prick the collective air of stuffiness, one morning Douglas arrived on the set accompanied by a mini-entourage that included two dogs. His prank was "greeted with stony silence. Nobody seemed even mildly amused." He received a veiled threat from

Brown, who took him aside and "murmured 'I hope you will never do any-thing like that again, Mr. Douglas.' I didn't."[10]

Douglas's account reveals the pettiness and the indulgence of "tempera-ment" that were commonplace on Hollywood sets, yet his description of Brown's handling of Crawford, while embellished, has a ring of truth. But what Douglas viewed as the massaging of the star's ego might more gener-ously be viewed as Brown's pragmatism in the face of the inevitable insecuri-ties that accompany stardom. Douglas could mock it, but Brown's job was to facilitate the star's performance, even if that meant endless reassurance or the indulgence of excessive demands (such as Garbo's request that her sets be closed). Much of the time it paid off—notably with the sometimes "difficult" Garbo or with inexperienced child actors—but on this occasion, his best efforts failed.

To contain rumors that all was not well on the set, MGM's publicity department went to work, building a sense of momentum and piquing fans' interest by feeding stories to the press about the actress's transformation into a nineteenth-century heroine. One journalist offered a somewhat wry account of Crawford in costume: "She is wearing a big, floppy hat with daisies on it and a gown with voluminous skirts. Her hair hangs down in long curls, her eye lashes are shorter than usual and her lips scarcely made up at all." (He also noted how easily she slipped out of her role, nonchalantly puffing on a ciga-rette between takes.) Brown revealed the secrets of successful directing to the more highbrow publication the *Hollywood Spectator* (presided over by some-time Brown fan Welford Beaton). Declaring that he favored "understated emotions" over grand displays, he promised that *The Gorgeous Hussy* would be a new kind of costume drama. Duly impressed, the journalist went on to describe the techniques Brown used: "Clarence moves his characters well up to the front to gain pictorial value by widening the composition behind them. He gives us a lot to look at. Moving his characters away from walls has another advantage. It permits back lighting." It was a technique Brown and Folsey came up with not merely to show off Crawford's perfect bone structure but also to disguise her elaborate and unflattering costumes.[11]

Filming finally wrapped at the end of June, but extensive editing and some retakes meant that the film's nationwide debut was delayed until Sep-tember. As expected, Frank Nugent of the *New York Times* was caustic and a little unfair—given his understanding of the influence exerted by PCA: "It is hoped that some day we may come to understand why Hollywood, when it selects a colorful personality for one of its themes, almost invariably chooses to divest the hapless character of that very color which seems to justify screen biography." The *Washington Post*'s Nelson Bell was more impressed, praising Brown's skillful direction of this "agreeable . . . picturesque bit of screen entertainment." Perhaps surprisingly, a journalist working for the *Hollywood Citizens News* (a publication with close ties to the industry) filed the most considered and perceptive review. Elizabeth Yeaman was critical of Brown for exercising "commercial rather than artistic judgment" and for the blatant glossing over of historical facts. However, she did identify one bright spark in the story—the dynamic between Andrew and Rachel Jackson, which she found more involving and well directed than anything else in the film. Although she complained that Barrymore "never quite submerges the Barrymore personality in his role," she was bowled over by Beulah Bondi: "Never is the Bondi personality glimpsed, so truly does she slip into her portrayals. Her Rachel in this picture is a little masterpiece—a portrait of a woman of the people who possesses common sense, deep understanding, devotion to her husband and country, and who is prone to pipe smoking."[12]

Yeaman was astute in her appraisal: apart from Bondi's beautifully realized portrait of Rachel Jackson and some moments of fine photography, *The Gorgeous Hussy* is rather dull and uninvolving. The focus on Crawford as Peg would have been fine if the actress had delivered a compelling portrayal of an intriguing character, but she was floundering in a part that had been stripped of its most provocative elements before the cameras even rolled. As critics pointed out, she may have been gorgeous, but she wasn't much of a hussy; her succession of romances is attributed to her disappointment at not finding true love, rather than a more interesting streak of wantonness. As Nugent observed, "Pot-house Peg" had been transformed, by Breen's careful hand, into "a maligned Anne of Green Gables, a persecuted Polyanna [*sic*], a dismayed Dolly Dimple."[13]

Although *The Gorgeous Hussy* was intended to advance Crawford's career, it probably had the opposite effect. Her performance—first as the ingénue, then as the prim but wise widow, then as the self-sacrificing martyr—ruthlessly exposed Crawford's tendency to be mannered and artificial, and she knew it. The poor reviews hurt in 1936, but with the benefit of hindsight, she assessed *The Gorgeous Hussy* with characteristic bluntness, admitting that she had been "so totally miscast, I think there's where the term 'credibility gap' originated." For his part, Brown remembered the film in largely negative terms, save for the pleasure of directing Bondi (even though her performance provoked protests back in his home state of Tennessee that her Rachel Jackson was too "country"). Bondi's scenes are the film's high point, but not only because she is totally immersed in the role and successfully brings to life a figure from the distant past. There is a sincerity of tone in Brown's lovingly crafted direction that entitles his Rachel Jackson to join the gallery of finely etched American folk heroines from his best work—including Louise Dresser's goose woman, Beulah Bondi's Mom in *Of Human Hearts,* Ma (Jane Wyman) in *The Yearling,* and Mrs. Habersham (Elizabeth Patterson) in *Intruder in the Dust.*[14]

The Gorgeous Hussy was the last time Brown was officially credited as Crawford's director, but it wasn't quite the end of the road for the pair. When the talents of Woody van Dyke were needed on a new *Thin Man* picture, Brown was asked to finish *Love on the Run.* Like many of his salvage jobs, it's unclear how much of the film he actually shot; according to some reports, he was brought in just to handle retakes, but others suggest he took four weeks to entirely reshoot what van Dyke had delivered in eighteen days. Brown later claimed he directed "80% of that [film] over again" after van Dyke left. Whoever directed the bulk of it, *Love on the Run* wasn't the worst way to end what had been a fairly productive collaboration between actress and director. Cast in a role that was more her style, and having called time on her marriage to Tone, Crawford was more relaxed. Even though comedy wasn't her forte, she delivered a reasonably good performance as madcap heiress Sally Parker opposite her favorite costar, Clark Gable. Brown may have dreaded the prospect of keeping the peace between Crawford, her on-and-off lover Gable, and her soon-to-be-ex-husband Tone (playing a supporting role), but there were surprisingly few problems, and the actress seemed to revel in the male attention: "[I] enjoyed the hell out of it, particularly with Clark and Franchot opposite. Not a big picture, but everyone I know who saw it seemed to love the thing." *Love on the Run* is unabashedly formulaic, but sometimes that can be a good thing. Brown (and presumably van Dyke) concocted an enjoyable if instantly forgettable piece of whimsy that audiences relished. The warm reception that greeted *Love on the Run* caused Mankiewicz to pause and consider what audiences really wanted: as he noted, the film "possesses not so much as an artistic [moment]," but it cleaned up at the box office.[15]

The eighteen months between the beginning of 1935 and the fall of 1936 had been hectic: Brown had completed five films, expanded his business interests and property portfolio in Los Angeles, and commenced extensive renovations on the Calabasas ranch. He had earned some time off, and he spent the early part of 1937 traveling, visiting Tourneur in Paris and arriving in London in time to witness the coronation of King Edward VIII in May. The pomp and spectacle of the ceremony might have provided some inspiration, because when he returned to Hollywood he was assigned to direct another historical epic. *Marie Walewska*—or *Conquest,* as it was titled for its American release— would bring to an end his productive, sometimes turbulent partnership with Greta Garbo.

20

Conquest

Waclaw Gasiorowski's novel *Pani Walewska* (and a 1933 play adapted from it by Helen Jerome) tells the story of Marie Walewska, a Polish countess who became one of Napoleon Bonaparte's lovers and even bore him a child. Set against a sprawling backdrop of European history in the 1800s to 1820s, Gasiorowski's novel melds fact and speculation to suggest that Walewska's liaison was inspired more by patriotism than by passion. Polish-born Salka Viertel read the novel in 1935, found it interesting, and identified it as a potential vehicle for Greta Garbo. Once again, Garbo refused the advice of David O. Selznick and, with the backing of Irving Thalberg, lined up *Marie Walewska* as her next project (after *Anna Karenina*).[1]

The subject matter was bound to create waves at the PCA office, and negotiations were so protracted that Garbo started shooting *Camille* while Thalberg continued to oversee consultations with screenwriter Viertel. Again, S. L. Behrman was tapped for cowriting duties, and although he wasn't especially interested in the subject matter, it was a lucrative assignment that gave him the opportunity to satirize Napoleon—a figure he considered "a disaster for the human race." Behrman soon discovered that "it was not easy to get sympathy for this point of view from a group of men who had busts of Napoleon in their offices, since he represented their secret wish-dreams of conquest." As he and Viertel worked on the script, Thalberg kept them briefed on the latest correspondence from Breen, who warned that the film would be "thoroughly acceptable" only if the "audience get out of it the feeling that living as a mistress, even to Napoleon, ends in disaster and unhappiness." Some of Breen's recommendations included writing a new character to take on the role of a chorus, offering commentary on events; adding several lines that expressed Marie's hopes for marriage; and excising any suggestion that Count Walewska pimped out his wife for the sake of Poland.[2]

The production was dealt a devastating blow in September when Thalberg died and Mayer instructed a reluctant Bernie Hyman to take over the project. Viertel soon realized that her dream of celebrating a brave and loyal Polish woman was unlikely to interest the unpretentious Hyman. He didn't care for the story or for her screenplay, complaining that it lacked "heart ... [it was] too sophisticated and cold. It did not make you cry." Viertel watched as she and Behrman lost control of the script and other writers were drafted. They included Samuel Hoffenstein, who Viertel claimed was hired to back up Hyman's criticisms of the script (he didn't); humorist Donald Ogden Stewart and Charles MacArthur (to supply, respectively, "zip" and "wit"); and Zoë Akins (to inject some "heart"). By the time the film made it to theaters in November 1937, it bore the marks of at least seventeen writers, but it was neither coherent nor absorbing. This was partly due to circumstances beyond anyone's control. With the deepening political crisis in Europe, the screenwriters had been advised to take "special care in writing Napoleon's dialogue"; thus, they had "carefully selected the speech in which Napoleon favors a United States of Europe and praises a democratic form of government." The script also studiously avoided the timely issue of whether absolute power corrupts absolutely, because MGM "didn't want to make him [Napoleon] a dictator and glorify all the Hitlers and Mussolinis." At least history had provided a PCA-acceptable punishment for the sinning lovers, as columnist Sidney Skolsky flippantly noted: the "picture has a tragic ending. Napoleon is defeated and crushed at Waterloo."[3]

Filming began in March 1937 with no final script in hand. In fact, Hyman had just managed to secure a director after the original choice, George Cukor, turned it down, fearing it would be a po-faced affair peopled by historical "waxworks." Once again, Brown was given Cukor's castoffs, but this time, Garbo was not convinced he was the right choice, allegedly grumbling, "I don't know if Brown is the man to do it, as a matter of fact he isn't." Her doubts were matched by Brown's. He had completed two historical epics in a twelve-month period and had little appetite for a third. He was far more enthusiastic about directing the film version of Emlyn Williams's smash hit *Night Must Fall*, but when MGM pressed, he capitulated. His pet project was handed over to Richard Thorpe, and Brown reported for his seventh film with Garbo.[4]

Problems surfaced almost immediately. Viertel, who liked and respected Brown and considered him an "excellent technician," noticed that he seemed to be switched off, and she suspected it was because *Marie Walewska* "went much against his grain." Although Brown's style could be as visually showy as anyone's, and although he had directed some large-scale, complicated productions (*The Eagle* and *Flesh and the Devil*), he was better at directing smaller projects that featured "ordinary folk." The epic sweep and "big history" of

Marie Walewska left him cold, and the lack of a final script drove him to despair. Within weeks, rumors began to circulate that the production was disorganized and Brown wasn't running the show. In an article published just before the film was released, gossip columnist Sidney Skolsky revealed some "fun facts" about it: "this is the first time that Garbo ever started a picture without having a final completed scenario. Hoffenstein and Viertel were still writing the scenario as the picture was shooting. Often there would be a conference on set and a scene rewritten before the shooting. And the only author who could go on the set and talk to Garbo was Salka Viertel." These were presented as interesting tidbits, but they revealed the haphazard progress and Brown's relative unimportance on the set. So it's hardly surprising that he delivered competent if uninspired service (Viertel accused him of more active "disgruntled obstructionism"). Brown later admitted that filming started badly and continued in that vein: "everything that could go wrong on a picture went wrong."[5]

It was a costly mess. MGM had poured vast resources into the film, building elaborate sets that included replicas of a Polish village, Napoleon's Warsaw headquarters, and a palace in Paris. The production traveled to Monterey (a stand-in for Elba) and central Los Angeles for location work. The 2,000 costumes added to the expense, as did the authentic jewelry worn by Garbo (reportedly belonging to Empress Marie Louise) and the $90,000 worth of antiques leased to the studio by Brown. MGM threw everything it had at the production, yet it hadn't addressed the key issue of furnishing a decent script. Certainly, the film's importance on MGM's roster of productions was underlined by the A-list cast: joining Garbo was Charles Boyer in his first leading role in a Hollywood film; Maria Ouspenskaya as Marie's mad aunt (a character that doesn't appear in the book); Dame May Whitty as Napoleon's mother; and Reginald Owen, Henry Stephenson, and Alan Marshall in supporting roles. Again, Charles Dorian served as Brown's assistant on the production, but Garbo's favorite cameraman, William Daniels, had been replaced by Karl Freund, a legend of European cinema. Garbo had worked with Freund on *Camille* (Daniels had been indisposed, allegedly because he was on a "drinking jag"), but this was Brown's first time collaborating with him. Brown was already an admirer, having been especially influenced by the films Freund made with F. W. Murnau, but he was soon exasperated by Freund's methodical and exceedingly "slow" approach.[6]

In the face of daily challenges and some ill health (director Gustav Machaty had to take over for a few days), Brown stuck with it. Once he had been critical of the costs incurred by von Stroheim, but now he was on a juggernaut of similar excess as *Marie Walewska* shaped up to be the 1930s equivalent of *Foolish Wives* (until *Gone with the Wind* stole that honor). Sensitive to criticism that MGM was producing a pretentious, wasteful "European" folly to indulge a Swedish diva, studio publicists planted stories of how relaxed the set was and how a jolly Garbo was playing practical jokes, pitching in to organize a birthday party for Brown, and even hitching up her skirts to participate in the softball games organized by him and Dorian. The reality was a little different, as Brown later admitted to Eyman: her increasing withdrawal negatively affected the atmosphere, and her churlish behavior sometimes offended him personally (such as her refusal to meet Brown's guest to the set, Leatrice Gilbert).[7]

Viertel and Behrman may have viewed Hyman as a crass moneyman with no understanding of art, but he proved remarkably prescient about the core problem of *Marie Walewska*. When the public finally got to see the film in November—after a shoot that took just under five months and cost nearly $3 million—they were shifting in their seats within minutes, bored by a plot that unfolded laboriously over 130 minutes. This time, Brown's leisurely style—employed here to preserve the "dignity" of the story and its star—only highlighted the stuffy, stilted quality of the proceedings. Admittedly, there were some bright sparks of action amid all the pageantry, such as an impressively staged and dynamically cut opening sequence of marauding Cossacks thundering through Count Walewska's home on horseback, but these were rare. It is interesting how much Brown cribbed from his own work for a number of (mainly nondialogue) sequences: the Cossack rampage is clearly inspired by similar ones in *The Eagle* and *Anna Karenina*, the Napoleonic army's trek through ice-bound Russia recalls the prospectors traversing the Chilkoot Pass in *Trail of '98*, and a shot of the power-hungry emperor silhouetted against a map of Europe is a nod to *Night Flight*. However, these "self-homages" seem to indicate a director who was looking to past glories and to more interesting projects for inspiration. For the most part, his direction was pedestrian, with a surfeit of medium shots of characters talking, broken only by montages of various battles in Napoleon's conquest of Europe.

Of course, Brown wasn't solely to blame. Pulling together a large-scale production that lacked a decent script would have been a challenge for most. Garbo's charm and skills had saved a fair share of mediocre films, but there was little she could do to bring *Marie Walewska* back from the brink. Hyman had been right about the story lacking "heart" and about the relationship between Marie and Napoleon being uninvolving. Admittedly, it would have been difficult for anyone to write a convincing film based on Napoleon's love affairs, unless it focused on his one true love (himself), but MGM's Marie was dull and pathetic, trailing after the self-absorbed Napoleon like a nineteenth-century groupie. Not helping was the distinct lack of chemistry between the leads and a mechanical quality that crept into Garbo's performance. Garbo and Boyer reportedly had little interaction between takes, and that probably contributed to the sense that they are two strangers "performing" passion. As the filming progressed, Garbo may have sensed that her character wasn't especially compelling, but Boyer's was. Indeed, the film's most amusing scene—in which a petty Napoleon squabbles with Marie's aunt over a game of cards—doesn't even feature her. In a profile published a year after the film's release, Boyer praised his leading lady as the "ideal choice" for the role, assuring American readers that "they idolise her" in France and noting that her performance as Marie was further evidence of her "genius," but he could afford to be generous: he had read the reviews, and he knew he had stolen the picture from under her nose.[8]

The film was released under the title *Conquest* for the American market, and critics were ruthless in sniffing out its weaknesses—the direction, Garbo's lackluster performance, the banalities of the script—but grudging in identifying its strengths (Boyer, Ouspenskaya). Frank Nugent lamented that the film demonstrated the pitfalls of conveying historical subject matter on a lavish scale, noting, "[it is] a surface show. It goes no deeper than the images its screen reflects. One can watch it and study it as academically as we would watch a procession of ants underneath a magnifying glass." Elizabeth Yeaman reserved most of her praise for the performances of the supporting players such as Ouspenskaya and Whitty, and she expressed surprise that "in almost every scene Garbo is the foil for Boyer's portrayal . . . she has few scenes of real dramatic importance." Louella Parsons agreed, observing that Garbo was "completely overshadowed by Boyer" and complaining that Garbo didn't even fulfill the basic requirements of a star: to look flawless and captivating. Parsons was critical of Garbo's costumes, which were "not particularly becoming to her, nor is her coiffure which accents her painful thinness . . . there are certain scenes where she is almost emaciated looking."[9]

Parsons may have been a little bitchy in her comments, but she wasn't entirely wrong. Garbo *was* looking haggard and thin, and the unflattering Empire-line dresses and Freund's flat lighting of her certainly didn't help. Creeping boredom with the whole Garbo phenomenon was detectable in the more highbrow reviews, such as John Mosher's for the *New Yorker*: "Madame Garbo's elegant anaemia, I fear, can pall a little. Her performance seems static, though the story covers a period of years. Beautiful, fragile and tired, she stands in the first scene among the Cossacks invading her husband's house; and quite unchanged, fragile and tired still, she waves her last farewell to Napoleon, as though she would assert and try to prove that loyalty is but a symptom of exhaustion." Across the Atlantic in Britain, Graham Greene opened his review with the admission that a "dreadful inertia always falls on me before a new Garbo film," and he ended by concluding that "one of the dullest films of the year" had done nothing to lift it. The failure of *Conquest* presented an accounting problem for the studio, but perhaps more serious was its impact on Garbo's career. She was already experiencing a decline in popularity, especially in America, and this stodgy epic merely accelerated it. Exhibitors outside the main urban areas reported poor box-office receipts and negative reactions from patrons. A. E. Hancock, a theater owner in Indiana, pulled no punches, complaining that *Conquest* "did not do any business here" because it is "too long, there are some draggy spots, and then again Garbo is supported largely by the sophisticates and our business comes from the rank and file. . . . It is a super colossal magnifco [*sic*], but a dog at the box office."[10]

For Brown, *Conquest* marked the end of his eleven-year professional relationship with the star. When he died in 1987, most obituaries mentioned that he was "Garbo's favorite director," despite some tense collaborations and a few mediocre films. Away from the lot, the two enjoyed a fairly amicable rapport, and they maintained a social friendship long after both had retired. Actor Gene Reynolds recalled that Garbo was genuinely fond of Brown, liking his seriousness and his sensitivity to her on-set demands. She occasionally showed her more playful side when the pressure of a shoot had passed (Reynolds relates one incident in which Brown, while window-shopping in Paris, was surprised by Garbo, who crept up behind him and covered his eyes with her hands. He knew instantly it was Greta). Yet, in their more candid moments, each admitted that their long professional collaboration didn't always yield the greatest films and that Garbo sometimes needed to be challenged in ways that Brown was reluctant to do. Brown was honest about his own limitations in directing Garbo, and he generously identified Cukor as her best director. He had reservations, too, about the impact the association with Garbo might have on his career. Around the time of *Conquest*'s release, the *Los Angeles Examiner* carried an interesting piece about the dangers of directors being too closely linked with particular stars, citing Brown as one who "wisely turned the direction of Garbo over to other directors when he began to feel that he was being classed as 'Garbo's director.' He did not wish to be dubbed as a single-star megaphonist."[11]

In the two decades that followed, rumors often surfaced about a possible reunion between Garbo and Brown. A color remake of *Flesh and the Devil* was discussed in the 1940s but came to nothing; nor did Garbo's cherished project, *Joan of Arc,* ever make it to the screen. Perhaps it was just as well; based on *Conquest,* it seemed their partnership had run its course. Garbo's final two films were lighter affairs that yielded mixed results, but for Brown, the termination of his professional relationship with Garbo led to a period of creativity and passion.[12]

Clarence Brown, ca. 1894. (Courtesy of Clarence Brown Collection, University of Tennessee, Knoxville)

Catherine, Larkin, and Clarence Brown, ca. 1896. (Courtesy of Barbara McRae)

Clarence Brown, ca. 1899. (Courtesy of Clarence Brown Collection, University of Tennessee, Knoxville)

Postcards of Lancaster Mills, Clinton, Massachusetts (top), and Brookside Mills, Knoxville, Tennessee (bottom).

Master Clarence Leon Brown
JUVENILE ENTERTAINER
Dramatic Reader, Impersonator and Imitator

Leaflet advertising Master
Clarence Leon Brown, Juvenile
Entertainer. (Courtesy of
Clarence Brown Collection,
University of Tennessee,
Knoxville)

ARTISTIC RECITALS
Tragedy, Humor, Pathos, Dialect, Wit, Scenes and Sketches

At

On

Admission

Clarence Brown, ca. 1901. (Courtesy of
Clarence Brown Collection, University
of Tennessee, Knoxville)

The Great Redeemer. (Courtesy of Clarence Brown Collection, University of Tennessee, Knoxville)

Hope Hampton and Lon Chaney in *The Light in the Dark.* (Courtesy of Clarence Brown Collection, University of Tennessee, Knoxville)

Brown directs the cast of *Butterfly*. (Courtesy of Clarence Brown Collection, University of Tennessee, Knoxville)

Filming *The Signal Tower.* (Courtesy of Clarence Brown Collection, University of Tennessee, Knoxville)

Frankie Darro and Rockliffe Fellowes in *The Signal Tower.* (Courtesy of Kevin Brownlow)

Pauline Frederick and Brown in a publicity still for *Smouldering Fires*. (Courtesy of Kevin Brownlow)

Malcolm MacGregor and Pauline Frederick in *Smouldering Fires*. (Courtesy of Kevin Brownlow)

Filming *Smouldering Fires* at Yosemite. (Courtesy of Clarence Brown Collection, University of Tennessee, Knoxville)

Shooting *The Eagle:* Brown, Rudolph Valentino, and Dev Jennings (cameraman).

Louise Dresser in *The Goose Woman*. (Courtesy of Kevin Brownlow)

Brown and Norma Talmadge in a publicity shot for *Kiki*.

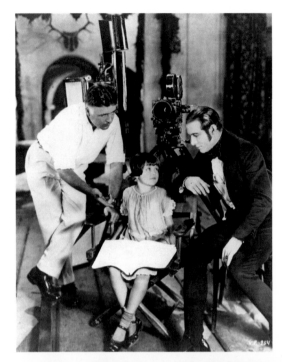

Brown, daughter Adrienne, and Rudolph Valentino in a 1925 publicity shot.

Garbo and Brown on the set of *Flesh and the Devil*. (Courtesy of Kevin Brownlow)

Ona Wilson-Brown and Clarence Brown, ca. 1926.

Brown directs Greta Garbo and John Gilbert in *Flesh and the Devil*. (Courtesy of Kevin Brownlow)

Brown between takes on *Flesh and the Devil*.

On the set of *The Trail of '98*. (Courtesy of Clarence Brown Collection, University of Tennessee, Knoxville)

Brown and Harry Carey on location for *The Trail of '98*.

Brown on the set of *Night Flight* (unidentified woman at the typewriter).

Brown, Dolores del Rio, and one of the huskies in *The Trail of '98*.

Brown and Garbo on the set of *A Woman of Affairs*. Hobart Bosworth is seated in the background, and William Daniels is the cameraman. (Courtesy of Kevin Brownlow)

Brown directs and William Daniels films Greta Garbo and John Gilbert in *A Woman of Affairs*. (Courtesy of Kevin Brownlow)

Catherine Brown and her son, ca. 1928. (Courtesy of Clarence Brown Collection, University of Tennessee, Knoxville)

Navy Blues. (Courtesy of Clarence Brown Collection, University of Tennessee, Knoxville)

Brown and pet, ca. 1920s.

Brown and Charles Dorian lunch at the MGM commissary.

Brown tries out early sound equipment.

Garbo and Brown on the set of *Anna Christie*.

Brown delivers *Romance*.

Greta Garbo in *Romance*. (Courtesy of Kevin Brownlow)

Clark Gable and Joan Crawford in *Possessed.*

Brown directs Lionel Barrymore and Eric Linden in *Ah Wilderness!*

John Barrymore in *Night Flight.* (Courtesy of Kevin Brownlow)

Brown directs William Gargan and Myrna Loy in *Night Flight*.

Edward Arnold, Joan Crawford, Brown, and Franchot Tone on the set of *Sadie McKee*.

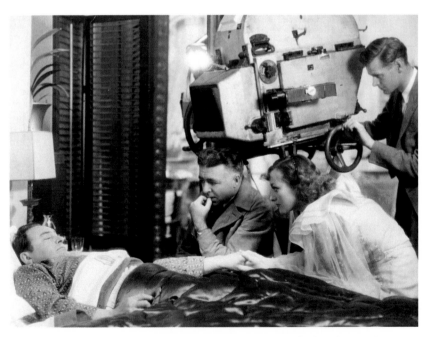

Brown directs Edward Arnold in *Sadie McKee* as Joan Crawford looks on. The cameraman is Oliver T. Marsh.

Brown and Alice Joyce, 1934.

Brown directs Greta Garbo and Fredric March in *Anna Karenina,* and William
Daniels films the scene. (Courtesy of Kevin Brownlow)

Brown and Garbo on the set of *Anna Karenina*. (Courtesy of Clarence Brown Collection, University of Tennessee, Knoxville)

Greta Garbo and Freddie Bartholomew in *Anna Karenina*.

Brown directs Clark Gable and Jean Harlow in *Wife vs. Secretary* as the crew looks on.

Filming a scene from *The Rains Came* with Brenda Joyce and George Brent. Joseph LaSalle is operating the camera, and Arthur Miller (in glasses) is watching.

Lionel Barrymore and Joan Crawford in *The Gorgeous Hussy*.

Filming *Conquest*. (Courtesy of Kevin Brownlow)

Clark Gable as "Harry" with his dance troupe in *Idiot's Delight.*

Alice Joyce and Brown, ca. late 1930s.

Peter Lorre, Clark Gable, and Rosalind Russell in a promotional still for *They Met in Bombay*.

Filming *The Human Comedy* with Jackie "Butch" Jenkins.

Fay Bainter and Mickey Rooney in a promotional still for *The Human Comedy*.

Jackie "Butch" Jenkins, Elizabeth Taylor, King Charles (the horse), and Mickey Rooney in a promotional still for *National Velvet*.

Publicity portrait of Brown, ca. 1940s. (Courtesy of Kevin Brownlow)

Claude Jarman Jr. and Jacqueline White on location in Florida for *The Yearling*. (Courtesy of Jacqueline White Anderson)

Brown and Claude Jarman Jr. on the set of *The Yearling*. (Courtesy of Claude Jarman Jr.)

Brown, Gregory Peck, and Claude Jarman Jr. on the set of *The Yearling*. (Courtesy of Claude Jarman Jr.)

Jarman and Brown mock fighting on the set of *The Yearling*. (Courtesy of Claude Jarman Jr.)

Brown and Jarman take a break on the set of *The Yearling*. (Courtesy of Claude Jarman Jr.)

Jarman, Brown, and cinematographer Leonard Smith (unconfirmed) on the set of *The Yearling*. (Courtesy of Claude Jarman Jr.)

Brown, Jane Wyman, and Jarman on the set of *The Yearling*. (Courtesy of Claude Jarman Jr.)

Jarman in a promotional still for *The Yearling*. (Courtesy of Clarence Brown Collection, University of Tennessee, Knoxville)

Brown and Gigi Perreau in a promotional still for *Song of Love*.

Brown gets a kiss from Joan Crawford. (Courtesy of Clarence Brown Collection, University of Tennessee, Knoxville)

Brown films Porter Hall in the quicksand scene in *Intruder in the Dust.*

Elzie Emanuel and Claude Jarman Jr. in a still from *Intruder in the Dust*.

Intruder in the Dust screens in Atlanta. (Courtesy of Clarence Brown Collection, University of Tennessee, Knoxville)

With the leads now in place, only the role of young Jason remained unfilled. MGM's casting department had sent Brown numerous boys to interview, but none of them matched his vision. There was some speculation that the Mauch twins, well-known child performers, might take the role if their schedule allowed. As Brown waited for confirmation, he diverted his attention to selecting the supporting roles. MGM may have been the studio of the stars, but it also boasted a colorful array of character actors who could deliver the kinds of performances that stole pictures. *Benefits Forgot* (renamed *Of Human Hearts*) proved to be a veritable showcase for the talents of these often under-appreciated performers: moon-faced Guy Kibbee took on the part of money-grabbing shop owner George Ames; Charles Coburn was the alcoholic Dr. Shingle; Robert McWade and Arthur Aylesworth played, respectively, the wonderfully named Dr. Lupus Crumm and Rufus Inchpin; and Clem Bevans and Leona Roberts appeared as a dotty church elder and an eccentric backwoods denizen. Working with such a talented cast helped Brown rediscover his passion for storytelling and brought back childhood memories of "local characters" in small-town Clinton and encounters with tough pioneer folk in the Great Smoky Mountains. Whereas *Ah Wilderness!* offered a rather comic and sentimental portrait of family life, *Of Human Hearts* took Brown in a new, more somber direction that anticipated the complex familial and parent-child relationships of *The Yearling* and *Intruder in the Dust*.

In a further confirmation of Brown's control over the production, he was granted the right to shoot most of it at his beloved Lake Arrowhead. There was just one problem: the Mauch twins were not available to start filming in October, and with everyone else ready to go, he had to find another child actor. It was a demanding role: much of the early story details the life of young Jason as he struggles to understand his father's harsh approach to parenting and seeks solace in his mother's warmth and gentleness. The part called for someone who looked and acted like an ordinary child, quite capable of holding his own against the tough kids of Pine Hill, but also possessing a quality of steeliness and ambition that sets him apart. In Brown's view, the problem was that so many of the child actors under contract at MGM were either too refined (Freddie Bartholomew), too urban (the Dead End Kids, for example), or too slickly professional (Mickey Rooney). A late casting call was put out, and Brown interviewed a stream of child actors, but again he was disappointed. Then one last boy was sent in. Gene Reynolds was fourteen and had appeared in some small roles. The moment he walked in, Brown exclaimed, "*That's* more like it," and hired him. In addition to having a physical resemblance to Stewart, Reynolds had the face of a child of the 1850s, with a natural, "unaffected" quality that was refreshing and rare in the artificial world of Hollywood.[5]

Reynolds recalled that it was all very last minute: he was told to immediately report for duty and join the rest of the company, which was already up at Lake Arrowhead. MGM had secured a lakefront site, and designer Harry Oliver was overseeing construction of the large set—a pioneer town—with animals and materials being transported by boat (Brown also used his Calabasas ranch for a couple of scenes). Publicity noted that Brown's engineering background proved essential during these preparations and that "no detail is too small for his notice." Reynolds confirmed that Brown meticulously monitored the sets' construction and their visual look. The village MGM built was a little stylized, but its rough-hewn quality was certainly more authentic than the opulent sets on which Brown had recently worked.[6]

The atmosphere was industrious and businesslike, but amiable. According to Reynolds, the location shooting fostered a sense of community, and all the actors had a little time to socialize, such as when Kibbee, Coburn, and Charlie Grapewin hosted a Halloween party at a lodge on the lake. Reynolds's previous experience had been working for the flamboyant and macho Victor Fleming on *Captains Courageous,* so he found Brown rather different. From the outset, the director made it clear that everyone was there to "work, not play," that deadlines had to be met, and that he was the boss. Even so, Brown didn't discourage breaks or slight diversions, because these often led to some interesting discoveries. He took everything in, even when he seemed relaxed, and Reynolds recounted one incident when Brown surprised everyone by stopping in the middle of a take to focus on a grip who had caught his eye. No doubt the crew member braced himself for a reprimand, but instead the man was told to drop what he was doing and take a small onscreen role as background color. Evidently, something about the man's face sparked Brown's interest, something "rural" and "pioneer" that would be a perfect fit. Reynolds also recalled that Brown's initially cool and intimidating demeanor began to thaw as the shoot progressed. When he noticed Reynolds showing off his acrobatic skills during a break, he was so amused and impressed that he incorporated the tricks into several scenes. Perhaps Reynolds reminded Brown of his own past as a child performer; he certainly developed a paternal affection for the young actor, which surprised many who saw him only as a tough boss, both on set and off. Reynolds hadn't known what to expect because he had heard mixed reports that Brown was too tough *and* too soft (the latter with Garbo). The man he encountered showed both traits: he was demanding with the crew, and although he was far from gushing with his actors, when he did

Richard Haydn, Clark Gable, and Bernard Miles in a promotional still for *Never Let Me Go.*

Brown shows Dore Schary a birthday present signed by the cast and crew of *The Plymouth Adventure.*

Jane Wyman and Brown in Knoxville. (Courtesy of Clarence Brown Collection, University of Tennessee, Knoxville)

Brown and Marian Spies-Brown, Palm Desert, ca. 1960s. (Courtesy of Clarence Brown Collection, University of Tennessee, Knoxville)

21

A Little Piece of Humanity

Of Human Hearts

As one writer observed in 1938, "Professionally speaking there are two Clarence Browns. One is the shepherd of great stars, leading people like Garbo, Crawford and Gable through million-dollars pastures. The other is the honest idealist director making for choice, simple human films like *Ah Wilderness!* and *Of Human Hearts* with a cast of unglamorous character players."[1] Brown had spent the two years since *Ah Wilderness!* as the conscientious "shepherd of great stars," but as his work on *Conquest* lurched toward its conclusion, he took stock of his career. His contract was coming to an end, and he was considering the possibility of going freelance, but MGM lured him back with the promise of a pay raise and, more important, greater control over his productions. Over the next decade, he still took his fair share of routine assignments, but he also began to fight for the right to make more personal projects that were better suited to his style. These films would turn out to be among the most accomplished of his sound career.

First up was a production of Honoré Morrow's 1917 story of life in small-town Ohio in the 1850s and 1860s. *Benefits Forgot: A Story of Lincoln and Mother Love* was a short novella, part of a collection of stories linked to Abraham Lincoln. It sketched out details of the life of a traveling preacher, Ethan, and his relationship with his wife, Mary, and their son, Jason. It was a moralistic yet affecting tale, focusing on themes of parental sacrifice and filial ingratitude, set against the backdrop of a vividly evoked rural community called Pine Hill. Brown had read the story soon after arriving in Hollywood in 1920, and its nostalgic evocation of small-town life evidently struck such a chord with him that he acquired the rights, with the intention of filming it after he wrapped *The Great Redeemer*. His hectic schedule for the next decade threatened to shelve the project permanently, but when he agreed to take on *Conquest*, it was with the proviso that he be allowed to make *Benefits Forgot* immediately thereafter. As Brown headed off to shoot his final film with Garbo, producer John Considine managed the *Benefits Forgot* team of Charles Whittaker (conducting research that included interviews with a ninety-two-year-old Civil War veteran) and screenwriter Bradbury Foote.[2]

Foote was almost finished with the script by July, but he wasn't sure how to end the story. In the original, the self-absorbed Jason, who has escaped the small town and the rigid rule of his father to train as a doctor, finally sees the error of his ways after the "nation's father," Lincoln, intervenes and shames him into returning home to look after his self-sacrificing mother (who is now a widow). Alongside cowriter Conrad Richter, Foote toyed with the idea of allowing one last encounter between father and son and a happy ending of sorts, before opting to retain the original conclusion. In the meantime, Considine was busy overseeing negotiations with Breen. It seems surprising that the PCA could find anything objectionable in such a gentle story, but Breen identified a few scenes of mildly bawdy humor and plain-speaking vulgarity, as well as a scene or two that featured excessive drinking. As Europe edged closer to war and America slowly extricated itself from the Depression, Breen had other important things on his mind: he fretted about the potentially horrifying effect of a brief shot of a cow's udder on moviegoers.[3]

By the fall of 1937, Brown was finished with *Conquest* and could immerse himself in preparations for *Benefits Forgot*. The first decisions concerned casting. Considine favored Lionel Barrymore for the role of Ethan—mainly because he believed the actor's befuddled persona could soften Morrow's rather harsh character—but Brown held out for Walter Huston. It was an inspired choice, not only because Huston was an accomplished and versatile actor but also because he had no qualms about portraying a stern, unyielding character. To play Ethan's gentle wife Mary, Brown selected Beulah Bondi, which necessitated a loan from Paramount. The role of Jason required two actors, one for the early scenes of his childhood and another for the adult character. For the latter, Brown turned to James Stewart, with whom he had worked on two previous productions (neither of which he rated highly). The part was an interesting one, a little risky and quite different from the charming, self-effacing roles with which Stewart was associated. Though his performance in this film is not well known, in many respects the petulant, self-absorbed character Stewart plays here anticipates the dark and troubled men he portrayed in postwar films by Frank Capra, Anthony Mann, and Alfred Hitchcock.[4]

and fascinating document." Nelson Bell of the *Washington Post* conceded it was "not a happy picture," given its focus on "family relationships, filial duty, the deprivations of life on a primitive frontier and the selfish aspirations of uncurbed character," but he found it so well directed and effectively cast that it "deserves to be seen." Only Dorothy Manners, who had been friends with Ona and Clarence Brown in the 1920s, expressed reservations. Although she commended his "fine feeling for the mood and era of his story," she thought it didn't quite rise to the level of "a great picture of the folksy, homespun variety," mainly because it failed to resolve the conflicts it raised: "This conflict between the man and the boy is gripping, and the intimate struggle of the preacher's wife, torn between her understanding of both her son and her husband is made very real by Beulah Bondi. But as the youth grows up the story slips into tangles from which it never quite clears itself." Manners implicitly attributed the sentimentality and implausible narrative twists of *Of Human Hearts* to Hollywood's influence, but in fact, these were also part of Morrow's novella.[10]

Why *Of Human Hearts* garnered such positive reviews and became one of Brown's personal favorites merits some consideration. Apart from the strong performances by a cast of exceptional actors, Brown's lighting and composition recall the best work of his silent career. Like *Butterfly* and *The Goose Woman*, this tale of complex familial relationships is told in a deceptively simple manner that eschews the showy techniques he sometimes employed. Instead, subtle camera movements, sparing close-ups, and atmospheric lighting evoke mood and reveal the characters' inner sentiments, especially in moments of emotional intensity. For this story, centered on father-son dynamics, Brown returns to the dark foregrounds and low-key lighting he learned from Tourneur. Particularly impressive is a scene in which the young Jason, accused of insolence by his father, is shown sobbing in a stable, illuminated by only a single lantern. The visual composition here, by Brown and veteran cinematographer Clyde De Vinna, is starkly effective, and the scene marks a turning point in the development of the father-son relationship. Ethan is revealed to be a deeply conflicted man who understands and empathizes with his son's need to rebel, but his sense of duty compels him to punish Jason and thereby instill in him the virtues of humility and respect.

In notes for an autobiographical article written around the time *Of Human Hearts* was released, Brown draws some revealing connections between the film and his relationship with his own father: "He [Larkin] was a cotton operator, and when I was a youngster and got into pictures he was disappointed. He wanted to make a cotton man out of me. 'I guess I didn't make any mistake, not becoming a cotton man as you wanted me to,' I remarked.

Dad looked me over. 'Humph!' he remarked. 'I guess you'd never know enough to be a good cotton man, anyhow.'" Intended as a humorous anecdote, it is interesting that the usually reticent Brown would use a personal memory of being unable to live up to his father's expectations to promote *Of Human Hearts*. It is telling, too, that he was so intent on casting the right actor to play Ethan, one who could show both his humility (best revealed in a scene with the eccentric Sister Clark) and his harshness. Like Ethan, Larkin Brown had a certain sparing quality when it came to according praise, and he was rather rigid in matters of morality and religion—his reactions to Brown's multiple marriages and ostentatious living aren't recorded—but he was also much loved and revered by his son. *Of Human Hearts*, which really came from Brown's heart, acknowledges that the bond between parent and child (his bond with Larkin, and his bond with daughter Adrienne) is complex and often leads to both disappointment and reward. Critic Donald Lyons has identified this as a central theme in Brown's work and regards *Of Human Hearts* as an outstanding example: "for all its softness of heart . . . [it] is unblinking in its treatment of generational conflict, of a healthy son's need to get away and grow, and in its depiction of civilization's struggle, of the raw cruelty of the very frontier that had bred Lincoln . . . this is not a film that prettifies or refuses pain."[11]

Of Human Hearts certainly shows Brown's long-standing interest in the complexities of family dynamics, but it also introduces another theme that would become central to his work: the role of animals in developing a child's personality and facilitating his or her passage from childhood to adulthood (explored in both *National Velvet* and *The Yearling*). Here, it is the family's horse, Pilgrim, rescued by Ethan from a cruel owner, that helps Jason recover from his father's harsh treatment. Ethan's brandishing of a whip so terrifies the animal that he cuts himself on the stall, forcing Jason to see beyond his own misery and, without flinching, stitch up the bloody wound. Pilgrim prompts both human compassion, the natural empathy between child and animal that Brown's work so often explores, and the ambition and determination that define the adult Jason. The animal as symbol, and as striking visual presence here, anticipates later Brown films. Like the Pie in *National Velvet*, Pilgrim literally "bursts" into the family's life and onto the screen: a wild horse, a great beauty (played in the film by an Arabian) possessing a strong will that makes him (like Jason) seemingly impossible to "break." Pilgrim is tamed by gentleness and by a willingness to respect him as a sentient and complex being, and the horse becomes a beloved member of the family. In *National Velvet*, the Pie deepens the connection between Velvet and her mother; likewise, Pilgrim becomes the means by which the estranged Jason finally makes his way home to his mother and to the moral code instilled in him by both his parents.

There is little doubt that *Of Human Hearts* is the most personal of Brown's films of the 1930s, not least because it looks, simultaneously, to his past and his future. He returns to the theme he explored in such detail in his earliest work—the relationship between man and nature. Freed from the confines of the studio lot, he and Clyde De Vinna used "special light filters" to "catch the beauty of the lake, towering pines, and sky" of the Lake Arrowhead location. Though these shots were the result of the collaboration between Brown and De Vinna (they had also worked together on *Ah Wilderness!*), they call to mind similar shots, used for like purpose, in *The Last of the Mohicans*, *The Signal Tower*, and *Smouldering Fires*. The striking shots of the fictional town of Pine Hill, nestled between the mountains and the glittering lake, offer viewers more than just a visual delight; they convey a sense of the town as an outpost, a world apart, reachable only by traversing the lake (which, like the bridge in *The Signal Tower*, is a means of both access and escape). The portrayal of the small town as both comforting and claustrophobic also looks back to *The Signal Tower* and *Butterfly* and anticipates *National Velvet*, *The Yearling*, and *Intruder in the Dust*.[12]

If the landscape of the film is invested with meaning, so too are the interiors, which fulfill a specific purpose. The domestic space is simple and "authentic," yet it imparts symbolic intent. Like Sally's building of a nest, which is then violated by Joe, in *The Signal Tower*, here it is Mary who transforms their simple house, filling it with reminders of her history and their shared values (in this regard, Brown's construction of domestic space is very similar to John Ford's in *Drums along the Mohawk* and *The Quiet Man*). In *Of Human Hearts*, Jason's loss of his moral code is indicated by the unrelenting pressure he puts on his parents to sell off all their "old things" to fund his education: a watch belonging to his grandfather; a hatbox his father gave to his mother when they were courting; a set of silver spoons passed down through the generations; and, most devastating of all, when there's nothing left to sell, his mother's wedding ring. The original title of the film—*Benefits Forgot*—is perhaps more fitting in describing how the simple, uncompromising childhood that Jason so vehemently rejects and resents is, in the end, all that really matters. MGM has often been criticized for the mawkish sentimentality of much of its output in the 1930s and 1940s, but it would be a mistake to assume this film mines the same vein. Instead of being "merely" sentimental, *Of Human*

Hearts is better viewed as an exploration of sentiment, of the emotions that drive us and the associations that define us. As John Baxter has noted, Brown is at his best when he explores the lives of "simple folk" against a distinctive yet instantly recognizable backdrop (be it a small-town or rural locale). As Baxter suggests, it is Brown's feel for landscape and for the people who inhabit it that aligns him with a distinguished tradition in American cinema that is best exemplified by the work of D. W. Griffith, Henry King (*Tol'able David*), Frank Borzage (*Seventh Heaven*), King Vidor (*The Jack Knife Man*), and John Ford (*Steamboat around the Bend*). Brown's "films of American life, and especially his celebrations of the nation's rural values," Baxter argues, are his true legacy, and they rank "among the most beautiful and true things ever put on film."[13]

Baxter concludes his analysis by offering a fascinating parallel between *Of Human Hearts* and its director: "Brown was the embodiment of canny C19th rural America. His films reflect a passionate but controlled response to people and places; his suspicion and foresight which have made him today a rich man show themselves in his work. Like Whitman, he hears America singing; but he does not sing himself." Baxter's observation implicitly acknowledges Brown's deftness at playing the game of being a studio director, but it also hints at a certain self-effacement that Jean Renoir, one of his admirers, also noted when he joked, "As a matter of fact, I think more of Brown than Brown does of himself." Like Renoir's own work, it is Brown's personal films, rooted in a distinctive landscape, that are most compelling in their revelation of the complexities of human nature and emotions.[14]

22

Foreign Affairs

Idiot's Delight and *The Rains Came*

Soon after he returned from Lake Arrowhead, Brown found himself back in the producer-led world of Hollywood filmmaking, lined up to direct another prestige film that was a far cry from the intimate dramas he hoped to make. In an interview published around that time, he seemed pragmatic about how the system worked: "Twenty five years of comparative success have not enabled me to do just what I want to do, I must still bow to the opinions of the men above me . . . so I do the best job I can of whatever I am asked to do." This time around, "the men above" wanted him to tackle the film adaptation of Robert Sherwood's controversial and topical play *Idiot's Delight*.[1]

When the play premiered on the Washington stage in March 1936, its political content and allusions to the tensions brewing in Europe ensured that it garnered considerable publicity, and its author won a Pulitzer Prize. For some critics and audiences, however, the chief draw was the star team of Alfred Lunt and Lynn Fontanne. A number of studios expressed an interest in buying the film rights, including Pioneer Pictures, RKO, and Warner, but their enthusiasm waned when the PCA declared that the play's "anti war propaganda" made it unsuitable for motion picture adaptation. The censors expressed particular reservations about Sherwood's references to communism, his generally pacifist message, and his suggestion of a sexual relationship between the two lead characters, Irene and Harry. Evidently, Warner decided it wasn't worth the trouble and bowed out, followed by the other interested parties. That left only MGM in the field.[2]

As the studio moved forward with production in 1937, it discovered that Will Hays had instructed Joseph Breen to "keep your eyes on the production if and when it occurs because it is full of dynamite." The project was also under scrutiny from abroad: the British and Italians didn't care for the political content in general, and the latter were especially offended by the Italian setting and Sherwood's explicit references to the aggressive policies of Mussolini. Breen had the difficult task of mediating between MGM and both parties throughout 1937–1938. The Italians, represented by consul R. Caracciolo, were fundamentally opposed to any screen version and warned that if MGM proceeded with references to Italy extant, it would have difficulty getting *any* of its films released in Italy. Hunt Stromberg indicated the studio's willingness to make a few concessions, including substituting a fictional country for Italy, but he ruled out some of Caracciolo's more ambitious demands, such as dropping the title and excising Sherwood's name. As he pointed out, MGM had paid a sizable sum for the rights to the play and the use of Sherwood's name, and it was unrealistic to expect the studio to "discard it in its entirety." However, he assured Breen and Caracciolo that the film would emphasize romantic over political elements and that prints released in Italy would be amended. On the matter of the play's pacifist message, he maintained, "there is no doubt that an argument against war will prevail in this underlying treatment of theme," but he pointed out that it would be expressed in the film by "private individuals with no governmental connections whatsoever and by characters of American and English nationality, definitely not Italian."[3]

In a bid to retain credibility, MGM hired Sherwood, for a fee of $135,000, to bowdlerize the play. Brown recalled working with him at the Calabasas ranch for three or four weeks, where they concentrated on opening up the action and excising the explicit political content. A prologue was added, introducing the character of Harry, an entertainer who returns from World War I and, during an engagement at a run-down theater in Omaha, has a one-night stand with dancer-acrobat Irene. The prologue ends as the two part ways. The action picks up many years later in a location somewhere in central Europe— definitely *not* Italy—where Harry, along with his dance troupe "Les Blondes," is stranded at a luxury ski resort, unable to leave because of the impending war. As they sit it out, they are joined by a motley array of travelers, including munitions magnate Achille Weber (Edward Arnold) and his glamorous Russian companion, Irene. Harry suspects that the flamboyant diva is actually the same little Irene he knew in Omaha, and only at the end of the film, as bombs rain down, does she confirm her identity.[4]

Given the troubles the production encountered even before the cameras rolled, it's no surprise that MGM considered postponing it altogether. As late as September 1938, it was being reported that Brown might direct *The Women* instead, but by the following month the studio had decided to forge ahead, submitting a revised script to Breen. With much of the political content now excised and a nonspecific European country substituted for Italy, MGM tried to stoke up interest by declaring that this would be the first film to showcase the universal language of Esperanto (as it turned out, that didn't happen). Breen's reaction to the amendments was cautious: he still had a few qualms about dialogue that might offend British audiences (words such as "bum," "lousy," and "punk"), and he was dismayed by the insinuation that Harry and Irene enjoyed a one-night stand in Omaha. He also advised MGM to make everyone's lives easier by deleting specific references to Germans and Austrians and eliminating the Salvation Army song "Onward Christian Soldiers" for the British release (the studio complied and opted for "Abide with Me"). MGM didn't implement all of Breen's suggestions; for instance, the fragility of democracy in the face of totalitarianism is still expressed by the character Quillery (Burgess Meredith), though he is muted from the avowed communist of Sherwood's play. Nevertheless, by the time Brown was assigned to direct it, few could deny that it was already a compromised production.

Shooting began in late October, mainly on the back lot, but with some exteriors shot at Brown's ranch. The content may have been insipid, but MGM spared no expense, lavishing resources and assigning the most distinguished actors. Clark Gable and Norma Shearer took the leads; they were supported by Brown favorites Charles Coburn, Edward Arnold, and Joseph Schildkraut. From the theater came Burgess Meredith, Laura Hope Crews (playing a phony clairvoyant, Madame Zuleika, who appears in one of the film's most amusing scenes), and former vaudevillian Skeets Gallagher. Intriguingly, Brown cast Barbara Bedford in a tiny and uncredited role as a nurse. Brown was delighted to be working with Gable again (this was their seventh collaboration), but he was less thrilled to be back with Shearer, who was once again accused of stealing the role from Joan Crawford. Crawford later admitted that she "cried buckets" when she heard that Mayer had blocked her from the role, but she perked up when she saw the finished film and gleefully crowed that Shearer "simply couldn't bring it off—no chemistry with Gable." Brown was dismissive of Shearer when he looked back at the film in the 1960s. As they were filming it, however, the two kept up appearances, even though both harbored doubts. Although she had pursued the role, Shearer apparently questioned the wisdom of putting herself in the shadow of the mighty Lynn Fontanne. In interviews on the set, she was quick to credit Fontanne as an influence, but she also claimed she intended to make the part her own, mainly by emphasizing its comedic aspects: "Most of the characters I have played [up to that point] have been sincere," Shearer gushed to journalist Harrison Carroll. The interviewer noted Brown's rather muted indifference on the set, observing that the director was "sitting back" as William Daniels called for another take. In his biography of the actress, Gavin Lambert calls Shearer's performance in *Idiot's Delight* one of the best of her career and maintains that it was largely self-directed because Brown oversaw "the picture like an undertaker." Certainly, Brown's interest seemed to be focused on the minor details, such as wardrobe (he requested that Gable's "Fifth Avenue" suit be replaced by a cheap off-the-rack model).[5]

As the filming ground on and enthusiasm dwindled, even the trade press began to take notice: "all publicity about *Idiot's Delight* has mysteriously ceased. It's quietly understood there's to be no campaign on the Gable-Shearer picture until after the previews." When journalists were finally presented with a rough cut in December, an air of gloom surrounded the film's prospects and the likely impact on Brown's career: "since so many restrictions were placed on this production by foreign governments, the wolves have smugly predicted that at last Brown's unblemished record for success had reached its limit." It was clear that the five-week shoot had yielded a mixed bag: Brown had directed the prologue with some energy, and it worked well to expand the play and satisfy Gable and Shearer fans, but thereafter all momentum was lost, and Brown's direction became markedly pedestrian.[6]

A few retakes in January didn't lead to any significant improvement, so it was with some trepidation that MGM released *Idiot's Delight* the following month. Reviewers on the West Coast seemed sympathetic about the compromises the studio had been forced to make, but even *Variety* commented that the film seemed "off kilter." Other critics were blunt. Nelson Bell of the *Washington Post*, while acknowledging that the film had "undergone a considerable amount of plastic surgery," did little to hide his irritation and disappointment with Shearer. Her interpretation of the role, he grumbled, had "taken on an artificiality and a vague sort of falsity that are betrayed by cheap theatrical tricks that seem a trifle below the highest fulfillment of Miss Shearer's brilliant talents." Predictably, the *New Republic's* Otis Ferguson was disgusted by the excision of all the political content, concluding that the film was "no more anti-war than a few squads of well-meaning and offended citizens, pelting a nasty old caterpillar tank with chocolate éclairs." Graham Greene was his usual opinionated self when he savaged the film's air of "heavy saturated ennui" and Sherwood's talents, which he dismissed as distinguished by "a moral pretentiousness, a kind of cellophaned intellectuality." Shearer, too, left him cold: "too powerful a personality. Over-acting could hardly go further" (though that had been the point of the role). Greene's disgruntlement at having to spend his "morning in the dark" watching *Idiot's Delight* was alleviated only by the few moments of enjoyment he derived from the film accompanying this grand production—a Disney short concerning "the adventures of Pluto with a rubber seahorse, coy, flippant and aerated."[7]

Ironically, MGM went all out to placate both American censors and foreign nations, with little tangible gain: by the time *Idiot's Delight* was released in Europe, most had accepted the inevitability of war, and the film seemed simultaneously naïve and threatening. French consul Raoul Duval had expressed concern about how his country would be represented, and the film's release was delayed in France due to "current events." Estonia, Spain, Portugal, and Switzerland rejected it on political grounds; Italy, which MGM and Breen had tried so hard to please, didn't even give the film a general release. MGM went to the trouble of shooting a more sober ending for the British release, only to discover that cinema owners there simply cut out the scenes with air-raid sirens, for fear they would frighten audiences.[8]

For his part, Brown largely erased the film from his memory, rarely giving it much attention in later interviews. Nevertheless, it is interesting to speculate on what the politically conservative Brown, and an early admirer of Mussolini, made of Sherwood's liberal play. The *New York Times* carried an intriguing piece in July 1938, as *Idiot's Delight* was being prepared for production. Pointing out that MGM planned to produce a "plea for peace" rather than a lampoon of dictatorship, it reported that Brown was doing research in Europe and even consulting with the Italian leader himself, whose philosophy was that "all things are attained by war." Back in 1936, Mussolini had expressed his admiration for Brown and had even offered him a leading role in the Italian film industry. Now, Mussolini was warning Brown that "no film will be tolerated which will undermine" his belligerent approach to European politics. By October, after political pressure and censorship concerns had radically transformed the play, and Mussolini's plans for a fascist Europe had become apparent to all, Brown was hastily doing damage control, quashing rumors that he and Il Duce had ever consulted on a script for *Idiot's Delight*. In an effort to prove his patriotism, Brown expressed his willingness to lend his experience as a pilot and as a director to the air force, backing it up with a generous donation to fund four scholarships for new recruits.[9]

Idiot's Delight hadn't been much of a delight, but Brown's next production proved more rewarding. Inspired by Ohio-born author Louis Bromfield's travels in India in 1932, *The Rains Came* started life as "Bitter Lotus," a serialization published in *Cosmopolitan* in December 1936. Its success led Bromfield to expand the story to novel length, retitle it *The Rains Came*, and publish it with Harper in June 1937. A spectacular earthquake and flood provide the backdrop to this story of the lives of English colonists, American missionaries, and Indian rulers in India, and its exotic setting, evocative prose, and portrayal of miscegenation created quite a stir. Hollywood was quick to take note. David O. Selznick toyed with the idea of buying the rights in 1937 but was put off by the PCA, which warned that the novel's risqué aspects and especially its critique of British rule in India made it too contentious to bring to the screen. Selznick moved on to other projects (namely, *Gone with the Wind*), leaving Darryl F. Zanuck, head of Twentieth Century–Fox, to swoop in and purchase the rights for $52,000 in March 1938.[10]

Zanuck assigned Philip Dunne and Julien Josephson to write the adaptation. Despite the potential difficulties, the duo urged their boss to let them shape a script in which Indians appeared not "as exotic Easterners, nor as an inferior race, but as human beings, the friends and equals of the Europeans in the story." The key theme, they suggested, should be "India and the struggle of its people for regeneration and deliverance from the darkness and superstitions of the past." In this clash between the forces of tradition and modernity, English aristocrat Lord Esketh would symbolize the "evils of British profiteering in India," while the progressive Indian doctor Major Safti would represent the face of the new India. Dunne and Josephson even suggested the addition of a foreword, dedicating the film to "progressive Indians." Zanuck was sympathetic, but as he negotiated with the PCA, it became clear that the India Office in Britain was already monitoring developments. Although it couldn't block the entire project, it could make specific requests that any "offensive" British characters be toned down and that the studio "avoid in dialogue or action any aspersions or reflections on Indian government by the British." Zanuck's willingness to comply was prompted less by any particular sympathy for Britain's rule in India than by business concerns: it would be disastrous if the film failed to secure a release in the still vast territories of the British Empire. Similarly, the writers' eagerness to incorporate a progressive message reflected both personal conviction and a general shift toward more nuanced representations of India and its peoples in Hollywood films of the late 1930s.[11]

Dunne and Josephson worked throughout the summer of 1938, with Zanuck as their guiding force. He could be overbearing and crude, but none could dispute that he was a dynamic producer, one of the few who truly appreciated creative talent (after all, he had started his career as a writer at Warner). Dunne remembered Zanuck as a "great creative executive: intelligent, decisive, totally in support of his subordinates." An example of his hands-on approach can be seen in the detailed notes Zanuck made on various drafts of the script: in annotations on the July 15 draft, he reiterated that political elements must be toned down and suggested a shift in focus toward the expatriates. In October he proffered advice on how the set should look and how one character's racism might be subtly conveyed, as well as how the writers might make Safti a "much more vital and human person" (by introducing humor). As might be expected, Zanuck was much more interested in conjuring an atmosphere of romance and exoticism, and wowing audiences with the groundbreaking special effects used to create the earthquake and flood, than in using the film to convey political insight.[12]

Zanuck spent months mulling over possible casting choices, consulting a list that included Hedy Lamarr, Marlene Dietrich, Tallulah Bankhead, and Rosalind Russell for the role of Lady Edwina Esketh; Reginald Owen for Lord Esketh; Ronald Colman for Tom Ransome; and Phyllis Brooks for Fern. As it turned out, when the film was released the following year, only one of his original choices, Maria Ouspenskaya as the Maharani, was included. Zanuck didn't give any serious thought to casting an Indian actor in the role of Safti, but he did consider a number of foreign-born actors such as Charles Boyer and Ramon Novarro before opting for Tyrone Power, then on the brink of huge box-office success. The selection of Power was a canny commercial decision, but it also neutralized any concerns about miscegenation—Power had dark and smoldering good looks, but he was also "reassuringly" white. The casting of his romantic interest, Lady Esketh, proved more contentious. Myrna Loy was identified as a possibility, but Zanuck seemed unsure; even when she was selected, there was a delay because she was under contract to MGM. Another loan, this time from Warner, brought Irish-born George Brent to play Ransome, a dissolute aristocrat and supporter of the British Empire (somewhat ironic, given the actor's alleged ties with Irish Republicanism). Rounding out the cast were character actors Nigel Bruce, who usually specialized in eccentric and bumbling characters but here took the role of a nasty bigot and cuckold, Lord Esketh; Jane Darwell; Henry Travers; H. B. Warner; Laura Hope Crews; and Joseph Schildkraut. For the part of the rebellious, "Lolita-like" Fern, who is hopelessly in love with Ransome, the studio selected newcomer Brenda Joyce, a UCLA coed. *Life* magazine reported that she had been cast after a lengthy star search, but a number of publicity sources suggest that she was discovered by the director.[13]

Zanuck had no shortage of superb directors on the lot (including John Ford, Henry Hathaway, Fritz Lang, and Henry King), but he opted for an outsider: Clarence Brown. His reasons aren't entirely clear, although it's safe to say that he admired some of Brown's work and probably anticipated that his name would lend prestige to the production. According to Brown, he got the job chiefly because Loy specifically requested him. But Loy maintained that Zanuck was intent on securing Brown and accepted her only as part of a package. The most likely explanation is that both loans were part of a bigger deal involving the transfer of talent between the two studios (around the same time, Zanuck also borrowed Spencer Tracy from MGM to make *Stanley and Livingstone*). There is no indication that Brown was foisted on Zanuck or that Brown manipulated Loy into demanding him so he could escape from MGM. In fact, Brown later revealed that he had been reluctant to meet with Zanuck and did so only as a favor to Irving Thalberg—although in this case his memory was certainly faulty, given that Thalberg had died before Bromfield's novel was published. The initial encounter between Zanuck and Brown was rather odd. Stopping by the Twentieth Century–Fox lot, Brown discovered Zanuck practicing his golf swing and, to put him off, blurted out his reservations: "I understand you are a son of a bitch to work for." Then Zanuck "really started swinging his golf club. After a while, he cooled off. 'Mr. Brown,' he said, 'if you make this picture, you'll reserve that statement until after the picture.'" Persuaded by the producer's confidence and by the generous offer of $100,000 for twenty weeks of work and an additional 3 percent for each week thereafter, Brown signed up in April 1939.[14]

The trio of Brown, Dunne, and Josephson developed a productive collaboration, both professionally and personally. Dunne was already an admirer of Brown, having been impressed by *Flesh and the Devil* back in his Harvard days. He found Brown to be a demanding perfectionist, yet also a respecter of and contributor to the script. Brown spent several weeks with Dunne and Josephson "exploring every nook and cranny" and making suggestions that "helped the script enormously." This collaboration continued in script conferences with Zanuck, as Brown came up with "bits of business," visual additions, and shifts in emphases in the delivery of certain speeches. The liberal Dunne also developed an unlikely friendship with the politically conservative Brown, one that impacted the course of Dunne's personal life: he met his future wife, Amanda Duff, at a barbecue at the Calabasas ranch. Later, when the pair decided to marry, Brown flew them to Virginia City, Nevada, and served as best man at the ceremony.[15]

Time for friendship was limited as pace picked up on the production. By mid-April, everything was in place, and filming commenced on the back lot and on location in Balboa Park (standing in for India). Having just extricated himself from a film that was "tired" before it even began, Brown was relieved that this new production was much more involving. Later, as he looked back over his experiences as a contract director, he singled out Twentieth Century–Fox, not MGM, as the studio that made him feel most appreciated: "at Metro I got what I wanted but I had to fight for it . . . at Fox, I didn't have to fight, just ask." And even though he was personally close to Mayer, he confessed that Zanuck, for all his ego and volatility, was actually the more supportive boss. Zanuck saw to it that Brown "had the run of the studio," including the use of "Shirley Temple's six room bungalow" (one assumes he wasn't sharing it with her). Brown also believed that Fred Sersen's technical department was far superior to MGM's, and his confidence was borne out when the spectacular earthquake and biblical flood helped win *The Rains Came* the first Academy Award for special effects (quite a coup in the year of *The Wizard of Oz*).[16]

It was the security of knowing that his demands would be met and his concerns listened to that helped Brown overcome his first hurdle on the set. He had been assigned veteran cinematographer Bert Glennon, who had been working in movies since the 1910s and had teamed with many of the industry's best, including Ford, DeMille, Walsh, and von Sternberg. Accomplished and talented as Glennon was, after three days of shooting Brown became convinced he wasn't the right man for the job. He later explained that the cinematographer favored a lighting style that was "too shadowy and soft," whereas he preferred something sharper and more pristine for this film. Glennon didn't take the criticism well and walked off the set. Zanuck circulated the story that illness had required Glennon to withdraw, but he was actually moved to Ford's *Drums along the Mohawk*, for which he won an Oscar. Glennon's replacement was Arthur Miller, one of the studio's top cinematographers, whose style was noted for its jewel-like clarity. With Brown, Miller developed a lighting schema to "make the whole thing . . . shine."[17]

One of Miller's first tasks was to shoot some color tests of Loy. He had worked with the actress before but had forgotten her little quirks about how she wanted to be filmed. She was convinced that she photographed better when a red gelatin filter was used to light her in close-ups. Neither Brown nor Miller thought it made much difference, but Brown ordered two tests—one with a filter and one without. Later, when everyone gathered to view the results, Brown made a speech in which he noted the negligible "difference in the quality of the eyes with the red gelatin on the light or without." Miller suspected the whole exercise was less an effort to assuage Loy's concerns and more a demonstration of Brown's authority on the set and, importantly, his technical know-how. Miller also learned an interesting lesson: "In reality, the red gelatin on the matchbox or eye light . . . lost its effectiveness in photographing blue eyes because of the brightness of the key and filler lights necessary. I continued using the matchbox to produce a catch light in the eyes when shooting close-ups but dispensed with the red gelatin from that day on."[18]

Each day brought fresh challenges and complications, often because of the host of special effects used in several sequences. Many of these were overseen by Sersen, but Miller recalled that he and Brown devoted hours to developing and finessing the striking effect whereby their lighting added a "glow" to "suggest a spiritual, transcendent quality" (used most effectively in the death scene of the Maharajah, played by H. B. Warner) or the storm scene in which they placed a sun arc behind a window to "enhance the shadows and contrasts." Over his long career, Miller turned in some astonishing work, but he identified *The Rains Came* as one of his personal highlights: "I guess in that picture I really 'got' my style of having shadows hard and very bright highlights indeed."[19]

The Rains Came turned out to be a highlight for Brown, too. He was doing what he loved best—immersing himself in the technical side of filmmaking with an inspiring cinematographer—and he was working with an enthusiastic and cooperative cast. In Loy's case, her cooperation was based in part on her sincere gratitude to Brown, who had defended her in the face of Zanuck's hostility. Even though the producer had had the final say over her casting, she had the niggling feeling he wasn't completely convinced that she was right for the role. When he saw the first rushes, she recalled, he "started in on me. Questioning my interpretation, but never being specific, he offered no constructive alternatives. That's a terrible thing to do to an actress." She turned to Brown, who was quick to dismiss his boss's criticism with a terse, "Forget it. Don't let him upset you." Thereafter he did everything he could to bolster Loy's confidence and reassure her that her portrayal of Lady Esketh was pitch perfect. With Brown's precise direction and unstinting encouragement, Loy turned in a performance that brilliantly captures her character's evolution from a brittle, careless socialite who regards India as just another playground to a vulnerable, complex woman transformed by romantic love and by a profound spiritual epiphany.[20]

Loy will forever be identified with the role she made her own—Nora Charles in the *Thin Man* series—but in *The Rains Came* she had the chance to play a character that is far less likable. When Zanuck first floated the idea of making a film version of Bromfield's novel, Breen had been most worried about the character of Lady Edwina Esketh. While Dunne and Josephson's script certainly made an effort to placate Breen's office, there remained plenty of scope for the suggestion of moral ambiguity. In one memorable early sequence, Lady Esketh's amoral outlook is hinted at when she initiates a casual yet passionate tryst with old flame Ransome. Though she is driven by hot passion, her management of their encounter is coolly efficient, and she succeeds in regaining her composure almost instantly when confronted by her jealous husband and the suspicious Maharani. Moments later, the still (sexually) frustrated Lady Esketh casts Ransome aside when she catches a glimpse of the "copper Apollo" Safti and resolves to make him hers. The expressionistic shadows and the exotic setting contribute to the sensual mood, and Loy's appraising gaze of desire conveys Lady Esketh's sexual voraciousness, with no need for dialogue.

Having worked with him on three previous occasions, Loy knew Brown "had a deft hand," but she was impressed by his willingness to let her push the boundaries. The results of this productive and imaginative collaboration can be seen in several scenes. In one that takes place late in the film, Edwina seems to be well on the path to moral redemption. Having fallen from lust into love with Safti, she has given up everything to help Ranchipur recover from the earthquake and floods. When the region is overcome by a cholera epidemic, Edwina abandons her life of meaningless luxury and becomes a nurse at the local hospital. The scene opens with her in the role of angel of mercy, tending to patients, giving them water, fanning them, and resting her cool hand on their fevered brows. Brown's camera remains at a distance during this long take, and we observe Edwina moving from background to foreground, slumping into a chair for a short break, and reaching for a glass of water. Sharp viewers will have noticed that she drinks from the same tumbler as a dying woman, but only after almost three minutes of largely wordless action does Edwina realize that, with a glass of water, she has sealed her fate. Only then does Brown's coolly observational camera work give way to a more directive (and scarcely required) fast track-in to the empty space where the contaminated glass should have been placed, followed by a dolly-in to a shot of the same glass from which she has just drunk. Moments like these demonstrate not only Loy's talent as an actress but also Brown's effective use of a long take and observational camera.

Striking, too, is the handling of Edwina's death scene. In her memoirs, Loy recalls that a suggestion from Brown made her rethink how she would "die." More conventional treatments would have had the victim slowly closing her eyes and perhaps exhaling one last breath before peacefully slipping away, but Brown urged her to approach it differently, pointing out that "people don't die with their eyes closed. . . . Why don't you try dying with your eyes open. You've just got to hold your breath." Loy complied: "I held my breath, staring at some fixed object until I began to see stars, and everything started to blur and run together. I was turning a little blue when he finally called 'Cut!' When you trust a director, you'll do anything for him."[21]

The Rains Came is one of the more accomplished films of Brown's decidedly mixed sound career, but not because it demonstrates a newfound ease with sound or dialogue. Instead, its chief merits are his use of the observational camera, atmospheric lighting, and symbolism—techniques he had developed in the silent era. Many of the most striking sequences owe a debt to his own catalog of work. The erotic encounter between Edwina and Ransome, which takes place in a lush garden where velvety shadows, latticed silhouettes, and a shared cigarette enhance the mood of intoxication and forbidden desire, recalls Felicitas and Leo's tryst in *Flesh and the Devil*. The play of dappled light on Edwina's face as she and Safti listen to a beautiful Hindi love song references moments of dreamy romanticism in both *Butterfly* and *Ah Wilderness!* And, as it is in those films, romantic love is fleeting and ultimately doomed.

Filming wrapped up in late June (with some retakes completed in July), and Zanuck readied *The Rains Came* for a September release. Though there was a wealth of strong acting on display, he was chiefly interested in using the film to promote Tyrone Power, the one actor whose performance had been something of a dud. Certainly, Power's physical beauty meant that he could pass as a "copper Apollo"—despite a rather distracting and alarmingly inconsistent mustache—but he was clearly ill at ease in the role and was stilted as Safti. More convincing, and with a more credible mustache, was George Brent, whose humorous turn as the self-deprecating Ransome showed just how engaging he could be when he was interested (which he rarely seemed to be for Warner, his home studio). Some reviewers picked up on Power's awkwardness and expressed reservations about the glossy tenor of the production. James Crow called *The Rains Came* a "typical Darryl Zanuck creation. It bears the Zanuck stamp in its use of panoramically picturized natural disaster. It bears the Zanuck stamp also in the assignment to the leading role of Tyrone Power, whom Zanuck herein calls upon again to play a role far beyond his normal capabilities." But Crow felt that Brown had done a reasonable job, turning in a "photoplay [that] remains . . . strong and convincing." Frank Nugent adopted a rather disgruntled tone in his review, betraying his dismay at the unacceptable cuts to Bromfield's novel and the changes made to the characters to suit established stars. Loy's performance, he complained, suggested "the hapless struggle of an actress who can't help being 'sympathetic,'" while Power had "all the depth of a coat of skin-dye." Mary Harris, writing in the *Washington Post*, was a little more sympathetic to the two leads but maintained that both had been miscast, with Loy "not so much a siren as an elegant piece of deliberate wickedness," and Power simply "too handsome." Only Graham Greene, who viewed the film under its British title, *Rains over India*, seemed to understand the challenges of screen adaptations; in his opinion, Brown had managed, through his "vivid camera," to transform a novel of "dim characterization" and "flat prose."[22]

In India, Fox publicized the film as a sympathetic and authentic representation of the subcontinent (even though it hadn't been shot there). Understandably, Indian nationalists were not convinced, seeing it as merely another variation on the imperialist discourse and finding its admiration for Indian princes misplaced. Those who sought authentic depictions of India and its peoples were best advised to look elsewhere, because *The Rains Came* offered nothing more than a slice of exotica designed to showcase beautiful stars and immerse viewers in a sumptuous spectacle that allowed them to escape their everyday woes. Even though Dunne and Josephson tried to offer some criticism of the dismissive, bigoted attitude of British and American expatriates, their unconscious prejudices shone through in their reiteration of the clichéd notion that behind the mask of Western education, the timeless and "primitive" face of India still lurks (most clearly expressed in the character of the educated Indian Banerjee, who "reverts" to irrational type when faced with the catastrophe).[23]

Despite the somewhat mixed response, Brown continued to be proud of *The Rains Came* and was impressed by what Twentieth Century–Fox had to offer. Zanuck may have hoped to secure Brown on a more permanent basis, and it was rumored that he was considering Brown for one of his newly acquired properties: John Steinbeck's *The Grapes of Wrath*. It was not to be, and Brown went back to MGM and negotiated a new contract that netted him $159,000 per week. The next twelve months saw him return to the fold and to a string of run-of-the-mill assignments.[24]

23

Inventions and Conventions

Edison the Man, Come Live with Me, and They Met in Bombay

Given his centrality in the invention of motion pictures, it wasn't surprising that Hollywood was keen to immortalize Thomas Alva Edison. Producer John Considine had long harbored ambitions to make a biopic of the "Wizard of Menlo Park," and in 1939 he set two hot young writers to the task. One was Dore Schary, who would accede to the throne of MGM following Mayer's deposing a few years later. The other was Hugo Butler, a talented writer who had worked on a number of family-friendly films during the 1930s (*A Christmas Carol, The Adventures of Huckleberry Finn*) but whose outspoken political views would damage his career when the House Un-American Activities Committee came to town in the late 1940s. The pair conducted extensive research that included trips to Henry Ford's Dearborn, Michigan, museum, where Edison's Menlo Park laboratory had been reproduced, and consultation with Edison's widow and son. They obtained a somewhat "mummified" official version of Edison's complicated life, and it became obvious to Considine that it might be difficult to bring such a revered figure to the screen, especially in a fashion that would be appeal to contemporary audiences. In fact, so much material had been gathered that he decided to split the project in two and cast Mickey Rooney as a young Edison in the first segment, the Norman Taurog–directed *Young Tom Edison*. Released in March 1940, it featured some additional work by Bradbury Foote, but Butler and Schary were given joint screenplay credit. According to his widow, Butler continued to work on the second installment, *Edison the Man*, although he was later denied official credit (instead, it went to Foote and Talbot Jennings).[1]

Considine figured that, as a former engineer, Brown would understand the forces that drove Edison. Brown was drawn to the subject matter, but he was also tempted by the caliber of the cast, which included a number of actors with whom he had recently worked (Gene Reynolds, Charles Coburn, Gene Lockhart, Arthur Aylesworth, and Henry Travers), as well as a few new faces (Lynne Overman and Rita Johnson). Without doubt, though, the chief attraction was the actor cast as Edison: Spencer Tracy. Their paths had crossed at MGM, but this would be Brown's first chance to direct Tracy. He was hopeful that it would be a rewarding experience, even though Tracy could be difficult. Brown had been assured that the actor was enthusiastic about the project and was already immersing himself in the role, making field trips to Dearborn to view the replica of the original lab, meeting with the Edison heirs in New Jersey, and viewing original 1920s footage of the inventor. The latter proved crucial because, although he was adamant that his performance would encapsulate "my idea of Edison," Tracy wanted to accurately capture the sound and cadence of Edison's speech (makeup artist Jack Dawn would take care of the visual transformation).[2]

Shooting took place in January and February 1940, amidst a flurry of publicity about Brown's attention to detail, especially in the "authentic" and "exciting" invention scenes. MGM's promotion capitalized on his engineering background, spinning stories that Brown had caught the "inventing bug" and was now investing time and energy into the construction of a "device . . . consisting of a small ultra-high frequency transmitter mounted on the top of a traffic light" that would warn drivers when they crossed the stop line. Brown may have dabbled in a few inventions, but they ultimately came to nothing. In any case, he was busy ensuring that the film would not be overly reliant on endless dialogue and speeches: "In *Edison* there is perhaps half a reel during the climactic sequence in which hardly a word is spoken. The sequence during the 40 hours test of electric light bulb I tried to relate entirely in pictorial terms." One of the cast members, Gene Reynolds, recalled that Brown actually "wasn't too tickled" by the project, but he maintained an air of professionalism and diligence that was broken only once when he lost his temper with a supporting player who was "mugging" to the camera. On another occasion, he had to temporarily suspend shooting to accommodate a visit to the set by Secretary of Labor Frances Perkins.[3]

It seems that Brown and Tracy had a harmonious relationship, especially when both acknowledged that Tracy would be allowed his own time and space to sculpt his performance. The production wrapped up on schedule in late March, and the release was slated for early summer. Butler and Schary had included a "timely" scene in which Edison delivers a final speech (to a 1929 audience) about the need for cooperation and balance among nations in this "troubled world," and when *Variety* reviewed the film in May 1940, it commended MGM for providing the public with an "inspirational antidote for the depressions of the day." In general, reviews were more respectful than enthusiastic, with many focusing on Tracy's handling of the role. Bosley Crowther was impressed that Tracy had "imbued the role with human and vital substantiality," but he had some reservations about the film: "When Metro deliberately distorts certain important details in Edison's career and boldly invents others—evidently done with the sanction of his family—the question arises as to whether this creation is intended to be a reliable portrait of the great inventor or just another fellow who looks something like him." Nor was he convinced by the screenwriters' "sort of obvious" attempts to transform the real Edison, who was often volatile and tyrannical, into an appealing, all-American guy who loves his mother and apple pie. Crowther described Brown's direction as "smooth and workmanlike"—an apt observation, given that he executed the material in a competent though self-effacing fashion. This style, which can also be detected in some of his work with Garbo, might be attributable to a desire not to "distract" from a great performance. Although Tracy's performance is undoubtedly good—and reportedly he was proud of his interpretation of Edison—the more memorable moments are those in which the character actors (Overman, Travers, and Bressart) are allowed to steal a scene and in which Brown's skills as an editor find expression in a series of visually pleasing montages.[4]

Perhaps the most puzzling aspect of MGM's retelling of Edison's life is the almost complete absence of any reference to his role in the invention of cinema. This "oversight" might have been related to an unwillingness to add fuel to the existing controversy over the extent of Edison's personal involvement in some of the inventions for which he took credit. However, this wasn't the omission picked up by the daughter of one of Edison's assistants: Julia C. Lieb wrote personally to Brown to express her dissatisfaction about a scene in which Edison is shown flicking the switch that gave New York City its first electricity. Lieb was offended that no actor had been cast as her father (who had apparently been with Edison that night) and that MGM hadn't bothered to consult with her or with any of the members of the "Edison Pioneers Association." By the time he received her letter, Brown was already on to his next assignment and had little desire to engage with any of *Edison*'s critics.[5]

Reminiscing about his life and career, James Stewart recalled the moment when he realized that movies could affect people in simple yet profound ways. During a break on the set of Anthony Mann's *The Far Country* (1954), he was approached by an elderly man who wanted to know if he was indeed *the* James Stewart. His identity confirmed, the man blurted out his reason for approaching Stewart: "'You did a thing in a picture once. . . . Can't remember the name of it, but you were in a room and you said a poem or something about fireflies. That was good.'" Stewart recalled, "I knew right away what he meant. That's all he said. He was talking about a scene in the picture *Come Live with Me* that had come out before the war in 1941. He couldn't remember the title, wasn't even sure I was the same guy, but that little thing—didn't even last a minute—he'd remembered all those years. And that's what's so great about the movies."[6]

Come Live with Me began life as a story by Virginia Van Upp, a screenwriter and producer who would find fame for her work with Rita Hayworth (*Cover Girl, Gilda*). Van Upp drew heavily from the best of Hollywood's screwball comedies of the 1930s—La Cava's *My Man Godfrey*, Capra's *It Happened One Night*, even Brown's *Love on the Run*—and added a dash of Lubitsch to tell the tale of a Viennese refugee, Johnny (Hedy Lamarr), who picks up a down-on-his-luck writer, Bill (James Stewart), and enters into a marriage of convenience so that she can stay in America. Predictably, what is a business deal for her soon becomes true love for Bill, and he resolves to lure her away from her superficial life of dinners and dancing with her married lover, Barton Kendrick (Ian Hunter). His plan involves "kidnapping" her and taking her to his grandmother's house, where she can encounter "real" Americans and learn what brings true happiness. As expected, she slowly falls under the charm of both Bill and his grandmother.

Brown signed up for the project in the summer of 1940, and it was reported that he conducted research on the émigré story line by visiting refugee camps in Tijuana and Ensenada to witness firsthand the living conditions of those who had been displaced from their homes. However, any pretense of a serious engagement with contemporary events was soon forgotten as screenwriter Patterson McNutt honed in on the romance and comedy elements. By the end of September, McNutt's script was ready, and it was duly submitted to the PCA for approval. It was coolly received, and Breen expressed amazement that MGM expected him to pass a script in which the central character is clearly a "kept woman" involved in a "travesty of marriage." He directed that all references to "modern marriage" be eliminated and that McNutt redraft the character of Johnny as a woman who is intent on being financially independent. Evidently, McNutt's efforts were not enough. When Breen received the revised draft, he declared it "thoroughly unacceptable" and demanded cuts to a scene showing that Johnny and Bill share a bedroom, as well as a general "cleaning up" of what he viewed as innuendo-laden dialogue. He especially fretted about how several "troublesome" scenes would be handled, including one in which Bill, dressed in his pajamas and thwarted in his romantic plans, positions himself under a needlecraft sampler bearing the proverb: "If at first you don't succeed, try, try again." Breen also regarded a scene in which Johnny is shown switching a flashlight on and off—thereby suggesting some receptiveness to a sexual overture—as a sly circumvention of the production code.[7]

MGM couldn't wait for full approval and put the film on its production roster for an October 1940 start. Filming took place on the back lot, but Brown also got to shoot in various locales in the San Fernando Valley and at his Calabasas ranch (for the final scenes), where it was reported that he drew on his engineering skills to design "a cantilever bridge . . . [that would traverse] an arroyo which cuts his ranch in two." There were no major hitches or incidents to delay shooting, and Brown apparently enjoyed the experience, particularly because he was able to work with Stewart again and also with a rather unusual star in the making: septuagenarian Adeline de Walt Reynolds. She was making her screen debut as Bill's Grandma, and she had reportedly been cast after Brown spotted her performing in amateur theater. As she prepared for the role, Brown encouraged her to draw on her own life experience, and she was certainly not lacking in that respect: she was old enough to remember the Civil War; she had survived the San Francisco earthquake of 1906; she had raised four children single-handedly after her husband (a juggler) died; and to top it off, she had recently graduated with a BA from the University of California. *Come Live with Me* kick-started what was a surprisingly prolific screen career for the actress, who worked in thirty-six productions over the next three decades (she was still working at age ninety-seven!).[8]

Filming finished in late November, and there was more negotiation with the PCA before the film was finally previewed in February 1941. In many respects, *Come Live with Me* was a routine vehicle, offering audiences a dash of escapism and some gentle comedy, but Lamarr's casting also played on the public's knowledge of her Austrian background and her noted anti-Nazi sympathies, while her character's status as a vulnerable, displaced person "looking for home" reminded viewers of the contentious issue of America's duty to such people. *Come Live with Me* turned out to be Stewart's final production before he departed Culver City for US Army Air Corps training, adding to its significance.

And yet, despite all its coincidental timeliness, *Come Live with Me* probably could have been made in any decade of Brown's career. Its finest moments are those in which the American heartland and its stoic folk are quietly celebrated. Stewart's knowledge that his Hollywood career would soon be temporarily halted in service to the greater good probably influenced how he played his character. In contrast to his petulant Jason in Brown's *Of Human Hearts,* here he is wistful and sincere, and his scenes opposite Reynolds are distinguished by a genuine warmth and humor. There is some irony that Bill seems far more entranced by Grandma than he is by Johnny, played by the "most beautiful" Lamarr. There is minimal chemistry between the two leads, and as a romantic comedy, *Come Live with* Me doesn't quite work. Lamarr's performance was especially lambasted. Yet, in her defense, the stilted quality she brings to the role is reasonably effective in conveying her (somewhat clichéd) cultural difference: the formal Viennese sophisticate who soon crumbles in the face of the easy charm of the "regular" American.

If Lamarr struggled a little, so did Brown. In private life, he appreciated sophisticated parties and the charms of racy singers such as Nan Blakstone, and he wasn't averse to making the occasional ribald joke—he once observed that screenwriter Ouida Bergere was "a dame so stuck on herself she needed a velvet cushion to fart on"—but professionally, risqué comedy just wasn't his forte. Consequently, the screwball elements of Van Upp's story remain largely unrealized. What works better are those scenes that depict the burgeoning romance between Johnny and Bill (nurtured by Grandma and her homespun wisdom), as well as one delicately directed and movingly performed scene in which Diane Kendrick (Verree Teasdale) realizes that her "open" marriage to Barton may be threatened by one of his flirtations.[9]

When *Come Live with Me* was released in February, critics commended Reynolds's performance and noted how deftly MGM had circumvented the censors. For the *New York Times,* Theodore Strauss observed, "Mr. Brown has found one of the neatest tricks of the year [in the final scene] for evading and/or undermining the Hays office," but he complained that the pacing of this "sentimental little lark" was all wrong ("dog-trot . . . too stiff in the joints for a madcap antic"). Although Stewart's unnamed fan had been especially moved by the actor's recitation of a Christopher Marlowe poem, Strauss was indifferent: "its sentiment is oversoft. Perhaps the fault lies in the fact that both author and director have tried to weave some homely emotion and philosophy in a story which is adequate enough for farce but much too artificial for more pretentious treatment." Strauss's criticisms were repeated, albeit in less harsh tones, by several other reviewers, yet *Come Live with Me* struck a chord with audiences, as exhibitors reported positive responses among their patrons. Brown, too, was generally pleased with his modest production, even as he grew restless at MGM. As it turned out, his simmering discontent would be further fueled by his next assignment.[10]

Viennese-born writer John Kafka provided the story for Brown's next star vehicle, which was set to team Hedy Lamarr and Clark Gable for the third time. Somewhere along the way, however, Lamarr was transferred to a Robert Z. Leonard film (*Ziegfeld Girl*), and Rosalind Russell was drafted to play jewel thief Anya von Duren, who embarks on a love-hate relationship with fellow grafter Gerald (Gable). What starts as a caper evolves into an espionage plot that requires Gerald to set aside his personal interests and defend American interests.

It was far-fetched material, but more worrying was the fact that Brown never got to see a final script. It wasn't for lack of effort. Producer Hunt Stromberg had assigned a crack team of screenwriters that included Leon Gordon, Edwin Justus Mayer, and the legendary author of *Gentlemen Prefer Blondes*, Anita Loos, but it seems that none of them could figure out what kind of film they were writing. Loos's biographer records that she was hired—much to her bafflement—to "inject some topical references into the script" because Stromberg wasn't convinced that audiences in 1941 would respond to a movie that was "just a lark." Mayer was also a gifted comedy writer (he wrote Lubitsch's *To Be or Not to Be*), but his skills were not in evidence in what passed as a script. Instead, months of work yielded a hodgepodge that grafted political content onto a standard romantic comedy and caused only confusion for both cast and director. The normally easygoing Gable was worried even before shooting began and voiced his concerns at script conferences, where Loos bore the brunt of his criticisms (she retaliated by calling him a "studio-cured ham" and walking off the production).[11]

Brown later revealed that whatever unity there was on the set was based on a shared sense of dismay and a creeping fear that their efforts were being wasted on a preordained flop. He was frustrated that, in the absence of a complete script, he had to make it up as he went along, shooting the first reel of the film in four different ways in the hope that one might work. Even the simple matter of the title seemed impossible to pin down: initially it was *The Uniform*, then it was changed to *Unholy Partners* before *They Met in Bombay* was finally settled on. There were compensations for Brown, in the form of a lucrative salary and another chance to collaborate with Gable, who was now both a friend and a business associate. It was some relief, too, that nobody had far to travel: the exotic settings of India and Hong Kong were all reproduced on the back lot, with some additional filming done at Brown's ranch and around the Malibu hills.[12]

Even in the face of these problems, appearances had to be maintained, and trade journalists did their part. Reporting from the set in April, Harrison Carroll explained that MGM's latest comedy would be an important barometer of current cultural tensions, as long as audiences could keep up with the convolutions of the plot. These include a twist in which the two jewel thieves, who have been outwitting each other in their mutual quest to steal the "Star of Asia," are drawn into an international espionage drama when they hop on a slow boat to Hong Kong (captained by Peter Lorre with the usual "Oriental" makeup) in a bid to evade Scotland Yard. Implausibly, and for reasons not entirely clear, Gable's character masquerades as a soldier and becomes involved in the emergency evacuation of colonial settlers and native Chinese in the face of Japanese invaders. His actions prove his heroism, and the film ends with the two thieves setting aside their criminal pasts and looking to a brighter future.

There is little of interest in the silly plot of *They Met in Bombay*, but its portrayal of Japanese aggression turned out to be rather timely: Pearl Harbor was attacked just a few months after its release. In fact, even before Japan became the official enemy of the United States, this innocuous film managed to spark controversy. When audiences in Japan were treated to screenings, they responded with hostility, not because their country was portrayed as an aggressor but because of Korean American actor Philip Ahn, who played the part of a Japanese general. Before he was cast, Ahn had explained to Stromberg that he couldn't speak Japanese, but the producer had assured him that he could deliver his lines in Korean because no one would know the difference. Unfortunately for MGM, Japanese audiences instantly noticed and were incensed when a translator revealed that the dialogue had been most unflattering to their nation. MGM was forced to make hasty deletions to subsequent prints.[13]

Whether Brown took notice of the controversy is difficult to say, because once he completed filming in late April, he participated only minimally in the film's promotion. His embarrassment is understandable, as *They Met in Bombay* is hardly the best showcase of his skills. Despite having the talents of William Daniels at his disposal (the two even appeared in an MGM promotional film, *You Can't Fool a Camera*, to plug *They Met in Bombay*'s innovative camera work, including the use of a rotary camera crane), Brown shot most of the action in uninspired medium shots, only occasionally alleviated by some clumsily inserted close-ups of "important information." The few scenes that exhibit any imagination draw on his past catalog; for instance, the scenes on board the boat to China are filmed with a melancholic moodiness that recalls *Anna Christie*. *They Met in Bombay* may have paid the bills, but it did little to enhance Brown's career or those of Gable and Russell. The latter was reportedly so disgusted by the whole MGM experience that she refused any further loan-outs once she had completed her agreed trio of assignments for the studio. Brown couldn't even bring himself to attend a preview—"I hid so I didn't have to go"—and he was certainly bemused when Eddie Mannix told him the audience had loved "the lousiest picture I ever made." If audiences seemed to appreciate this slapdash effort, reviewers weren't so easily won over: Bosley Crowther dismissed it as a B movie masquerading as an A, while Nelson Bell observed it could be tolerated only if one overlooked the fact that it was hokum: "to those who can assimilate the indigestible inconsistency of the picture's developments . . . [it] . . . will not be too hard to take."[14]

Putting *They Met in Bombay* behind him, Brown took an extended working vacation, traveling first to New York to catch some plays before making his annual visit to Europe. Over the next twelve months, he went on a buying spree, purchasing the rights to a number of novels and plays, including J. H. Wallis's *Once Off Guard* (which he later sold to producer William Goetz, who released it as Fritz Lang's noir *The Woman in the Window* in 1943); *Cumberland*, a "novel of deepest Alabama"; and *Resin-Puss*, about an unsuccessful prizefighter. One purchase he had a more personal interest in was Baynard Kendrick's *Lights Out*, the story of a blind war veteran's adjustment to civilian life. Brown paid $10,000 for it but eventually decided against making it and sold it to Robert Montgomery (it was eventually produced as *Bright Victory* in 1951).[15]

Even though his recent career had seen its fair share of flops, profiles of Brown in the early 1940s accorded him the status of industry elder, a businessman of some importance in the Greater Los Angeles area. In addition to the literary properties he was buying in a bid to develop his producing career, he was expanding his real estate portfolio. By the mid-1940s, he owned prime lots in Beverly Hills, Calabasas, and Lake Arrowhead; he was also an investor in a new racetrack in Oakland. Horse racing was less of a passion for Brown than it was for Louis Mayer, but a shared interest in the sport certainly helped deepen the friendship between the two men. When Brown was not working, he spent much of his time at the Calabasas ranch, dabbling in the role of gentleman farmer and hosting weekend parties and the annual MGM Fourth of July barbecue. One profile describes him as "ruddy-cheeked, fifty years old, a little laconic and given to under rather than over-statement, but very purposeful," and it details his passion for experimenting with new methods of crop cultivation and animal husbandry, as well as his continued interest in tinkering with machinery.[16]

These profiles painted a picture of a contented man supported by a loving wife who, happily retired from acting, concerned herself with overseeing the smooth running of the household. But Gene Reynolds recalled that all was not as it seemed. Tensions between the couple had emerged back in the late 1930s, and by the early 1940s, they were pretty much living separate lives, albeit at the same address. Brown could escape his marital problems by burying himself in his work, and he often slept in his bungalow at the studio when he was in the middle of a shoot. But for Alice Joyce, who had been a star when Brown was "just" a car salesman, it must have been difficult to find a purpose. Even if she had wanted to make a comeback, there were precious few roles for older women in Hollywood. She had a few jobs in radio in the early 1940s, but as her daughters grew up and her husband kept his distance, she turned more and more to alcohol for comfort, much to Brown's disapproval. Her drinking was something of an open secret in Hollywood, though out of deference to her past stardom and Brown's current status, it was not revealed in the press. Few were surprised, however, when the couple announced their intention to divorce in 1945, listing 1942 as the start of their separation. There wasn't much surprise, either, when Brown wed his fourth wife, his longtime secretary Marian Spies, a few months after the divorce became final. Like Joyce's drinking, Brown's relationship with Spies was common knowledge, despite their discretion.

It is interesting that when Alice Joyce divorced Brown, her petition used much the same language as Ona's had seventeen years before. In it she complained that her husband had treated her in a "cool manner," and as a consequence she had "suffered humiliation and mental anguish and become extremely nervous and distressed." The split with Ona had been a bitter one, but this time around, Brown treated his ex-wife in a more compassionate manner. He always maintained that she was "a lady" and that the marriage had just run its course. When Joyce was seriously injured in a car accident in 1946, Brown was the first one at the hospital, assuring her that all her medical expenses would be taken care of and continuing to visit her as she slowly recovered. When she died in 1953, her liver damaged from years of heavy drinking, Brown paid her funeral expenses and erected a memorial stone in her honor.[17]

24

Representing the War Front at Home and Away

The Human Comedy and *The White Cliffs of Dover*

Unlike *They Met in Bombay*, which crudely grafted contemporary anxieties about an impending war onto a formulaic star vehicle, Brown's next two films were more considered and affecting engagements with the zeitgeist. In an early profile published in 1928, Jim Tully had called Brown a "shrewd" man who "knew his nation," and with both *The Human Comedy* and *The White Cliffs of Dover*, Brown certainly gauged Americans' attitudes well. Like many Hollywood productions of the time, both reflect a jingoistic sentiment and offer reiterations of rather than challenges to contemporary ideologies, but their commercial success suggests they profoundly moved audiences.[1]

The first, *The Human Comedy*, would become one of MGM's most successful wartime films, but it had a rocky start. It was drawn from Pulitzer Prize–winning author William Saroyan's exploration of American identity and immigrants' place in the melting pot. The story's self-conscious poeticism and the unabashed sentimentality with which Saroyan traced war's impact on one small-town family attracted the attention of Louis B. Mayer. With producer Arthur Freed serving as a go-between, Saroyan entered into what one account termed a "gentleman's agreement" with MGM in December 1941.[2]

Snaring Saroyan was a coup for Mayer, and he paid the author a generous fee of $60,000 to expand his story. After several months, he submitted a grossly overlong script—accounts vary from 900 pages to 240 pages—with the stipulation that only he could direct it. As news of Saroyan's demands leaked out, the reactions of the highly experienced directors on the MGM lot were predictably derisive. Composer David Diamond, who was then experimenting with a career as a Hollywood writer, recalled that Saroyan's clash with the studio was the subject of much gossip, with the consensus being that he was an arrogant upstart ("Where the hell does this guy get off?") and delusional if he believed he was "the most important thing that hit M-G-M." In an effort to placate him, or simply to fob him off, Mayer suggested that Saroyan "prove" himself by writing and directing a short, and they would take it from there. Saroyan set to work and in April submitted *The Good Job*, which was met with the coolest of receptions. The wily Mayer had smoothly outmaneuvered Saroyan, distracting him with this side project as he cast around to identify which contract director he would entrust with *The Human Comedy*.[3]

There were rumors that Mayer was lining up King Vidor and Sidney Franklin for the project. Franklin was likely tapped as a possible producer—he hadn't directed a film since 1939—and he certainly got involved enough to seek advice on how to fix the script. Lillie Messenger, one of MGM's chief readers, identified the main problems with Saroyan's "overwritten" script as its length and its approach to characterization: "The characters all talk the same way. They are all philosophers. They are all Saroyans." Certainly, it was going to be a challenge to produce a new script that would retain the poetic tone and still be credible to a general audience. Franklin, it seems, lost interest and took over producing duties on two Greer Garson films (*Random Harvest* and *Madame Curie*). Although Vidor had been announced as director, he too dropped out to concentrate on the development of *An American Romance* (which took until 1944 to complete). In the meantime, Saroyan was still hovering in the wings. He tried to persuade Victor Fleming to put himself forward as director—and then consult with Saroyan on every shot—before switching his allegiance to William Wyler. In fact, neither Fleming nor Wyler wanted to be involved, and once again, Saroyan was left out in the cold.[4]

By June, Mayer was anxious to get started, so he offered the film to Brown. The selection of Brown was an acknowledgment that his talents were well suited to this sentimental celebration of ordinary folk, but it was also a bid to make amends for the *They Met in Bombay* debacle. Brown made no effort to hide his dissatisfaction with MGM and even leaked to the press his intention to defect to another studio or go freelance; a decent assignment was needed to win him over. As it turned out, Brown was an excellent choice. He was certainly one of the most gifted directors of Americana (along with Vidor), and he was enthusiastic about Saroyan's story, even if he regarded the author as a pompous ass. MGM assigned Howard Estabrook to work with Brown on the script throughout July and August. The duo was ruthless in trimming the dialogue, cutting out some key scenes (such as one featuring the youngest Macauley child, Ulysses, getting caught in a bear trap, and another of a man holding up the telegraph office), and expanding a few minor ones (Ulysses's encounter with the Mechanical Man). The team also benefited from the contributions of screenwriter William Ludwig, who was best known for his work on the Andy Hardy films. As Ludwig remembered, he had been instructed "to take the script and cut sequences out and put some in and not lose the story. It was much more than bridging. I had to develop character scenes that would pull the script together and leave it at a reasonable length." He built up several of Saroyan's more poetic scenes, including the memorable one in which Ulysses watches a train rumble by, a scene in a drugstore, and one in the Macauley house where Mother plays the harp. Some scenes were added that elaborated, perhaps unwisely, Saroyan's spiritual subtext: a new credit sequence that includes an image of Mr. Macauley, superimposed on a shot of clouds, revealing that he's been dead for two years, but it's okay because the "end is just the beginning"; and an amended ending in which it is divulged that the dead Marcus Macauley will be symbolically replaced by his soldier friend, who, on a visit to Ithaca, realizes he has "come home."[5]

As work on the script progressed, casting decisions were finalized. The headliner was Mickey Rooney playing the second Macauley son, Homer, who transforms (like the nation) from a carefree boy larking around to a mature and responsible young adult who must confront death and accept the reality of evil in the world. This was Brown's third time directing Rooney, who, in the seven years since *Ah Wilderness!* had become one of MGM's most bankable stars (largely because of the success of the Andy Hardy series). Brown liked and admired him—so much so that he later called Rooney the most gifted actor he had ever worked with—but he wasn't sure he had the maturity to infuse the character of Homer with real depth. Up to this point, Rooney's stock-in-trade had been the roguish, hyperactive kid with a heart of gold, a kind of 1930s variation on George Peck's Bad Boy, and his vaudeville roots often surfaced in a shameless mugging for the camera. A skeptical Brown warned Rooney, "The first time you shed an unnecessary tear or start any of that mugging you're famous for, I'm going to halt everything, walk right out in the middle of the set, and give you a swift kick in the pants." Undoubtedly there was some embellishment for the MGM publicity campaign—which promoted *The Human Comedy* as the film that introduced a more mature Rooney to the world—but the sentiment rang true.[6]

A humbler Rooney reported to the set in late August, joining a cast that included veterans Fay Bainter as Mrs. Macauley, Frank Morgan as telegrapher Willie Grogan, and Ray Collins as the "spirit" of Mr. Macauley, as well as newcomers Van Johnson, Marsha Hunt, James Craig, Donna Reed, and, in a small role, Robert Mitchum. For the part of Ulysses, the youngest Macauley boy, Brown cast a new child actor, five-year-old Jackie "Butch" Jenkins. Publicity trumpeted that he had been discovered by either Brown or his secretary (and future wife), Marian Spies, as he played on a beach at Santa Monica. Perhaps it was a random encounter, but it's more likely that Jenkins's mother, actress Doris Dudley (daughter of well-known theater critic Bide Dudley), introduced her son to Brown or Spies. Whatever the case, Jenkins was a complete novice, and he soon enchanted Brown. Whereas Rooney had years of training and experience, Jenkins was more like a force of nature. As Brown remembered, Jenkins was largely oblivious to the filmmaking process: "he never knew he was making a picture . . . he thought he was playing all the time." For Brown, he was a welcome relief from the children being churned out of stage schools and out of MGM's own talent department. Jenkins was amenable to direction and had nothing to unlearn. Brown was able to coax from him a performance that had "authenticity" and naturalness—qualities he increasingly valued.[7]

Actress Marsha Hunt, who plays Diana, the aristocratic love interest of James Craig's character (the manager of the telegraph office where both Grogan and Homer work), remembered that Brown ran the set in an "orderly . . . congenial" manner. She was under contract and had been given the role with "no discussion or options" offered. Although her character initially seemed like "a bit of a caricature," she ended up enjoying the experience. Interestingly, she had few memories of Brown because she had little to do with him: "he saw that I 'had a handle' on the role . . . [and] he just turned me loose to play her as I chose." Brown's "hands off" approach was, she confessed, a little underwhelming, and at one point she thought, "So this is the great Clarence Brown?" Later she realized it was less a symptom of disinterest and more a matter of his confidence in her abilities as an actress. Her recollections confirm what other actors had already deduced: Brown was the kind of director who preferred to intervene only when an actor was struggling or inexperienced. Hunt was neither, and she delivered a charming, humorous performance as the sparky Diana—a far cry from the other drab females (played by Donna Reed and Dorothy Morris) in the film.[8]

If Hunt recalled Brown as a rather distant figure, it may have been because the production was turning out to be a large and complicated operation. Jenkins needed quite a bit of attention, as did Rooney. The latter took his work seriously, but perhaps not as seriously as Brown had hoped. The star was at an awkward juncture in both his career and his private life: now in his early twenties, and with more money than he knew what to do with, Rooney was distracted by his extremely colorful social life, and he was keen to sate his voracious appetite for women, gambling, and alcohol. To the public, however, he was still a boyish teenager, and Howard Strickling had gone to considerable lengths to create a squeaky-clean persona that, according to Rooney, "had little or nothing to do with reality. Instead of collecting blondes, brunettes, and redheads, they had me collecting stamps, coins, and matchboxes." Mayer might have wished to keep America's favorite teenager frozen in time, but it was increasingly difficult to maintain that image when Rooney had already been married and divorced (to Ava Gardner, the first of eight wives) and was clearly of an age that he should have been serving in the armed forces. To facilitate *The Human Comedy*, Eddie Mannix had pulled some strings to delay his being drafted, but the consequences were guilt for Rooney and negative criticism in the press.[9]

Given the exertions of his private life, it was a miracle that Rooney managed to make it to the set, but even Brown had to admit that he always delivered a credible performance. Forty years later, Marian Brown recalled how her husband had always marveled that Rooney "needed no rehearsal. Tell him what to do and he did it. Perfectly. The first time." Rooney could usually deliver on the first take, although some scenes, such as the one in which he reads a telegram containing the news that his brother Marcus has been killed, "we must have shot . . . four or five times." That was normal for any actor, but what struck Brown was Rooney's ability to muster an air of spontaneity with every new take: "each time he'd read it as though he'd seen it for the first time." His devil-may-care attitude and the unabashed flaunting of his vices probably drove the straitlaced Brown to distraction, but Rooney's natural talents were such that Brown later admitted the "little bastard" could "do no wrong in my book." For his part, Rooney was tactful and complimentary about his frequent director, remembering him as a "consummate gentleman," a "director of taste, energy and credibility, and imagination" who "never raised his voice, never criticized anyone in front of another." And while he may not have appreciated Brown's firmness on the set of *The Human Comedy*, he later realized that the director's insistence on "simplicity and restraint" profoundly influenced the development of his craft, "bringing out the best in me—by simply telling me to be Homer Macauley, in my own way."[10]

In his autobiography, Rooney remembered Brown of *The Human Comedy* as a man of sophistication, "dressed in impeccable, tailor-made English tweeds and white turtlenecks . . . his shoes always shone." Brown's self-assured air meant that the cast and crew viewed him as a figure of some authority, but their respect deepened when they saw his commitment to getting the best out of each performer. For eleven-year-old Darryl Hickman, playing Ulysses's mentally challenged friend Lionel, Brown was among a small group of directors that impacted his own development as an actor: "[he] would say just the right words at the right moment to guide an actor's performance" and was "*very* methodical. *Very* painstaking. He took his time until he was good and satisfied." Initially, Hickman had struggled to get into character, and he turned to Brown for advice: "he made a decision that unlocked Lionel for me. A dentist fitted me for removable buck teeth, and the prop department provided a pair of thick glasses. The moment I put on the teeth and glasses, I was the slow witted boy Saroyan had created so sensitively on paper. Then Brown helped me with explicit, succinct direction before every take: 'blink a little less the next time,' he'd say, and I would zero in on the characterization. Lionel was living in my teeth, my bad eyesight, my whole being." Today, many might regard the character of Lionel, and all the attendant props, as a thoughtless or even offensive caricature, but at the time, it was intended as a sincere and sympathetic portrait of a boy who views the world with an undimmed sense of wonder and possesses a naïveté intertwined with instinctual wisdom. In one of the most memorable scenes, Lionel takes Ulysses to the library—where an intent reader is played by none other than Gibson Gowland, star of von Stroheim's *Greed*—and although neither boy can read, Lionel shows his companion the wonders of "all these books." Lionel is, of course, a Saroyan invention, but he is not so different from Brown's other child protagonists, most notably Jody in *The Yearling* and Velvet in *National Velvet*. All are dreamers whose "uncluttered" view of the world and of human nature makes them timeless and appealing.[11]

Brown finished filming in November, and four months later *The Human Comedy* was unveiled to critics, accompanied by an aggressive promotional campaign. Then, as now, the movie prompted mixed reactions. Legendary Hollywood mogul Jesse Lasky Sr. viewed it at a private screening in Jack Warner's house and hastily wrote to his son, urging him to see this "gem" that is "beyond description . . . it is an emotional experience that you will never forget." Admittedly, Lasky's reaction was rhapsodic—he compared the experience to being "under the influence of a prayer"—but even the most cynical of viewers had to concede that *The Human Comedy* got under the skin. Bosley Crowther commented that it featured "cheek by jowl and overlapping . . . some most charming bits of fine motion-picture expression and some most maudlin gobs of cinematic goo," but he appreciated its "moments of extraordinary beauty" and the "textural firmness" with which it depicts life in a small town. For Crowther, the film's flaws were attributable mainly to Saroyan, but the author's overemphasis on goodness had undoubtedly been exacerbated by the MGM treatment: "When Mr. Saroyan states these ageless and elemental facts by having his characters give out with speeches which sound upon the screen like sermons delivered from pulpits; when Clarence Brown, the producer, backs them up with soulful and tear-jerking music or with aureoles about the head, then the dignity and simplicity of the ideas shade off into cheap pretentiousness." Rooney's performance, however, was a revelation to him: "There is a tenderness and restraint in his characterization, along with a genuine youthfulness, such as he has not shown for a long time." The reviewer for the *Los Angeles Times* agreed, declaring, "to all intents and purposes, brash, bumptious Andy Hardy is dead."[12]

Reviewers outside the United States were less susceptible to the film's charms, and many noted its elision of the complicated and brutal facts of war. In his review for the British publication the *Spectator*, Edgar Anstey dryly noted that the film's central message ("the thesis that all men are really angels") was naïve, and it avoided dealing with "the fact that it takes two sides to make a war." However, he admitted that there were a couple of reasons why someone might be drawn to it: "The first is that every scene in which Jack Jenkins, the little five year old, appears is a joy; and secondly you may have a grudge against Americans." There was a grudging note, too, in the two reviews written by Brown's fellow Knoxville native, the quirky James Agee, for the *Nation*. In the first, published shortly after the film's premiere, he pondered the rather embarrassing appeal of tearjerkers, admitting that his intellect told him *The Human Comedy* was "mainly a mess," but for all that, it "interests me more than any other film I have seen for a good while." The best moments, for him, were those that displayed the kind of the visual innovation that had characterized Brown's strongest work in the silent era—scenes in which the camera, in conjunction with a finely etched performance, told the story and pretentious or mawkish dialogue was secondary or absent. However, in his opinion, there were not enough of these moments, and he panned the unevenness of Brown's treatment: "[it] wobbles between that stultifying kind of slick-paper competence which is worse than no competence at all and unforgiveable errors of taste and judgment ... the best one can say of it ... is that it tries on the whole to be 'faithful' to Saroyan; not invariably a good idea." Agee was candid enough to admit that he liked *The Human Comedy*, flaws and all. The scenes featuring Jenkins and Rooney gave it "a rare and honorable right to existence," while

Rooney's performance proved "how sensitive and earnest an actor this usually unfortunate young man can be."[13]

Lasky had been instantly enchanted, and as the weeks went on, it dawned on Agee that *The Human Comedy* had cast a spell on him, too. In May he wrote another review in which he offered a qualified apology to Brown for his prior "ill-directed nastiness . . . which should have been more accurately directed. . . . I think of Clarence Brown . . . in the most praise-worthy and respectful terms, as the man who piloted Garbo's best films, and who, before that, made the excellent and bold films *Smoldering Fires* and *The Signal Tower*." Given Brown's undoubted talent, Agee found it regrettable that he too frequently succumbed to the seductiveness of the glossy MGM style and forgot his natural instincts: "I still have to insist that he has become a dope, and to offer the negligences in *The Human Comedy* as proof." It's unknown whether Brown ever discussed his inadequacies with Agee, but it's intriguing to speculate about how the two would have gotten along or how Brown might have filmed Agee's evocative Knoxville-set novel *A Death in the Family*. In any case, Agee wasn't the only one paying attention. Brown received copious correspondence about *The Human Comedy* both from the general public and from high-profile figures. Among his papers are letters from novelist Fannie Hurst, fellow directors Allan Dwan and Mervyn LeRoy, Broadway writer Damon Runyon, and, most touchingly, the wife of comedian Joe E. Brown, who wrote that she had been deeply affected by the film, having recently lost her son in the war.[14]

Years later, Brown would often say that of all his films, he retained the most affection for *The Human Comedy*. Its warm sentiment and sincere appreciation of ordinary folk and family bonds held immense appeal for him, despite his own struggles with marriage and fatherhood. There is some poignancy that he made this film about love and death, and about fathers and sons, as he was mourning the loss of his father. Larkin Brown, who had moved with Catherine to Los Angeles in the 1930s to be closer to his son, died in March 1942, just weeks before production commenced on *The Human Comedy*. The lapses into mawkishness and the inclusion of a spectral father, which can so easily be dismissed as risible, might be read in a more compassionate light as Brown's reaction to this loss. The reassurance that "death is only the beginning" offered hope to Brown, as well as to the countless viewers who had been bereaved by the war.[15]

There is no doubt that Brown was personally invested in the film, but *The Human Comedy* can also be ranked among his most accomplished work of the sound era, notably because of the deftness with which it fuses innovative visuals and evocative sound. Nowhere is this more evident than in the opening, later cited by Brown as one of the best demonstrations of his theories on the selective use of the mobile camera: "There's a scene in *The Human Comedy* where I had the camera up on a five ton truck with . . . [the] crane on top . . . and I brought that camera down from the long shot to a little boy in the distance looking in the ground, without a cut, until I came right to a close-up of a gofer [*sic*] coming out of a hole without a cut." The sweeping shot serves not only as a fitting introduction to one of the film's most charming characters but also as the visual expression of an emotional reaction—Ulysses's awe as he observes the gopher's vigorous activity. To a more jaded eye, the gopher's industry might seem banal—after all, it is simply doing what gophers do, digging a hole—but to the boy, this small creature is part of the wondrous world of nature. Ulysses is introduced, in the most cinematically elegant terms, as a "Brown child," one who sees beauty in nature and has an instinctive empathy for animals. Romantic poeticism may drive Brown's use of a crane shot here, but it is not without a precise narrative purpose: it links back to the opening scene in which a spectral Mr. Macauley is shown watching over his family and, it is assumed, his youngest son. In this one shot, the innocence, curiosity, and freedom of childhood are suggested, as well as the bond between fathers and sons, which, as Donald Lyons notes, is central to a number of Brown films.[16]

The freedom of the crane shot, mirroring the fluid and carefree movement of the child, is carried through in a series of tracking shots Brown uses to capture Ulysses as, distracted by the sound of a distant train, he runs up the dusty streets of Ithaca into its hinterland. Brown was lucky to be working with gifted cinematographer Harry Stradling, and the two came up with an evocative, magical scene that anticipates the work of Andrew Wyeth and Terrence Malick but also looks back to a seminal influence on Brown: F. W. Murnau's *Sunrise*. As the camera tracks Ulysses moving through the high grass and up onto a mound, he pauses to greet the train and is rewarded by a wave and a burst of song from a black traveler (Ernest Whitman), who sings, in a Paul Robeson–style baritone, "Weep no more" and joyfully declares that he's "going home." Though contrived, this is still a lovely scene, and it introduces the theme of home—as a place and as a state of mind—that underpins the film. Scenes like these, so effortless and graceful, were achieved only through immense effort and inventiveness on the part of Brown and his crew. As he later recalled: "They took . . . time and money to do them but I think they were worth it."[17]

This technically intricate, somewhat showy style is tempered by quieter moments in the film when Brown employs an observational camera to record the unfurling of emotion or the seeming spontaneous chemistry between two actors. In several scenes between Rooney and Jenkins—one in which they discuss Homer's morning fitness regimen and his plans to travel the world, and another in which Homer reassures Ulysses after his frightening encounter with the sinister Mechanical Man—Brown wisely holds back, letting the experienced Rooney play off the more natural Jenkins. Rooney is crucial to the success of these scenes, not only because of his skill as an actor but also because he is willing to coach the inexperienced Jenkins and wait it out until he hits the right note. It takes time and some manipulation, but a sense of naturalness and spontaneity is eventually achieved. These qualities also surface in Rooney's scenes with gifted character actor Frank Morgan, playing the alcoholic Willie Grogan. The film takes some care in building up their relationship, showing its deepening from a strictly professional one to a more emotionally intimate dynamic that suggests a quasi-paternal solicitude on the older man's part. This makes it all the more devastating when Homer arrives at the office one morning to find Grogan unresponsive. Initially assuming he's drunk, Homer attempts to revive him, only to realize that Grogan is dead. Having been forewarned by Brown not to mug in the scene, Rooney conveys Homer's sense of loss not through large gestures or emotional dialogue but through stillness, remaining in the background of the shot as others rush in to manage the crisis.

For the contemporary viewer, it may be the pared-down scenes or the ones that express childhood exhilaration that are the most deeply affecting, but for audiences in 1943, those that referenced the war carried a particular resonance. William Ludwig didn't regard Brown as "an emotional director," but he remembered being struck by Brown's sensitivity and how intent he was on extracting the right response from the audience:

> There was the scene in the troop train—they're on their way to the West
> Coast to ship out, kids going to war. Lionel Stander [according to
> author Lee Server, it was actually Frank Jenks] was in the scene and he
> starts singing, "Leaning on the Everlasting Arms." And he says, "Now
> come on, sing everybody." And all the people on the train join in the
> singing. Well, they got paid for it. But nobody else, nobody in the
> theater, is singing. After, we get out of the theater and into the car and
> Clarence says, "Goddammit, that scene . . . I wanted everybody in the
> audience to start to sing. I really wanted them to get into it. But
> nothing." We all went home, but Clarence went to the studio. He had
> quarters there, and he used to be able to sleep right on the lot. About

4.30 A.M. my phone rings. It's Clarence. He says, "Get over here as fast as you can. Meet me in my projection room." So I go over and meet him. He says, "We're going to take the picture out again tomorrow night, and this time we're going to have that audience singing." He had Dutch Shearer, head of the sound department, there with us, and he told him what he wanted. And, oh, he was a smart man. We took it out that night and when Stander [*sic*] comes on and says, "Come on, sing everybody," the troops start to sing, and then you hear—from somewhere in the back—an untrained woman's voice starts to sing. And then another. And someone else. And the people in the audience are convinced that other people in the audience have started to sing, and pretty soon the whole goddamn house was singing. And Clarence had done it. He had dubbed those other voices on the track to sound as if they were coming from the theater. The audience stopped being self-conscious when they believed others were singing, and they sang, too. It was wonderful to see.[18]

Undoubtedly, *The Human Comedy* is a product of a particular era, yet it still retains the power to impress, to move, and to inspire new filmmakers (Meg Ryan directed a remake in 2016). For its cast, *The Human Comedy* acquired special significance. Rooney regarded it as "one of the best I ever did." Hunt observed that even though it was "pretty heavily sentimental," it "was what America needed to see and believe, in a time of universal stress and anxiety: that the family is strong and firm, was what counted most and together could weather whatever came. Today's revved-up, cynical America, with no memory of then, must find it pretty soapy. But I love it." Others loved it too, and Brown was nominated for an Oscar, but he lost to the very deserving Michael Curtiz (for *Casablanca*). He was disappointed, of course, but he buried himself in his work, fending off rumors that he was going to reunite with Garbo for an adaptation of Shaw's *Saint Joan* (shelved because MGM was worried that her main market in Europe could not be guaranteed). More of a sure bet was a film adaptation of George Martin's story of small-town life, *Our Vines Have Tender Grapes;* it had the same kind of homey atmosphere as *The Human Comedy* and also featured child protagonists (one of whom would be played by Jenkins). However, due to a delay in production, Brown had to pass the film on to Roy Rowland and return to a previous project. *The White Cliffs of Dover* would turn out to be one of his most commercially successful films.[19]

The White Cliffs of Dover had originally been conceived shortly after war broke out in Europe. Its author, Alice Duer Miller, had worked in Hollywood since the 1920s and had collaborated with Brown on *Wife vs. Secretary*. She was a committed Anglophile and was keen to foster Anglo-American relations during this time of crisis. Using the form of a long prose poem, she tells the story of Susan Dunn, a young American who visits England in 1914 and, following a whirlwind romance, marries an English lord, only to lose him in World War I. Choosing to remain in England, she raises their son and becomes part of the upper-class world. When World War II breaks out, she must face the possibility of losing her only son in another war. Miller's poem evidently struck a chord on both sides of the Atlantic, and its popularity increased following a radio adaptation (featuring Lynn Fontanne) that was broadcast soon after the attack on Pearl Harbor. English actor Ronald Colman, himself a veteran of World War I, bought the rights to it, hoping to produce it (with Bette Davis in the lead) and donate a share of the profits to British war-relief charities. There was certainly interest from Hollywood: the success of English-themed films such as Wyler's *Mrs. Miniver* and, later, *Random Harvest* meant that studios (and especially MGM) were indulging in something of a love affair with England in 1942. For reasons not entirely clear, Colman vacillated and sold the rights to Clarence Brown in June 1942. The upper-class English world of *The White Cliffs of Dover* might have seemed a million miles from his avowed interest in Americana, but Brown was a cosmopolitan, a Europhile, and a fan of English culture (according to one 1944 profile, he "dresses like an English squire with a passion for Tattersall vests"). It seems that Brown liked everything about England except its press, which had made a snide comment about his mispronunciation of conductor Leopold Stokowski's name back in the 1930s, and he never forgave them for it.[20]

By 1941, Brown had recovered from his mild flirtation with Mussolini and was firmly pro-Allies. In July he traveled to England to see the war's effects firsthand and to do some research for a possible film. The *Los Angeles Times* reported the visit in rather gung-ho terms, as if the fifty-one-year-old Brown had parachuted into the thick of the action: "[Brown] who was an aviator in World War I, has been spoiling for a look at today's action." The purchase of Miller's poem reflected Brown's Anglophilia, but even more, it revealed a shrewd appreciation that it was the right time to cash in on audience interest in European developments. Originally, he considered shooting the film in Britain and releasing it through United Artists, but as the summer of 1942 wore on, he and his agent, Jules Goldstone, carried on negotiations with several studios, until it was reported that MGM had offered a lucrative deal. The studio wanted to retain Brown as director, adding Sidney Franklin as producer and Colman as star. Brown was reluctant to commit and continued to consider other proposals, including one from William Goetz (Mayer's son-in-law) to join forces and set up a new independent company. Of course, MGM won him over, mainly because it offered him a decent assignment, *The Human Comedy*, with an immediate start and a contract that promised to give him greater control over the kinds of projects he accepted. *The White Cliffs of Dover* was temporarily put on hold while he tackled the Saroyan adaptation.[21]

In Brown's absence, Franklin managed the preproduction work on *The White Cliffs*. The decision to involve Franklin was a wise one, not only because he was an industry veteran but also because he was an Anglophile and had the credentials (*Mrs. Miniver* and *Random Harvest*) to prove it. He assigned English-born Claudine West and two staff writers, George Froeschel and Jan Lustig, to write the script. The three consulted through the spring of 1943, trying to come up with a solid melodrama that would also have some timely, but not overly propagandist, content. Irene Dunne was expected to take the lead role, and that posed a problem for the writers, given that the story follows her character from her late teens to her early forties (one of the writers noted in a memo that it was "going to be a touchy question"). The final script made no explicit mention of the character's age, and audiences were expected to suspend disbelief at the sight of the forty-five-year-old Dunne playing a woman in her late teens in the early scenes. In line with MGM's general approach in wartime films, and in deference to Dunne's legion of female fans, the content was shaped to emphasize the human story over the ideological message.[22]

Even so, liaising with the Office of War Information (OWI) was one of Franklin's main tasks. The OWI kept a close eye on productions with war themes, and although *The White Cliffs* raised no questions about the war itself, it did portray England as a class-divided society. Few could argue that this wasn't an accurate portrayal, but the OWI feared that if the differences between England and America were emphasized, it could "actually raise resentment on both sides of the Atlantic." Those elements that Claudine West felt were "natural" and proper in the story, such as Susan's eagerness to attend a royal ball, were a source of some concern for the OWI, which thought American audiences might see Susan as a "snob." The OWI was worried, too, that the portrayal of the aristocratic Ashwoods—the family Susan marries into—could spark resentment from American audiences, especially when tenant farmers on the Ashwood estate are represented as submissive and fearful that the war's impact "was worse for the gentry than it is for us" (the OWI suggested instead: "Ben was saying it is as bad for the gentry as for us"). The OWI's specific concerns about references to the war and to isolationist and détente positions also resulted in discussions about how the character of Susan's father should be shaped: early drafts featured him criticizing England as a colonial power and a class-ridden society and expressing his vehement opposition to his daughter's marriage to an aristocrat. Robert Nathan was drafted to do some additional (uncredited) work on the character and to give him dialogue that conveyed his grudging appreciation of English stoicism and his prescient realization that Germany was no longer a defeated nation. As a result, the brittle character was softened, permitting the masterly Frank Morgan to depict him as a comic character conducting an unending battle with English manners and the country's weather.[23]

By May, the script was ready, and Brown had returned from a short break after completing *The Human Comedy*. The original plan to shoot in England had been scrapped as the war intensified; instead, MGM poured money into building sets—the studio reportedly spent $250,000 to reproduce the port of Dieppe—pushing the final budget to $1.5 million. Brown also made occasional excursions to shoot on location, using his ranch for a couple of background shots as well as the landmark Bradbury building in downtown Los Angeles for scenes that bookend the film and depict the hospital where Susan is a nurse (and where her son succumbs to his injuries). Brown had spotted the impressive building many years before, when he was working for Maurice Tourneur, and he had vowed to use it someday in one of his films. Apart from a couple of striking shots of the interior's gridlike stairs, Brown didn't exploit its extraordinary architecture, and it would be up to Ridley Scott to realize its full potential in *Blade Runner* forty years later.[24]

The White Cliffs of Dover took on some significance in terms of Brown's future career and life. It was his first collaboration with Sidney Franklin, even though the two had known each other socially since the 1920s. The business relationship that developed between them could be difficult and fraught at times, but it inevitably deepened their personal bond. The two men could not have been more different: Franklin was generally regarded as warm, extroverted, and witty, while most people characterized Brown as tough, introverted, and sometimes humorless (although he had a penchant for off-color stories). Despite their differences, both men were sentimental and romantic (Franklin was inclined to express this more openly in both his films and his personal demeanor). Over the years, their friendship evolved, and in retirement, Franklin was one of the few who could cajole Brown out of his black moods. Franklin's mischievous nature occasionally annoyed Brown, and he found much to criticize in his films (he saw them as simply "too good," in that they overemphasized goodness), but he also conceded that Franklin was "the closest friend I have in the picture business."[25]

Their first collaboration was, on the whole, a smooth one, after some initial casting disappointments. Although Ronald Colman had envisaged Bette Davis in the lead role, MGM chose Irene Dunne because she was under contract and a considerable box-office draw in 1942. An early request by Brown to have Laurence Olivier play the role of Sir John Ashwood was turned down, and MGM assigned the less charismatic Alan Marshall. The cast was filled out by a selection of English actors (Dame May Whitty, Gladys Cooper, Miles Mander, and C. Aubrey Smith) and some American ones (Van Johnson and Frank Morgan)—a solid ensemble for a solid film. The appearance of two beautiful child actors, Roddy McDowall and Elizabeth Taylor, added some spark. Each of them had a striking screen presence and a timely backstory: both were wartime evacuees, of a sort. It was Brown's first time working with them, and he treated them with kid gloves. McDowall later ranked Brown as one of the best directors he worked with, praising his patience and the atmosphere of taste ("pure Cartier") he fostered on the set. Taylor had a very minor role, but her raw talent and extraordinary beauty made an impression on Brown. Although it can't be said with certainty that he immediately lined her up to play Velvet Brown in his next film, there is no doubt she was on his mind when it came time to cast it. As he directed Taylor's key scene in *The White Cliffs of Dover*, in which she swings off a fence to suggest her coy flirtation with McDowall's character, he once more drew from his back catalog, subtly referencing a similar scene featuring Leatrice Gilbert in *Of Human Hearts;* he returned to another variation of it with Taylor in *National Velvet.*[26]

The small parts played by McDowall and Taylor were significant, but without a doubt, *The White Cliffs of Dover* was shaped around the persona and performance of Irene Dunne as Susan. The shoot proved quite a challenge for the actress: in addition to having to "age" from her late teens to late forties, she was juggling a killer schedule that required her to work simultaneously on another production, the war-themed *A Guy Named Joe*. She delivered a polished performance that includes moments of poignancy and occasional fire— such as the scene in which she takes the English to task for their casual dismissal of Americans—but she was saddled with a rather one-dimensional role that, compared with the protagonists of other "women's films" of the day, lacked depth or ambiguity. It would also be hard to read Susan as a "Brown heroine" because, apart from her one act of rebellion—marrying a man she hardly knows and staying in England with him—she unfolds as a consistently passive, stoic character. Even though the project was his from the start, Brown's overall handling of the material and the cast was rather stolid, showing none of the zest he brought to *The Human Comedy*. In a piece in *Lion's Roar*, he revealed that he saw it not as a "war picture" but as a "beautiful love story," and in directing it he was "guided by simple rules. . . . Humanness, Brown points out, is the first element he looks for in a story." *The White Cliffs of Dover* most definitely emphasizes the *human* cost of war, but its message is conveyed by characters so impossibly noble, and by a voice-over so mawkishly sentimental, that the "humanness" of the story seems lifeless.[27]

Following some retakes in January, *The White Cliffs of Dover* was released in May 1944. The reviews were polite at best, and dismissive at worst. Doris Arden, writing for the *Chicago Sun Times*, was disappointed that the film was "sentimental instead of realistic . . . there is no hint that any of the characters are moved by anything other than the noblest of motives, the highest of principles and the most unselfish of intentions." Bosley Crowther was exasperated by its obsequious tone, complaining that the film "has supplemented the handshake with a tug on its forelock and a bow. As a matter of fact, it has virtually gotten down on its knees and kissed the ground—the ground, that is, of England and all that it represents . . . [it] is such a tribute to English gentility as only an American studio would dare to make." James Agee, with his usual flair, compared the experience of watching the film to "drinking cup after cup of tepid orange pekoe at a rained-out garden party staged by some deep-provincial local of the English-speaking Union." Audiences were more forgiving of its flaws, and *The White Cliffs of Dover* registered box-office receipts of almost $6.5 million, making it one of Brown's most profitable films. He was sanguine about it all, later noting that it worked for audiences chiefly because it was "timely."[28]

25

Velvet and the Pie

National Velvet

The success of *The White Cliffs of Dover* consolidated Brown's position at MGM, and in the months that followed, the trade press was filled with rumors about what his next film would be. Some of the possibilities included an adaptation of the Gershwin musical *Porgy and Bess* and a film version of the Paul Gallico story *The Clock*, but instead he opted for a project that had been floating around Hollywood for almost a decade. English author Enid Bagnold had written *National Velvet* in 1934—the story of Velvet Brown, a girl who wins a wild piebald horse in a raffle and then rides him to victory in the Grand National. For this "study in a girl's relationship with her pony," Bagnold had been inspired by "all the fantastic joy and fun" of her own life with her children in the Sussex countryside.[1]

Despite an initial rejection from publisher George Morrow, which predicted "this little story won't sell in America," the first print run of *National Velvet* sold out, catching the attention of several Hollywood studios. Following a battle between Paramount and RKO's Pandro S. Berman (who wanted it as a vehicle for Katharine Hepburn), Paramount acquired the rights for £8,000. The studio announced that Leo McCarey would direct the film, with Arthur Hornblow Jr. as producer and W. P. Lipscomb as writer. In February 1937 Lipscomb turned in a script that closely followed the novel in depicting all aspects of the Browns' family life, presenting a nostalgic image of rural 1920s England in the village of "Sewels"—a misspelled homage to the author of *Black Beauty*—and elaborating on Bagnold's exploration of how compassion and cruelty are intertwined in human attitudes toward animals. He continued the novel's delineation of the human-imposed hierarchy of animals in which some are pets (the Pie, Jacob the terrier, canaries), others are workers (Miss

Ada the cart horse, the spaniels banished to the outhouse, the unnamed dog perpetually chained up and ignored), and the rest are meat (the sheep and horses slaughtered in a room adjacent to the family home). It was a surprisingly brutal script, but by the time *National Velvet* made it to the screen, much of it had been reworked in a bid to appeal to the family market.[2]

During the time that *National Velvet* was under development at Paramount, many of the studio's biggest stars, including Claudette Colbert, Carole Lombard, and Margaret Sullavan, were linked to the role of Velvet Brown. There were also rumors that Paramount would seek new talent or negotiate a loan of Shirley Temple from Fox. Louella Parsons even reported that Leslie Howard was actively campaigning "for the delectable part" on behalf of his daughter, Leslie Ruth (other accounts suggest he did so only after MGM acquired the property). As it turned out, finding the right girl to play Velvet became another studio's problem. Paramount lost interest in 1937 and sold the rights to MGM. Producer Hunt Stromberg ordered a complete overhaul, going back to the source novel to identify what might be eliminated, such as a subplot in which Velvet "inherits" a stable of horses; it was decided to focus on her relationship with just one horse, the Pie. Stromberg also explored casting options and seemed hopeful that he might secure Spencer Tracy for the role of stable hand Mi Taylor, thereby balancing the risk posed by casting a newcomer as Velvet. At the top of his list for that role was a not entirely unknown name, Leatrice Gilbert, who had recently appeared in *Of Human Hearts* and was being backed by her ambitious mother, former star Leatrice Joy. Gilbert recalled that her mother mounted a formidable campaign: "Auntie Mame couldn't have done it any better. She got me all dressed up and trotted me down to the studio and we called on Ida Koverman [Mayer's assistant]. I'd sit in her lap, then we'd go and see Hunt Stromberg." According to Gilbert, MGM went so far as to announce her in the role, before doing an abrupt U-turn and shelving the production.[3]

In a piece published shortly after *National Velvet*'s release in 1944, writer H. P. Mooring outlined the factors that led to MGM's decision. Stromberg had always known that "no matter how the story were written, the character of Velvet Brown had to be the starring one," but when Tracy rejected the role of Mi the stable hand (saying he "didn't care for it"), Stromberg's enthusiasm waned. He hadn't discovered a young girl charismatic enough to carry the film, and without someone of Tracy's caliber, he feared a box-office failure. There was a brief flicker of renewed activity in 1939 when Jules Furthman submitted a draft that concentrated on developing the character of Mi (with Mickey Rooney in mind), but the outbreak of war in Europe scuppered plans to shoot it on location in Sussex, and it was shelved again. In 1941, buoyed by the success of a spate of English-themed films, MGM had a change of heart and put newly hired staff member Pandro S. Berman in charge. He had been a fan of the novel and had tried to acquire it for RKO; now that he was at the studio that owned the rights, he was determined to see it through. Berman hired *New Yorker* writer Sally Benson (of *Cabaret* fame), and she submitted a novella-style script in June 1942 that stuck closely to Bagnold's story. Staff writer Albert Mannheimer also submitted a treatment shortly thereafter. Neither satisfied Berman, so he turned to Helen Deutsch (whose main experience was as a songwriter) and veteran screenwriter Theodore Reeves. The team worked on it for the better part of 1943 (January–October), with Berman advising them to concentrate on developing the character of Mi Taylor (intended for Mickey Rooney). Deutsch and Reeves duly bulked up that character, adding bookend scenes that featured his arrival in Sewels and his departure. Their script devoted more attention to the dynamics of the Brown family, building up the character of Araminty Brown and emphasizing her special relationship with her youngest daughter, Velvet. The writers also had to anticipate possible objections from the PCA, so an insect jar replaced the beloved "spit bottle" possessed by Donald, the youngest of the Brown clan, and they eliminated Bagnold's references to the slaughterhouse's proximity to the Browns' living space. Gone, too, was a scene in which Velvet drinks alcohol before the big race, as well as her tendency to vomit when she is nervous (replaced by a more ladylike predisposition to fainting). Finally, in an acknowledgment of its screen potential, the Grand National race was expanded to become the film's dramatic set piece.[4]

By November 1943, a viable script for *National Velvet* was finally in place, and Berman turned to decisions on cast and crew. Mervyn LeRoy had originally been expected to direct, but the script delays meant that he was now caught up in *Thirty Seconds over Tokyo*. Berman turned to Brown, who had recently enjoyed a productive collaboration with Rooney and Jenkins and also happened to be enthusiastic about the subject matter. Their first task was to finalize the cast: Bagnold had described Mrs. Brown as an "enormous woman," but Brown and Berman had other ideas, and Judith Anderson, Sara Allgood, and Anne Revere were all tested for the part. Revere was selected, and she was joined by veteran actor-director Donald Crisp playing her husband; veteran character actors Reginald Owen, Arthur Treacher, and Arthur Shields; and some emerging talent in the form of Angela Lansbury, Juanita Quigley, and Jackie Jenkins. Lansbury had been attracting considerable attention for her performance in two period productions (Cukor's *Gaslight* and Lewin's *The*

Picture of Dorian Gray), but she recalled that she had little say over her casting (by Benny Thau) as Edwina Brown, Velvet's bossy big sister: "I was hired to do it because MGM put me in the part, there was no question about that. I was under contract, I was a natural to play that part and they had me there, so they put me into it." She had mixed feelings about playing a boy-crazy teenager: "I was getting to be . . . of an age where I was aware of myself as a woman, and I was coming into myself," and the role seemed something of a step back for her, both professionally and personally.[5]

The search for Velvet had commenced back in January 1943, when the studio had announced it was reigniting the project. A nationwide quest for raw talent had been promised, but in fact, MGM was looking to cast someone with a little experience. *Variety* reported that novice Patricia Hitchcock was trying out for the role and that talent agent Billy Grady was testing a number of experienced Broadway actresses, including Patsy Lee Parsons, Pat Arno, and Alix de Kauffman. At one point, rumors surfaced that an as-yet-undiscovered English girl would play Velvet, but Britain's child labor laws apparently put MGM off. A nationwide appeal to film reviewers yielded one interesting suggestion: Shirley Catlin, the daughter of writer Vera Brittain and a resident of St. Paul, Minnesota (Catlin didn't get called, but years later she found her own calling as politician Shirley Williams). By November, interest in the search was beginning to wane, and the pressure was on MGM to make an announcement.[6]

Just *how* Elizabeth Taylor came to be cast is the stuff of wildly conflicting accounts, with everyone involved laying claim to one of the most fortuitous decisions in Hollywood history. Mooring's 1944 piece in *Picturegoer* reported that it was Brown who had pointed out the obvious: the little English girl who had lit up the screen in his *White Cliffs of Dover* and had worked so well with animals in *Lassie Come Home* was the perfect choice to play Bagnold's heroine. Interviewed by one of Taylor's many biographers, Clarence Brown later related a slightly different account of being cornered by "two diminutive but formidable females"—Taylor and her mother, Sara—in an encounter that took place *before* he directed her in *The White Cliffs of Dover*. Though impressed by the eleven-year-old's conviction, he found her overt manipulation and inappropriate flirtation off-putting and was embarrassed when he received a series of gifts from her (designed to ensure that she remained on his radar). The account has a ring of truth because Taylor's mother was certainly pushy enough to approach Brown, and Taylor herself freely admitted that she was desperate to play the part. In fact, so fierce was her determination that she took the initiative and approached Lucille Ryman Carroll in MGM's talent department and asked her to get her a test (shot by Fred Zinnemann). Brown, Berman, and Mayer remained unconvinced that this slight girl could handle the physical exertion required, and so, in a hubristic account that has become part of her legend, Taylor embarked on a regimen to "will" herself taller and put on some weight. Perhaps. It is a romantic account, but one that has been disputed by Berman, who claimed he had earmarked Taylor for the part of Velvet as far back as 1941, when she was under contract at Universal, and that he had delayed production for two years so she could "grow into" the role.[7]

Whatever the circumstances of her casting, Taylor was announced in the role in late 1943. There remained just one crucial part to fill: the Pie. It would take a very special horse to play the high-strung piebald, one with the ability "to simulate sickness, to recover, to run away, show affection and do everything but speak lines." It was reported that as soon as Brown signed on, he initiated a special talent search, sifting through photos and visiting local stables for a horse that was malleable enough to train and gentle enough for Taylor to manage, but spirited enough to be convincing as a Grand National contender. Undoubtedly, the publicity department embellished a little, but it's possible that Brown got personally involved, given his interest in horses and racing. It was a hobby that grew out of his friendship with Mayer, who sometimes boarded horses at Brown's ranch. Brown was a frequent visitor to the Santa Anita racetrack and even accompanied Mayer on trips to Ireland in the 1950s to check out the bloodstock there. Brown's search for the Pie led him to inspect horses of all types, and he was close to casting a pinto when Taylor persuaded him to look at a sorrel Thoroughbred she had been riding at her local stable and had grown attached to. In the end, Taylor got her way, and "King Charles" was cast as the Pie (when the film wrapped, she got to keep the horse as MGM's gift). The selection of a Thoroughbred to depict Bagnold's "thick-necked, muscular, short" piebald horse was in some respects a typical Hollywood concession to beauty, but in the end, it was a good decision. The preexisting bond between Taylor and the horse meant that she had few qualms about doing most of the riding scenes herself. Contrary to the publicity that raved about how accomplished and instinctual a rider she was, Taylor wasn't a very proficient horsewoman, and a stunt double was used for the riskier jumping shots. Bagnold's daughter Laurian, who had been the model for Velvet, later dismissed Taylor's skills, noting, "It was a shame. She rode so badly."[8]

Filming on *National Velvet* commenced in January 1944 on the back lot. MGM had no intention of going to the original Sussex location, but it poured money into creating its own version of a quaint English village, complete with half-timbered houses, imitation foliage, and a village green. It was a distinctly artificial simulation, though Mooring was impressed that "the Hollywood people had managed to capture, fairly accurately, the atmosphere of British village life." For those working in this "village," it was less idyllic. Angela Lansbury recalled that the combination of low ceilings and bright lights needed for Technicolor meant that the heat was "oppressive," and everyone was relieved when the production decamped to Monterey (Pebble Beach) and Alhambra for location work.[9]

Brown later remembered *National Velvet* as one of his happier shoots because of his personal interest in the material and because he had the privilege of directing an accomplished cast. Initially, most were under the impression that the film was a Rooney vehicle, and a special one at that: it would be his last film before he left for army training. Rooney remembered that Brown seemed uncharacteristically relaxed, confident that the film was going to be a winner: "He'd just sit back, away from the camera, and say, with his great moon face breaking in a smile, 'okay, whenever you're ready.' When we finished the scene, he wouldn't say, 'Cut,' or 'Stop,' or even 'Okay.' He'd just be sitting there chuckling softly. Then he'd get up and you'd hear an assistant in the background say to cut the cameras." During filming of *The Human Comedy* Brown had helped Rooney appreciate that understatement and reaction can convey as much as a highly demonstrative style. Here, he gave Rooney more leeway, allowing him to improvise and "find" the character; he even allowed the actor to experiment briefly, albeit not too successfully, with an Irish accent. Consequently, Rooney turned in a mature and generous performance in what was a rather delicate role: a man in his twenties who forms a close relationship with a pubescent girl. For Rooney, the set was relaxed, and his relationship with Brown was easy, but others had slightly different memories. Angela Lansbury recalled being "awed by him [Brown] and afraid of him, quite frankly, and I think we all were a bit." Though she conceded that when the cameras stopped he was "congenial, a nice man," while shooting he could be "a bit gruff," and there was no doubt that he was the boss: "[he was] numero uno, there was no question, and he ruled the set, and I think he was particularly like that."[10]

At the Directors Guild of America tribute to Brown, held thirty years after the release of *National Velvet*, Elizabeth Taylor expressed her admiration and appreciation for Brown's "genius" and "his willingness to allow her time to find her way" in the role that remained her favorite. During *The White Cliffs of Dover*, Brown had noticed that for all her precociousness off the set, Taylor was actually very sensitive, and she responded far better to quiet encouragement than direct orders. In that respect she was similar to Garbo, and the two stars certainly had comparable chemistry with the camera. Brown spent much of his career showcasing the somber eyes of Garbo as she expressed loss and doomed love for a series of unworthy men. *National Velvet* is filled with similarly exquisite close-ups of what Brown called Taylor's "Act of God" face and her violet eyes as she falls under the spell of a passionate love. Unlike the disloyal men of Garbo films, however, the object of Velvet's devotion proves entirely deserving: having been the recipient of Velvet's compassion and tenderness, the Pie almost "burst[s] himself" to please her and win the Grand National.[11]

It wasn't just Taylor's beauty or charisma that impressed Brown. He could see that despite her youth, she was capable of delivering a performance of great emotional depth, of conveying *feeling* in a manner that seemed totally sincere. There is no doubt that a significant factor in generating this authenticity was Taylor's personal identification with the character of Velvet. An animal lover himself, Brown could understand Taylor's feelings for King Charles, so he offered her only the subtlest direction, suggesting that she draw from her real emotions in her scenes with the horse. The look of pure joy and exhilaration when she first glimpses the wild Pie seems entirely spontaneous; similarly, the quiet authority with which she calms the horse reveals her knowledge of his temperament. Taylor's natural empathy for animals also proved crucial in a later scene, when she must appear distraught at the sight of a gravely ill Pie. Rooney was on hand to offer advice on how to reach an emotional peak, suggesting that she picture the horse as a family member on the brink of death, but there was no need to fabricate elaborate scenarios: all Taylor had to do was imagine how she would feel if the horse were actually sick, and the tears flowed.[12]

Brown and Taylor generally worked well together, and Brown liked her—in spite of her overbearing mother and her (limited) stage-school training. He appreciated her innate honesty and the instinctual quality of her acting. Occasionally, however, her strong character and her tendency to engage in "diva behavior" surfaced, much to Brown's dismay. Everyone could see that *National Velvet* was shaping up to be a showcase for Taylor, and some at the studio were anxious to demonstrate due deference: when a star with "Miss Taylor" appeared on her dressing room door, Brown reacted with horror and ordered its immediate removal. At the time, Taylor was outraged because she felt entitled to the recognition, but she later admitted that Brown had been wise: "[he was] afraid it might go to my head . . . he wanted me always to stay the same . . . and I promised him with all my heart that I would never, never change." Although in this instance she acquiesced to Brown's wishes and even massaged his ego, Taylor's famous iron will emerged when she steadfastly refused to cut her hair, on camera, for the scene in which she prepares to disguise herself as a male jockey. Brown may have been feeling a little nostalgic when he came up with the plan, as twenty years before he had directed Laura La Plante in a similar scene in *Butterfly*. However, even at this tender age, Taylor knew how to make men feel like they were in charge: she went straight to studio hairdresser Sydney Guilaroff and ordered a wig, which was cut for the scene. Whether Brown discovered the switch is unclear, but he probably wouldn't have forced the issue. Perhaps there was an element of mutual bluff going on, and the incident seems to have developed into something of a gag between the two. In the congratulatory telegram she sent on the occasion of Brown's tribute in 1977, she quipped that she "would still cut my hair off for you any day."[13]

Taylor's deep identification with her character meant that Brown could easily extract a "natural" performance from her, but he had more of a challenge with the less disciplined Butch Jenkins, playing Donald. MGM publicity cast Brown as the kindly yet firm father figure who, using a combination of orders and bribes, knew how to handle the sometimes restless and unruly six-year-old. In Bagnold's novel, Donald is a minor but memorable character, given to fabricating fantastical tales and charming everyone with his "film-eyes . . . [and] platinum-blond Hollywood head." Physically, Jenkins was a perfect fit, but Brown—with some help from Rooney—had to coax a performance from him, and it turned out to be one that illustrates the general shift toward a naturalistic style for child actors of the 1940s. In an interview with Oscar Rimoldi, Brown was asked to reveal the secret of his success at directing children. He claimed to have "no tricks at all . . . I direct children as I direct adults, always trying to understand their personalities, and to make them trust me wholeheartedly. Children have a very keen mental perception. They know when you speak to them condescendingly or try to trick them into doing something." As a former juvenile performer himself, Brown undoubtedly understood what it was like to be railroaded or silenced by adults; when he directed children, he appreciated how important it was to listen and to build trust. Critic Manny Farber would later offer an intriguing insight about the essence of Jenkins's appeal, observing that he seemed very different from other child actors because he "still seems cut off from this civilization and has been wisely left." Yet, as neorealist directors such as Vittorio de Sica and Roberto Rossellini would soon realize, spontaneity is usually the result of much artifice, planning, and manipulation. Jenkins had to be firmly controlled to elicit a performance that translated to the screen as "wild" and unstructured. Claude Jarman

Jr., another Brown "discovery," remembered that the director's method of coaxing a "natural" performance from him was very hands-on, and there were many takes before the desired results were achieved (Brown's catchphrase was "one more take for Paris"). Brown's interventionist approach to directing children, then, seems diametrically opposed to his method with adults.[14]

A number of Brown films associate a child or young adolescent with instinct, emotions, and clarity of vision (an "uncluttered" view). In *National Velvet* these traits are most obviously embodied in Velvet, but there is also a hint of them in the character of Donald. Having observed how Jenkins expressed his will and his temper when he was off-guard, Brown sought to capture these mercurial qualities on camera. The result was the creation of an arresting character, a young boy who is given to illogical outbursts and hysteria, as well as moments of self-conscious manipulation and charm. Farber was perceptive in identifying the "uncivilized" aspect of Jenkins as Donald, who gives every appearance of being a child not yet fully integrated into social (and familial) structures. In one particularly memorable scene (which was also in the novel), Donald reacts hysterically to Mi's story of a horse left shipwrecked on an island. When Mi realizes that his entertaining story has had a devastating effect on the child, he hastily concocts a happy ending in which the horse is rescued and goes on to win the Grand National. Donald, however, is not foolish enough to believe him and proclaims that he "knows" the truth because he "was there." He is adamant that the horse actually starved to death in the "salty place." It is an extremely strange moment in this seemingly cozy vision of family life—not least because Jenkins so rapidly spirals into a very convincing hysteria—and it suggests that Brown was intrigued by the idea of exploring both the mechanics and the emotional impact of storytelling. In fact, Donald's function in *National Velvet* seems to be as a "weaver of tales," constantly coming up with bizarre stories and instant shifts in emotion to ensure that the spotlight remains on him. In one scene, he claims that he's been bitten by a "stinging ant" and has "been sick all night." In another, he declares that he hates the nail polish Edwina has put on him, only to insist that he "doesn't mind" it when his father sympathizes with him.

In scenes like these, Jenkins charms and even threatens to steal the film from its stars (Taylor and Rooney), but Brown also introduces moments that depict him as a curious mix of sweetness and cruelty. In doing so, he counteracts any tendency toward cloying sentimentality. *National Velvet* is often remembered as a feel-good family movie, and although MGM excised Bagnold's starker references to human cruelty toward animals, traces of a darker side remain in the character of Donald. Like the rest of his family, he is collector of everything, from the insects he stores in a bottle to the baby tooth he wears around his neck (reclaimed by less than sanitary means). Slightly disturbing, yet entirely authentic, is Donald's fascination with the trapped insects whose destiny he controls. His innate cruelty, and the sense that his capacity for empathy is not yet fully formed, is revealed in several scenes. He seems to clinically observe Velvet's emotional collapse when she fears that she has lost the Pie to colic. As her mother attempts to comfort her, Donald examines her as if she were one of his specimens: noting her chattering teeth, he imitates her. Yet for all these "savage" elements—the acknowledgment of a certain opaque, unexplainable quality in children—*National Velvet* also features the winning Jenkins charm. This is particularly in evidence in the scenes he shares with Donald Crisp, playing the embattled Brown patriarch whose authority is constantly undermined by his wife, his children, and even the family dog.[15]

National Velvet was the last time Brown worked with Jenkins, and although the boy appeared in a few films in the 1940s—most notably *Our Vines Have Tender Grapes*—his performances never quite matched those he delivered for Brown (he was, however, startling in the Fred Zinnemann programmer *My Brother Talks to Horses*). Jenkins is a rare example of a child star with a parent who put his interests first: when he developed a stutter and confessed that he was bored and unhappy, his mother let him return to a normal life. He reportedly had a career as a businessman in Texas and later retired to a farm near Asheville, North Carolina, where an interviewer caught up with him in 1970. He stated: "I have never regretted leaving the picture business and am very grateful to my mother for taking me away from it. I enjoyed the first few years of acting in movies but I certainly don't miss it." And he definitely ruled out a comeback: "There may be a better way to live than on a lake with a couple of cows, a wife, and children but being a movie star is not one."[16]

National Velvet involved a long and intense shoot—they were still filming exteriors in April—but the effort was rewarded when the film was released to overwhelmingly positive reviews in December 1944. *Variety* noted its "charm, deeply probing human-heart interest [and] magnificent spectacle," and even the grumpy Bosley Crowther acknowledged that although it was "far-fetched," this "fresh and delightful Metro picture" was "wholly captivating." The press reported how Brown and cinematographer Leonard Smith had come up with the film's unique aesthetic and, drawing from an extensive color palette and soft lighting, captured the astonishing beauty of Taylor. This tale of family life, imbued with both nostalgia and warm sentiment, as well as the charming story of one girl's act of "breathtaking folly," appealed to audiences traumatized by the horrors of war and human suffering. English reviewer H. P. Mooring noted that the film would do its part in helping to "temper some of the anti-British feeling which has spread over the American continent as a result of slightly different political views on Poland and Greece."[17]

James Agee's review playfully subverted the readers' expectation that he would offer a definitive opinion of the film's flaws and merits, and he managed to raise more than a few eyebrows while doing so. Expressing his admiration for certain aspects of Brown's handling, he nevertheless complained that it seemed like a lost opportunity: "The makers of the film had an all but ideal movie: a nominally very simple story, expressing itself abundantly in visual and active terms, which inclosed and might have illuminated almost endless recessions and inter-reverberations of emotions and meaning into religious and sexual psychology and into naturalistic legend." The avoidance of any exploration of the psychosexual impulses that drove Velvet, according to Agee, resulted in a film that seemed rather *muted*: "If the audience could have experienced what the girl experienced, with anything like the same razorlike distinctiveness of detail and intensity of action and spirit, they would have been practically annihilated." Agee's claim that *National Velvet* failed to convey Velvet's intense passion and to provoke a similar response from the audience seems highly contestable, given its status as an enduring classic. However, the most controversial aspect of his review was his description of the feelings the fourteen-year-old Taylor provoked in him. He didn't rate her as an actress ("she seems, rather, to turn things off and on, much as she is told"), but he confessed that he found her "rapturously beautiful" and was drawn to her expressions of "semi-hysterical emotion, such as ecstasy, an odd sort of pre-specific erotic sentience, and the anguish of overstrained hope, imagination, and faith." Rather like Donald's abrupt shifts of emotions, Agee concluded his review with the declaration that for all Taylor's faults and those of the film as a whole, both were "wonderful."[18]

Agee's identification of a sexual undercurrent in *National Velvet* may have made some readers uncomfortable, but he wasn't alone in noting it. The reviewer for *Time* magazine called the film an "interesting psychological study of hysterical obsession, conversion mania, [and] pre-adolescent sexuality." A few months later, Manny Farber alluded to the connection between Velvet's "passion" for the Pie and her emerging sexuality in a piece he wrote for the *New Republic*. Parker Tyler's examination of the importance of the horse in American cinema, written for the British publication *Sight and Sound*, doesn't explicitly mention *National Velvet*, but the connection it makes between animals, human sexuality, and processes of identification and empathy ("temperamentally unruly horses . . . [that] yield mysteriously to gifted individuals") is applicable to Brown's film. In MGM's view, Taylor was a gifted individual, and this film transformed her into a bona fide star. According to Susan Smith, the studio handled the tricky issue of her burgeoning sexuality by initially evading it and using animals to "sell" a particular image of Taylor that would appeal to parents (and not to grown men like Agee). Within weeks of the release of *National Velvet,* the studio published Taylor's ode to her pet gerbil, *Nibbles and Me,* and it rapidly became a best seller.[19]

National Velvet was one of MGM's top box-office hits of 1944–1945, and of course it has become a classic. In a reappraisal published thirty years after its release, Pauline Kael expressed her view that although *National Velvet* is a flawed film, it still possesses "a rare and memorable quality: it touches areas in our experience that movies rarely touch—the passions and obsessions of childhood. It's one of the most likable movies of all time." In their respective studies of Brown, Allen Estrin and Patrick McGilligan rank it among Brown's best, even though the film's soft center was specifically designed to appeal to wartime audiences. For Estrin, *National Velvet* marks a welcome return to the experimentation that had been the cornerstone of Brown's early career: "[it] experiments extensively with new sources of light to illuminate colour film— overcast skies and interiors that seem to be lit by kerosene lamps—and exhibits objects like trees, fences . . . to frame the action."[20]

W. C. Fields once warned against working with children and animals, but Brown, it seems, was a glutton for punishment. He had directed horses and adolescents (*Of Human Hearts, National Velvet*) and children and gophers (*The Human Comedy*); up next was the prospect of directing a boy and a host of wild animals. *The Yearling* had already defeated the formidable Victor Fleming and had cost MGM a fortune. When it was announced in January 1945 that Brown had agreed to take over the project and shoot it on location in the Florida scrubland, there were many who doubted that the aging director would have the stamina and determination to see it through.

26

A Year with *The Yearling*

Marjorie Kinnan Rawlings's Pulitzer Prize–winning novel *The Yearling* is a beautifully observed coming-of-age tale set in the post–Civil War period and told through the eyes of the sensitive Jody, the only child of Penny and Ora Baxter. When his father shoots a doe while on a hunting trip, Jody adopts her orphaned fawn and raises it as a pet, but when the deer gets older and threatens the family's crops, he must take responsibility and shoot this symbol of his youth. Back in 1938, a reader at MGM, Philip Shapiro, had filed a positive report on the novel, and, driven by the interest of producer Sidney Franklin and writer John Lee Mahin, the studio had purchased the rights. Franklin was drawn to Rawlings's story, with its themes of nature, childhood, and the intrusion of the adult world, in part because it was similar to Felix Salten's 1923 novel *Bambi*, which he had once hoped to adapt as a live-action film. He had eventually concluded that coordinating a cast of animal performers would be a production nightmare, and so he had passed *Bambi* on to Walt Disney. *The Yearling* seemed to promise a more straightforward production, but Franklin would soon come to regret his involvement.[1]

In his biography of director Victor Fleming, Michael Sragow has extensively detailed *The Yearling*'s many false starts at MGM, featuring clashes between Franklin and Mahin over fidelity to Rawlings's novel; the succession of writers, including Claudine West, Paul Osborn, and Mark Connolly, who worked on the script over the three-year period from 1939 to 1941; and the headaches Fleming endured after he finally received the script and commenced shooting in Florida in 1941. Sragow also records MGM's incredible investment to replicate Rawlings's scrubland world and fill it with animal actors—even initiating a breeding program to ensure an ample supply of deer. Despite all these efforts and a solid cast that included Spencer Tracy as Penny, Anne Revere as Ma, and newcomer Gene Eckman as Jody, the production collapsed within weeks. An attempt was made to revive it the following month, with King Vidor at the helm and a new cinematographer replacing Hal Ros-

son. Vidor seemed the ideal choice, given his excellent track record in directing Americana (starting with *The Jack-Knife Man* in 1920), but he was less
than enthused. He reportedly told Mayer he'd be "damned if he would get a
sunstroke in any swamp" to shoot a story of "a boy falling [in] love with a
fawn. . . . This sounds to me pretty corny for a three hour show." In his own
account, Vidor blamed MGM's unwieldy system and nature's refusal to cooperate—by the time he was assigned, the does had stopped breeding and
couldn't be persuaded otherwise—for the collapse of the production. Despite
a reported investment of almost $1 million and Franklin's readiness to take
over as director, interest in *The Yearling* dwindled as America moved closer to
war.[2]

Franklin, however, wasn't ready to give up. While working with Brown on
The White Cliffs of Dover, he speculated that his friend might have "the forti-
tude to stay on location and fight it out until he'd licked it." He was heartened
when Brown received the Paul Osborn script and reacted with enthusiasm,
which "was like a shot in the arm." Actually, it was relatively easy to win Brown
over. *The Yearling* was a slice of Americana that featured a child protagonist,
animals, strong sentiments, and plain folk—in short, everything Brown liked
in a film. He would later explain that he was drawn to the story because of
both its timelessness and its timeliness: "it epitomizes everything we fought
for in two wars." As a friend of Fleming's, Brown would have heard about the
horrors he had endured in Florida, but even after his own traumatic shoot on
Trail of '98, he remained convinced that the benefits of working on location
outweighed the risks. A couple of years later, during publicity for *Intruder in
the Dust,* he noted that "a location troupe, in my experience, quickly picks up
an indefinite but important 'mood' or 'spirit' of a sector. After a few days on
location you find your actors are speaking much more convincingly in the
native dialect."[3]

In this instance, Brown's enthusiasm may have been colored by personal
problems. His marriage to Alice formally ended when she filed for divorce in
March, and he responded by burying himself in work and consulting with
Franklin and Osborn on amendments to a script that was now four years old.
Franklin agreed with Brown that the character of Ma might be better developed to explain her emotional distance from Jody—she's afraid to express her
love because she has lost all her other children to malnutrition and disease.
Osborn was commissioned to submit some new scenes, including one of Ma
searching for Jody after he runs away from home and another of her breaking
down when he returns. As they worked to finalize the script, the first rum-
blings of discontent surfaced. According to one-time contributor Mahin,

Franklin was keen on "softening" the hard edges of both the plot and the characters (especially Ma), and he even suggested a less emotionally devastating ending. He met resistance from Brown on both fronts, and on this occasion, producer conceded to director.[4]

Putting the finishing touches on the script was important, but even more pressing in the spring of 1945 was casting the main roles. Tracy had moved on and wouldn't countenance another jaunt to Florida; child actor Gene Eckman was now too old, and in any case, he had been afraid of animals, much to Fleming's exasperation; and even though he had worked with her on *National Velvet*, Brown wasn't pushing for Anne Revere. Instead, they decided to bring in new blood. To play Penny, Franklin and Brown chose an up-and-coming star who was then under contract to David O. Selznick. Gregory Peck had recently appeared in a string of films beginning with *Days of Glory* (for Brown's old rival Jacques Tourneur) before hitting his stride with *The Keys of the Kingdom* and Hitchcock's *Spellbound*. Peck was already embroiled in the production of *Duel in the Sun*, but a strike at the studio in April 1945 had led to a temporary suspension of shooting, freeing him to take on *The Yearling*. Peck's striking good looks hardly fitted Rawlings's Penny, who was "no bigger than a boy. His feet were small, his shoulders narrow, his ribs and hips jointed together in a continuous fragile framework." However, the actor was likable and had charisma; he could anchor the cast and balance the harsher performance required from the actress playing Ma. For that role, several actresses were considered, and it was even reported that Ingrid Bergman would reunite with Peck following their successful collaboration on *Spellbound*. It surprised many when the studio opted to cast a contract player, Jacqueline White, in the part. White, a UCLA coed, had been "discovered" by MGM talent scout Billy Grady following an appearance in a college production. She had had some minor roles in major productions such as *A Guy Named Joe* (1943) and in not-so-major ones such as the Laurel and Hardy vehicle *Air Raid Wardens* (1943). According to White, Grady suggested her for the role of Ma, even though, at twenty-three, she was significantly younger than Rawlings's character. Newspapers would later report that Brown's initial doubts were dispelled when she donned the "deep lined, leathery make up of a pioneer woman" and played a scene for him. White was "overjoyed" when she learned that she had the part, and in a matter of weeks MGM had dispatched her to Florida. Little did she know that her promised "big break" would soon end in disappointment and sadness.[5]

Just as he had been determined not to change Rawlings's ending, Brown was adamant that the part of Jody could be played only by an unknown non-professional, "unspoiled" by the stage school. He was "particularly anxious to avoid any even sub-conscious touch of sophistication in the boy actor. He had to be a little awkward, a little self-conscious, but very appealing." Brown's determination to cast a newcomer was motivated in part by his realization that a shift was taking place in audience preferences. The 1940s saw the ascent of child stars such as Jackie Jenkins, Margaret O'Brien, Peggy Ann Garner, Roddy McDowall, Dean Stockwell, and Enzo Staiola (of de Sica's *Bicycle Thieves*), all of whom had a more natural, authentic style shaped less by formal training and more by instinct and emotion. Leaving MGM scouts to search through their lists, Brown embarked on his own expedition, flying his plane to the South and touring six cities, hoping to make a discovery. After several disappointing days, he made a last stop in Nashville, where, posing as a school inspector, he observed a class of eleven-year-olds going about their daily routine. His eye was drawn to one blond, blue-eyed boy who was unpinning a Valentine's Day display. The child, Claude Jarman Jr., had a rare combination of awkwardness and dreaminess, qualities so intrinsic to Rawlings's Jody. Brown later told Franklin that Jarman interested him because he had an unsophisticated air, as well the right "look"—his hair was quite long, just right for a kid living in the Florida scrub, cut off from education and culture. Jarman was the son of a railroad executive and had appeared in some school plays and community theater, but he was more interested in sports than in acting. When Brown approached his parents and told them he wanted young Claude to star in a major Hollywood production, they were stunned. Claude Jarman Sr. later admitted to a Florida newspaper that he "didn't know what to think . . . I wouldn't let my wife tell it for a while for fear it might not be true." Like Jackie Jenkins, Jarman Jr. wasn't being pushed into acting by overbearing parents, and he was enthusiastic about participating. Brown later observed to columnist Hedda Hopper that it was Jarman's appealing personality that made his performances (in two films for Brown, as well as a memorable turn in John Ford's *Rio Grande*) so effective and affective, but his humility and easygoing nature sabotaged his career in the long run: "Claude was never an actor at heart. He had none of the extrovert characteristics of an actor. He was very natural and had none of the ambitions of an actor."[6]

In an email to the author, Claude Jarman Jr. remembered how he and his family were brought to Hollywood so he could prepare for the role. As both his director and a quasi-paternal mentor, Brown formed a close relationship with him: "Clarence Brown basically had me living with him once I was finally selected." Brown made it clear that he was heavily invested in Jarman both professionally and personally, "since I was the only boy brought in for a test that was selected personally by him." Over the course of a year, Brown coached Jarman on the back lot and on location in Florida and California ("we read the script a lot and talked endlessly"), guiding him through retakes and preparing him for the hoopla his performance would inevitably attract. Like Gene Reynolds before him, he was invited to the Calabasas ranch on weekends, where he socialized with Brown's mother, his daughter Adrienne (now an adult), and his newest fiancée, Marian Spies.[7]

By April, the cast was ready, and as they left for Florida, Brown must have been reasonably confident that he could cope with any challenges presented by the location. After all, he had shot two Olga Petrova films in the state back in 1917. But now he was a man in his late fifties, and this was a much more high-stakes production. Doing little to boost his confidence, the *New York Times* noted the departure of this latest *Yearling* team by reminding readers of the two previous attempts and of the fact that the production was already running at a deficit of $500,000 (it was actually a lot more). Just as his predecessor Fleming had watched things unravel, Brown realized within days what he had gotten himself into. First off was the matter of the accommodations: the Silver Springs Court Hotel and Cottages may have advertised itself as "different" and "in the open," but the natural breeze couldn't offset the Florida humidity, and air-conditioning units had to be hastily sourced and installed. Unsurprisingly, the arrival of a big Hollywood production sparked huge interest among the locals and the press, and Brown had to contend with curious visitors, surveillance, and near-constant reports on the film's progress. One profile noted that Brown was a "perfectionist, a stickler for detail," and that he had personally flown across Marion County in a search for the best spots, choosing thirty-eight sites spread over a 300,000-acre area. It was also reported that his passion for authenticity prompted him to demand that Rawlings's original backwoods cabin be transported over fifty miles of rough roads and reassembled "piece by piece and set up" in the main location.[8]

Many of the stories in the press concerned the Hollywood folks' attempts to control the one thing they couldn't: nature. As the shoot wore on, the obstacles they encountered were detailed in increasingly gleeful tones. In a piece for *Collier's* published shortly after Brown's unit had beat a retreat to California, Amy Porter offered an amusing account of nature's revenge in all its forms, from "red bugs and wood ticks" enthusiastically doing their bit to "add to the boiling discomfort of the hundred or so people working" to the "supreme annoyance" caused by the persistent cloud cover that blocked the sunlight and ruined every shot. Writer John Maloney sided with the "vastly amused" Floridians who viewed "those Hollywood nuts" and their muddled attempts to deal with the resident wildlife as proof that they "just didn't act quite bright." He quoted one local who pointed out that the "'fool folks' frantically dousing themselves with DDT to ward off the 'chiggers' should simply concede defeat and 'let them critters git their fill. Then they'll stop bitin.'" Maloney recounted tall tales of vomiting buzzards that targeted the crew, a horse too drunk on beer to perform, and a recalcitrant bear (playing Slewfoot) that, when hit with a slingshot full of BBs in an effort to make him run for a chase scene, "calmly sat down in the water, held up a paw as if asking for time out, and proceeded to pick the BBs out."[9]

Journalist George Bartlett was on the set in May 1945 and contributed a firsthand account of how Brown coordinated his company and dealt with the constant challenges:

Director Brown appears, looking something like a jungle hunter in his pith helmet, khaki pants and snake boots. He and Leonard Smith, photography director, squint up the road through their "finders." "It would be grand if we could see some sky down that road," Brown says. Having come so far for his effects he is anxious to make every shot tell. "We trimmed some of the oaks back," an aid[e] assures him. . . . The director nods. "Let's see if the horse can pull that wagon," he suggests, leaving nothing to chance. . . . "Get Jody over here!" Brown shouts. . . . Brown takes the boy on his knee and whispers advice. Script Girl Eyla Jacobus, who keeps the important log of production, kneels at their side. Claude nods understandingly as the director talks. . . . Brown is ready. An assistant director blows a whistle to give Jody warning. "Camera!" yells Brown through a megaphone. Jody starts running. But something is wrong. An auto hood protrudes somewhere in the background. In a picture only slightly post Civil war, that won't do.[10]

While Bartlett's account presents a picture of an organized set presided over by a calm director who is in total control, the truth was somewhat different. Brown's nerves were soon at a breaking point as he grappled with a cast of unpredictable animals, an increasingly cranky crew, and actors with varying levels of experience. He later recalled that the experience in Florida easily took the title of "worst shoots he ever endured," with the "heat and rattlesnakes and mosquitoes" taking an immense toll: "I never went through a seizure like that in my life, I lost 20 pounds on that picture." Everyone was under siege from the voracious insects and worn out by the sweltering heat and humidity; some were even battling bouts of dysentery from drinking contaminated water.

Brown's letters to Franklin—who was comfortably ensconced in California—reveal his increasing frustration at the slow pace and his fears that the production was going to fail. Like Fleming and Vidor before him, Brown was beginning to realize that as much as he liked animals, deer were another matter. For a start, the fawns and the pregnant does needed a tremendous amount of care, with the small fawns requiring feeding every two hours. They also proved none too interested in being directed. As Claude Jarman remembered, "A deer is impossible to train. You just have to keep filming over time until the deer does what you want it to do. . . . We had one scene where we had to film it over seventy times." An exasperated Brown complained to Franklin that just as the child actor was easing himself into a scene, his animal costar would stop "performing": "I tell you right now that if we get it [a scene between Jarman and the fawn] it will be a miracle to get emotion and the deer at the same time." For one key scene in which Jody goes in search of the orphaned fawn, Brown needed the tiny creature to sit still while the boy comes upon the spot, pushes back the vegetation, and discovers it. The fawn had other ideas, and take after take was ruined as it sprang up. Even assistant Chester Franklin was baffled, and he knew something about handling deer—back in 1934, he had directed the rather extraordinary *Sequoia*, the tale of a deer's unexpected friendship with a mountain lion. Brown finally figured out what was making the fawn so jittery: it wasn't fear of Jarman but discomfort at sitting on the baking earth. Former engineer Brown came up with the simple idea of burying a block of ice underneath the soil. It had the desired effect—the fawn settled down, and he got the shot.[11]

It wasn't just the animals that required careful handling. In contrast to the more "hands-off" approach he employed with adult actors (including Peck), Brown would later admit that Jarman's performance was "semi-synthetic," the result of a "labor of love." Jarman confirmed that it took him a long time to ease into the "natural" performance Brown demanded: "I think it was only after four months into filming that I felt comfortable. . . . Before that time I was lost. I can look at that film today and spot the early scenes and still cringe at how dreadful I was." Jarman wanted to please his mentor, but he was also a little intimidated because Brown could be a very formidable presence on the set and "a very tough guy to work for. He was a driving person with his crew and actors. He wasn't a screamer, he just kept striving for perfection. We worked Saturdays, we worked Sundays. He did what he asked everybody to do, but he was a hard person. Never difficult with me, but a real perfectionist." There were occasions when Brown snapped: Jarman recalled him hurling his safari hat at one of the crew after a take was ruined.[12]

The source of much of Brown's grumpiness was Chester "Chet" Franklin (Sidney's brother), who was heading the second unit. Obviously, Brown had spent his career working with second units, but everyone on the set understood that the director was the boss, to whom all others deferred. In an interview with Kevin Brownlow, producer Sidney Franklin admitted that Brown was not happy about the sizable second unit shooting on *The Yearling* or that Franklin's brother was in charge of it. Both Sidney Franklin and Jarman recalled that Brown permitted Chet to handle only the animal action scenes, not the closer scenes between Jody and the deer Flag. Brown's distrust was probably due, in part, to a professional difference of opinion: Chet Franklin was evidently not shy about expressing his opinions about how sequences involving the animals and Jody should be filmed, and he had clashed with Fleming on that issue years before. Yet it is also possible that the rift between Brown and Franklin was prompted by Brown's deep feelings of insecurity, which shaped him into the hypersensitive, prickly, and sometimes cold character he was. Chet Franklin had a much longer involvement in the project, and this may have caused Brown some anxiety that his authority on set would be undermined. Added to this was his awareness that Chet was regularly reporting back to his brother in California.[13]

It seems the resentment was mutual: in letters to Sidney, Chet expressed his exasperation with Brown, blasting his unwillingness to praise the hard-pressed second unit. According to Chet, Brown would view the daily footage and then request retakes, fully aware that the light was fading and the animals were becoming increasingly uncooperative. It made Chet wonder whether some part of Brown wanted the second unit to fail; the director certainly seemed determined to constantly challenge him. Tensions came to a head during the shooting of one scene showing Jody's encounter with some raccoons beside the river. Using a second camera to shoot reaction shots of the boy's face, Brown voiced his skepticism that Franklin could capture the animals in one unbroken take. Franklin, however, had planned the scene in some detail, precisely marking out everyone's positions and ensuring that the animals' sight line was on the camera (so that when a cut-in of Jarman's face was added, they would seem to be looking at him). Cinematographer Len Smith had also devised a special camera boom to create a sweeping shot, showing it all. As it turned out, the scene was shot in just one take, and both the human and animal actors behaved impeccably. Everyone was thrilled, except for Brown: "He wanted to try again, so we sat and sat and sat while the light went and it started to rain and that was it. Len Smith was sore as hell at Clarence because he never said a word to me about how smooth the scene went."[14]

The problems on the set were not simply the result of a personality clash between two strong-willed individuals. Chet Franklin complained that Brown's slow approach and his failure to make decisions quickly were frustrating the rest of the crew: "I know now why things go so slow with Brown. He won't say yes or no and will not help the boys [crew] keep ahead of him." In a final attack, he reported that Brown frequently lost his cool and that no one escaped his wrath, not even his discovery, Jarman: "I know now why the boy looks a bit stiff at times—it's because Clarence swears at him and scares him to a point where he is speechless. I felt like telling Clarence something the other day when he let the kid have it. If I was the kid's father, I'd knock all of Brown's teeth out." If Franklin's account can be believed, it would certainly cast doubt on Brown's reputation as a sensitive and patient director of children, but Jarman himself disputed it, although he conceded that working with Brown could be challenging: "Was he tough on me? . . . You bet, but he was tough on everyone. He strove for perfection and it took some effort to get what he wanted out of a ten year old with no professional acting experience." But Jarman was adamant that Brown never aimed his anger at him personally: "[he was] very patient with me . . . he liked me . . . I was his protégé, he had a lot riding on me." Nor did he have any memory of being cursed at or of being petrified of his director, but he had plenty of recollections of seemingly endless retakes and the dread of hearing Brown say, "One more take for Paris." Jarman's account mirrored that of Gene Reynolds: both recalled that despite Brown's reputation for being cold or grumpy, he rarely displayed that side to them and seemed genuinely proud and fond of them.[15]

If there were tense moments on the set of The Yearling, it was entirely understandable. The harsh conditions would have been tolerable if the results of each day's filming were satisfactory, but that was far from the case. Technicolor specialist Harry Wolf had initially been enchanted by the location and by the beauty of the Florida sun, gushing to the local press, "It has a different quality from the California sun . . . in some ways it's softer. For certain effects it is best. When the Florida sky is right I get wonderful color." However, he soon realized that the soft sun was all but obscured by the persistent cloud cover. When the dailies were viewed, it was clear that almost all the footage was below par, and some of it was simply unusable. Hiring a plane, Brown took to the skies to assess the weather conditions and returned with bad news. As he explained to Franklin, there was "a complete blanket of smoke covering the whole state [from scrub fires raging through Florida that summer]. When the sun is shining, we get only about one third intensity of light. We open natural exposure on the ground, we shoot wide open, and still are underexposed.

The sky which is white still overexposes. We have clouds in the sky, but in exposing for the under-lit foreground, everything goes out in the sky. The scenes we thought were beautiful are mud." Charles Rosher, who was working with Smith in Florida and would later take over principal photography, remembered that in the brief moments when the smoke lifted, the rain almost invariably began to fall.[16]

In the end, the three-month stint in Florida yielded little viable footage, but it did help the cast settle into their roles. All the care Brown took with Jarman paid off, as the child began to relax and deliver a more natural performance. Crucially, and unlike his predecessor Eckman, Jarman had no fear of his animal costars and formed a close bond with one of fawns that appeared in most of the scenes and, like Flag, grew up as the shoot progressed. Nicknamed "Bambi," the fawn was docile enough to be picked up and hugged, and it didn't even require sedation for a scene in which it lies down beside Jody for a night's sleep. Jarman interacted well with his human costars too, and he remembered Peck as being particularly kind, a "saint," who was "very patient" with him. The warm rapport that developed between them, on set and off, helped color the relaxed dynamic in their scenes together. Peck won fans among the inhabitants of Silver Springs, too. The press approvingly reported that he was always willing to stop and talk to locals who accosted him to communicate their thoughts on how Penny Baxter should be played. Brown got along fine with the always professional and courteous actor, and although they didn't develop a close friendship off the set, Peck was one of the first to speak at the Directors Guild of America tribute to Brown in 1977. In an unpublished interview with Scott Eyman, he remembered Brown as "a great, quiet, technical man," but confessed to being a little puzzled by his directing style: "At first, I couldn't figure it out. I knew he was Garbo's favorite, but it didn't make any sense because he didn't seem to actually direct. And then I realized that she must have liked him because what he did was leave her alone and set everything up for her." He may have been a little underwhelmed by Brown's method of directing actors, but Peck was impressed by his precise camera work: "He knew *exactly* what to do with the camera; he was the best technical director I ever had."[17]

Peck and Jarman were working out well, but Jacqueline White became a source of contention. Shortly after her arrival in Florida, she encountered her first obstacle: Marjorie Kinnan Rawlings. White got all dressed up to attend a meeting with the author and was taken aback by her reaction: "[Rawlings] said I was too young and pretty for the part" (the author hadn't liked Anne Revere either). Undeterred, White threw herself into the role, put up with the conditions ("big mosquitoes, big spiders, snakes . . . heat and humidity"), and followed her "gut instinct" to shape a performance that was pared down and de-glamorized. Because many of her scenes were exteriors and long shots, she had only minimal contact with Brown on the set, but between takes the two bonded over the humorous letters her father sent her ("he [Brown] always seemed to get a kick out of them"). She recalled that Brown was "very passionate about his work," and he seemed to warm to her when she declared her determination to prove the skeptics wrong. For the few weeks she was on the set with him, Brown seemed pleased with her work.[18]

However, if Brown was willing to give White a chance, Sidney Franklin was less receptive. In his memoirs he quotes from letters he exchanged with Brown in which he expressed his disquiet that the Ma he saw in the rushes was far from the MGM ideal of an American mom. In one letter written in July, just as the company was leaving Florida, Franklin complained that the director was allowing White to look "awfully depressed . . . [she] looked sort of unpleasant . . . there [in a scene that takes place after the storm, as Jody and Penny begin replanting] she should be happy." It wasn't just her performance that Franklin found off-putting; he complained, "With that face of hers you've got to watch—we've got to look out for self-pity . . . I want to be sorry for Ma, and I don't want her to be sorry for herself." Referring to a scene in which Ma is shown walking home after Jody has run away, Franklin expressed his concern that the audience might find her attitude disconcerting: "when she was walking home you got the feeling she's a sour sort of person, instead of carrying a burden in her soul." Brown's response to Franklin's criticism was uncompromising: he wrote back in support of White's performance. To justify the style he had used to film her, he pointed out that the character *should* be played as downbeat and sullen, shaped by years of poverty and grief. It was, he observed, hardly likely that "[Ma] was happy very often, especially after doing a hard day's wash." Displaying a grasp of the changing expectations of a postwar audience, he also explained to Franklin that he was trying to extract the kind of "natural" performance from White that Elia Kazan had recently coaxed from Dorothy Malone in *A Tree Grows in Brooklyn* (1945).[19]

It is interesting that Brown was so adamant that the character of Ma should be played as a withdrawn, emotionally inexpressive woman who is fearful of showing her love for Jody because she has been so scarred by loss. In favoring that interpretation, he was making a subtle distinction between his Ma and Rawlings's. In the novel, Ma is undoubtedly reluctant to show love, but she expresses emotion through bouts of temper, general cantankerousness, and, on occasion, comic posturing. One might speculate that Brown emotionally identified with the characters that exhibited the traits he himself possessed—the sensitivity of Jody and his otherworldly friend, Fodderwing, and the prickliness of Ma—and he lavished most of his attention on these characters and the actors portraying them. In any case, we will never know how effective Jacqueline White might have been in the role: while in Florida she received word that her father was seriously ill, and she went home to be with him (sadly, he died before she got there). Shortly afterward, MGM announced that the cast and crew were being recalled to California and that White would no longer be part of the production. Why MGM dispensed with White has been the subject of some speculation. Franklin's resistance may have played a part, but Jarman has suggested that she was simply too young and "too pretty," and perhaps her performance lacked the depth and world-weariness an older and more experienced actress might have brought to the role. Brown's correspondence with Franklin and White's memories of their working relationship indicate that the director was happy with her, but in truth, she had not been his first choice. According to White, when Billy Grady first escorted her to the screen test, he admitted that Brown (and MGM) wanted Jane Wyman, but she wasn't available. By September, Wyman's schedule had cleared, allowing her to take over the role.[20]

The decision to cast Wyman took many by surprise. Her physical appearance was the polar opposite of Rawlings's conception of Ma, and the actress was best known for lighter, more comedic roles. According to one biographer, producer Benny Thau summoned Wyman to MGM for an interview shortly after Brown and company had returned to Culver City. When she arrived, all blonde and glamorous, Franklin seemed taken aback and expressed doubt that she was right for the role. Brown, however, argued that the lightness of her hair would work as a contrast to the very dark Peck and provide a logical explanation for their fair-haired child. It was not only Wyman's physical appearance that intrigued Brown; he had almost certainly seen a prerelease cut of her latest production, Billy Wilder's *The Lost Weekend,* and been impressed by her. Brown must have known that casting Wyman would have a devastating impact on Jacqueline White, but business was business.[21]

There was still one person left to convince: Wyman herself. Brown later revealed that the actress had her doubts—she "thought she was incompetent for the part"—so he had to "build up her ego a little." Brown's faith and encouragement not only helped Wyman find her way in a tough role but also led to a lifelong friendship between the two (she called him "Pappy" and credited him with giving her the first "real" part of her career). In September 1945 Wyman was confirmed. She faced a grueling schedule, commuting between MGM, external locations, and the Burbank lot (where she was finishing retakes on a Warner production, *Night and Day*). However, she maintained a professional air, immersing herself in the role by staying in character on set, wearing minimal makeup, and taking little time off. Her efforts were worthwhile: at the heart of *The Yearling* is her powerful performance as a woman so scarred and crushed by life that she has closed in on herself. Fearful of loving Jody lest she lose him, too, she expresses her love in quiet, understated ways that recall the poignant tenderness of the selfless sisters in *Butterfly* and *Smouldering Fires* or the devoted mothers in *Of Human Hearts* and *National Velvet*. Wyman would come to regard her performance as Ma Baxter as one of her best and the production as a crucial turning point in both her personal life and her career: "For the first time in my life, I was no longer shy, or afraid of being ridiculed for my ambition."[22]

As Wyman settled in, Brown began to relax. The collapse of the Florida shoot devastated Brown, who admitted to Franklin that he was worried about the effect it might have on his career: "[it is] very serious from my point of view because we worked like hell to get the right thing." For MGM, it only confirmed that once a company left the back lot, expensive logistical difficulties ensued. It was with some reluctance that the studio sanctioned Brown's request to shoot again on location, this time at the more manageable Lake Arrowhead. He used some of the leftover sets from *Of Human Hearts* and collaborated with Charles Rosher—who had assumed principal photography after Len Smith was taken ill—to create the distinctive visual design. Rosher had a reputation as a painstaking perfectionist who didn't always see eye to eye with directors, but Brown admired him and had been influenced by his work, especially on Murnau's *Sunrise*. Rosher had high regard for Brown, too, praising his "incredible patience" and voicing his appreciation of Brown's efforts to achieve "complete realism." For instance, he wanted to "dispense with all artificial make-up. It was a bold step and a photographic challenge." Responding to Brown's request for a look that was similar to the N. C. Wyeth illustrations in the original novel, Rosher came up with a very specific lighting schema:

> The dramatic mood of the majority of the scenes laid in the interior of
> the cabins suggested a low key lighting. But, in going to a low key, I
> wanted to inject a quality of warmth that seemed to emanate from this
> little family group. Warm tones were emphasized whenever the
> fireplace appeared to be the dominant source of illumination. To

accentuate the pathos of Fodderwing's funeral, the entire sequence was photographed in a cold light. The same effect was achieved in the roving shot over the grave stones of the Baxter children in the early scenes.

The carefully planned design drew from Brown's work on *The Signal Tower*, *Of Human Hearts*, and *Flesh and the Devil*, as well as from Rosher's cinematography on *Sunrise* and on the Mary Pickford vehicle *Sparrows* (1926). Charmingly, Brown even included a tribute to Rosher in the "discovery of Flag scene," where a *Sunrise*-style roving camera tracks the marks left by the orphaned fawn.[23]

Getting the technical side right was always one of Brown's chief concerns, but he also had to manage the demands of a now-expanded cast, many of whom were already exhausted. The "veterans" of the Florida shoot now mingled with Wyman and a host of new faces such as Henry Travers, June Lockhart, and Donn Gift. According to Jarman, Gift had originally auditioned for the lead but was cast as Jody's otherworldly friend, the "crookedy" boy Fodderwing, who identifies more with animals than with humans and whose death is Jody's first experience of loss. Although Gift was as inexperienced as Jarman, his touching performance makes his scenes among the most moving of the film. Both Gift and Jarman were under immense pressure, working "at least six days a week." In Jarman's case, he was in virtually every scene, and he was also required to complete the mandatory three hours of school each day. He remembered feeling like he "never had a break." Adding to his exhaustion was Sidney Franklin's insistence that he spend time with MGM's resident acting coach, Lillian Burns, to get some pointers. When Brown detected some of the Burns method filtering into Jarman's performance, he ordered an immediate halt to the lessons.[24]

All in all, the production went smoothly, with the California climate proving more amenable than Florida's and the daily footage being of a higher quality than many Technicolor films of the time. After several weeks at Lake Arrowhead, the company returned to Culver City to shoot some interiors scenes, with a few pickup shots and retakes done in Florida in January 1946. Brown retained some footage from the original Florida shoot— mostly second-unit work, but also some brief scenes in which White can be glimpsed in long shot—as well as a few action sequences and miscellaneous shots salvaged from Fleming's shoot (such as an opening shot of Lake George by cinematographer Charles Boyle). Finally, after almost a year on the project (and seven years after Franklin had first convinced MGM to make the film), Brown had achieved what had once seemed impossible: *The Yearling* was in the can.[25]

Directors weren't usually personally involved in editing their films at MGM, but given his intense work on the project and his extensive experience as an editor, few objected when Brown announced that he would supervise the process. It was a daunting task: there was a lot of footage, and Brown faced the usual pressure to cut it down to the standard length of an MGM film. The final film ran a little over two hours—perhaps longer than the studio would have liked—and as Eyman and Gillam have noted, its leisurely pacing seems appropriate for this lyrical evocation of a world apart from society.[26]

Brown introduces a dreamlike mood in the film's opening voice-over as Penny relates how he returned from the Civil War intent on leaving "civilization" behind. In the spirit of America's first pioneers, he ventured deep into the Florida scrub and carved out his own "island" with his bride, Ora. Shots showing dense scrubland, ominous overhanging trees, and a network of rivers conjure up a mysterious, even primeval, landscape and hint that there is a deeper level to Penny's physical journey. References to his Civil War past introduce the key theme of psychological trauma, which has driven Penny to leave society behind and will eventually form the bedrock of Jody's progression from child to adult. The atmospheric opening is followed by our introduction to Jody. Using a dramatic crane shot, Brown sweeps down to his small figure lying next to a watering hole, deep in the forest. Dreamily whiling away the day watching animals and building frivolities like a toy waterwheel, Jody is a child of nature. He is mesmerized by the sights and sounds that envelop him, causing him to forget his domestic chores and, indeed, time itself. Undoubtedly, Jody is Rawlings's creation, but he is brought to life here by a director whose work often features dreamy, sensitive children: most notably, little Ulysses, who is entranced by birds and a gopher in *The Human Comedy* and is similarly introduced with a swooping crane shot. The drama of the crane shot and what Eyman terms the film's subsequent "languorous" pace may seem at odds, but in fact they work well together to capture Jody's sensual yet dangerous world, one where life and death, violence and gentleness, cruelty and compassion are natural bedfellows. In the scenes that follow, Brown beautifully relates Jody's development from the lonely child who yearns for something to nurture, "something with dependence to it," to the young adult who must confront the consequences of his decision to "save" Flag from certain death.

Many viewers probably remember *The Yearling* with nostalgia—all those warm, touching scenes of a boy frolicking with his beloved fawn, accompanied by the evocative music of Frederic Delius's *Appalachia*—but the film is, in fact, surprisingly tough and uncompromising. Unlike Rawlings, Brown doesn't fully explore humans' dual attitudes toward animals—as both pets and meat—and he shies away from the graphic details of Jody's killing of Flag, but what he presents is far from reassuring. MGM films, and indeed, Brown films, have often been justifiably criticized for their overly sentimental depictions of family life, childhood, and animals, but in *The Yearling*, Brown refuses to sugarcoat the realities of an existence defined by, and subject to, nature. Joyful scenes of Jody playing with his deer, and comic interludes involving visits to neighbors and to the town of Volusia, are balanced by somber, melancholic moments. Advertising touted the film's glorious Technicolor, but Brown's use of Expressionist-influenced photography reminds us how closely life is intertwined with death, joy with sorrow. Particularly effective is the panning shot of Ma bleakly looking at the tumbledown gravestones of all her dead children, as well as the scene in which dark shadows envelop Jody as he is ushered into the room where Fodderwing lies dead. Fodderwing's funeral, too, is strikingly presented, shot with such a starkly Expressionistic palette that not even the crass addition of spiritual music—what critic Bosley Crowther described as the moment when "the Aurora Borealis is turned on and the heavenly choir starts singing"—can diminish its power.[27]

Of course, the film's most traumatic scene comes toward the end, when Jody is forced to shoot his deer. In an interview with Eyman, Brown admitted to using "every trick in the book" to coax an emotionally wrenching performance from Jarman, including telling him to pretend his mother was dying. However, in an interview with the author, Jarman revealed that he had established such a strong bond with "Bambi" that he simply imagined what it would be like to lose him. The results were powerful, but the scene almost didn't make it into the film: Franklin tried to argue for a happy ending, but Brown refused. Brown often took a firm stand when confronted with producers and studio personnel, and in this case it is clear that he had a firmer grasp of Rawlings's novel and the realities of the rural folk she depicted than Franklin. Visually and thematically, *The Yearling* fits perfectly into Brown's oeuvre, in which he explores themes of life, loss, and death and the clash between innocence and experience. His decision to retain the original ending respects the integrity of Rawlings's novel, but it also adheres to the logic of the narrative. Jody's execution of his pet ends his usurpation of the natural order, initiated by his well-intentioned action in saving the fawn from the brutal Darwinian universe. The world of *The Yearling* is one of predators and prey, where the weak are eliminated and the strong must ruthlessly fight to retain their supremacy.

Nowhere is this more clearly expressed than in the early scene in which Penny must shoot the doe to ensure his own survival: with her carcass still warm, the buzzards arrive, eager to pick her clean and wait for her fawn to succumb. Jody's intervention, which to the audience seems so right, so *natural,* is revealed to be misguided because it creates an animal that exists in a kind of artificial limbo. It may seem a giant leap from Garbo to a fawn, but like her Anna Karenina, Flag is tainted by death, living on borrowed time, and doomed to fulfill its natural destiny. And so, in this "feel-good" family movie, Brown offers the rather distressing lesson that humans' attempts to interfere with nature will end only in loss, and the pure emotion of childhood will inevitably succumb to the realities of the adult world.[28]

Such bleak themes were not highlighted in MGM's elaborate promotional campaign for *The Yearling.* The publicity department declared 1947 to be "The Year of the Yearling," and a lavish premiere was held in Los Angeles at the Cathay Circle Theater, featuring foliage in the foyer, a full orchestra, and a live deer giving autographs using a hoof dipped in ink. Brown's reactions to such hoopla were not recorded, but Franklin was delighted, pronouncing it "the most beautifully vulgar thing I've ever seen." The studio solicited and received Rawlings's endorsement; privately, she had mixed feelings, but she praised Brown and company for doing such "a beautiful job." Unsurprisingly, much of the campaign centered on Jarman, and soon after the premiere, the *New York Times* carried a profile of him. He was described as the same dreamy little boy he had always been, bashful and eager to deflect the praise heaped on him by assuring readers he had simply done "what Mr. Brown . . . told me to." It was revealed that his future plans included the University of Tennessee, but first there were a few more film projects in the works (a version of *The Secret Garden,* to be directed by Brown, was announced, but Jarman didn't appear in it). Unlike Elizabeth Taylor, Jarman didn't get to keep his animal costar—"Bambi" apparently went to a zoo—but he reportedly pocketed a bonus of $25,000.[29]

Reviews for *The Yearling* were mainly warm and appreciative. Bosley Crowther noted that the film "caught much of the feeling which a lonesome lad has for wild things, expressed with such tenderness and eloquence in Mrs. Rawlings' classic work," yet it also captured "the adult pain and struggle in a frontier farmer's life, the humor and spunk of rawboned rustics and the strength that derives from patient toil." Although critical of the occasional lapses into cliché, he was complimentary about Brown, who "revealed both his heart and intelligence in keeping the whole thing restrained. By simple pictorial indications, devoid of gesture or 'gush,' he has shown the fabric and its shading which bind the father, the mother, and the boy." *Variety's* critic also commended Brown's choice to do everything "in a minor key," noting that although "the underplaying is sometimes too static," that is usually turned around because, "just as the interest lags, director Clarence Brown injects another highlight. The underlying power is impressive." More recently, *The Yearling* has been appreciated by both Brown's defenders and his detractors. In his perceptive study of fathers in Brown films, Donald Lyons argues that *The Yearling* occupies a central place, with Claude Jarman Jr. "perhaps the greatest of Brown's luminous kids." For Lyons, even its occasional mawkishness fails to detract from what is "an amazingly hard film" featuring an "unpretty backwoods society . . . a world so consuming in its struggle as to leave little room for Oedipal drama—little, but just enough." Allen Estrin regards it as one of Brown's more "contemplative and disturbing" films, "told with an unflinching eye for the realities of the setting." Even Brown's chief detractor, Barry Gillam, expressed somewhat grudging admiration: "Ironically, the same slow pacing and laborious narrative style that choke off other Brown films manages here to breathe life into the project by giving it time to develop. The narrative events have little impact and the climactic shooting is flubbed, but the sense of atmosphere, of place, of life close to the earth and synchronized with the seasons is strong and appealing." Perhaps the greatest praise, though, was the telegram Brown received from Maurice Tourneur, who commended him for his "superb motion picture." Brown was so moved that he had it framed and hung it on his office wall, where it stayed for the rest of his life.[30]

The Yearling was one of the most popular releases of 1947, but it netted only a modest profit, chiefly because of the debts incurred during the previous failed productions. Brown often measured success by box-office returns, but on this occasion, he focused on the reviews and on his personal satisfaction in achieving what everyone had thought impossible. His efforts did not go unnoticed in the industry, either. He was nominated, alongside Wyman, Peck, and Rosher, for an Academy Award. Once again he lost, this time to William Wyler for *The Best Years of Our Lives*. In truth, he may have been more disappointed that Wyman didn't win—the award went to Olivia de Havilland—but he derived some consolation from the special Oscar (with a miniature statuette) awarded to Jarman. Rosher and Cedric Gibbons also walked away with awards for cinematography and design.

Brown's plan was to team up with Jarman for an adaptation of *The Secret Garden,* but he soon discovered that MGM had other ideas. The studio wanted him to direct one of the screen's most iconoclastic stars, Katharine Hepburn, in a film about the turbulent life of composer Robert Schumann.

27

Songs and the South

Song of Love and *Intruder in the Dust*

After the travails of *The Yearling*, *Song of Love* was a more staid affair, a foray into nineteenth-century Germany based on an unproduced play by Bernard Schubert and Mario Silva about the turbulent lives of composer Robert Schumann and his wife Clara Wieck. It was touted as Brown's "first musical production assignment" (evidently, *The Wonder of Women* [1929] had been forgotten). *Song of Love* recounts the story of Wieck, a talented pianist groomed for international stardom by her ambitious father. She falls in love with up-and-coming composer Schumann, and they conduct a clandestine courtship that leads to an elopement when she comes of age. Clara bears her husband eight children while juggling domestic duties, maintaining her own profile as a concert performer, and nurturing his career. On the surface, it was ideal material for an MGM biopic: young love threatened by a tyrannical father (shades of the studio's hugely successful *The Barretts of Wimpole Street*), a selfless woman who gives up her own dreams to devote herself to her husband and family, and a classic message that love overcomes adversity. Yet the Schumanns' story was more complex, marred by disappointments, financial difficulties, and deep sadness. Robert Schumann suffered from depression and attempted suicide more than once. It ended with him being committed to an insane asylum in 1854, where he died two years later.[1]

The more "controversial" elements of the Schumanns' life story, then, had to be managed carefully by MGM, as always operating under the watchful eye of the censor. Scriptwriters Irmgard von Cube and Allen Vincent were encouraged to introduce some light into the dark, balancing the "gloominess" of the story with comedy and romance. For MGM, it was especially important to avoid any suggestion of impropriety in the courtship between Robert and

288

Clara and, later, in the couple's friendship with a young admirer, Johannes Brahms. Robert's mental illness, too, had to be delicately negotiated, especially as there was some speculation that it had been triggered by syphilis: a proposed scene of Robert having hallucinations at a carnival and attempting suicide was scrapped. After some negotiation—the censors cautioned that the film should "avoid any undue emphasis on the pains of childbirth," and they insisted that the women's costumes should cover their breasts at all times—the script was passed in the fall of 1946. A few unusual moments, such as a brief shot of Clara breastfeeding, made it into the final film, but the script generally adhered to a familiar formula in a bid to win over a diverse audience. Accordingly, it features early scenes of the young Clara and Robert falling in love, building a home together, and breaking the rules. Their relationship with the good-natured Brahms starts out on a comic note as he arrives at his idol's house only to encounter a chaotic domestic scene involving countless children, a tetchy cook, and a chicken. It continues in that vein as he moves in, becomes the unpaid babysitter, and secretly harbors a chaste and unrequited yearning for Clara.[2]

Brown rarely mentioned *Song of Love* in later interviews, so it was likely one of his more impersonal assignments. Still, it gave him the opportunity to work with an actress he had not directed before: Katharine Hepburn. Initially, MGM had considered borrowing Ingrid Bergman from David Selznick—having acted in two versions of *Intermezzo*, Bergman had seemingly cornered the market on playing women who fall in love with volatile musicians. Instead, MGM announced in July 1946 that Hepburn would play Clara. After some notable peaks as well as some distinct troughs, Hepburn's career was enjoying something of a renaissance in the early 1940s, in part due to her onscreen teaming with Spencer Tracy. Early in her career she had seemed indifferent to public opinion, sometimes to her detriment; however, by the 1940s she was actively choosing roles that would win moviegoers' hearts, playing characters who were a little less brittle and a little more tamed. In taking on the role of Clara Schumann, Hepburn hoped to broaden her range even further by playing a mother for the first time, thus appealing to the increasingly conservative postwar zeitgeist. Although Hepburn wasn't especially passionate about the role, she may have recognized parallels between Clara's life and that of her own mother, Katharine Houghton. Both women possessed fierce intellects and juggled busy family lives while maintaining public profiles. Brown later revealed that Hepburn had pushed for the movie to include all eight Schumann children when, in a spirit of puritanical prudishness, MGM had suggested cutting them down to four.[3]

The studio's publicity department made much of the involvement of acclaimed pianist Arthur Rubinstein, who was drafted to play some of the musical sequences, and of Hepburn's meticulous preparation as she sought to convince the audience of her piano-playing skills. The press carried details of the lavish budget and the three sound stages used to reconstruct nineteenth-century Germany, including a replica of Cologne's historic Gürzenich concert hall, all intended to emphasize MGM's commitment to ensure the film's historical "authenticity." The casting of the Yankee Hepburn as Wieck admittedly stretched credulity, but MGM figured that if a few "real" Europeans, such as Viennese actor Paul Henreid and Englishman Henry Daniell (as Franz Liszt), were added to the mix, the audience would accept the deception. In a bid to attract a younger crowd, Robert Walker was cast as Brahms. The actor's star was on the rise following his appearances in Vincente Minnelli's *The Clock* and the Selznick-produced *Since You Went Away*, and he had just finished working with Hepburn on *Sea of Grass* (playing her son). Walker was plagued by profound personal problems and deepening mental illness, but there was no indication that he brought his troubles to the set, and his performance was offbeat and charming. Henreid remembered the film as "a delight to make" and expressed his appreciation of Brown's skills ("thoroughly professional and exciting"). His preconceived notions of Hepburn as unbearably "mannered" and difficult to work with were soon dispelled; he found her self-deprecating (especially when Spencer Tracy came to visit) and noted that she "had a bright, incisive mind of her own and an intelligent, political view of things." Indeed, it would be Hepburn's politics that generated a buzz when *Song of Love* hit theaters.[4]

The release took almost a year, and neither the critics nor the public thought it was worth the wait. Bosley Crowther of the *New York Times* couldn't have been more dismissive; he found nothing to like, apart from the music, and that could hardly be credited to MGM. Calling the film "boldly imitative" of the studio's own *A Song to Remember*, he despaired of its "clichés of false and sentimental romance" and a "visual element" that was "mawkish beyond temperate words and abuses the spirit of the music in the most vulgar and patronizing way." He was irritated by Brown's handling of the material, too: "More vulgar, however, than this story is the persistent way in which Clarence Brown has directed his actors and his camera to achieve the most tear-drenched effects. Not content to let beautiful music, plus a sugary drama, do the job, he has pushed the weepy face of Katharine Hepburn and the St. Bernard orbs of Paul Henreid right up against the eyes of the audience and practically said, 'Look, they're suffering! This is sad!'"

Most reviewers, as well as the public, agreed with Crowther, and *Song of Love* sunk at the box office.[5]

Paul Henreid—he of the St. Bernard orbs—attributed its failure not to inadequacies in the script, direction, or performances but to the dark forces enveloping America in 1947. In his autobiography, he claimed that conservative elements in the media had stoked up resentment against Hepburn because of her appearance at a political rally in support of presidential candidate Henry Wallace in Los Angeles's Gilmore stadium in May 1947. Wearing an eye-catching red dress, she delivered a speech written by Dalton Trumbo in which she was critical of attempts by the House Un-American Activities Committee to curb individual freedoms, censor political debate, and restrict artists' rights. The speech served as a rallying cry for liberals, but it provoked a backlash from conservatives, who had never warmed to Hepburn anyway. Observing these developments was Hepburn's boss, Louis B. Mayer; though not especially interested in the political allegiances of his staff, he could scarcely turn a blind eye when they impacted box-office receipts. Somewhat surprisingly, Hepburn and Mayer enjoyed a friendly relationship: she respected him because he truly loved films, and she had allegedly declared him to be "the most honest man I ever met in Hollywood." Swimming star Esther Williams bumped into Mayer as he emerged from a meeting with Hepburn and recalled that he was so tense he could barely talk: "Don't! I had to spend the day talking to Katharine Hepburn about wearing a red dress to a rally." His anger was further inflamed when Eric Johnston, head of the Motion Picture Producers Association, told him that Hepburn's political activism, and specifically her appearance at the rally, had had a tangible impact on the profits of one MGM production (most likely *Song of Love*). He also reported an alleged incident in a North Carolina theater, claiming that audiences had stoned the screen when the actress's name appeared in the credits.[6]

The vitriol hurled at Hepburn must have prompted some interesting conversations with Brown. She was a committed liberal, whereas Brown's conservatism only deepened in the 1940s as he became more actively involved in the Motion Picture Alliance for the Preservation of American Ideals (he was its treasurer). His busy production schedule and his side career in real estate, however, ensured that he had little time to join fellow directors Sam Wood and Cecil B. DeMille in their near-hysterical rooting out of "subversives." He was occasionally on hand to make pronouncements to the press on the state of national politics and his concerns about the "crackpot foreign and domestic isms and ologies that plague us today," but for all these declarations, Brown was really not much of a political animal. His support for the Motion Picture

Alliance was rather passive, sometimes even lukewarm. He later admitted to Kevin Brownlow that he was certainly proud of being a "red hot conservative," but he disapproved of the extreme tactics used by his fellow committee members. Actor Adolphe Menjou, he ruefully observed, "went berserk over the thing [anticommunist campaign]. Way over the line." Brown's opposition to blacklisting was also remembered by one of its victims, Bernard Gordon. As was often the case with Brown, there was an intriguing disjuncture between his actions and his declarations. In terms of his politics, this became eminently clear when, just as the Motion Picture Alliance was stepping up its campaign to expose "subversives" and silence liberal dissenters in the late 1940s, Brown decamped to Mississippi to shoot a film that would end up being feted by liberals.[7]

Meanwhile, Brown had to deal with the failure of *Song of Love*. Movie fans in North Carolina might have stoned it as a political protest, but *Song of Love*'s greatest enemy was itself. With its ragbag approach—a little bit of history, a little bit of slapstick comedy, and a lot of sentimentality—it must have seemed somewhat naïve and derivative compared with sophisticated postwar fare such as *The Best Years of Our Lives* and *The Lost Weekend* or the moody style and pessimistic tone of film noir. It is difficult to see *Song of Love* as anything but a misfire, with its faintly ludicrous approach (even by Hollywood standards) to historical fact. Yet there were a few sparks: Brown coaxed a charming performance from six-year-old Gigi Perreau, who had been "discovered" by Mervyn LeRoy. Cast as Julie, one of the Schumanns' many children, the rather unconventional-looking child played the role with sincerity and seriousness (the scenes between her and Walker are especially compelling). Brown's preference for understatement also proved effective in some of the more highly wrought scenes, such as when Brahms confesses his love to Clara. Likewise, Brown and cinematographer Harry Stradling shot the asylum scene showing the incarcerated Schumann in a muted, melancholic tone that anticipates Hitchcock's darker *Vertigo*. And even if Brown had little interest in the material, he did slip a personal reference into the final sequence: Clara is shown performing a farewell concert on May 10, 1890, Brown's birthdate.

When *Song of Love* failed to live up to expectations, any plans to continue the Hepburn-Brown collaboration were dropped. The film had almost been forgotten when, in November 1954, the *Los Angeles Times* ran a piece about a lawsuit filed by the ancestors of Robert Schumann against Loews (MGM's parent company), asking $900,000 in damages for "libel, invasion of privacy and misappropriation of property right." The suit claimed, "Since the movie revealed that the composer had been in an insane asylum for two years, the public might believe a 'strain of insanity' runs through his descendants." Just as audiences and critics dismissed the film, the lawsuit was thrown out by the courts.[8]

As he always did after a failure, Brown moved on to other projects, both personal and professional. Proving that optimism triumphs over experience, in November he married his longtime secretary Marian Spies. Spies had started her career as a schoolteacher in her home state of Ohio, before moving to Los Angeles in the early 1930s to work as journalist (including a stint as a stringer for Ed Sullivan). She met Brown at a party and became his secretary in the early 1940s, around the time he was making *Come Live with Me*. Although Spies was not listed as a corespondent in Alice Joyce's divorce suit, she was working for Brown at the time and was probably involved in a romantic relationship with him. They were married in a Methodist church on Long Island on November 7, 1946. Marian recalled that her new husband was overwhelmed with emotion during the ceremony and thereafter always referred to her as his "first real wife," but tellingly, his pragmatic side was revealed in his selection of Nicholas Schenck as his best man.[9]

Brown's choice of Schenck was perhaps not all that strange, given that the two men had known each other since the early 1920s. However, viewed in the context of the increasingly troubled environment at MGM in 1947–1948, it takes on some significance. There was no love lost between Mayer and Schenck (nicknamed "Skunk" by Mayer), and cultivating a friendship with one ran the risk of antagonizing the other. Brown's fostering of cordial relations with both men suggests that he was enough of a pragmatist to realize that changes at MGM were inevitable, and he would be wise to keep his options open. He proved correct: just a few months after he returned from his honeymoon in Ireland, he and other MGM employees learned that a new vice president of production had been installed. It was none other than Dore Schary, who had worked for Brown as a writer on *Edison, the Man*. Since then, Schary had clambered up the corporate ladder and become head of production at RKO, overseeing some interesting examples of postwar noir and "message" movies. Mayer initially welcomed Schary back to the MGM fold, but it soon became clear that the two held vastly different views on how MGM should be run and what kind of movies it should be releasing. Schary felt it was high time to dispense with flabby star vehicles and champion more "meaningful" films with pared-down aesthetics and "real" people. As far as Mayer was concerned, MGM had built its reputation on the proven formula of family fare; earnest message movies and the grubby world of noir were better left to other studios. It was against this backdrop of corporate upheaval that *Song of Love*—precisely the kind of family-friendly, high-gloss star vehicle that Mayer liked—flopped. Its failure, and perhaps his growing awareness that the old studio system was under threat, impelled Brown to make some changes. Reinvigorated by developments in his personal life, and still basking in the triumph of *The Yearling,* he resolved to take on his riskiest project to date.[10]

In the spring of 1948 Brown went to Mayer and proposed an adaptation of a novel by a prize-winning author, to be shot on location on a relatively low budget. "Prize-winning" was a phrase that warmed Mayer's heart, but his initial enthusiasm was dampened when he learned that the novel in question was *Intruder in the Dust* and the author was the "difficult" William Faulkner. Brown had received Faulkner's novel as a manuscript in late 1947 and had been captivated by the story about the attempted lynching of a black man, Lucas Beauchamp, for the murder of a white neighbor and the lengths to which a white teenager, Chick Mallison, goes to expose the real culprit. What appealed to Brown was probably Faulkner's emphasis on the murder-mystery angle and his focus on Chick's progression from adolescent naïveté to jaded maturity. He bought the rights and, with the tacit support of Schary, approached Mayer. Reminding him of his years of devoted service, he urged Mayer to let him make what would be the most personal film of his career. "If you owe me anything," he said, "you owe me a chance to make this picture."[11]

That Brown was interested in Faulkner surprised many. He hardly cultivated the image of an intellectual, and it seemed strange that he would champion a writer whose works were often perceived as inaccessible, given his stream-of-consciousness technique and complex representations of the South and race issues. Brown was also a businessman, and he must have known that previous screen adaptations of Faulkner's works had been less than successful (Paramount's 1933 *The Story of Temple Drake,* a heavily censored adaptation of *Sanctuary,* scored negative press and a tepid box office). At the same time, civil rights and integration were important issues in postwar America, and Hollywood was showing an interest in making films that engaged in the debate. In 1948, as Brown was canvassing Mayer, Stanley Kramer was working to convert a play about anti-Semitism into a movie about racism (*Home of the Brave*), Fox was planning a film about miscegenation (*Pinky*), and independent producer Louis De Rochemont was adapting a true story of racial passing for his film *Lost Boundaries.* Brown's enthusiasm for *Intruder* was partially motivated by a desire to cash in on a hot topic, but it was also prompted by something deeper and more personal. Faulkner's exploration of the complicated relations between the races in the South, his vivid and intricate re-creation of the specific landscape of Yoknapatawpha County (the fictional stand-in for Oxford, Mississippi, and its surrounds), his obsessive concern with the past and its ghosts, and his wariness in dealing with the thorny topic of racial integration ignited both passion and determination in Brown.

The novel "spoke" to him in a way that took him back to his youth and allowed him to revisit a traumatic incident that had a profound influence on the man he would become. Although born in Massachusetts, Brown always considered himself a child of the South; his father had deep roots in Georgia, and Brown's own personality had been shaped by his Tennessee upbringing. Growing up in Knoxville in the early part of the twentieth century, he was not exposed to the same level of racial volatility that was more commonplace in the Deep South (including Faulkner's own Oxford). In fact, Knoxville was progressive when it came to race relations, with a sizable black middle class springing up in the city from the 1880s onward. Even so, it was a resolutely segregated city, and its minority black population was subject to Jim Crow laws. In Brown's boyhood community, whites held "natural" assumptions of racial superiority, and the churches and schools he attended were exclusively white. Whatever contact he had with the black community was minimal, but it helped shape the complex and contradictory attitudes he held. There is no evidence that he harbored any deep-seated prejudice against African Americans; in fact, he supported, at least in theory, the principle of racial equality. Even so, Brown occasionally exhibited some of the casual racism common to many of his generation (and not just southerners).[12]

In interviews with Kevin Brownlow in the 1960s, for instance, Brown was quick to express his respect for Martin Luther King and his belief that "the Negro should get all he can hold," yet at the same time, he confessed to having concerns about the fast pace of desegregation: "What are we going to do about the color question? God knows. But they're going too fast. Even Martin Luther King realizes that. Some white folks who were sympathetic are thinking again. I hate to use the phrase, but some of my best friends are black." Brown's support for Dr. King, and his hasty declaration that he regarded African Americans as his equals, hinted at the contradictions in his own thinking on race relations, betraying both an eagerness to demonstrate that he was sympathetic to the concerns of the black community and a certain white paternalism ("some of my best friends are black"), which, to his credit, he sheepishly acknowledged. There is no doubt that Brown was a man of his time and of his upbringing; for instance, in the same Brownlow interview, he casually used the words "nigger," "buck," and "darkies." Even more revealing, perhaps, was an anecdote he told about a feud he had with actress Louise Brooks over an incident that occurred back in the 1920s. While attending a party at her house, he had been shocked that she permitted her black guests to share the swimming pool with whites: "If I've been sour to Louise Brooks it's because she and Eddie Sutherland [Brooks's then husband] didn't draw the color line. I'd seen some darkies in their pool and I come from Tennessee! I've enough Southern blood not to be able to stomach that." Brown's still visceral reaction to the memory of a racially mixed swimming pool was striking, especially when, in the same conversation, he made a connection between the sharing of communal space and sexual activity: "I believe the Negro should get all he can hold, but I draw the line at the sex question." Brown's assumption that social interaction would result in sexual relations revealed the complexity of his own feelings toward blacks, ones he shared with Faulkner. Novelist and filmmaker were equally fascinated with exploring the *intimacy* of race relations and—related but not exclusively linked to that—invoking the specter that haunted the South and arguably all of America: miscegenation.[13]

Brown's Knoxville childhood may have resulted in only a passing acquaintance with black communities and racial tensions, but childhood visits to Georgia and, later, time spent in Alabama exposed him to the viciousness of prejudice and the undisguised volatility of the Deep South. One incident in particular profoundly shaped his thinking and laid the groundwork for his future investment in *Intruder in the Dust*. In September 1906, while sixteen-year-old Brown was visiting his paternal grandparents in Atlanta, he became caught up in the bloodiest race riots the city ever witnessed. After a summer of growing tensions between the black and white communities, stoked by an increasingly hysterical (white) press that warned the "natural order" of racial segregation was threatened by a black populace demanding their rights, the city erupted in violence on the evening of September 22. The streets of Atlanta were enveloped by a white mob made up of what contemporary commentators called "excitable boys," as well as a number of well-dressed, middle-class participants. They roamed the thoroughfares, smashing black-owned businesses, maiming unarmed African Americans, and ultimately killing as many as twenty-five black men. One of those who witnessed the violence was Walter White, the future head of the National Association for the Advancement of Colored People (NAACP) and a consultant on many "race issue" films (including *Intruder*) in the 1940s. Traveling down Peachtree Avenue, White saw "a lame Negro bootblack from Herndon's barber shop pathetically trying to outrun a mob of whites. Less than a hundred yards from us the chase ended. We saw clubs and fists descending to the accompaniment of savage shouting and cursing. Suddenly a voice cried, 'There goes another nigger!' Its work done, the mob went after new prey. The body with the withered foot lay dead in a pool of blood on the street."[14]

For all the whites who participated in the vicious attacks, many more simply stood by and watched the bloodbath, afraid or unwilling to intervene. A few attempted to halt the violence, moved to action by a sense of common decency perhaps flavored by a paternal benevolence toward blacks. Historian Charles Crowe cites one such intervention: "A Bijou Theater employee, named J. D. Belsa, reached his baggage men almost simultaneously with a murderous mob and daringly rushed them to safety behind locked doors. When the rioters tried to storm the theater doors, Belsa, armed with a shotgun, forced them to retreat and stood guard for the rest of the night." Upstairs in the Bijou was a young college freshman, recently enrolled at the University of Tennessee, who had gone to the theater for an evening of entertainment. Sixty years later, Clarence Brown was still emotional when he recalled that, from his vantage point in the balcony, he looked out on the street and saw "15 Negroes murdered by a goddamned mob of white men." The memories of the "poor innocent negroes who came in out of the country on Saturday night in the streetcar to do their shopping . . . [and] . . . the mob . . . [that] drag[ged] them off the streets" stayed with him. When he read *Intruder in the Dust,* he realized that the ghosts of his past must finally be exorcised.[15]

Brown set to work in August 1948 and hired Ben Maddow to write a script. Maddow was an interesting choice: as "David Wolff," he had been involved in left-wing documentaries produced by Frontier Films in the 1930s, and in 1942 he took cowriting credit on the Leo Hurwitz–Paul Strand film *Native Land.* Fellow screenwriter Walter Bernstein remembered that Maddow had a unique "film sense . . . he wrote for the eye as well as the mind." A writer of his caliber was essential to transform an opaque novel into an audience-friendly script, and Brown put aside any reservations about Maddow's politics to concentrate on building a cooperative relationship with him. He later claimed the two "wrote it together," but he had to maintain tight control ("I kept him in rein all the time") because he feared that Maddow's liberalism might radically transform the novel's core sentiment. In an interview with the *Los Angeles Times,* conducted while he was filming in Mississippi, Brown revealed that he had bought the rights to Faulkner's book because he "liked the subject, felt it would do a lot to set the South right in its thinking. That thinking must come from within [southerners] themselves and they're doing a hell of a good job of it."

While his statement probably reflects an eagerness to win over the Oxford townsfolk, even in later conversations with Brownlow, his advocacy of a gradualist approach was in evidence: "Evolution not revolution. That was what the picture was about."[16]

Unsurprisingly, Maddow had mixed memories of working with Brown. In an interview in the 1970s, he acknowledged being impressed by Brown's sincere commitment to the project—"he told me he wanted to make amends for this part of his history that he could never forget"—but puzzled by his lack of decisiveness—"[he] didn't know what the hell to do with it." According to Maddow, "Clarence Brown couldn't think his way through the script . . . I had to explain the novel to him, though I think that any bright person that was interested in the story could have worked it . . . out." It seems doubtful that Brown had no understanding of the novel, but it's possible he feigned a strain of anti-intellectualism in the face of a writer who, by all accounts, took himself very seriously. Like his peer John Ford, Brown was a sensitive man who concealed his nature under a brusque exterior, reiterating in interview after interview that he was a no-nonsense troubleshooter, a pragmatic studio director who made films for the general public, not a scholarly elite. Still, Maddow's most abiding memory of their script consultations concerned the antics of Brown's pet parakeet, which he brought to the office and which served as an alarm clock for when its master nodded off.[17]

Maddow may have had his doubts, but *Intruder* was viewed around the studio as a project of some importance. The *New York Times* reported that Dore Schary thought so highly of *Intruder* that he had selected it as his inaugural production and was planning to cast Spencer Tracy. In his memoirs, Schary acknowledged that Brown had "buttonholed" him almost as soon as he arrived on the MGM lot and quickly won him over with his passion for the project. Thereafter, Schary took an active part in the film's development, even contributing its final line: lawyer Stevens refers to Lucas as the "keeper" of "their [whites'] conscience," and Chick adds, "our conscience." To ensure that the issue of race was dealt with sensitively, Schary consulted the president of the NAACP, Walter White. White warned that black audiences might object to the script's use of "nigger"—employed both as a slur and to refer to whites wanting Lucas to "play the nigger"—but he commended it as "an excellent script . . . the kind of film we can endorse." By the end of 1948, what Maddow considered a "very poor and complicated novel" had been transformed into a streamlined script that eliminated several subplots and incidental characters, emphasized the murder mystery, and adapted the complicated stream-of-consciousness device used by Faulkner into more film-friendly voice-overs and flashbacks.[18]

Brown spent the first weeks of February 1949 visiting locations near Oxford and looking for suitable actors to support the central protagonist, Chick Mallison. For that part, he had already selected his protégé Claude Jarman Jr., now a gangling six-footer with all the awkwardness of a teenager. Both he and Schary were hopeful that a big-name actor would take the role of Chick's uncle John (changed from Gavin) Stevens, who represents Lucas Beauchamp when he is accused of killing a white man. Spencer Tracy had been mentioned, as had Joel McCrea, but neither was available, and Brown had to be satisfied with a contract player, the less-than-stellar David Brian. The supporting cast of white actors proved more interesting: Porter Hall as Nub Gowrie, the patriarch of the clan that accuses Lucas of murder; Tennessee-born Elizabeth Patterson as the redoubtable Mrs. Habersham, an elderly woman who keeps a lynch mob at bay; Will Geer as Sheriff Hampton; and Charles Kemper as Crawford Gowrie, brother of the murdered man. For the black cast, Brown had reportedly seen "200 negroes" and was "talking to Amos and Andy about their radio actors." If some of them were cast, they secured only minor roles. Apart from the central role of Lucas Beauchamp, the film features just three black characters of significance: Lucas's wife Molly, played by Georgia-born Julia Marshbanks; Paralee, the Mallisons' house-keeper, played by educator and actress Alberta Dishmon; and Aleck Sander, Chick's closest friend and fellow investigator in the murder-mystery plot. Elzie Emanuel took the role of Aleck and, as it turned out, experienced a rather unhappy shoot with Brown.[19]

Brown may have seen *Intruder* as another chance to explore the transition from adolescence to adulthood and provide his protégé Jarman with a substantial part, but as the project evolved, the role of Lucas Beauchamp became increasingly important. This was chiefly due to the performance of actor Juano Hernandez. Born in Puerto Rico in 1896 to a Brazilian mother and a Puerto Rican father, Hernandez had crammed in more careers by the time he was twenty than most people do in a lifetime. He'd had stints as an acrobat, a street singer, and a boxer in both his native country and Brazil before coming to America, where he reportedly landed a bit part in the D. W. Griffith production *The Life of General Villa* (1914). Within a few years he was appearing on the New York stage—including in a production of *Showboat*—and at the legendary Cotton Club. He also took roles in a number of films directed by pioneering African American filmmaker Oscar Micheaux (*The Girl from Chicago* [1932] and *Lying Lips* [1939]). Having lived such a cosmopolitan life, Hernandez was accustomed to racism and prejudice, but he needed all the self-assurance he had to tolerate the brand of southern hospitality that greeted him in Oxford. Brown later claimed that Hernandez initially stayed at the same hotel as the rest of the cast but moved out after he befriended G. W. Bankhead, the town's black undertaker, and accepted an invitation to stay at his home. Hernandez had a different recollection. In an interview with *Ebony* in August 1949, he remembered Brown and Maddow as "wonderful, fighting for the dignity of Lucas Beauchamp in every scene," but "as for Oxford . . . I went down there with an idea of what I'd find and I didn't get to change my mind." Hernandez found his own way to protest, however: he refused to enter any of the stores in town that required "Negroes . . . to take their hats off when entering."[20]

The wary reception Hernandez got in Oxford was undoubtedly related to the color of his skin, but the locals greeted the whole Hollywood juggernaut with a degree of skepticism when it rolled in in March. Faulkner himself observed that an air of unease prevailed, with many townsfolk openly declaring themselves ready to oppose the production: "we don't want no one comin' into our town to make no movie about lynchin." *Ebony* reported that "there were mumblings from some in Oxford who cracked about what 'we would do if these weren't Hollywood Negroes,'" and it repeated the rumor that "one of the town's leading citizens who appears briefly in the film is the local Ku Klux Klan chief." Anxious to defuse any tensions, Brown embarked on a charm offensive, telling the local newspaper that the film would be an "eloquent statement of the true Southern viewpoint of racial relations" and pointing out that the presence of a major production would surely lead to a boom for local businesses. Once the white population had been assured that money was available, they "took us into their homes and their bosoms," as Brown remembered. It took a bit more work to win over the black citizens, who had no reason to believe they would profit from involvement in a production by "white" Hollywood. Brown called on Juano Hernandez and, more effectively, local church figures to persuade the black townspeople to take small roles. According to *Ebony*, up to 120 locals "pitched in eagerly to help in making the picture" (although this number seems high). The "selling" of *Intruder* was given hearty support by the *Oxford Eagle*, which stoked the town's excitement by carrying almost daily updates, interviews with Brown in which he commended the town's friendliness and the superiority of its locations, and stories about locals who had snagged parts, including twins Edmund and Ephraim Lowe and Mayor R. X. Williams. The latter was an interesting piece of casting: the mayor plays Mr. Lilley, a thoroughly respectable neighbor of the Mallisons who, in one scene, declares his support for the upcoming lynching of Lucas Beauchamp and then serenely continues to water his garden. It is indeed a striking irony that Oxfordians participated so enthusiastically in a film that laid bare their prejudices and referenced the dark history of their town, where lynchings were a relatively recent occurrence.[21]

At first, Faulkner had been slow to lend his wholehearted support, mainly because he had been burned by Hollywood before. He observed, with detached amusement, the frenzy that greeted the commencement of filming, but he gradually capitulated to curiosity and met with Brown and his cast. It turned out that he and Brown had a lot in common: both men were reserved rather than verbose, and both were passionate about cars and planes. In the end, Faulkner was so intrigued by the production that he offered some contributions to the script, provided a little dialect coaching to Hernandez (whose delivery lacked a proper southern drawl), and loaned his beloved horse Highboy to Jarman to ride in the film. Yet, even if Faulkner was happy to collaborate with Hernandez, he didn't invite him to the dinner for cast and crew that he arranged at Rowan Oak.[22]

Faulkner's implicit endorsement of racial segregation mirrored the content of the almost daily editorials in the *Oxford Eagle* that assured both residents and outsiders that the town's system of racial segregation was entirely normal and that even Hernandez could understand its purpose:

> Hernandez and the other visitors learned how false is most Northern
> publicity about Southern racial conditions. . . . Even though he is
> recognized as one of the outstanding dramatic artists of the day,
> Hernandez quickly agreed that he would follow the *natural pattern of
> social segregation* in his stay in Oxford. . . . Just as he worked closely
> with director Brown and the white actors of the company, so he
> discovered that in Oxford Negroes and white men work closely
> together in all fields of endeavor and enjoy the same mutual respect and
> affection.[23]

Hernandez and Brown certainly enjoyed a relationship of mutual respect, but Elzie Emanuel experienced something quite different. The young actor frequently clashed with the director, mainly over how the character of Aleck Sander should be played. Brown could be very authoritative when dealing with young performers, especially those with little experience, but there was a troubling aspect to his treatment of Emanuel. Evidently, Brown saw no great contradiction in the fact that, in this film about racism featuring a dignified and nuanced black character, he transformed the relatively progressive character of Aleck into a "comic coon." The contentious scene, in which Chick,

Aleck, and Mrs. Habersham make a nocturnal expedition to "Beat Nine" to dig up Vinson Gowrie's grave (to prove he was not shot by a bullet from Lucas's gun), was filmed a few miles from Oxford, at Holly Springs National Park. The scene needed to be handled delicately, and problems arose when Brown instructed Emanuel to emphasize Aleck's horror and terror at the imminent opening of a coffin. Consciously or unconsciously, Brown apparently assumed that the black character would be more susceptible to superstition and fear of the supernatural than the white character Chick. In any case, Emanuel refused to cooperate. To break the impasse, cinematographer Robert Surtees recalled that Brown "played several practical jokes on [Emanuel] . . . including the use of a white sheet floating down from a tree and a loudspeaker emitting eerie sounds, in order to frighten him and make him respond properly." It is doubly striking here that both Brown, in his alleged direction of the scene, and Surtees, in his retelling of the incident, assumed that the "practical joke" would affect only the black actor, not the white actors sharing the scene. The scene is a standout, largely because it so effectively builds tension and perfectly marries evocative sound (the nocturnal calls of animals) and a moody aesthetic. However, the brief shot of Emanuel rolling his eyes and acting "the coon" prompted a justifiable backlash from the African American press and from Emanuel himself.[24]

Navigating the complexities of racial politics on the set and in Oxford certainly kept Brown busy, but shooting on location also brought technical problems that required ingenuity to solve. Brown was again blessed with a talented cinematographer in Surtees, who was in the middle of a long career that won him several Oscars. Although Harry Stradling contributed a little studio work for *Intruder*, it was Surtees who went on location and helped Brown develop the film's unique style featuring Expressionistic scenes of nocturnal encounters in jails and in graveyards juxtaposed with scenes that, in their starkness and unsympathetic lighting of faces, have a photorealistic feel. A former apprentice to Gregg Toland, Surtees was very experienced and had worked with many directors who had simply ceded responsibility for the technical work to him, and he was surprised at how proficient the "perfectionist" Brown was. When the crew encountered a practical problem, Brown was usually the first to devise a solution, often one he had used in the past. For the scene in which Nub Gowrie discovers the corpse of his son Vinson in quicksand, Brown ordered that oatmeal be mixed and flooded on to the riverbank, assuring the skeptical crew that, on film, it would have the appearance and consistency of quicksand. He knew this because he had already used it on a silent production (possibly the Tourneur film *Lorna Doone*). Brown also drew from his past catalog, specifically *The Goose Woman*, to devise the Expressionistic lighting of the graveyard scene, which begins with a shot of a startled black family peeping out of their cabin to watch the passing car and continues as Chick, Aleck, and Mrs. Habersham desecrate a grave to solve the murder.

There were some logistical problems that proved more challenging to overcome. March and April 1949 were unexpectedly damp, and the flooding of the local dirt roads made it difficult for the crew to move equipment and, consequently, stick to the tight schedule. More serious was the issue that arose over the recording of sound on location. When *Intruder in the Dust* was released in October 1949, many commentators praised the "authenticity" of its sound, with renowned documentary filmmaker and critic Paul Rotha comparing Brown's work to the distinguished directors of postwar Italian cinema. However, as with the films of Rossellini and de Sica, the "realism" here was achieved only through considerable artifice. When Brown arrived back in Culver City, he realized that the sound recorded on location was unusable, and the accents of the locals appearing in minor roles were so thick that they were incomprehensible to anyone raised outside of Mississippi. He ordered the principal actors back to the studio to loop their dialogue, and then added sound effects of birds and animals and some scene music. Amusingly, when the film premiered in Oxford, the locals patted themselves on the back for the slickness of their performances and the clarity of their delivery, but the voices they heard were those of the professional actors Brown had hired to dub them.[25]

Principal photography on *Intruder* finished up in late April, and when an emotional Brown said good-bye to the locals, he promised that their town would host the world premiere. He spent weeks supervising the editing and preparing a print for a grand unveiling to the still-skeptical Mayer. As the lights went up after the screening, Mayer expressed astonishment, but not of the admiring kind: he simply couldn't imagine how a "picture [that] was about a colored man who had no respect for white people" could play at the box office. It was mainly Brown's resolute defense of his handling of Hernandez and of the picture's message—"[it was about] the dignity of the negro who walked upstage at the end of the picture—he's as big as any man in the world"— that finally won Mayer over.[26]

Brown and Schary continued to have high expectations, but as they put the final touches to the film, their hearts sank at the news that other "race issue" films were performing poorly at the box office. They pressed on, and by

October they had a final cut ready for the eagerly anticipated premiere in Oxford. It was attended by the Browns, Porter Hall, Elizabeth Patterson, and, rather unexpectedly, Faulkner himself, who gave the film his endorsement, observing, "You can't say the same thing with a picture as you can with a book . . . Mr. Brown knows his medium and he's made a fine picture . . . I wish I had made it." For the most part, the locals were delighted with the film and seemed oblivious to the largely negative portrait it painted of their town and themselves. Reviews in the southern press confirmed that a kind of selective memory was in operation, with some critics overlooking the race angle entirely or simply concluding that Lucas was "hardly typical of the Southern Negro" and, in any case, he found justice in the end. If much of the white press saw only what it wanted to see, others viewed the film in more contemplative terms. In her piece for the *Charlotte News*, Emily Wister pointed out that "the South, particularly Mississippi, comes in for some hearty slaps in this picture and the sad thing about it is most of the charges are true."[27]

The fact that the southern press ignored or faintly dismissed the film's treatment of race suited both MGM and Brown. He pitched in on a promotional strategy that sold *Intruder* as a cracking "who-dunnit"; this was helpfully reiterated by *Variety*, which suggested to nervous exhibitors that "in smaller situations where social aspects of the film can't be sold, it'll stand up as straight murder-mystery fare." *Intruder* also garnered some good reviews, which proved useful in selling it, especially in large urban centers and overseas. In perhaps the most positive review he had ever written for a Brown film, Bosley Crowther commented on the auteur touches on display: "He has photographed most of his picture right there in that genuine locale with a sharpness of realistic detail that has staggering fidelity. He has placed his principal characters in stunning relation to crowds, and he has searched their expressive faces in striking close-ups for key effects. Most conspicuously, the director has shunned 'mood music' throughout . . . the sounds, which are full of minor drama, are intrinsic to the action of the film and the boldness of the message."[28]

Even more interesting was the press coverage that gave African American audiences and commentators a chance to air their views. Archer Winsten, a white reviewer writing for the *New York Post*, reported the reaction of a racially mixed audience at New York's Mayfair Theater: "Negro observers had experienced great enthusiasm . . . and three white observers had not," but almost all present regarded *Intruder* as superior to any of the previous "race films" released by Hollywood. In her column in the *Chicago Defender*, a newspaper with a majority black readership, Lillian Scott praised Brown's spare aesthetic style peppered with rich symbolism, noting that the film effectively conveyed the "cancerous tissue of Southern life." She confessed to being thrilled by the sight of Hernandez as the "unbending Lucas striding down the street with his broad belt, swallowtail coat, preacher's hat and gold toothpick." The Mississippi-based *Mound Bayou News-Digest* (published in a town founded by ex-slaves) was similarly appreciative, with reviewer Ruby Berkeley Goodwin commending *Intruder* as "by far the most adult and satisfying" of all the "race films" and urging her readers to "get the cramp out of your arm and write them [the Hollywood studios] your appreciation for the recognition they have accorded the Negro."[29]

Not all black commentators were won over, however. The left-wing *California Eagle*, which had followed the production with interest, now viewed the finished film with mixed feelings. Columnist Robert Ellis complimented Brown on producing a "dynamic movie" and noted the irony of the locals participating in a film that exposes their "true bigotry and hate," but he was disappointed at the lack of effort to show Lucas within his black community. For Ellis, that omission reinforced the sense that he was neither representative of the black South nor viewed as such by his people. Although Ellis was impressed that a white man had produced such an insightful film about racism, he was dismayed by the graveyard scene, observing that it was "cruel" of "producer Brown to jockey the young Negro player . . . into a Willie-Best-eye-rolling comedy part." Ellis's review prompted a response from Brown himself, who wrote to Ellis to thank him for the praise and acknowledge the rightness of some of his criticisms (in a later column, Ellis quoted from Brown's letter). If Ellis's review was generally favorable, his colleague John M. Lee's was less so, and he used *Intruder's* release to offer a resounding critique of all of Hollywood's "race issue" films, which he claimed were motivated entirely by financial considerations ("untapped wealth sources in stories about Negroes"). "As revolutionary as they seem to appear," he argued, all four films were "nothing more than representations of condescension from men who know something has been wrong, but who do not care to disturb the balance too much." He offered some harsh words for Brown's film, calling it "a devious picture with a devious purpose" that offered an endorsement of "what apologists for the backward South have been saying for generations. It says only the unwashed, ignorant white trash make up the lynch mobs. It says the 'good' white folks in the South can take care of the Negro problem without any help from outsiders."[30]

Lee's stance against the film was extreme, but he did pick up on a certain feeling of unease within the black press. Acclaimed novelist Ralph Ellison

(*Invisible Man*), in a thoughtful review, offered an appraisal of the film's merits as well as its flaws. *Intruder*, he claimed, was "the only film that could be shown in Harlem without arousing unintended laughter. For it is the only one of the four in which Negroes can make complete identification with their screen image." He expressed his appreciation that Brown (and Maddow) had given Hernandez free rein to imbue the character of Lucas Beauchamp with real authority and presence. He was tickled by the "sharply amusing" scenes in which Lucas bests Chick at his attempts to "pay him" for his hospitality, and he admitted that the film was in many respects progressive because "we see Chick recognizing Lucas as representative of those virtues of courage, pride and independence, and patience that are usually attributed to white men." Yet for all that, he could hardly overlook the fact that Lucas's primary function seemed to be to facilitate a white boy's progression, and he couldn't help but conclude that *Intruder* was "not *about* Negroes at all . . . [but] about what whites think and feel about Negroes."[31]

Intruder in the Dust may have been Brown's most acclaimed film, but that didn't translate to the box office, and the production reportedly lost $614,000. Brown attributed the failure to audiences' indifference to race films in late 1949, as well as to lackluster promotion by MGM. He remained bitter about the studio's lack of loyalty, and this edged him closer to a final break with MGM. However, in the years that followed, Brown could derive some comfort from the fact that commentators continued to analyze *Intruder*, and festivals and retrospectives occasionally revived it. This afterlife began when screenwriter, novelist, and political activist Dorothy B. Jones published an in-depth examination of this adaptation of Faulkner's novel and Brown's role in it. For her, *Intruder* was an immensely important film because "[it] does more than portray an unquestioned acceptance of white supremacy in the South; it suggests also that basic assumptions of hatred and violence underlie this idea and consequently underlie all Negro-white relations in the South." She admired the film's "objective" style but also made an interesting observation, wondering whether its coolness in some moments might be related to Brown's own sense of conflict: "[Brown] is evidently so on guard against his own mixed emotions as a southerner that he creates a sheen of impersonality which detracts from the vitality of [the lynch mob] scene." Discussing that scene, in which the townspeople line the streets in expectation of Lucas's lynching, she was critical of its "flat, mechanical quality." Her analysis of the film was perceptive and important, in that it drew connections between content and a certain directorial vision, but in her criticism of the mob scene, she may have overlooked Brown's intentions. His use of long takes, with select close-ups of the rather bovine faces of the townsfolk, lays bare the *banality* of the white mob, which sees the crucifying of a fellow human being as simply an entertaining diversion from the mundaneness of their ordinary lives. It is Brown's eschewal of the overheated "Southern Gothic" style—used in other lynching films such as *In the Heat of the Night* and *The Intruder*—and his avoidance of devices such as rapid cutting and music (designed to cue emotional response) that makes it such a powerful and unsettling scene. Even more striking is the fact that a director formerly known for his nostalgic, warm representations of small-town America should depict Oxford, with its dusty, sun-bleached center and its prissy, picket-fenced homes, as a stagnating, claustrophobic town where a neat exterior hides an ugly truth.[32]

Jones's article also paid close attention to both Hernandez's performance and the methods Brown used to present his character. She noted several scenes in which Lucas is shown in positions of authority, such as Chick's first encounter with him and a subsequent one at Lucas's house. In the former, Chick falls into a creek during a hunting expedition and, as he struggles to emerge, a point-of-view shot shows the imposing figure of Lucas on the bank, directing his rescue. The later scene shows Chick's attempt to restore the "natural order" of white supremacy, first by refusing offers of hospitality and then by throwing money on the floor of Lucas's home. Both scenes, in their quiet way, visually establish Lucas as the master of his land and his home, a symbol of adult authority who demands (and gets) respect and obedience from Chick. At the heart of these scenes—and, of course, of the film as a whole—is the astonishing performance by Juano Hernandez, an actor with immense screen charisma who develops Faulkner's rather thin character into a fully realized human being. His cool authority as he strides down the main street of Oxford, his contemptuous laugh in the face of racist slurs directed at him by the Gowrie brothers, and his thinly veiled boredom as he listens to the empty rhetoric of lawyer Stevens make Lucas Beauchamp one of the most compelling portraits of masculinity in postwar cinema.[33]

Intruder in the Dust is one of the few Brown films that has continued to attract critical attention. Pauline Kael, writing in the 1960s, claimed that it opened her eyes to the talents of a director she had previously dismissed as simply a servant of the MGM style ("a man whose sensibility and taste have been less publicized than his ability to handle stars"). Her high regard for the film prompted her to reassess how film history had been written—specifically, how the "pantheon" approach spearheaded by critic Andrew Sarris, which elevated

307

some directors to special status, had the unfortunate effect of neglecting or ignoring important works by directors who hadn't made the grade. As she wrote of *Intruder*, "if this movie had been produced in Europe, it would probably be widely acclaimed among American students of the film as a subtle, sensitive, neorealist work." Regina Fadiman's extensive study of the film, which concentrated on the process of adaptation and drew extensively from interviews with most of its participants, also played an important role in the critical reappraisal *Intruder* has enjoyed since the late 1970s. Unsurprisingly, many of the subsequent analyses have emerged from the field of Faulkner studies, and although some are less than sensitive in their understanding of film as a distinct medium, most agree that of all Faulkner adaptations, *Intruder in the Dust* remains the most satisfying.[34]

The jury is still out on which of Brown's film is his greatest work, but there is no doubt that, as a cultural text, *Intruder in the Dust* is his most important film. He certainly saw it as his most personal project, and in many respects it served not only as an exorcism of earlier events that haunted him but also as the culmination of a cinematic career. Thirty-five years before, armed with a double degree in engineering, he had entered the film industry because he was excited by the prospect of tinkering with machines and discovering the technical capabilities of the medium. As he served his apprenticeship with Tourneur, he came to realize that films could be art, and once he struck out on his own, he directed some of the most innovative films of the American silent screen. In the years that followed, Brown sometimes lost touch with his inventive side, succumbing too easily to a direct-by-number approach that served the studio and its stars, even as it muted his creative expression. Only as he faced the prospect of retirement did he have an epiphany, a realization that time was running out. Starting with *The Rains Came*, many of his films in the 1940s display a renewed vigor by a director who was once again excited by his medium. In his best work, the enduring influence of the silent era is present: in *Intruder*, the rich visual symbolism "says" more—about race, about self-knowledge—than any dialogue could. Consider the interlacing of hands, black and white, across the prison bars as the jailed Lucas asks Chick for help; the close-up of his eye as he urges the boy to move beyond his blinkered view of the world; the tension created by the stark shot of a coin, magnified, rolling on the floor, as Chick experiences shame at his disrespectful behavior in Lucas's home; the witty juxtaposition of the porcine Crawford Gowrie with a pigpen. Certainly these examples attest to the continued importance of the methods Brown learned as a silent director, yet *Intruder* also reveals his most complex use of audio. The use of natural sounds, and of silence, evokes atmosphere and suggests a mistrust of human voices, but it also functions on more symbolic levels. The accomplished fusion of sound and image is best demonstrated in a beautifully realized scene in which the patriarch of the Gowrie clan discovers the body of his dead son and, as the bloodhounds commence a mournful chorus, ministers to his violated body with tenderness and love, wiping the quicksand from his eyes before covering their blankness with his battered hat. It is in such scenes, handled so delicately and in such a characteristically restrained fashion, that Brown reveals profound truths about the universal nature of human emotions.

28

The Twilight of a Career

As Brown entered his fifth decade in the film industry and celebrated his sixtieth birthday, he began to look toward a departure from MGM. He had threatened to leave on many occasions, but this time his personal disillusionment, brought into sharp focus by what he perceived as the studio's indifference to *Intruder,* was exacerbated by developments unfolding at Culver City. As audience tastes changed and television lured away once-devoted fans, box-office receipts dipped for most studios, but the atmosphere at MGM was particularly poisonous as the estrangement between Schary and Mayer deepened. By the mid-1950s, MGM's galaxy of stars was also looking decidedly less luminous: Clark Gable was still under contract, but he was aging and tired, and it showed; youngbloods such as Howard Keel and Van Johnson were hardly in the same league.

Brown observed the corporate upheavals, the gradual sidelining of Mayer, and the deterioration of old alliances and partnerships within the Hollywood community and began to wonder whether it was worth the effort anymore. He retained his membership in several right-wing organizations, including the Motion Picture Alliance, but he was reluctant to be drawn into the controversies surrounding loyalty oaths and blacklists. As he later admitted to Brownlow, he just couldn't stomach the atmosphere of paranoia and backstabbing that permeated the industry. He would not officially check out of MGM until 1955, but his frequent absences from the lot, both for location work and for vacations, suggest that he began the process of withdrawal soon after he returned from Mississippi.[1]

Brown still had some commitments to honor, however. Shortly after he wrapped up publicity for *Intruder,* he received an assignment that he hoped might hit the mark with the public and offer him some distraction. *To Please a Lady* was a romantic drama set against the backdrop of professional auto racing, drawn from a story by former journalist and now screenwriter Barré Lyndon (pen name of Alfred Edgar). It had been making the rounds for a while when MGM acquired it for Lana Turner, with Clark Gable lined up as her romantic interest. One of its unique selling points was that the racing sequences would be filmed at the Indianapolis racetrack, and it was this prospect, as well as the opportunity to work with Gable again, that probably persuaded Brown to accept the project. However, he seemed lukewarm about it from the start, declaring to one interviewer that it was "essentially a studio picture." By September 1949, the cast had changed: Turner had moved on to another project, and Barbara Stanwyck was brought in to replace her. Further delays were encountered when a dispute arose between original screenwriter Robert Pirosh and producer Dore Schary; it ended when Pirosh left the production in December and Lyndon and Marge Decker assumed script duties. More upheaval followed when Charles Dorian left Brown's employ after five decades and Howard Koch (not the same Koch of *Casablanca* fame) replaced him. Finally, in time for May's Speedway Decoration Day at Indianapolis, *To Please a Lady* commenced filming in early 1950.[2]

Brown had been looking forward to working with Gable, but he found that the once cheerful, down-to-earth actor had become cynical and world-weary. Evidently, he was still struggling to cope with the loss of Carole Lombard in 1942. Even though Indianapolis offered Brown and Gable plenty of opportunity to indulge their love of fast cars, it was also the city from which Lombard had departed on her doomed flight. Scheduling conflicts most likely dictated the decision to replace Turner with Stanwyck, but there were rumors that Gable and Turner had been having an affair in 1942 and that Lombard had boarded that flight to return to Los Angeles and try to salvage her marriage. There was no such complicated history with Stanwyck. The two had known each other since *Night Nurse* (1931), directed by William Wellman and featuring Gable in a very early role. Since that first onscreen encounter, both had enjoyed success and battled some personal woes, and they were now acutely conscious of their increasingly precarious positions on the Hollywood ladder as they aged.[3]

No one seemed particularly thrilled to be making *To Please a Lady*, but they soldiered on: Gable delivered his "treat her mean and keep her keen" shtick, Stanwyck gave her usual "steely-yet-soft" interpretation of a career woman, and Brown concentrated on capturing the spirit of the Indianapolis racetrack. Working with cinematographer Hal Rosson, and advised by Wilbur Shaw, president of the Speedway Association, he filmed the races at actual speed—rather than undercranking the camera—using multiple cameras and real drivers. This aspect of the film won some acclaim, and most critics couldn't help but notice that in this romantic drama, the visual delights lay less in the starry cast than in the lovingly filmed shots of sleek, gleaming cars. Location work wrapped up by June, and MGM unveiled its promotional strategy, which was uninspired, to say the least: taglines promised a "Thrill a Minute Romance of a Dare Devil and a Darling!" But the critics who saw *To Please a Lady* were just as bored as Brown and the cast had been making it. The embarrassment of having to deliver weak dialogue and trying to instill energy into cardboard characters came through in the performances by Gable and Stanwyck, and reviewers picked up on it. The *Washington Post* concluded the film was an "anachronism" that might have worked "20 years ago," revealing how out of step MGM had become and how tired Gable was: "Gable is the same old Gable," the critic wrote. "He crinkles up his forehead, he waggles his eyebrows, he puckers up his lips, he speaks roughly to the lady, he slaps her, he masterfully kisses her." Critics were disappointed, too, by Stanwyck. But in her defense, the material she had to work with was quite a leap from her earlier whip-smart dialogue penned by the likes of Preston Sturges and Charles Brackett. Here, she sashays through the racetrack and is forced to feign delight when she is greeted by a wolf whistle and an admiring "take a look at that chassis" from one of the mechanics. There is little to like about *To Please a Lady*—unless one is partial to racing scenes. The brash tone, signaled by the rousting music introducing the credits, seems intended to reassure audiences of the studio's all-Americanism, but it was not a quality that Brown was particularly comfortable with.[4]

Undoubtedly one of his lesser films, *To Please a Lady* may hold some interest for those looking to gauge the zeitgeist of the time. Stanwyck's character offers ample proof of the swing toward conservatism in the onscreen depiction of gender roles in the 1950s. Her transformation from the ruthless and cynical Regina to a kittenish, submissive "woman in love" also has some parallels with the character of Jane in *Smouldering Fires*. Whereas the earlier film offered a commentary on American society in the 1920s—the concern with youth, the generation gap, the restrictions placed on women even in an age of apparent freedom—*To Please a Lady*, set in the terrifyingly competitive world of racing, recognized the dangers of contemporary cultural obsessions—in this case, a "win at any cost" ethos that can devastate both the individual and society. However, in comparison to other releases that year—*All about Eve, Sunset Boulevard, The Asphalt Jungle*—the conventionality and direct-by-number approach of *To Please a Lady* are all too apparent. The scathing reviews should have sunk it at the box office, but audiences seemed to like this forgettable film, and it returned a modest profit.

Just as *To Please a Lady* appeared in theaters, the trouble that had long been brewing in the Hollywood community came to an explosive climax. At its center was Cecil B. DeMille, industry veteran, member of the Motion Picture Alliance, and kingpin of the Screen Directors Guild. Believing that the industry must make a public demonstration of its loyalty and its support of the campaign to root out "subversives," he proposed a mandatory loyalty oath for all employees of the guild. He turned first to the powerful board, which included respected veterans John Ford, Frank Borzage, Frank Capra, Merian Cooper, and Clarence Brown. It was a logical step because it was generally assumed that the conservatives on the board would sympathize with his cause; however, it didn't go as planned, and he encountered strong opposition from liberal members such as William Wyler and John Huston. The division in the guild extended beyond political ideologies and was indicative of a wider generational gap in Hollywood. On one side (DeMille's) were the grizzled old-timers Ford, Borzage, and Brown, veterans of the silent era who had been instrumental in building the industry but whose output in the 1940s was decidedly mixed (especially in the case of Borzage). In opposition to DeMille was a dynamic group that included Wyler and Huston, directors whose films more effectively tapped into the mood of postwar American society. They had also been active participants in the war, an experience that shaped their political liberalism and motivated many of them to defend the Hollywood Ten in 1947. Though talented, the liberal wing was less organized and less influential within the guild, and its members sometimes seemed cowed by the dominant personalities of DeMille and company. In the climate of fear that prevailed, DeMille found it relatively easy to orchestrate the installation of the board in 1948, influence the guild's presidential election the following year, and then move to implement the mandatory loyalty oath. As it turned out, the most serious threat to his preeminence came not from his avowed opponents in the liberal wing but from a man whose position had been engineered, in part, by DeMille himself: Joseph Mankiewicz.

With films such as *A Letter to Three Wives* (1949) and the soon-to-be-released *All about Eve* to his name, Joseph Mankiewicz was one of the "hot" directors of the postwar era. He was far from being a Hollywood newcomer, however; he had been involved in the industry, as a writer and later as a producer, since the late 1920s and had worked with Brown on *The Gorgeous Hussy*. Like Brown, Mankiewicz had been a political conservative at the time, a registered Republican and an astute businessman who could maintain good relations with anyone who mattered, including DeMille. In fact, in 1950 he formed an unofficial alliance with DeMille that helped him win the guild presidency. As DeMille drew up his plans for the loyalty oath, he expected both Mankiewicz and the board to be supportive, but tellingly, he waited until Mankiewicz was on a European vacation to bring the resolution first to the board and then to all members in an *open* ballot. With such tactics, it was no great surprise when the motion passed, 547 in favor and 14 against. But the battle had just begun.[5]

Mankiewicz was furious when he learned of DeMille's coup, and at a meeting of the guild on October 9 he delivered an eloquent speech that railed against DeMille's methods, objected to the loyalty oath, and voiced concerns about a proposal to circulate a list of members who had refused to sign the oath (in effect, a blacklist). Reporting on the proceedings two days later, *Variety* noted that Mankiewicz had been so compelling that he "won the support of board members Frank Capra, Mark Robson, John Ford and Clarence Brown." The inclusion of Brown's name here is surprising, given his proud declarations of "red-hot" conservatism and the unlikelihood of him building an alliance with a noted liberal like Robson. To add to the confusion, Brown's name appeared, along with Capra's, on a petition issued just days after the October 9 meeting to "recall" Mankiewicz as president (it was not signed by either Ford or Robson). It is difficult to account for Brown's shifting position over a three-day period; he never explained why he supported Mankiewicz and then signed a petition to depose him. Mankiewicz's biographer Kenneth Geist has expressed doubts that the October 9 meeting could have "turned" either Capra or Brown, so firmly entrenched were their political beliefs. Yet both voted against the oath and then signed the recall petition on October 13.[6]

Some clues to their rationale may be uncovered by examining the case of Frank Capra. According to his biographer Joseph McBride, Mankiewicz's October 9 speech won over many of the most conservative board members, but when they picked up *Variety* just two days later, they were shocked to see that sensitive details of the guild's internal conflict had been reported—including concerns about a possible blacklist—and that specific directors and their stances on the issue had been listed. Quite apart from qualms about procedural matters and the guild's private business being made public, Brown and Capra may have been fearful that in the atmosphere of paranoia that prevailed in 1950, they, too, might come under suspicion from the FBI and House Un-American Activities Committee (HUAC). To some extent, their fears were not outrageous, given that the FBI had been keeping detailed files on all members of the guild for two decades, and even a donation to an innocuous humanitarian organization back in the 1930s could arouse suspicion in the 1950s. In Brown's case, his most recent work had been with Ben Maddow, a left-wing (and soon-to-be-blacklisted) writer, on a film that was generally grouped with other liberal "message movies." Capra had even more reason to be worried, as his back catalog was far more "progressive" than Brown's; his fears were realized within months when he became the subject of an HUAC investigation (he asked Brown to be a character witness).[7]

A desire to act according to individual conscience may have motivated both men to support Mankiewicz and vote against the oath. Then, as they reflected on the possible fallout, the instinct for self-preservation probably caused them to shift their positions. Capra's vacillation was more evident and public. Having signed the recall notice, he opened himself to the charge of being a turncoat; he wavered in the days that followed and, disapproving of the cloak-and-dagger tactics used by the main instigators of the recall petition, began to move away from the DeMille cohort. When his attempts to cancel the recall notice were headed off, and upon learning from the editor of *Variety* that Mankiewicz had not been the one who leaked the details of the October 9 meeting, Capra took a decisive step away from the board and tendered his resignation. He thus neatly avoided being on the losing side at the legendary October 22 meeting of the guild in the Crystal Room of the Beverly Hills Hotel, which resulted in a discrediting of the conservative wing, a humiliating defeat for DeMille, and the subsequent resignation of the entire board.[8]

Brown's actions were not as public. Faced with the unpleasant situation and no longer sure of his own position in the wake of DeMille's increasing truculence, he withdrew, explaining that he had pressing business in Italy. At the October 22 showdown, DeMille found himself alone as he faced a savage attack from both liberals (such as Don Hartman) and conservatives (such as John Ford). In a speech that demolished DeMille, George Stevens revealed that Brown was "no longer" on the committee that had signed the petition to recall Mankiewicz. Guild members could draw their own conclusions as to why Brown failed to show up: he may have been taking a principled stand against DeMille's tactics; more likely, he was reluctant to become further embroiled in the debacle and lose Capra's friendship. How much DeMille resented Brown's absence isn't known, but he took a rather phlegmatic attitude when he realized the fight was over. The next day he telegrammed Brown in Rome, curtly noting: "the 'boys' now in complete control. Attack upon Board and me led by Huston, Hartman, Wyler, Cromwell, Stevens, Potter, et cetera. Regrets and Regards."[9]

At the meeting of the Screen Directors Guild on October 9, one of the four directors won over by Mankiewicz—probably John Ford—grumbled that they should all "get out of politics and back to directing pictures." It seems that Brown was of the same opinion, and when he returned, he shot an episode of

Dore Schary's pet project, *It's a Big Country*. The film, which had been germinating for some time, had been announced at the start of 1950 as a "propaganda" piece that would promote a liberal vision of an America founded on tolerance and diversity. It would feature an all-star cast, both behind the camera and in front of it, and consist of nine unrelated episodes. By the fall of that year, Schary's ambitious plans had been scaled back, chiefly on the advice of the production code office, which advised him that the planned Asian American episode might be poorly received, and an African American narrative would inevitably present "problems." Schary took the easiest option, excising the former narrative and relegating the latter to a sloppy episode that used newsreel and stock footage of noted black figures in American history to suggest that they, too, had contributed to the nation. The eight-part film that was green-lighted was a veritable mishmash that included a sentimental John Sturges–directed drama about an elderly Irish American woman (played by Ethel Barrymore) who determinedly fights to be included in a census; a romantic comedy about a Hungarian and Greek conflict featuring Gene Kelly and Janet Leigh and directed by Hungarian-born Charles Vidor; a poignant story of a widow (played by the great character actor Marjorie Main) meeting with her dead son's soldier friend; a po-faced drama, written by Schary himself and directed by William Wellman, about a minister (Van Johnson) and his efforts to communicate with his congregation; and a humorous tale of an Italian American father's struggle to come to terms with his son's shortsightedness (in this thin story, MGM saw fit to cast the decidedly WASPish actor Fredric March as the hysterical father). Brown's contribution to the mix was the shortest episode, "Texas," a wry look at Americans' popular assumptions about the Lone Star State: a laconic Gary Cooper narrates to the camera, while stock footage undermines everything he says. It was far from spectacular, but at least it made no pretensions to seriousness and presumably gave both its highly paid director and its star something to do for a couple of days.[10]

It's a Big Country was finally released at the beginning of 1952 and was generally dismissed as inconsequential, although Bosley Crowther was surprisingly kind in his summation (a "cheery, sentimental estimation of life in the United States"). The usually pandering *Los Angeles Examiner* was critical of the elision of the racial issue, observing that "the dignity of our Negro citizens can surely be dramatized, rather than brushed off with newsreel shots." Perhaps reflecting some of its staff's sympathy for the ousted Mayer and animosity toward Schary, the *Hollywood Reporter* blasted the film's "pointed preaching and editorializing as entertainment." Brown probably gave it little thought; for him, *It's a Big Country* was just a quick filler project. His mind was focused on his future at MGM and the challenges involved in shooting four films back-to-back.[11]

Although he had hosted the Tennessee Volunteers football team a couple of times and dabbled in horse racing, Brown wasn't an avid sports fan, so his decision to direct another sports-related film may have come as a surprise. In fact, Richard Conlin's story, about a cantankerous baseball coach who is transformed when he starts to see angels, was right up Brown's alley. Hokey and sentimental, *Angels in the Outfield* uses baseball mainly as the setting for an unlikely romance between career woman Jennifer Paige (Janet Leigh) and bachelor Aloysius X. "Guffy" McGovern (Paul Douglas). The film gave Brown a chance to collaborate with Dorothy Kingsley, whose mother Alma Hanlon had worked with him many years before on the Tourneur film *The Whip*. Kingsley not only provided the screenplay but also negotiated MGM's use of Forbes Field, the home of the Pittsburgh Pirates.

As is often the case in Hollywood movies, the romance in *Angels* is the May-December kind, with a forty-four-year-old actor playing the love interest of a twenty-four-year-old actress. Paul Douglas specialized in playing gruff characters onscreen—sometimes villains, sometimes slobs—and he had recently appeared in another baseball film, Lloyd Bacon's *It Happens Every Spring*. He seemed ideal for the role of Guffy, but he wasn't the studio's first choice. When the project was initially announced in January 1951 (under its original title, *The Angels and the Pirates*), the studio hoped to cast Spencer Tracy, but his work on *The People against O'Hara* meant that he was not available. Instead, it was decided that Clark Gable would take the lead. But by the time Brown started shooting in March 1951, Gable's long-running battle with MGM had resulted in his suspension, and Douglas had to be hastily substituted. As it happened, it was a stroke of luck because, apart from Tracy, no one could have played Guffy so well. Douglas's blustering performance revealed the character's soft heart hidden by a deliciously grumpy exterior, and it later influenced actors playing similar roles (Tom Hanks in *A League of Their Own* and Danny Glover in the remake of *Angels*, released in 1994).

Cast as the tenacious yet sweet Jennifer Paige, Janet Leigh was reportedly a "discovery" of Norma Shearer's. MGM had signed Leigh in 1947, and she had already appeared in an impressive number of films, including as the object of Gene Kelly's love in *It's a Big Country*. Her character in *Angels* didn't require much effort, but she enjoyed the three weeks of location shooting in Pittsburgh for what she called a "charming story." In her memoirs, Leigh admitted she had been a little awestruck at the prospect of working with the "unmatchable Clarence Brown," and like many before her, she discovered he could be quite tough. When she stumbled over her lines and ground to a halt during one take, she braced herself for his reaction. It came, but it wasn't what she expected. Brown told her: "'Never, never cut a scene. I will say cut when it is the appropriate time. This girl would not have these names at the tip of her tongue. Your stammering made it believable, normal. The importance is the intent of the scene—the makeup of the character—not to show the audience how well you memorize.'"[12]

Generally, Leigh found the director supportive and encouraging, but another cast member witnessed Brown's harsher side. New York–born Marvin Kaplan appeared in two short but memorable comedy scenes, playing a journalist friend of Jennifer's. Kaplan had been "discovered" by Katharine Hepburn while working in a theater production, and she had convinced George Cukor to cast him in a small part as a court stenographer in *Adam's Rib.* Shortly after wrapping that film, Kaplan's agent Meyer Mishkin received overtures from Brown's office, and they were summoned to the MGM lot. Though something of Hollywood outsider, Kaplan was an avid movie fan and knew Brown's reputation as an A-list director and a demanding taskmaster; Brown had also directed one of Kaplan's favorite films, *The Human Comedy.* So it was with a sense of awe that he entered the all-white office, its grandiose columns and huge raised desk only adding to his trepidation. Mishkin shoved Kaplan behind a column as Brown stopped what he was doing—practicing his golf swing on an indoor putting green—and approached them. But Brown had no interest in talking to the agent; he complimented Kaplan on his performances in *Adam's Rib* and *Francis, the Talking Mule* and then got down to the matter at hand. Brown had decided, it seemed, that no one but Kaplan could play the part, and when Mishkin chanced his luck and asked for $1,000 a day, Brown nonchalantly agreed.

After this pleasant initial meeting, Kaplan expected more of the same on the set. However, he soon realized that, in contrast to the friendly, creative atmosphere Cukor fostered, Brown ran the set in a formal, businesslike manner that left little time for socializing or small talk. Whereas Cukor "gave you everything," according to Kaplan, Brown was not overly generous with the actors and believed that, as professionals, it was up to them to "find" their characters. This "hands-off" approach continued as long as an actor was performing to Brown's satisfaction, but the moment the actor slipped up or didn't convey what he wanted, the director swooped in. Kaplan soon learned that the running joke on the set was that the day's shoot wasn't complete until Brown had fired someone (usually an actor). With such a buildup, Kaplan was naturally a bundle of nerves when it came time to shoot his first scene: as he dines with Jennifer, he delivers some wry observations on the wisdom of approaching the fearsome Guffy, while sipping from a coffee cup. Kaplan was naturally gifted when it came to comic timing, so he didn't find the scene difficult, but then Brown insisted that he hold the cup in his left hand—the actor was right-handed—and gesticulate as he talked. It was a puzzling, seemingly irrelevant requirement, and Kaplan felt that Brown was testing him. To his relief, he passed the test and delivered the scene in one take (without spilling a drop). But another actor featured in the same scene wasn't so lucky: required to do a double take to convey his disgust at Guffy's boorishness, he failed to meet Brown's expectations and was axed. Kaplan's insight, as an actor's actor, is especially interesting in light of Leigh's rather affectionate recollection of Brown's helpfulness and his industry-wide reputation for his sensitive handling of the most temperamental stars, human and nonhuman. These contrasting accounts reveal that, when faced with an actor whose nerves were getting the better of him, Brown was a most sensitive and patient supporter; with an actor who was being lazy or difficult or was simply not up to the role (for example, Franchot Tone or Ralph Forbes), he could be harsh and sarcastic. With actors cast in small and therefore dispensable roles, one wrong move could result in public humiliation and dismissal, often to serve as an example to others.[13]

Brown's talent for directing children wasn't in question, and he found an outlet for it on the set of *Angels*. Nine-year-old Donna Corcoran had been cast as the orphan who, in an unlikely plot turn, helps bring Guffy and Jennifer together. According to publicity, she was the daughter of an MGM employee— either a studio policeman or a maintenance man—and had been "discovered" by Dorothy Kingsley on the lot (in another version, Kingsley claimed she spotted the girl at Sunday Mass). The story of Corcoran's "chance discovery" was used extensively in publicity for *Angels*, highlighting the fairy-tale aspect of the film itself and enhancing Brown's reputation as a "starmaker." In truth, however, most of the Corcoran kids were already involved in acting, and Donna's selection was probably not the result of serendipity. In any case, she emerged as one of the brightest sparks in the film. Her performance as Bridget conveys a serious, shy quality that makes it one of the more "natural" elements of an unashamedly hokey film.[14]

Much was made of *Angels'* close connection to baseball, with press reports noting its use of real locations and cameos by popular players such as Ty Cobb and Joe DiMaggio, as well as a blink-and-you'll-miss-it appearance by the part owner of the Pirates, Bing Crosby. Hundreds turned out for the premiere, which was held in Pittsburgh in September, and the film was enthusiastically received. Outside the city, reviewers were more measured, with Orval Hopkins of the *Los Angeles Times* noting that *Angels* worked only if audiences went into it with the "proper frame of mind" and accepted the warm appeal of this "batch of nonsense." *Variety* had no such qualms, commending it as a "tremendously human, humorous and lovable chunk of celluloid." *Angels in the Outfield* isn't a complex film, but there's no doubt that it has its charms. Leonard Maltin cited it as one of his favorite Brown films, complimenting its "lightness of touch." Although the conditions on the set were sometimes less than relaxed and congenial, *Angels'* message—that we should be kinder to one another and that a belief in God, in whatever incarnation, makes for a better America—was certainly warm and fuzzy. Unfortunately, it didn't translate at the box office, where ticket sales were disappointing. However, Brown could derive some consolation from the fact that President Dwight Eisenhower named *Angels in the Outfield* his all-time favorite movie, and years later, when he ran into the former president on a golf course in Los Angeles, he was delighted when Eisenhower admitted that he "was crazy about that movie" and "had personally worn out three copies of [it]."[15]

Brown's next film, the penultimate film of his directing career, also had a religious element and teamed him once again with Dorothy Kingsley and Paul Douglas (this time the third choice after Jimmy Durante and Spencer Tracy proved unavailable). The plot of *Angels* had stretched credibility, and so did the gossamer-thin story line of *When in Rome*, a "bromance" between a con man (Douglas) and a naïve priest (played by the still fresh-faced Van Johnson) who meet on a sea voyage to Italy. Joe Brewster, Douglas's Runyonesque character, is on the lam, while Johnson's Father John Halligan is on his first trip to Europe to participate in the 1950 Holy Year celebrations. Complications ensue when Brewster steals both Halligan's clothes and his identity in an effort to evade an arrest warrant.[16]

What drew Brown to the Robert Bruckner story is not clear: though raised to be a churchgoer, he was not especially devout (in contrast to practicing Catholic Kingsley). There is no indication that Schary worked on the project, but the film's moral—that all people are worthy of a second chance and can be "redeemed"—points to his involvement. Brown might have found some aspects of the story appealing: the development of a relationship between two opposites and the tracing of a journey that transcends the physical are core to *Intruder*; the theme of spiritual awakening and redemption features in his first film, *The Great Redeemer*; and belief in the essential goodness of humans is a sentiment that runs throughout his work. However, he had more selfish and immediate reasons for signing up: MGM planned to shoot in Rome and Genoa because the studio had frozen assets in Italy that needed to be released. The prospect of an overseas jaunt was a welcome one for Brown, who was increasingly miserable at MGM (his departure for Rome coincided with Mayer's final leave-taking from MGM in June).

By early July, cast and crew were ready to start shooting, and their presence was causing quite a stir in Rome. Van Johnson's flamboyant fashion sense, which included red socks and "opera pumps," reportedly startled the natives, who were still emerging from postwar austerity. It was a short but pleasant shoot, and it reunited Brown with William Daniels for the first time since 1941's *They Met in Bombay*. What emerged is a good-natured buddy movie set against the backdrop of a tourist's view of Rome (the Colosseum, the Spanish Steps, St. Peter's, and so forth, all of which are somewhat pertinent to the narrative of a spiritual quest but not exactly essential). MGM's reluctance to commit to an overt religious theme is evident in the opening credit, which assures viewers that although the story is set in Rome during Holy Year, this won't be taken too seriously ("God may move in mysterious ways, but He gets there just the same"). Douglas and Johnson turned in amiable performances, even though they were not exactly Crosby and Hope. Brown's direction, designed to showcase the mild brand of humor, was leisurely at best. The comic moments (such as they are) arise from the central conceit of Brewster's pretense of being a priest—saying grace, singing in Latin—and Halligan's grappling with his conscience (should he be a snitch and turn Brewster in, or track him down and encourage him to repent?). In an era in which audiences lapped up the frenetic slapstick and camp outings of Frank Tashlin films and the comedy duo of Lewis and Martin, *When in Rome* was rather old-fashioned, its comedy more of the slow-burn, character-driven variety. Yet it has moments of appeal and, on occasion, some visual flair: in one scene, as Joe Brewster enters a monastery, the monks' cells recall enclosures of the more penal kind, and Brown suggests Brewster's repulsion via a Tourneuresque dissolve to an *Alias Jimmy Valentine*-style jail. The film's ending, which has Brewster repenting and entering a monastery under a vow of silence, may seem like a typically neat (and unlikely) MGM conclusion. Yet it takes on some resonance within the careful plotting that introduces Brewster's verbosity as core to his successful career as a con man; suggests the beginning of his disempowerment and, in turn, his redemption as he struggles with Latin; and culminates in his total surrender to a life of goodness with the voluntary muting of his voice.

The release of *When in Rome* was delayed until April 1952, and although the *New York Times* expressed warmth toward the director and the principal cast, it concluded that MGM had gone to "great expense and great lengths to come up with a strangely unspectacular and often commonplace offering." The Hollywood press was more favorable, with *Variety* expressing some relief that MGM had "avoided any stuffing dealing with the religious angle." Unfortunately for the studio, the lukewarm reviews and disinterested audiences meant that *When in Rome* soon petered out at the box office.[17]

In a further demonstration of MGM's patriotic credentials and its penchant for lavish productions, in the spring of 1951 Dore Schary seized on the idea of recounting, in garish Technicolor, the story of the 1620 arrival of the Pilgrims on the *Mayflower*. He acquired the rights to a best-selling novel on the subject by Irish writer Ernest Gébler and decided to personally supervise what became *The Plymouth Adventure*. He explained that he was excited by the "opportunity to tell the historically significant Pilgrim story in highly cinematic terms. . . . This story of the Pilgrims' conflict with the captain . . . offers a chance to express what it was they were seeking in America." Perhaps he saw parallels between the struggles of the Pilgrims, driven from their land by religious intolerance and seeking to build a new society shaped by their convictions, and his own battles with Mayer. Or maybe he regarded their story as a parable for the fraught atmosphere of Hollywood in the early 1950s. Whatever his motivation, Schary was enough of a realist to know that ideological messages needed to be balanced with a little romance, and although he hired Gébler as a consultant, it was the experienced screenwriter Helene Deutsch (of *National Velvet* fame) who adapted the novel. Schary threw everything he had at the production, assigning an A-list cast that featured Spencer Tracy as Christopher Jones, the captain of the *Mayflower*; Van Johnson as a boyish carpenter; Lloyd Bridges as Jones's sneering sidekick; and Gene Tierney as the romantic interest (his first choice, Deborah Kerr, was unavailable). William Daniels was behind the camera, and after a number of other MGM directors ducked the assignment, Brown was announced as the "captain" of the production in July 1951.[18]

As the Massachusetts-born son of an immigrant and a director experienced in historical drama and Americana, Brown seemed the perfect choice, and he dutifully expressed his enthusiasm to the press. In truth, he was skeptical about the whole project, and after directing back-to-back films, he probably lacked the energy to keep a large-scale and, as it turned out, difficult production on an even keel. Preproduction took months as the studio's technical departments constructed a to-scale reproduction of the *Mayflower* and a Hollywood version of a seventeenth-century English village (recycling a set used in Brown's *Conquest* many years before). When filming was finally ready to start in March 1952, Brown found the cast and crew unsure about the project and in some cases actively resistant to it. Despite his good-humored persona, Van Johnson was a troubled man plagued by personal demons; he did little to disguise his boredom with the paper-thin character he had been asked to play. Though Gene Tierney's performance in Stahl's *Leave Her to Heaven* had shown her to be more than just a beautiful face, the actress brought a world of emotional problems—including a complicated love life and undiagnosed manic-depression—to the set. But neither of them was a match for the very grumpy Spencer Tracy, who made it known how much he *didn't* want to be there and complained from the moment he reported to the set to the moment filming wrapped that he despised the "boring story," the two-month shoot, and the storm sequences that left him drenched in his less-than-flattering costume. Regarding the latter, his complaints were well justified. While the women were attired in an array of richly colored and beautifully cut costumes, Tracy's tight-fitting outfits showcased his gut and were topped off by a hat more ludicrous than Garbo's folly in *Ninotchka*. As Tracy's biographer notes, the effect was a "gnomelike appearance" that made Captain Jones look like "a sort of malevolent Mr. Pickwick of the high seas." It was little wonder that the actor remained in a permanently foul mood, seething at the injustice of it all, and firing off correspondence to the man he viewed as the architect of his humiliation: Schary.[19]

Whatever his difficulties with other members of the cast—he sneered that Lloyd Bridges was "just" a radio actor—Tracy was on fairly cordial terms with Brown. The press reported that he socialized with the Browns, although at least one account suggests that this was only because Tracy appreciated the director allowing him to do as he pleased on the set. Reggie Callow, an assistant director on the production, suggested that Tracy, not Brown, was calling the shots: "I never heard him [Brown] tell anyone in the cast what to do . . . I never saw him tell anybody anything." If Callow regarded Brown as disengaged, Gene Tierney was appreciative of his attentiveness and kindness. She had hoped that *The Plymouth Adventure* would offer a respite from her turbulent personal life and that playing opposite Tracy would help her develop as an actress, but she soon realized that her abysmally written character demanded little of her: a few dewy looks, a couple of steely ones, and some light exercise around the ship's decks. Tracy had little interest in giving her acting lessons but plenty of interest in sleeping with her, and despite her mother's warnings to steer clear of this "most tormented" of men, the two drifted into a brief and tortured affair. Those who viewed Brown as unapproachable and cold would have been surprised that the increasingly distressed Tierney turned to him, and the two developed a warm "father-daughter" relationship. The unhappy Tierney became another of the damaged, sensitive women Brown looked out for. Tierney would later write to thank him, confessing that he had helped pull her from a dark melancholia: "you are personally responsible for a brand new outlook and enthusiasm . . . your confidence in me has been like a shot in the arm and the timing was perfect." But her expression of gratitude for their "wonderful & happy voyage" disguised her bitter dismay at how badly the shoot had gone.[20]

At the heart of the problem was Helene Deutsch's script: the po-faced preaching and weak exposition of both plot and character ensured that the talented cast had little opportunity to inject realism or energy into their roles, and audiences had to endure long stretches when they sermonize or simply stand around exchanging meaningful looks. Faced with such material, Brown poured his energies into getting the technical side right, and he seemed enthusiastic about drawing from his engineering background. It was certainly a challenge, as Daniels recalled: "We had the whole ship hinged at one end. The camera was suspended on a long boom. We wanted to show the people leaning. It was hard to light: we had little units . . . it was so crowded there with beams and everything; the moment you moved your set the lights would be seen. We kept the camera moving constantly. The special effects of the storm were the best I've ever photographed." Although it was far from the *best* film he ever worked on, Daniels later listed *The Plymouth Adventure* as among the most *rewarding* ones. And the film's delights are mainly visual—shots of the majestic ship and the impressive storm sequence—winning praise and, later, an Oscar for special effects.[21]

In his memoir *Heyday*, Schary wryly admits that *The Plymouth Adventure*, released over the Thanksgiving weekend in 1952, turned out to be something of a turkey. Although he claimed the film was scuttled at the box office by American filmgoers—"there weren't enough direct descendants of the original *Mayflower* passengers to help it cross over to success"—the film did make a profit. It was Schary's ego, rather than the studio's bank account, that took the bigger hit, as reviewers bemoaned the clunky script, the leaden pacing, the distortion of facts, and the misrepresentation of historical figures. Commentators took particular exception to the suggestion that Dorothy Bradford committed suicide because of a stymied on-board romance with Captain Jones, and all were quick to point out the MGM gloss that gave the

Pilgrims a happy ending (in the film, most of the settlers survive their first winter in America, but in fact, almost half the colony died). *Variety's* review complained about the dull story and characters that lacked "dimensions as real people," while *Time* conceded that "the picture has a spectacular Atlantic storm," but "most of the time the Pilgrims—and the audience—are merely awash in a sea of florid dialogue." Intriguingly, *The Plymouth Adventure* elicited some curiosity from writer and future filmmaker François Truffaut, whose review contained some interesting—if deliberately elusive—observations about both the film and its director: "[The] Plymouth Adventure constitutes a film as boring as rain, or as fascinating as a 'thriller,' depending on the goodwill of the viewer. With Clarence Brown, the viewer has to make the first move. The attention that one is willing to bring to it from the beginning is always well rewarded."[22]

For Brown, the new MGM no longer felt like home. During the final months of his contract, he concentrated on wrapping up *The Plymouth Adventure* and overseeing one last project. *Never Let Me Go*, a product of Cold War unease, centers on the love affair between an American journalist and a Russian ballerina and their attempts to escape the Iron Curtain and find happiness in the "free" West. Its formulaic plot, with shades of MGM's earlier *Comrade X* and *Ninotchka*, was in fact based on the real-life story of American Pulitzer Prize–winning journalist Eddy Gilmore's romance with Tamara Chernashova, a ballerina he met while working as a foreign correspondent in the Soviet Union in the late 1940s. Roger Bax—pen name of the prolific crime novelist Paul Winterton—was inspired by their story and, conscious of the plight of so-called Russian brides who were being prevented from joining their husbands abroad, wrote a novel, *Come the Dawn*, which MGM acquired. The plan was to shoot it at MGM's British facility at Borehamwood in the spring of 1952 and to feature Clark Gable (fresh from suspension) and Gene Tierney (on Brown's suggestion). Tierney was excited by the prospect and assured Brown she would "do everything within my power to retain your vote even to becoming permanently muscle-bound trying to emulate a ballerina." Gable was probably not as bowled over, but he saw it as a good opportunity to take advantage of European tax exemptions and put some distance between himself and his soon-to-be ex-wife Sylvia Ashley.[23]

As production on *Plymouth* dragged on, the schedule for *Never Let Me Go* was pushed back, allowing Tierney extra time to prepare for the physically demanding role of Marya. As she remembered: "to prepare myself I had to endure six weeks of ballet lessons, two hours a day, just to master enough technique to get on my toes and do the few steps that would be required of me. The Russian ballerina Natalie Leslie doubled for me in the long shots. I was thirty-two then, not an ideal age to be taking up so strenuous an activity as ballet." For Brown, the delay merely confirmed his decision that he was done with directing: he handed *Never Let Me Go* over to director-producer Delmer Daves. Daves, whom Brown had taken under his wing, had recently turned out some interesting westerns and noirs. Like Brown, he was politically conservative and not averse to the anticommunist material of *Never Let Me Go*, but he shared Brown's doubts about the wisdom of the actions of Hollywood's conservatives (at the October 22 meeting of the Screen Directors Guild, Daves had been vocal in his criticism of the "completely undemocratic" and "secretive" tactics used by those responsible for the petition to recall Mankiewicz). Daves and Brown enjoyed a friendly relationship, and *Never Let Me Go* became an interesting fusion of their very different styles and sensibilities.[24]

Brown stayed on as producer, and he traveled to Borehamwood to join the unit. He still had mixed feelings about England and the English, but he had to admit that both the MGM facility and the pool of talent were impressive. Distinguished actors such as Richard Haydn, Kenneth More, and Bernard Miles filled the character roles; behind the camera, Michael Powell favorite Alfred Junge handled production design duties, and Australian Robert "*Third Man*" Krasker oversaw cinematography. Several weeks were spent shooting at Borehamwood and in picturesque Cornwall, which was standing in for Tallin in Estonia. Unlike the rather tense set of *The Plymouth Adventure*, Daves cultivated a friendlier atmosphere, and although the Americans complained about the damp English weather that often delayed shooting, the mood was generally relaxed. Gable was emerging from the cloud that had enveloped him on *To Please a Lady*, and he spent his time shuttling from Borehamwood to Cornwall (where he raced his new Jaguar and made friends with some of the locals) to Paris (where he romanced his latest lover, Suzanne Dadolle). Tierney, too, had a complicated love life—she had recently become involved with Rita Hayworth's ex, the Aly Khan, in another affair that would end unhappily. Gable's reputation as an incorrigible womanizer led many to assume that he would make a play for the beautiful Tierney, but somewhat surprisingly, his attentions remained strictly platonic. She found him unexpectedly sensitive and vulnerable, and she was touched when he confided in her about his loneliness following the death of Lombard, his regrets over his brief marriage to Ashley, and his excitement at the prospect of shooting his next film, John Ford's *Mogambo*, in Kenya. Tierney recalled that, distracted as he was, he was kind enough to remember her on a trip to Paris: he bought her a special salve to apply to her bruised feet.

With a cast that was getting along fine and a director who seemed to be handling both the studio and location shooting with ease, a more casual side of Brown emerged. Tierney recalled his visits to the set as pleasant occasions during which he took time to interact with her young daughter: "Whenever she came to the set, Clarence Brown would lift Tina onto his shoulders and say, 'Now, let's watch Mommy dance.'" With the pressure off him, and perhaps relieved that he had finally decided to leave MGM, Brown was respectful of Daves's authority. Despite a silly plot and thin characters, Krasker's noirish cinematography enlivened scenes of Marya's rescue, and the supporting cast of English character actors lent some welcome comic moments. The finished product remains something of a curiosity, and not just in the political sense. Daves paced it better than the jaded Brown might have done, but the specter of Brown lingered. As one critic noted: "*Never Let Me Go* feels less like a 'real' Daves movie . . . than a work of producer Clarence Brown, whose romantic sensibility dominates a starry-eyed love story against a background of Cold War politics." At times, it seems that the younger director was keen to pay homage to the master: a comedy scene that features Haydn's character recalling the drunken banquet where he met his Russian wife (played by Anna Valentina) explicitly references the "Russian work" of Brown's *The Eagle* and *Anna Karenina*, with almost identical camera work—a traveling camera moving up a long table, intercut with off-kilter close-ups of the attendees—and tone. Shades of Brown are also evident in a scene showing Marya and Philip's escape through the streets of Tallin: the Expressionism of *Flesh and the Devil* is fused with the distinctive Krasker–Carol Reed aesthetic of *Odd Man Out* and *The Third Man*.[25]

It took some time for *Never Let Me Go* to see the light of day, but when it did, reviewers agreed that the plot was pretty much a rehash of *Comrade X*, albeit with a degree of visual flair and not a little comedy. *Variety* conceded that the "plot reeks of implausibility, but this is compensated by bold direction, nimble scripting and lively performances and there is suspense and action in good measure." Bosley Crowther described it as ludicrous but not without appeal: "the writing is brash and eventful, the texture of the production is fairly real and the performances by all the actors are in the appropriate make-believe style. To be sure, the whole film is romantic and just this side of ridiculous farce in an area that isn't quite that funny." Though the reviews encouraged audiences to suspend their disbelief and just enjoy ninety minutes of Gable looking dashing and quizzical and Tierney looking sweet and adorable, they didn't, and *Never Let Me Go* slipped out of theaters barely noticed.[26]

Despite this, *Never Let Me Go* wasn't such a bad final production for Brown. With none of the day-to-day pressures of directing, he had enjoyed the experience of mentoring Daves, but he also knew it marked the end of an era. Returning from Britain, he packed up his office and, on April Fools' Day 1953, *Variety* carried a short piece noting that Brown had "checked out" of Culver City for the last time, with no immediate plans for any future productions.

29

Slow Fade-out

Brown in Retirement

There was no dramatic exit, no scandal, no effort to renegotiate a more lucrative contract. As he finished up *Never Let Me Go,* Brown, in his understated way, let go of a long career. In the years that followed, there was the occasional rumor of a comeback—including a couple of projects with Garbo—but it came to nothing. Brown may not have planned to make such a definitive break, but as time passed and the industry changed, he maintained his distance. It wasn't as if he needed to work: thanks to his business sense and his investment portfolio, he was a very rich man. This allowed him to avoid the fate of many of his peers, who spent the 1960s drifting around Europe and directing the occasional swords-and-sandals epic.

Brown rejected the new Hollywood where the actor was king and the moguls were relics of the past, but he also turned away from the art form he had helped shape. In later interviews he admitted that he rarely attended the movies and could name only two—*Born Free* and *Dr. Zhivago*—that had made any impression on him. Like many of his generation who had grappled with the production code and had found subtle ways to convey sex and sin onscreen, he was repelled by gratuitous violence and crude sex scenes as censorship lost its grip in the 1960s. Television fascinated him only for its technology: Sidney Franklin recalled visiting Brown in the 1960s and watching as he obsessively scanned muted TV channels, captivated by the flickering colors.[1]

Although Mrs. Frank Capra described Brown as living a "dead life," and Franklin recoiled at the thought of his friend "holed up in that hovel in the desert," the Browns' retirement was hardly a reclusive or a squalid one. They sold the ranch in 1952 to a religious order (it was eventually acquired by the

National Park Service), but the Browns maintained a Los Angeles residence before finally leaving the city in the 1960s, moving to a luxurious bungalow at the El Dorado country club in Palm Desert. Brown held on to an office at the L. B. Mayer Foundation well into the 1970s, and he continued to make business deals and travel to Europe to purchase luxury cars and visit Tourneur until his death in 1961. Brown had remained close to his mentor and even supported him financially in the aftermath of an accident that led to the amputation of his leg. And despite Brown's reputation for being a difficult person, it appears that his marriage to Marian was a happy one. Though he sometimes "growled at her like an old bear," she understood him and remained devoted. It was Marian who brought him along to social functions and golf tournaments and, more significantly, persuaded him to respond to the courting by the University of Tennessee (UT) Development Office in the late 1960s. In time, the Tennessee link would become a "second life" to Brown, and once he put aside his initial reservations, he became a very active and very generous alumnus.[2]

The Tennessee connection may not have been visible during Brown's years in Hollywood—expressed more in his folksy films and in their affection for the rural lives of ordinary folk than in frequent visits home—but he remained attached to Knoxville and, as is so often the case, his affection deepened as he aged. Over the years he stayed in sporadic touch with cousins who still lived in the South, but his first tangible reconnection began when, ironically, he faced a Tennessean backlash to the earthy Rachel Jackson character in *The Gorgeous Hussy*. Once his interest in his "home state" was piqued, he was happy to play host when the UT Volunteers football team visited Los Angeles in the late 1930s and again in the early 1940s, and he helped drum up publicity for their games. When the team returned in 1967, the university's development office organized a reception to coincide with the big game at the Los Angeles Coliseum. Of the many invitations sent out by the office's president, Ed Boling, only the Browns accepted, and they turned up at the Century Plaza Hotel for a trip down memory lane. Offers of alcohol refused, Brown warmed up when he was treated to a slide show of the UT campus, and then he began to share reminiscences of growing up in Knoxville: visiting his father at Brookside Mills, watching his mother learn to drive a horse and buggy at Circle Park, and memories of high school, college, and first love. As development offices tend to do, its representatives tactfully broached the subject of "giving back" to the university, and although he was initially noncommittal, Brown had a change of heart in the months that followed and donated $50,000, with the promise of more. Urged on by Marian, he presented plans for a death legacy and agreed to fund the development of a theater on campus. He was soon fired up and totally involved, as Charles Brakebill—then on staff but later the vice president of development—recalled: Brown wanted to be consulted on everything about the design of the building, its interior layout, and even the type of seating. When the cornerstone ceremony took place in 1970, the usually reticent Brown took pride of place alongside guests such as Claude Jarman Jr. and Jane Wyman.[3]

The University of Tennessee would eventually benefit from a Brown legacy of $12 million, as well as the donation of his papers and some personal effects. His involvement certainly yielded much for his alma mater, but Brown benefited too, taking considerable pride in having a structure on campus that bore his name and encouraged new generations to get involved in creative practices. He met many of these young people at a festival featuring his films held at UT in 1973, and though he often seemed out of step with the liberal politics and student protests sweeping American campuses in the late 1960s and early 1970s, both Brakebill and former UT president Joe Johnson recalled that he had a good rapport with the "hippie" students who crowded in to hear him speak.[4]

Brown's dislike of biographers and memoirs, along with his reluctance to stay in touch with the industry, meant that he was his own worst enemy when it came to safeguarding his reputation. As others became the darlings of auteur-inclined critics who gullibly swallowed tall tales of fighting for personal artistic vision while bucking the system, Brown kept himself apart. The fact that he spent most of his career at MGM—the studio regarded as Hollywood's most stolid and impersonal—didn't help. In his beloved France, home of cinephiles who passionately argued for the recognition of individual auteurs within the system, Brown looked on as John Ford, Orson Welles, Raoul Walsh, and Sam Fuller were feted. He was not the only one left out in the cold, of course, but even when historians mentioned him, it was usually as Garbo's director or as a "subject for further research." As William Everson, one of the first to examine Brown's work, has noted, "Perhaps even more irksome than being an under-rated director or neglected director (he at least stands a chance of being discovered and celebrated belatedly) is the fate of the director who is acknowledged, casually, as a craftsman and thereafter so taken for granted that his art is rarely discussed at all."[5]

By the time Everson published his overview of Brown's career in 1973, there were hopeful signs that this critical neglect was going to be addressed. Leading the way was Kevin Brownlow, filmmaker, historian, and collector (and restorer) of silent films. Having come across Brown's work as a teenager—when he acquired a print of *The Goose Woman* and was astonished by its sophistication and subtlety—Brownlow approached Brown in the early 1960s, as he embarked on his seminal study of silent film, *The Parade's Gone By*. While many of those he interviewed proved willing participants, happy that someone remembered them and their films, Brown turned out to be elusive quarry. Persisting in the face of some tough rebuffs, Brownlow eventually conducted a series of interviews—recorded as Brown pretended not to notice—that yielded a treasure trove of reminiscences that cast light not only on his own films but also on the spirit of innovation and spontaneity that reigned in the earliest years of the industry. With his memory still sharp, Brown revealed the mechanics behind single shots; the technical challenges that fascinated his engineer's mind; the daily compromises he made to please the studio, the star, or the public; the personal projects that brought him joy but sometimes ended in commercial failure. And in doing so, Brown may have revealed much more than he intended: despite repeated claims that he was in the business "just" to entertain the public and to keep the stars busy, it was clear how emotionally invested he was in many of his films. An interview by Brownlow and Donald Knox for an American Film Institute oral history project in 1969 turned into a marathon session of eight hours, with the near-octogenarian director demonstrating impressive stamina as well as recall: he was able to remember the details of camera setups for Tourneur, coaching techniques he had developed for Pauline Frederick, and even the names of crew members he had worked with in the 1920s. Brownlow followed up with a screening of Brown's silent films at Paris's Cinémathèque, and as he watched the images he had created four decades before, his tough exterior melted away, and he was overcome with emotion.

Brown was always wary of attempts to "intellectualize" or "analyze" his work, but in his interviews with Brownlow and later with Scott Eyman, Harry Haun, and Patrick McGilligan, he was quick to identify both his strengths and his weaknesses. He acknowledged that he was primarily a visual director, one who sometimes struggled to pull off dialogue-heavy productions. In an interview with Eyman, Brown revealed the reason for his reluctance to grant interviews that might lead to a reappraisal of his work: he was afraid the films he held most dear might seem quaint and sentimental to a 1970s audience. Indeed, he identified sentimentality as a flaw in his oeuvre, associating it with an "old-fashioned" quality. In some respects, he was doing himself a disservice; even though some of his work seems sentimental to the modern viewer, there are moments in his films (notably, *The Yearling* and *Intruder in the Dust*) that continue to surprise with their level of toughness and candor. It might be more fruitful, in fact, to view Brown's oeuvre as one in which myriad sentiments are expressed and happy endings are often qualified or muted.

Brown's work enjoyed a flurry of renewed critical interest in the late 1960s and early 1970s when French critics such as Gilles Cèbe, Patrick Brion, and Christian Vivani began to take note and John Baxter and Allen Estrin published excellent short studies. But as he aged and his memories faded, Brown began to withdraw from public events. It was only after some persuading from Charlie Brakebill that he attended his own Directors Guild of America tribute in July 1977, which was presided over by Gene Reynolds and featured memories from a host of actors, writers, and directors with whom he had worked—although, predictably, Garbo was otherwise engaged. It was an evening of celebration, and as one critic noted, the visual "spoke" more eloquently than any of the speeches or telegrams: "The words used by Brown's collaborators in an attempt to explain his talent (some used the word genius) were mostly fumbling and inadequate in comparison to the evidence of the clips. Brown's craft was so largely visual, his style so subtly and unobtrusively sophisticated and most of his co-workers so inarticulate that it was hard at the tribute to pinpoint much about his working methods."[6]

In the decade that followed, Brown's profile receded, as a shift away from auteurist studies led to a decline in interest in excavating the work of studio directors. When Brown finally succumbed to old age (he was ninety-seven), obituary writers remembered him as "Garbo's favorite director" or as a stolid, old-fashioned MGM hack. The more generous were respectful but a little disinterested. The *Hollywood Reporter* noted that Brown may have been a victim of the selective writing of American film history, in which those who toed the line and served the studio directive would always be considered less glamorous and less interesting to writers accustomed to the flamboyance of Sam Fuller or Raoul Walsh, the cantankerousness of John Ford, or the charisma of Alfred Hitchcock.[7]

When Brown donated his papers to the University of Tennessee, he seemed unsure whether future generations would find anything of interest: "Let them make what they can of it. . . . Maybe it means something. Maybe not. We did our best, usually. . . . You had to fight for everything you got onto the screen. That's how things were set up with the old studio system, and it worked out for the best most of the time. But you did have to fight. . . . Anything worth wanting is worth fighting for. Isn't it?"[8] Over his long career, Brown fought for the right to express his creativity, to put onscreen some of the sentiments he held most dear. His fellow aviator Antoine de Saint-Exupéry once remarked, "I fly because it releases my mind from the tyranny of petty things." Brown never quite freed himself from the tyranny of the system, but at times he soared in flights of poeticism and romanticism that are still unequaled on the American screen.

Acknowledgments

Two people have been instrumental in helping me research and complete this book: Patrick McGilligan and Kevin Brownlow. I owe an enormous debt to them both for their patience and kindness, their encouragement and support, and their generosity in sharing their own research with me. Pat and Kevin constantly reminded me it was worthwhile, and they were always ready to drop everything to help me. I thank them most sincerely.

I am greatly indebted to Barbara McRae, cousin of Clarence Brown, for her generosity in sharing her genealogical research on Brown's ancestry with me.

Thanks also must go to Mike Malone, retired from the National Park Service, who shared his research on Brown's Calabasas ranch and on Brown more generally.

In Knoxville, a huge thanks to Charlie Brakebill, retired from the University of Tennessee–Knoxville Alumni Foundation, who shared his memories of Brown and his involvement in his alma mater. Thanks, too, to Joe Johnson, former president of the university, and to all the staff at the archive, especially Bill Eigelsbach.

Also, much appreciation to journalist and historian Jack Neely, who took the time to give me a guided tour of Knoxville and share his wealth of knowledge about its history. Thanks to Terry Ingano of Clinton, Massachusetts, who helped me fill in some of Brown's New England background.

At the archives: thanks to all the staff at the Clarence Brown Collection at the University of Tennessee, Knoxville; Barbara Hall, Kristine Krueger, and all the staff of the Margaret Herrick Library, Academy of Motion Picture Arts and Sciences; Ned Comstock of USC; the staff at the UCLA archive; the staff at the David O. Selznick Collection at the Harry Ransom Center, University of Texas, Austin; the staff at the Beinecke Library, Yale; the staff at the Harold B. Lee Library, Brigham Young University; the late Charles Silver at the Museum of Modern Art; and Caroline Yeager and all the staff at George Eastman House. I am particularly grateful for Caroline's help in furnishing a copy of the restored *Light in the Dark* on DVD.

Thanks to those who granted personal interviews or emailed me their anecdotes: Marsha Hunt, the late Leatrice Gilbert Fountain, Gene Reynolds, Allen Estrin, the late Marvin Kaplan, and especially Jacqueline White and her family and Claude Jarman Jr. Thanks to those who answered my queries by email: Daniel Selznick, Scott Eyman, Glen Lovell, Leonard Maltin, Lea Williams, Richard Koszarski, Andre Soares, Emily Leider, Roger Memos, Carmen Guilraut, and Carlo Gebler.

I thank the staff at the University Press of Kentucky, especially my very patient, very efficient editor Anne Dean Dotson and also Leila Salisbury, Patrick O'Dowd, Ila McEntire, and Jacqueline Wilson. I would like to express my sincere gratitude to copyeditor Linda Lotz, who gave the manuscript such meticulous attention.

My thanks to Emily Leider and Lucy Fischer, writers I hold in great esteem, for supplying endorsements of the book.

Thank you to all my kind and cheerful colleagues in the School of English and Film and Screen Media at University College Cork (UCC). I especially thank Barry Reilly and Dan O'Connell for their technical help and Anne Fitzgerald and Laura Rascaroli for a lot of encouragement and support. I am grateful for the support of the UCC Library, especially the staff of the Inter-Library Loans Department and Ronan Madden. A note of thanks to Patrick O'Donovan, who in his capacity as head of college granted me a sabbatical that allowed me to finish the book. Thanks, too, to Jill Murphy, whose offer of teaching cover facilitated my sabbatical.

Thank you to all my friends and family (human and canine) who supported me over the long gestation of this book. I am especially grateful to Maria Pramaggiore and Tom Wallis, who always maintained that the project was worthwhile and even took the time to drive me from Boston to Clinton so that I could visit Brown's birthplace. I also want to say "merci" to Frédéric Lorente and Laurence Couderc for the wi-fi and endless kindness and humor during my time spent in France writing (and rewriting) the book. Also, a special note of gratitude goes to Cathrina Gaffney for her proofreading skills and support.

I would like to acknowledge the financial support received through the publication funds offered by the College of Arts, Celtic Studies and Social Sciences, UCC, and by the National University of Ireland.

Most of all, I thank my parents, Phil and Keith Young. I know you had given up hope that the book would ever be finished, but here it is!

Notes

Abbreviations

AMPAS   Academy of Motion Picture Arts and Sciences
MPPDA   Motion Picture Producers and Distributors of America
PCA   Production Code Administration
SDG   Screen Directors Guild
SRC   Studio Relations Committee
USC   University of Southern California

1. A Brown Boy

1. *Variety*, July 20, 1977.

2. Some confusion exists over her birth date. Genealogical records note the birth of a Catherine Ann Gaw on February 8, 1865, which is the date listed on her gravestone in Forest Lawn cemetery in Los Angeles. However, in a profile of the Browns published in one scholarly source on Tennessee, her birth date is listed as February 17, 1867; see John Trotwood Moore, *Tennessee: The Volunteer State, 1769–1923* (Chicago: S.J. Clarke, 1923). Her obituary in the *Los Angeles Times* lists her age as ninety-one, which makes a birth date of 1865 more likely.

3. I am indebted to Clarence Brown's cousin, Barbara McRae, for sharing her genealogical research with me.

4. Twain quoted in A. J. Bastarche, *An Extraordinary Town: How One of America's Smallest Towns Shaped the World* (Clinton, MA: Angus MacGregor Publishing, 2005), 78.

5. William Bruce Wheeler, *Knoxville, Tennessee: A Mountain City in the New South* (Knoxville: University of Tennessee Press, 2005), ix.

6. Ibid., 20.

7. "Brookside Mills," *Knoxville News-Sentinel*, January 18, 1988.

8. See James Agee, "TVA: Work in the Valley," https://www.tva.gov/About-TVA/Our-History/heritage/The-Great-Experiment.

9. Jack Neely, "The Forgotten Director: Who Was Clarence Brown? *Metro Pulse*, March 6, 2008, 78.

2. The Master's Apprentice

1. Allen Estrin, *The Hollywood Professionals* (South Brunswick, NJ: A. S. Barnes, 1980), 147,

2. Jim Tully, "Clarence Brown: Estimate," *Vanity Fair*, April 1928, 79.

3. Clarence Brown, "I Remember," *Film Weekly* 20 (1939): 47.

4. On NOLA, see *Moving Picture World*, January 30, 1915, 651. The account of Brown's audition is from Leatrice Gilbert Fountain, email to Young, June 22, 2000.

5. For a history of Fort Lee, see Richard Koszarski, *Fort Lee: The Film Town* (Rome, Italy: John Libbey, 2004).

6. "The Men behind the Stars: Clarence Brown," *Movie Play*, July 1952, 95.

7. Kevin Brownlow, *The Parade's Gone By* (New York: Alfred Knopf, 1968), 140.

8. Tully, "Clarence Brown: Estimate," 79.

9. Christine Leteux, *Maurice Tourneur: Réalisateur sans frontières* (Paris: La tour verte, 2015), 15.

10. For more on Tourneur's war record, see ibid., 36; Gerard Perron, "Maurice Tourneur," *Lumière du Cinéma*, July–August 1977, 51; Harry Waldman, *Maurice Tourneur: The Life and Films* (Jefferson, NC: McFarland, 2001), 3.

11. "The Wishing Ring," *Variety*, October 30, 1914.

12. *Motography*, February 27, 1915.

13. Maurice Tourneur, "Movies Create Art," *Harper's Weekly*, April 29, 1916, 459.

14. Maurice Tourneur, "Impressionistic Art Is Coming into Its Own on the Screen," *Vanity Fair*, September 1919, 104.

15. "Maurice Tourneur Is a Master Screen Magician," *Brooklyn Eagle*, March 3, 1918.

16. Harrison Haskins, "The Big Six Directors," *Motion Picture Classic*, September 1918, 17.

17. For more on Tourneur's style, see Richard Koszarski, "Maurice Tourneur: The First of the Visual Stylists," *Film Comment* 9 (March–April 1973): 24–31.

18. Waldman, *Maurice Tourneur*, 42.

19. *Los Angeles Times*, July 20, 1924.

20. Clarence Brown, unpublished interview with Kevin Brownlow and Donald Knox, 1969, Library of Congress.

21. According to Brownlow, and confirmed by Ben Carré, one of these students was Cedric Gibbons, who would become a close friend of Tourneur's and one of the major forces at MGM in the 1920s and 1930s. See Kevin Brownlow, "Ben Carré," *Sight and Sound* 49 (Winter 1979–1980): 46.

22. Brownlow, *Parade's Gone By*, 141.

23. Anthony Slide, *Fifty Great American Silent Films, 1912–1920: A Pictorial Survey* (New York: Dover, 1980), 74.

24. Van Enger quoted in Richard Koszarski, "Career in Shadows: Interview with Charles Van Enger," *Film History* 3, no. 3 (1989): 276.

25. Ibid.

26. Scott Eyman, *Mary Pickford* (New York: Dutton, 1990), 92.

27. Frances Marion, *Off with Their Heads! A Serio-Comic Tale of Hollywood* (New York: Macmillan, 1972), 43–44.

28. Gary Carey, *Doug & Mary: A Biography of Douglas Fairbanks & Mary Pickford* (New York: E. P. Dutton, 1977), 54.

29. Frances Wood, "Tourneur: A Weaver of Dreams," *Picture Play*, June 1918, 215.

30. Maurice Tourneur, "Meeting the Public Demands," *Shadowland*, May 1920, reprinted in *Film Comment*, July–August 1976, 32.

31. Brown quoted in *Variety*, July 1920. Charles Brakebill shared Brown's recollection in an interview with the author conducted on November 5, 2008, in Knoxville, Tennessee.

32. Brownlow, *Parade's Gone By*, 141.

33. Jacques Tourneur revealed the details of his complex relationship with his father in an unpublished interview with Kevin Brownlow in June 1969.

34. Lea Williams, email to Young, December 8, 2008.

35. Brakebill, interview with author, 2008.

36. Jacques Tourneur, interview with Brownlow, 1969.

37. Richard Koszarski, *The Rivals of D. W. Griffith: Alternate Auteurs, 1913–1918* (Minneapolis: Walker Art Center, 1976), 41.

38. Kristian Moen, "The Blue Bird," in *Films and Fairy Tales: The Birth of Modern Fantasy* (London: I. B. Tauris, 2013), 98–136.

39. Those who praised *The Bluebird* included the reviewer in *Photoplay*, May 1918, 90. The critic writing in *Motion Picture Magazine*, May 1918, 104, found it a little tiresome.

40. Charles van Enger offered an eyewitness account of the tragedy in an unpublished interview with Kevin Brownlow, December 4, 1969, Los Angeles. A similar version appears in Koszarski, "Career in the Shadows," 227–28.

41. *Exhibitors Trade Review*, July 20, 1918, reported van den Broek's death and Tourneur's anguish. Tourneur quoted in *Moving Picture World*, July 20, 1918, 391.

3. Brown Goes to War ... and Returns to Tourneur

1. Clarence Brown, unpublished interview with Kevin Brownlow, October 1966, Paris; *The Scott Field Army Book, 1918* (copy in Clarence Brown Collection, University of Tennessee, Knoxville), 134.

2. Letter from Charles van Enger to Richard Koszarski, quoted in *Griffithiana*, September 1988, 243; Brown, interview with Brownlow and Knox, 1969. See also George Geltzer, "Maurice Tourneur," *Films in Review* 12 (April 4, 1961): 200; Koszarski, "Career in Shadows," 278.

3. Brown, interview with Brownlow, 1966; Charles van Enger, *Wid's Daily*, July 14, 1919, 1, quoted in Leteux, *Maurice Tourneur*, 189n.

4. Brownlow, *Parade's Gone By*, 142.

5. For the acquisition of H. H. Van Loan's story, see "The Story behind a Play," *Washington Post*, October 17, 1920, 54. For Brown's collaboration with Gilbert, see

Leatrice Fountain, *Dark Star: The Meteoric Rise and Eclipse of John Gilbert* (London: Sidgwick & Jackson, 1985), 48.

6. Brownlow, *Parade's Gone By*, 142.

7. *New York Times*, October 25, 1920, 22; *Screenland*, October 16, 1920; letter from James Bramlay to Brown and Tourneur, September 8, 1920, Brown Collection, University of Tennessee.

8. Brownlow, *Parade's Gone By*, 142, notes that Tourneur sustained an injury after a fall. *Variety*, October 15, 1920, 42, and Geltzer, "Maurice Tourneur," 202, record that his absence was due to pleurisy and ptomaine poisoning. Mueller quoted in Geltzer, "Maurice Tourneur," 202; Jacques Tourneur, interview with Brownlow, 1969; Koszarski, "Career in Shadows," 280.

9. Brownlow, *Parade's Gone By*, 144.

10. Koszarski, "Career in Shadows," 279, 281.

11. Jacques Tourneur, interview with Brownlow, 1969.

12. For Sarris's assessment of Bedford, see Andrew Sarris, *The American Cinema* (New York: Dutton, 1968), 236.

13. Brown, interview with Brownlow and Knox, 1969.

14. Jan-Christopher Horak, "Maurice Tourneur's Tragic Romance," in *The Classic American Novel and the Movies*, ed. Gerald Peary and Roger Shatzkin (New York: Frederick Ungar, 1977), 4–20. See also Hubert Niogret, "Le Dernier des Mohicans, de Maurice Tourneur et Clarence Brown, et Le Dernier des Mohicans de Michael Mann," *Positif* (1992): 58–59, for a comparison of this version and Michael Mann's 1992 film. The other version of the novel filmed in 1920 was a German production directed by Arthur Wellin and starring a pre-*Dracula* Bela Lugosi.

15. *Photoplay*, April 1921, 78; *Life*, undated clipping, Brown Collection, University of Tennessee.

16. For the filming of *Foolish Matrons*, see Geltzer, "Maurice Tourneur," 204; Brown, interview with Brownlow, 1966.

17. For Kingsley's review, see undated clipping, Brown Collection, University of Tennessee.

18. Brown quoted in Brownlow, *Parade's Gone By*, 153.

19. Jacques Tourneur, interview with Brownlow, 1969; Brown quoted in Fountain, *Dark Star*, 47.

20. Dorothy Nutting, "Monsieur Tourneur," *Photoplay*, July 1918, 56.

4. Striking Out

1. Van Enger recalled Hampton as a talented dancer and a woman who could be self-deprecating; see Charles van Enger to Kevin Brownlow, October 8, 1971, private collection of Kevin Brownlow, London. This seems to be borne out by a November 1923 profile of her in *Photoplay*, in which an initially cynical Bland Johaneson confesses to being charmed by this "fiery, redheaded little Irishwoman, reckless, blunt, almost tactless in the frankness with which she voices her opinions of things and people," and amused at how blithely she dismisses her detractors,

declaring that she gives "back as good as they give me . . . and when they see they can't fuss me, they simply settle down." Quoted in Koszarski, *Fort Lee*, 247.

2. Details of the negotiation of the Brulatour deal are in van Enger to Brownlow, October 8, 1971. Brown's fears about Tourneur's reaction were recorded by Leatrice Gilbert Fountain and relayed in an email to Young, June 26, 2000.

3. For Brown on why he accepted the assignment, see Brownlow, *Parade's Gone By*, 144.

4. Brown, interview with Brownlow, 1966.

5. *New York Times*, June 25, 1922; Brownlow, *Parade's Gone By*, 144. A contemporary news report noted the shooting of a stunt on the corner of Columbus Avenue and 72nd Street; see *Variety*, September 1, 1922, 46. Brown gave a short account of the filming in his unpublished manuscript "Fifty Million Feet of Hollywood Romance," n.d., Brown Collection, University of Tennessee.

6. Lewis quoted in Florice Whyte Kovan, *Rediscovering Ben Hecht: Selling the Celluloid Serpent* (New York: Snickersee Press, 1998), 60; Carré's unpublished memoirs, n.d., 21, Brownlow collection; Brown quoted in Brownlow, *Parade's Gone By*, 144.

7. On the film's duration, see email from Caroline Yeager (George Eastman House, Rochester, NY) to Kevin Brownlow, May 9, 2011, Brownlow collection. For the initial review and audience reaction, see *Variety*, September 1, 1922, 42; *Motion Picture News*, September 9, 1922, 1295; *Variety*, September 9, 1922.

8. Brown was reluctant to talk about the film even fifty years after its release; see Brownlow, *Parade's Gone By*, 144. For Chaney's letters from prisoners, see Jeanine Basinger, *Silent Stars* (New York: Alfred A. Knopf, 2000), 350.

9. Van Enger to Brownlow, October 8, 1971; Fountain, *Dark Star*, 66, 67.

10. "Still the formula" was how *Photoplay*'s November 1923 review put it; *Los Angeles Examiner*, December 22, 1923, commented on moral lessons; Williams's review in *Los Angeles Times*, December 23, 1924.

5. Early Years at Universal

1. Frederica Sagor Maas, *The Shocking Miss Pilgrim* (Lexington: University Press of Kentucky, 1999), 35.

2. On building up Brown's career, see *Los Angeles Times*, March 17, 1927, A2; on Ona as press agent, see *Los Angeles Times*, June 17, 1925, C10.

3. Review of *The Acquittal*, *New York Times*, January 6, 1920. Schatz estimates that only one-twelfth of all Universal productions released each year would have been "Jewels"; see Thomas Schatz, *The Genius of the System* (New York: Metropolitan Books, 1996), 22. According to the American Film Institute catalog (see https://catalog.afi.com), the original release ran approximately 6,523 feet. The Library of Congress's print was donated from the Raymond Rohauer collection.

4. Brown's fond memories of the cast and the need to shoot around the injured Kerry are in "Fifty Million Feet of Hollywood Romance," *Picturegoer*, May 13, 1939, 10. On Brown's preparation for his cameo, see *Los Angeles Times*, July 13, 1924.

5. *Photoplay*, January 1924, 68; *Variety*, December 20, 1923.

6. For Brown's acquisition of the Camp story, see *Exhibitors Herald*, February 20, 1924.

7. Locations listed in *New York Times*, January 20, 1924, X5; *Los Angeles Times*, July 27, 1924, B16. For the Skunk train line, see http://www.filmmendocino.com/films.htm. Brown also remembered the shoot in Brownlow, *Parade's Gone By*, 145. According to Brown's foreword for Frederica Sagor Maas's memoirs, Kay Knudsen designed "an important set" for the film, but her contribution wasn't credited. Maas, *Shocking Miss Pilgrim*, ix.

8. Brown recalled Dorian's accident and the conditions at Mendocino in "Fifty Million Feet of Hollywood Romance," 10. Mayer quoted in Mickey Rooney, *Life Is Too Short* (London: Hutchison, 1992), 77.

9. Brown, interview with Brownlow, 1966.

10. *Los Angeles Times*, July 13, 1924; Taylor review in *Los Angeles Times*, August 2, 1924, A7.

6. Brown and the Universal Women

1. Estrin, *Hollywood Professionals*, 142; George Landy, *Screen News*, October 18, 1924.

2. Kathleen Norris, *Poor Butterfly* (London: William Heinemann, 1923).

3. For the Valli rumor, see *New York Morning Telegraph*, March 2, 1924. For the Dempsey rumor, see "Conqueror Seeks New Worlds," *Los Angeles Times*, June 1, 1924, B15. Brown's recollections of Harlan were recorded by Brownlow in unpublished, undated notes on *Butterfly*, Brownlow collection.

4. Ruth Clifford quoted in a letter from Anthony Slide to Kevin Brownlow, December 26, 1997, Brownlow collection; Ruth Clifford, unpublished interview with Sue McConachy, ca. 1976, 24 (on casting), 20 (on acting), Brownlow collection; Brown on actors quoted in Brownlow, *Parade's Gone By*, 151.

5. Brown's directions to the set designer are recalled in "Fifty Million Feet of Hollywood Romance," *Picturegoer*, May 13, 1939, 10. For more on American culture and the fascination with youth and beauty, see Kathy Peiss, *Hope in a Jar: The Making of America's Beauty Culture* (New York: Owl Books, 1996); Gaylyn Studlar, *This Mad Masquerade: Stardom and Masculinity in the Jazz Age* (New York: Columbia University Press, 1996); Lois Banner, *American Beauty* (Chicago: University of Chicago Press, 1983); Heather Addison, *Hollywood and the Rise of Physical Culture* (New York: Routledge, 2003).

6. Edwin Schallert, *Los Angeles Times*, July 25, 1924, A9; *Photoplay*, November 1924, 63; Clifford, interview with McConachy, 23.

7. Brownlow, *Parade's Gone By*, 145; Brown, interview with Brownlow and Knox, 1969.

8. Brown, interview with Brownlow, 1966.

9. *Los Angeles Times*, January 4, 1925, 27. Interestingly, a review that appeared before the Lipke piece was critical of the ending, noting that the film would have

rung truer had it depicted Jane returning to the life she once had. Tamar Lane, "Views and Reviews," *Film Mercury*, December 19, 1924, 6.

10. Herbert Moulton, *Los Angeles Times*, November 19, 1924, C12; Edwin Schallert, *Los Angeles Times*, January 5, 1925, 5; Alma Whitaker, *Los Angeles Times*, January 9, 1925, A7.

11. Maas, *Shocking Miss Pilgrim*, 43. Her recollection of the sum of $20,000 is probably incorrect, as a copy of the legal agreement between Universal and Rex Beach, dated December 5, 1924, states that Beach was to receive $32,000, payable over a period of ten months (Brown Collection, University of Tennessee). Rex Beach, *The Goose Woman and Other Stories* (London: Hodder & Stoughton, 1925).

12. On Frederick's departure, see *Los Angeles Times*, September 30, 1928, C26; on Dresser's contract and the geese, see Brownlow, *Parade's Gone By*, 145; on Dresser's cooperation, see *Los Angeles Times*, February 8, 1925, D17.

13. *Screen News*, February 21, 1925.

14. *Los Angeles Times*, April 9, 1925, A9. In a letter to Lillian Gish, Mary Pickford mentions that her brother is traveling to New York to see an eye specialist and that the production will have to shoot around his absence; see Pickford to Gish, March 26, 1925, Brownlow collection. Although Jack Pickford's illness was likely due to "kliegl eyes," he was already on the road to chronic alcoholism, and this might have been a factor as well.

15. Mordaunt Hall, *New York Times*, August 4, 1925, 14; "Mae Tinee," *Chicago Daily Tribune*, January 2, 1927, D1; Paul Rotha, *The Film Till Now* (London: Spring Books, 1967), 197; Everson's notes on the film, dated January 30, 1968, Brownlow collection.

16. Letter from Dresser to Brownlow, November 12, 1960, Brownlow collection.

7. Brown at United Artists

1. See Emily Leider, *Dark Lover: The Life and Death of Rudolph Valentino* (London: Faber & Faber, 2004); Studlar, *This Mad Masquerade*; Miriam Hansen, "Pleasure, Ambivalence, Identification: Valentino and Female Spectatorship," *Cinema Journal* 25 (Summer 1986): 6–32.

2. *Hollywood Citizen News*, May 6, 1925; Grace Kingsley, "Rudy Forsakes Role of Latin Lover for that of Dignified Comique in Latest Effort," *Los Angeles Times*, August 23, 1925, 17.

3. *Moving Picture World*, April 25, 1925, 804. Fairbanks was also a partner in United Artists; see Leider, *Dark Lover*, p. 342.

4. Brownlow, *Parade's Gone By*, 146.

5. Andrew Sarris, *You Ain't Heard Nothin' Yet: The American Talking Film History & Memory, 1927–1949* (New York: Oxford University Press, 1998), 386.

6. Leider, *Dark Lover*, 347. Valentino and the bear, wrestling at the junction of Ventura Boulevard and Laurel Canyon, was reported by the *Los Angeles Times*, September 9, 1925, A9.

7. *Los Angeles Times*, August 23, 1925, 17; Leider, *Dark Lover*, 342.

8. *Los Angeles Times*, November 15, 1925, 13.

9. Norbert Lusk, *New York Telegraph*, November 15, 1925; Mordaunt Hall, *New York Times*, November 15, 1925, X5; Basinger, *Silent Stars*, 296; Leider, *Dark Lover*, 349.

10. Harry Carr, "The Status of the Directors: The Men with the Megaphones," *Motion Picture Classic*, November 1925, 20; Kingsley, "Rudy Forsakes Role of Latin Lover," 17.

11. "The Man on the Cover," *Motion Picture: The Director*, February 1926, 22.

12. Franklin quoted in Kevin Brownlow, *Hollywood* (London: Collins, 1979), 157.

13. *Los Angeles Times*, January 28, 1926, A9; *Los Angeles Times*, February 14, 1926, 15; Brown, interview with Brownlow and Knox, 1969; Brownlow, *Parade's Gone By*, 146.

14. Scott Eyman, "Clarence Brown: Garbo and Beyond," *Velvet Light Trap* 18 (Spring 1978): 20; Scott Eyman, *Lion of Hollywood: The Life and Legend of Louis B. Mayer* (New York: Simon & Schuster, 2005), 113.

15. *Photoplay*, June 1926, 52; Mordaunt Hall, *New York Times*, April 6, 1926, 26; *Cinémagazine*, June 18, 1926, 620; Grace Kingsley, *Los Angeles Times*, May 2, 1926, 14; *Variety*, April 7, 1926, http://web.stanford.edu/~gdegroat/NT/oldreviews/kiki.htm.

16. Basinger, *Silent Stars*, 157.

8. Brown Meets Garbo

1. On the final years of Tourneur's American career, see Leteux, *Maurice Tourneur*, 239–56.

2. Schatz, *Genius of the System*, 36.

3. Alice Williamson, *Alice in Wonderland* (London: Philpot, 1927), 222; Schatz, *Genius of the System*, 42; Gary Carey, *All the Stars in Heaven: The Story of Louis B. Mayer and M.G.M.* (London: Robson Books, 1981), 117.

4. Eyman, *Lion of Hollywood*, 145.

5. *Los Angeles Times*, June 27, 1926, C26.

6. Treatments and drafts of the script are in the MGM collection at the University of Southern California (USC). Michael Williams, *Film Stardom, Myth and Classicism: The Rise of Hollywood's Gods* (London: Palgrave-Macmillan, 2012), examines the script's evolution; Maas to Marcin, November 15, 1925, MGM collection, USC.

7. Barry Paris, *Garbo* (London: Pan Books, 1996), 102; Ruth Biery, "The Story of Greta Garbo," *Photoplay*, April–June 1928, 144; Alexander Walker, *Garbo* (London: Weidenfeld & Nicolson, 1980), 10.

8. Fountain, *Dark Star*, 125.

9. Brownlow, *Parade's Gone By*, 147.

10. Daniels quoted in Charles Higham, *Hollywood Cameramen* (Bloomington: Indiana University Press, 1970), 71, 57.

11. *Los Angeles Times,* February 6, 1927, C19; Higham, *Hollywood Cameramen,* 71; *Los Angeles Times,* February 6, 1927, C19.

12. Mark Glancy, "MGM Film Grosses, 1924–1948: The Eddie Mannix Ledger," *Historical Journal of Film, Radio and Television* 12, no. 2 (1992): 129. The film returned $1,261,000 (in the United States and beyond), a profit of $466,000. The *Los Angeles Times,* August 18, 1926, A8, reported that shopgirl Barbara Kent had won a "Miss Hollywood" competition that resulted in a bit part in the Universal film Prowlers of the Night, which Brown had seen while he was casting *Flesh and the Devil.* For Kent on Brown's directing style, see Michael Ankerich, *The Sound of Silence: Conversations with 16 Film and Stage Personalities* (Jefferson, NC: McFarland, 2011), 157.

13. Brown's initial encounters with Garbo are recalled in a number of sources, including Carey, *All the Stars in Heaven,* 103, and Brownlow, *Parade's Gone By,* 146. On Brown's influence, see Mark Vieira, *Garbo: A Cinematic Legacy* (New York: Harry N. Abrams, 2005), 34.

14. Eyman, "Clarence Brown: Garbo and Beyond," 20; Brownlow, *Parade's Gone By,* 149. The original ending has since been put back in *Photoplay's* restored version.

15. Brownlow, *Parade's Gone By,* 146.

16. John Howard Lawson, *Film, the Creative Process* (New York: Hill & Wang, 1967), 104; Mark Vieira, *Hollywood Dreams Made Real: Irving Thalberg and the Rise of M-G-M* (New York: Harry N. Abrams, 2008), 115.

17. Karen Swenson, *Greta Garbo: A Life Apart* (New York: Lisa Drew/Scribner, 1997), 143; Mordaunt Hall, *New York Times,* January 16, 1927, 20; "Mae Tinee," *Chicago Daily Tribune,* February 27, 1927, G1; Herbert Moulton, *Los Angeles Times,* January 30, 1927, C22; Rudolf Arnheim, "Greta Garbo" (1928), in *Film Essays and Criticism,* trans. Brenda Benthien (Madison: University of Wisconsin Press, 1997), 217.

18. *Variety,* January 12, 1927, 14; Welford Beaton, *Film Spectator,* February 5, 1927, 2; *New York Times,* September 18, 1927, X5; Philip Dunne quoted in Patrick McGilligan, ed., *Backstory: Interviews with Screenwriters of Hollywood's Golden Age* (Berkeley: University of California Press, 1988), 155; *Los Angeles Examiner,* February 16, 1951.

19. Vieira, *Garbo,* 38; Kathleen Lipke, *Los Angeles Times,* October 17, 1926, C19; Cohen quoted in Scott Eyman, *Speed of Sound: Hollywood and the Talkie Revolution, 1926–1930* (New York: Simon & Schuster, 1997), 302; letter from Louise Brooks to Kevin Brownlow, October 19, 1968, Brownlow collection.

20. *New York Times,* May 16, 1926, X5.

21. *Los Angeles Times,* December 2, 1926, A2; *Los Angeles Times,* March 1, 1927, A1; *Los Angeles Times,* March 17, 1927, A2.

22. Alma Whitaker, *Los Angeles Times,* August 29, C32; Maas, *Shocking Miss Pilgrim,* 44; "Ona Brown Announces Betrothal," *Los Angeles Times,* September 1, 1928, A1; *Los Angeles Times,* March 28, 1937.

9. On the *Trail of '98*

1. Brownlow, *Parade's Gone By*, 152.

2. *Los Angeles Times*, December 9, 1926, A8; *Chicago Daily Tribune*, May 15, 1927, H3; Eyman, *Lion of Hollywood*, 118; memo from Stromberg to Glazer and Young, February 13, 1928, MGM collection, USC.

3. For more on the research conducted, see "Newspapers Aided '98 Film," *New York Times*, March 18, 1928, 123; John Shelton, "Life in the Raw," *Motion Picture Magazine*, January 1928, 28–29, 98.

4. *Los Angeles Times*, December 25, 1926, A6. Some of the animals had more success than the actors in the immediate postrelease period, with their trainers cashing in on their brief fame by featuring them in roadshows. Some of the huskies were adopted by members of the cast and crew. *New York Times*, February 19, 1928, 113.

5. Shelton, "Life in the Raw," 29; Jacques Tourneur, interview with Brownlow, 1969; *Los Angeles Times*, May 6, 1928, C12; Brown, interview with Brownlow and Knox, 1969; Vieira, *Hollywood Dreams Made Real*, 87.

6. *New York Times*, July 17, 1927, X5; Jacques Tourneur, interview with Brownlow, 1969. Maurice Rapf, son of producer Harry Rapf, also remembered seeing some segments of the Chilkoot Pass sequence being filmed at Culver City. Maurice Rapf, *Back Lot: Growing up with the Movies* (Lanham, MD: Scarecrow Press, 1999), 47.

7. Brownlow, *Parade's Gone By*, 150; Brown quoted in *Los Angeles Times*, March 26, 1927, A6; *New York Times*, February 19, 1928, 113; Brownlow, *Parade's Gone By*, 149.

8. Brownlow, *Parade's Gone By*, 149.

9. The plight of extras was referred to in Brownlow and Gill, *Hollywood* (TV series, 1980).

10. Bob Rose quoted in Brownlow and Gill, *Hollywood*; Brownlow, *Parade's Gone By*, 149; *Los Angeles Times*, December 23, 1928, C22.

11. Booth quoted in Directors Guild of America tribute to Brown, July 16, 1977, Los Angeles.

12. Edwin Schallert, *Los Angeles Times*, May 9, 1928, A9.

13. Mordaunt Hall, *New York Times*, March 25, 1928, 125; Norbert Lusk, *Los Angeles Times*, March 25, 1928, C13.

14. Dorothy Manners, "Without Benefit of Blow-ups," *Motion Picture Classic*, April 1928, 26.

15. Brown's involvement in *The Cossacks* was noted in *Los Angeles Times*, June 24, 1928, 14. For Brown's recollections of the film, see Fountain, *Dark Star*, 149.

10. An "Uplifting" Film

1. Vieira, *Garbo*, 68.

2. Thalberg to Hays, June 25, 1928, MGM collection, USC; Vieira, *Garbo*, 68.

3. The topic of venereal disease was not unknown in American cinema, but it was generally dealt with in B movies or "educational" films. See Jeremy Geltzer, *Dirty Words and Filthy Pictures: Film and the First Amendment* (Austin: University of Texas Press, 2016).

4. Hays to Thalberg, July 10, 1928, MGM collection, USC.

5. Edward Steichen, *A Life in Photography* (London: W. H. Allen, 1963), 8.

6. Jacques Feyder and Françoise Rosay, *Le Cinéma, Notre Métier* (Vésenaz-Genève: Editions Pierre Cailler, 1946), 53–55.

7. Harry Haun, "The UT Grad Who Engineered Dreams," *Tennessee Sunday Magazine,* July 2, 1972, 6.

8. For a closer analysis of this scene and its meanings, see Carmen Guiralt, "Self-Censorship in Hollywood during the Silent Era: *A Woman of Affairs* (1928) by Clarence Brown," *Film History* 28, no. 2 (2016): 81–113; Paris, *Garbo,* 132; Swenson, *Greta Garbo,* 175; Richard Corliss, *Greta Garbo* (New York: Pyramid Publications, 1974), 66.

9. Gilbert to Brown, in Fountain, *Dark Star,* 160.

10. Leatrice Gilbert Fountain, email to Young, June 26, 2000.

11. Swenson, *Greta Garbo,* 174; Douglas Fairbanks Jr., *The Salad Days: An Autobiography* (London: Fontana Books, 1989), 193.

12. Paris, *Garbo,* 132; Lenore Coffee, *Storyline: Recollections of a Hollywood Screenwriter* (London: Cassell, 1973), 144.

13. *Photoplay,* October 1928, 112.

14. Tim McCoy and Ronald McCoy, *Tim McCoy Remembers the West* (New York: Doubleday, 1977), 238.

15. Letter from Louise Brooks to Brownlow, quoted in Paris, *Garbo,* 202.

16. *Variety* review quoted in Vieira, *Garbo,* 72; Lorentz review quoted in Vieira, *Garbo,* 73, and Michael Conway, Dion McGregor, and Mark Ricci, *The Films of Greta Garbo* (New York: Bonanza Books, 1963), 73; Mordaunt Hall, *New York Times,* January 21, 1929, 26; Norbert Lusk, *Los Angeles Times,* January 27, 1929, C13.

17. Vieira, *Garbo,* 74; Manners, "Without Benefit of Blow-ups," 78.

18. *Washington Post,* December 30, 1928, A2.

11. Transition to Sound

1. Brown quoted in Eyman, *Speed of Sound,* 192.

2. *New York Times,* February 3, 1929, 112; Eyman, "Clarence Brown: Garbo and Beyond," 21; Brownlow, *Parade's Gone By,* 150.

3. Correspondence on the script, MGM collection, USC.

4. *New York Times,* February 3, 1929, 112; *Los Angeles Times,* January 30, 1929, A11; *Los Angeles Times,* February 21, 1929, A10.

5. *Wonder of Women* shooting script, 106, Brown Collection, University of Tennessee.

6. MGM cutting continuity, July 3, 1929, MGM collection, USC.

7. *Los Angeles Times*, April 4, 1929, A7; *Los Angeles Times*, April 24, 1929, A11; Haun, "UT Grad Who Engineered Dreams," 6.

8. *New York Times*, July 22, 1929, 16; *Variety*, July 24, 1929, 29.

9. William J. Mann, *Wisecracker: The Life and Times of William Haines, Hollywood's First Openly Gay Star* (New York: Viking Press, 1988), 164; Ankerich, *Sound of Silence*, 191.

10. Kenneth Porter, *Los Angeles Examiner*, January 10, 1930; Edwin Schallert, *Los Angeles Times*, January 10, 1930, A13.

12. A Year with Garbo

1. Vieira, *Garbo*, 104; Barbara Gelb and Arthur Gelb, *O'Neill* (New York: Delta Books, 1964), 126; Sam Marx, *Deadly Illusions: Jean Harlow and the Murder of Paul Bern* (New York: Dell, 1990), 111–12.

2. Marion, *Off with Their Heads*; Bengt Forslund, *Victor Sjöström: His Life and His Work* (New York: Zoetrope, 1988), 228; *Los Angeles Times*, November 10, 1929, B13.

3. The files of the Studio Relations Committee (SRC) of the Motion Picture Producers and Distributors of America (MPPDA) on *Anna Christie* are housed at the Margaret Herrick Library, Academy of Motion Picture Arts and Sciences (AMPAS).

4. Marion, *Off with Their Heads*, 198; Wilhelm Sörensen, "The Day that Garbo Dreaded," in Peter Haining, *The Legend of Garbo* (London: W. H. Allen, 1990), 144.

5. Vieira, *Garbo*, 107; Sidney Skolsky, *Don't Get Me Wrong—I Love Hollywood* (New York: G. P. Putnam & Sons, 1975), 55; Charles Bickford, *Bulls, Balls, Bicycles and Actors* (New York: Paul Ericksson, 1965), 239; John Loder, "Diary," *Film Weekly*, March 25, 1932, 150.

6. Marie Dressler, *My Own Story* (Boston: Little, Brown, 1934), 247; *New York Times*, June 22, 1930, X2; Betty Lee, *Marie Dressler: The Unlikeliest Star* (Lexington: University Press of Kentucky, 1998), 175.

7. Swenson, *Greta Garbo*, 217; Marion, *Off with Their Heads*, 198; *Los Angeles Times*, January 26, 1930, B15; Daily Production Records, October 19, 1929, MGM collection, USC.

8. Stuart Jackson, "Clarence Brown, Her Famous Director, Gives You an Intimate Glimpse of Garbo," *Film Weekly*, June 24, 1932, 8; Marion, *Off with Their Heads*, 192; Dressler, *My Own Story*, 252.

9. *Los Angeles Times*, December 12, 1929, A17; Willis to Joy, December 26, 1929, SRC/MPPDA files, Margaret Herrick Library, AMPAS.

10. Marion, *Off with Their Heads*, 204; Beth Day, *This Was Hollywood: An Affectionate History of Filmland's Golden Years* (London: Sidgwick & Jackson, 1960), 99; Sörensen, "The Day that Garbo Dreaded," 145; Brownlow, *Parade's Gone By*, 147.

11. Peet, writing in *Outlook* magazine, quoted in John Orlandello, *O'Neill on*

Film (Rutherford, NJ: Fairleigh Dickinson University Press, 1982), 29; Mordaunt Hall, *New York Times*, March 15, 1930, 22; Alexander Bakshy, *Nation*, April 2, 1930, quoted in Matthew Kennedy, *Marie Dressler: A Biography* (Jefferson, NC: McFarland, 2003), 115; Corliss, *Greta Garbo*, 80.

12. Lawson, *Film, the Creative Process*, 106; Higham, *Hollywood Cameramen*, 71; John Baxter, *Hollywood in the Thirties* (New York: Paperback Library, 1970), 24.

13. Lawson, *Film, the Creative Process*, 106.

14. Richard Schickel, *D. W. Griffith and the Birth of Film* (London: Pavilion Books, 1984), 427.

15. *Los Angeles Times*, July 5, 1928, A11; Brown's notes on *Romance*, December 11, 1929, MGM collection, USC.

16. Paris, *Garbo*, 178.

17. Vieira, *Garbo*, 115. According to Wilhelm Sörensen, Gordon said that Garbo was kind to him on the set. "Garbo Was My Friend," *Sunday Express*, July 3, 1955.

18. *New York Times*, May 4, 1930, X6; Jackson, "Clarence Brown," 8.

19. Howard quoted in Larry Carr, *Four Fabulous Faces: Garbo, Swanson, Crawford, Dietrich* (New York: Arlington, 1970), 121.

20. Vieira, *Garbo*, 115; Rudy Behlmer, *Henry Hathaway: Directors Guild Oral History: Interviews with Polly Platt* (Metuchen, NJ: Scarecrow Press, 2001), 362.

21. Trotti to Joy, July 21, 1930, SRC/MPPDA files, Margaret Herrick Library, AMPAS; Joy, memo on *Romance*, July 7, 1930, ibid.

22. *New York Times*, August 23, 1930, 12; Monroe Lathrop, *Los Angeles Evening Express*, July 18, 1930; Corliss, *Greta Garbo*, 86.

23. Vieira, *Garbo*, 121; Marx, *Deadly Illusions*, 114; Jackson, "Clarence Brown," 8; Michael Sragow, "Karen Morley: Still Sexy after All These Blacklisted Years," *San Francisco Weekly*, April 21, 1999, http://archives.sfweekly.com/sanfrancisco/karen-morley-still-sexy-after-all-these-blacklisted-years.

24. Joy quoted in Ruth Vasey, *The World According to Hollywood, 1918–39* (Devon, UK: University of Exeter Press, 1997), 111; Mark Vieira, *Sin in Soft Focus: Pre-Code Hollywood* (New York: Harry N. Abrams, 1999), 51.

25. Cecil Beaton, "Why Garbo Shuns the World," quoted in Haining, *Legend of Garbo*, 162; Vieira, *Garbo*, 123.

26. *Daily Variety*, December 6, 1930; Katherine Albert, "Did Brown and Garbo Fight?" *Photoplay*, March 1931, 33, 131; Ted Le Berthon, *Los Angeles Review*, December 9, 1930; Jackson, "Clarence Brown," 8.

27. Brown elaborated on how the shot was achieved in his interview with Brownlow and Knox, 1969.

28. *Los Angeles Examiner*, February 13, 1931; Elizabeth Yeaman, *Hollywood Daily Citizen*, March 13, 1931; Mordaunt Hall, *New York Times*, February 9, 1931; DeWitt Bodeen, "Memories of Garbo," in Haining, *Legend of Garbo*, 264; Corliss, *Greta Garbo*, 88.

29. Baxter, *Hollywood in the Thirties*, 24; Corliss, *Greta Garbo*, 26; Freda Lockhart, "Shepherd of the Stars," *Film Weekly*, April 2, 1938, 6.

30. Alfonso Pinto, "Mona Maris," *Films in Review* 31 (1980): 145–59; Louella Parsons, *Los Angeles Examiner,* January 21, 1932; Grace Kingsley, *Los Angeles Times,* February 7, 1932, B10.

31. *Los Angeles Examiner,* September 21, 1935; *Los Angeles Examiner,* February 6, 1936.

13. Starmaker

1. Vieira, *Hollywood Dreams Made Real,* 156; Adela Rogers St. Johns, *Love, Laughter and Tears: My Hollywood Story* (Garden City, NY: Doubleday, 1978), 32.

2. *Exhibitors Herald,* June 27, 1931; Chrystopher Spicer, *Clark Gable: Biography, Filmography* (Jefferson, NC: McFarland, 2002), 74. According to another account, Norma Shearer claimed credit for selecting Gable. Vieira, *Hollywood Dreams Made Real,* 156; Haun, "UT Grad Who Engineered Dreams," 6.

3. Joy quoted in Vasey, *World According to Hollywood,* 111; Vieira, *Sin in Soft Focus,* 52; correspondence between Hyman and Joy is in SRC/MPPDA files, Margaret Herrick Library, AMPAS.

4. Brown quoted in Jack Jacobs and Myron Braum, *The Films of Norma Shearer* (South Brunswick, NJ: A. S. Barnes, 1976), 32; Brown quoted in Gavin Lambert, *Norma Shearer* (London: Hodder & Stoughton, 1990), 214.

5. Eyman, "Clarence Brown: Garbo and Beyond," 21.

6. Whitney Stine and George Hurrell, *50 Years of Photographing Hollywood: The Hurrell Style* (New York: Greenwich House/Crown Publishers, 1976), 70 (emphasis in original).

7. Charles Samuels, *The King: A Biography of Clark Gable* (New York: Coward McCann, 1962), 165; Charles Foster, *Stardust and Shadows: Canadians in Early Hollywood* (Toronto: Dundurn, 2000), 378.

8. Lionel Barrymore, as told to Cameron Shipp, *We Barrymores* (London: Peter Davies, 1951), 196.

9. Mordaunt Hall, *New York Times,* June 3, 1931, (http://www.nytimes.com/movie/review?res=9B06E7D8153BE23ABC4B53DFB066838A629EDE); Edwin Schallert, *Los Angeles Times,* July 1, 1931, A11; Peet quoted in Jacobs and Braum, *Films of Norma Shearer,* 176.

10. For more on the promotional campaign, see Mary Beth Haralovich, "Flirting with Hetero Diversity: Film Promotion of A Free Soul," in *Hetero: Queering Representations of Straightness,* ed. Sean Griffin (New York: SUNY, 2009), 37–51; Gladys Hall, "Norma Shearer Tells What a 'Free Soul' Really Means," *Motion Picture,* April 1932, 48–49, 96.

11. *Los Angeles Evening Examiner,* June 23, 1931; Charlotte Chandler, *Joan Crawford: Not the Girl Next Door* (London: Simon & Schuster/Pocket Books, 2008), 97.

12. *Los Angeles Record,* July 24, 1931. Grindé claimed in an interview with Kevin Brownlow that Brown directed only a few days of footage; Brownlow, email to Young, May 3, 2006. Lawrence Quirke and William Schoell, *Joan Crawford: The*

Essential Biography (Lexington: University Press of Kentucky, 2002), 56; "This Modern Age," American Film Institute catalog, https://catalog.afi.com/Catalog/moviedetails/6926?sid=97209954-b334-41aa-ba6b-786e42ac385f&sr=4.266556&cp=1&pos=0.

13. Coffee, *Storyline*, 182.

14. Ibid.; Vieira, *Hollywood Dreams Made Real*, 145. Script drafts are in the MGM collection, USC.

15. Coffee, *Storyline*, 183–85.

16. Script discussions, *Possessed* file, SRC/MPPDA files, Margaret Herrick Library, AMPAS.

17. Warne Marsh quoted in Whitney Balliett, *American Musicians II: Seventy-One Portraits in Jazz* (Jackson: University Press of Mississippi, 2006), 489.

18. Brown quoted in Haun, "UT Grad Who Engineered Dreams," 6.

19. John Kobal, *People Will Talk: Personal Conversations with the Legends of Hollywood* (London: Aurum Press, 1986), 152; Coffee, *Storyline*, 184.

20. James Sanders, *Celluloid Skyline: New York and the Movies* (New York: Alfred Knopf, 2003), 281–82.

21. On Joy's reaction to the film, see Vieira, *Sin in Soft Focus*, 54–55; Trotti to Joy, October 21, 1931, SRC/MPPDA files, Margaret Herrick Library, AMPAS; Hays's correspondence to Schenck, ibid.; Beeston to Thalberg, October 22, 1931, ibid.; Vieira, *Hollywood Dreams Made Real*, 157.

22. Joy to Breen quoted in American Film Institute catalog; Warner to Joy, June 10, 1932, SRC/MPPDA files, Margaret Herrick Library, AMPAS.

23. Letter dated December 7, 1931, SRC/MPPDA files, Margaret Herrick Library, AMPAS; *Variety*, December 1, 1931, 15; letter from Thalberg to Lenore Coffee, February 23, 1932, MGM collection, USC. For more on the British censor's dispute with MGM, see Alexander Walker, *Joan Crawford: The Ultimate Star* (London: Wiedenfeld & Nicolson, 1983), 84; Vieira, *Sin in Soft Focus*, 155.

24. *Los Angeles Evening Express*, October 24, 1931; *New York Times*, November 28, 1931, 20; Norbert Lusk, *Los Angeles Times*, December 6, 1931, B13; *Variety*, December 1, 1931, 15.

25. Chandler, *Joan Crawford*, 98 (Crawford's recollection was a little off: it's a fur coat, not pearls, that drops to the floor); Coffee, *Storyline*, 105.

14. Devotion and Deceit

1. Myrna Loy with Kotsilibas-Davis, *Myrna Loy: Being and Becoming* (London: Bloomsbury, 1987), 71; Ankerich, *Sound of Silence*, 161.

2. *New York Times*, January 24, 1932, X4; MGM conference notes, December 7, 1931, MGM collection, USC.

3. *Los Angeles Times*, January 17, 1932, H3; *New York Times*, February 6, 1932, 14.

4. Dressler's biographer has also noted the *King Lear* connection. See Kennedy, *Marie Dressler*, 179.

5. On *Dishonored Lady*, see Amnon Kabatchnik, *Blood on the Stage, 1925–1950: Milestone Plays of Crime, Mystery, and Detection* (Metuchen, NJ: Scarecrow Press, 2010), 270–75; on negotiations over rights, see Vieira, *Hollywood Dreams Made Real*, 187.

6. See Douglas MacGowan, *The Strange Affair of Madeleine Smith: Victorian Scotland's Trial of the Century* (Edinburgh: Mercat Press, 2007); Marie Belloc Lowndes, *Mrs. Letty Lynton* (1932; reprint, London: Hutchinson, 1976).

7. Stromberg notes, January 11, 1932, MGM collection, USC; Joy to Stromberg, January 12, 1932, and Stromberg to Joy, February 12, 1932, SRC/MPPDA files, Margaret Herrick Library, AMPAS.

8. Walker, *Joan Crawford*, 84; Shaun Considine, *Bette and Joan: The Divine Feud* (New York: Dell, 1989), 54; visitor quoted in Vieira, *Hollywood Dreams Made Real*, 148.

9. Wood Soanes, "What I Think of Censors: Opinion of Clarence Brown, as Expressed by the Screen Director Himself to Wood Soanes," *Screen & Radio Weekly*, ca. 1932, Brownlow collection.

10. Trotti to Thalberg, April 13, 1932, SRC/MPPDA files, Margaret Herrick Library, AMPAS; Joy to Hays, June 7, 1932, ibid.; Vieira, *Sin in Soft Focus*, 82.

11. Philip Scheuer, *Los Angeles Times*, May 23, 1932, 17; *Washington Post*, May 14, 1932, 12; Mordaunt Hall, *New York Times*, April 30, 1932, 19.

12. Ruth Biery, "The New 'Shady Dames' of the Screen," *Photoplay*, August 1932, 28; *Photoplay*, June 1932 and August 1932; Charlotte Herzog and Jane Gaines, "Puffed Sleeves Before Tea-Time," in *Stardom: Industry of Desire*, ed. Christine Gledhill (London: Routledge, 1991), 77–95; Sarah Berry, *Screen Style: Fashion and Femininity in 1930s Hollywood* (Minneapolis: University of Minnesota Press, 2000), 88. The number of dresses sold is in dispute: see Charles Eckert, "The Carole Lombard in Macy's Window," in Gledhill, *Stardom*, 30–40; Herzog and Gaines, "Puffed Sleeves," 91.

13. *Washington Post*, June 25, 1932, 4; Wilson to Joy, June 29, 1932, SRC/MPPDA files, Margaret Herrick Library, AMPAS; *New York Times*, August 1, 1934, 14; *New York Times*, August 5, 1936; *New York Times*, August 1, 1937, 33. For more on the legal proceedings and the importance of the Sheldon-Barnes case, see Siva Vaidhyanathan, *Copyrights and Copywrongs: The Rise of Intellectual Property and How It Threatens Creativity* (New York: NYU Press, 2003), 107–10.

14. Roy Newquist, *Conversations with Joan Crawford* (Secaucus, NJ: Citadel Press, 1980), 76; *Hollywood Citizen News*, March 31, 1932; *Los Angeles Times*, August 29, 1932, 9; *Los Angeles Times*, January 26, 1932, A3.

15. *Hollywood Citizen News*, August 2, 1932.

15. Service and Passion

1. *Variety*, October 4, 1932, 6.

2. *New York Times*, April 16, 1933, X4.

3. American Film Institute catalog, https://catalog.afi.com/; Brown, interview

with Brownlow, 1966; *Variety,* November 29, 1932, 7; James Wingate notes, December 23, 1932, SRC/MPPDA files, Margaret Herrick Library, AMPAS.

4. *New York Times,* January 2, 1933, 29; *Variety,* January 3, 1933, 27; *Motion Picture Herald,* January 14, 1933, 44; *Motion Picture Herald,* July 1, 1933, 50; Andre Soares, *Beyond Paradise: The Life of Ramon Novarro* (New York: St. Martin's Press, 2002), 199.

5. Eyman, "Clarence Brown: Garbo and Beyond," 21.

6. Harwood, undated notes on treatment of *Service,* MGM collection, USC.

7. Brown, interview with Brownlow, 1966.

8. *Film Daily,* April 29, 1933, 3; Michael Moore, "Brown Study," *Film Weekly,* October 24, 1936, 26; *Los Angeles Times,* May 26, 1933, A9; *Motion Picture Herald,* June 17, 1933, 46.

9. *Los Angeles Evening Herald Express,* March 25, 1933.

10. David Thomson, *Showman: The Life of David O. Selznick* (New York: Abacus, 1993), 161.

11. Conference notes, April 12, 1933, MGM collection, USC; Sam Marx, *Mayer and Thalberg: The Make-Believe Saints* (London: W. H. Allen, 1976), 97.

12. *Hollywood Reporter,* May 12, 1933, 1; Loy, *Being and Becoming,* 84; Brown, undated interview with Kevin Brownlow, Brownlow collection.

13. Eyman, *Lion of Hollywood,* 183; Jimmy Starr, *Los Angeles Evening Herald,* August 12, 1933; *Los Angeles Times,* August 13, 1933, A1.

14. *New York Times,* October 15, 1933, X3; *Washington Post,* October 21, 1933, 16; *Motion Picture Herald,* January 6, 1934, 52.

15. Julia Gwin, "The Greatest Success," *Silver Screen,* December 1934, 65; Cooper quoted in unpublished interview with Brownlow and Haver, American Film Institute Oral History, 1971, Brownlow collection; Dunne quoted in Lee Server, *Screenwriter: Words Become Pictures* (Pittstown, NJ: Main Street Press, 1987), 106.

16. Leonard Maltin, "Night Flight," http://www.tcm.com/tcmdb/title/2589/Night-Flight/.

16. Back with Crawford

1. *Los Angeles Times,* May 15, 1934, 13; *Los Angeles Times,* April 16, 1934, 8; *Los Angeles Times,* May 26, 1934, 14; *Los Angeles Times,* April 26, 1935, 2.

2. Reine Davies, *Los Angeles Examiner,* October 2, 1935. Brown later hired László to redesign business premises on Wilshire Boulevard. *Los Angeles Times,* November 1, 1936, A7.

3. Brown quoted in Debra Weiner and Patrick McGilligan, "Clarence Brown at 85," *Focus on Film* 23 (Winter 1975–1976): 32; Viña Delmar, "Pretty Sadie McKee," *Liberty,* June 24–September 9, 1933. See also Jeff Cohen, "Vina Del Mar," http://vitaphone.blogspot.com/2007_07_01_archive.html.

4. Reader's report: A. Cunningham, April 20, 1933, MGM collection, USC.

5. *Saturday Evening Post,* 1948, cited in American Film Institute catalog, https://catalog.afi.com/.

6. Esther Ralston, *Some Day We'll Laugh: An Autobiography* (Metuchen, NJ: Scarecrow Press, 1985), 148; Michael Ankerich, "Interview with Esther Ralston," in *Broken Silence: Conversations with 23 Silent Film Stars* (Jefferson, NC: McFarland, 1993), 269.

7. For more on censorship and the production, see Vieira, *Sin in Soft Focus*, 178.

8. Mordaunt Hall, *New York Times*, May 18, 1934, 18; Muriel Babcock, *Los Angeles Examiner*, June 14, 1934; *Variety*, May 22, 1934, 15; Leonard Wallace, *Film Weekly*, October 12, 1934.

9. Crawford to Genie Chester, quoted in Michelle Vogel, *Joan Crawford: Her Life in Letters* (Shelbyville, KY: Wasteland Press, 2005), 47; Newquist, *Conversations with Joan Crawford*, 80.

10. Chandler, *Joan Crawford*, 124–25.

11. Newquist, *Conversations with Joan Crawford*, 114; Fitzgerald quoted in Bob Thomas, *Joan Crawford: A Biography* (New York: Simon & Schuster, 1978), 100.

12. Muriel Babcock, *Los Angeles Examiner*, September 21, 1934; Mordaunt Hall, *New York Times*, September 1, 1934, 16; *Daily Variety*, August 13, 1934, 3; *Motion Picture Herald*, February 2, 1935, 87.

17. Reunited

1. Memo from Selznick to Garbo, January 7, 1935, reprinted in Rudy Behlmer, *Memo from David O. Selznick* (New York: Viking Press, 1972), 75–76; Swenson, *Greta Garbo*, 331.

2. Salka Viertel, *The Kindness of Strangers* (New York: Holt, Rinehart & Winston, 1969), 198.

3. Breen to Selznick, December 20, 1934, and January 3, 1935, PCA files, Margaret Herrick Library, AMPAS; Ted Shane, report on script dated March 9, March 15, 1935, Selznick Collection, Harry Ransom Center, University of Texas, Austin; memos from Corbaley to Selznick, February 25 and 27, 1935, ibid.; S. L. Behrman, *People in a Diary: A Memoir* (Boston: Little, Brown, 1972), 151.

4. Selznick's notes on Bucknall's memo, March 4, 1935, Selznick Collection.

5. Lewton's numerous memos to Selznick and to J. Robert Rubin of MGM's Legal Department are in the Selznick Collection at the University of Texas.

6. *Los Angeles Times*, April 17, 1935, A13. Some of these suggestions are contained in a memo from von Stroheim to Selznick and Brown, March 21, 1935, Selznick Collection; Selznick to von Stroheim, March 23, 1935, ibid.

7. Selznick to Breen, March 7, 1935, quoted in Swenson, *Greta Garbo*, 335; Breen to Selznick, March 12, 1935, PCA files, Margaret Herrick Library, AMPAS.

8. Kazan was so impressed by the film and its director that he admitted he was tongue-tied when he later ran into Brown at the MGM commissary. Elia Kazan, *A Life* (New York: Da Capo, 1997), 384.

9. *Hollywood Citizens News*, March 12, 1935; March quoted in memo from Selznick to Garbo, January 7, 1935, in Behlmer, *Memo from Selznick*, 75–76; Paris, *Garbo*, 301; and Haining, *Legend of Garbo*, 30; Swenson, *Greta Garbo*, 336.

10. Basil Rathbone, *In and out of Character* (1956; reprint, New York: Limelight Editions, 1991), 139.

11. Basil Rathbone, "A Journey with Karenina" (1936), reprinted in Haining, *Legend of Garbo*, 223–25.

12. Owen quoted in Swenson, *Greta Garbo*, 337; Rathbone, *In and out of Character*, 142; Rathbone, "Journey with Karenina," 224; O'Sullivan quoted in Paris, *Garbo*, 30.

13. Swenson, *Greta Garbo*, 337; Skolsky, *Don't Get Me Wrong*, 133; *Hollywood Citizen News*, August 30, 1935.

14. Brown, interview with Brownlow, 1966.

15. Estrin, *Hollywood Professionals*, 142; memo from Lewton to Selznick, March 26, 1935, MGM collection, USC.

16. Vieira, *Garbo*, 213.

17. Behrman, *People in a Diary*, 151–52; Brown to Selznick, May 2, 1935, MGM collection, USC; Selznick to Schenck, June 6, 1935, Selznick Collection; "Guide to the Study of the Screen Version of Tolstoy's *Anna Karenina*," ibid.

18. Selznick to Dietz, June 3, 1935, Selznick Collection. See also Day, *This Was Hollywood*, 261–62; W. H. Mooring, "Secrets of Garbo's New Film," *Film Weekly*, September 27, 1935, 8–9.

19. *Variety*, September 4, 1935, 14; *New York Times*, August 31, 1935, 16.

20. Alistair Cooke quoted in Paris, *Garbo*, 300; Brown, interview with Brownlow, 1966.

21. *Motion Picture Herald*, January 18, 1936, 288.

18. Going Home

1. Barbara Gelb and Arthur Gelb, *O'Neill* (New York: Delta Books, 1964), 762.

2. Wingate to MGM, October 26, 1933, SRC/MPPDA files, Margaret Herrick Library, AMPAS; Breen to Mayer, March 7, 1934, PCA files, ibid.

3. *Los Angeles Times*, June 17, 1934, 3; David Goodrich, *The Real Nick and Nora: Frances Goodrich and Albert Hackett, Writers of Stage and Screen Classics* (Carbondale: Southern Illinois University Press, 2001), 89; Hunt Stromberg to Frances Goodrich and Albert Hackett, January 22, 1935, MGM collection, USC. Joan Crawford identified Stromberg as one of the few producers she regarded as a "creative person." Newquist, *Conversations with Joan Crawford*, 114.

4. Stromberg to Goodrich and Hackett, May 5, 1935, and January 19, 1935, MGM collection, USC.

5. Breen to Stromberg, June 14, 1935, PCA files, Margaret Herrick Library, AMPAS.

6. *Los Angeles Times*, August 6, 1935, 19; Goodrich, *Real Nick and Nora*, 90.

7. Goodrich, *Real Nick and Nora*, 90; *Los Angeles Times*, August 11, 1935, A1.

8. *Exhibitors Herald Express*, August 23, 1935.

9. *Los Angeles Times*, August 12, 1935, 10.

10. Terrance Ingano, "Clarence Brown," in *Twice Told Tales of Clinton* (Clinton, MA: Angus MacGregor Books, 2007), 55–56.

11. *Los Angeles Times*, December 26, 1937, H13.

12. *Chicago Daily Tribune*, October 4, 1935, 28.

13. *Ah Wilderness!* file, PCA files, Margaret Herrick Library, AMPAS.

14. *Hollywood Spectator*, November 23, 1935, 23; *New York Times*, December 25, 1935, 30; Estrin, *Hollywood Professionals*, 139; Orlandello, *O'Neill on Film*, 70, 72, 68; Barry Gillam, "Clarence Brown," in *American Directors*, vol. 1, ed. Jean Pierre Coursodon with Pierre Sauvage (New York: McGraw-Hill, 1983), 33.

15. Notes for Haun's "Starmarker," 4, Brown Collection, University of Tennessee; Goodrich, *Real Nick and Nora*, 89; Frances Goodrich and Albert Hackett quoted in "A Tribute to Clarence Brown," Directors Guild of America, July 16, 1977; Rooney, *Life Is Too Short*, 76.

19. Back to the Formula

1. Breen to Mayer, November 18, 1935, PCA files, Margaret Herrick Library, AMPAS.

2. Brown quoted in Lockhart, "Shepherd of the Stars," 6–7; Loy, *Being and Becoming*, 124, 123.

3. Haun, "UT Grad Who Engineered Dreams," 7.

4. Donald Dewey, *James Stewart: A Biography* (London: Warner Books, 1997), 147; Stewart quoted in Directors Guild of America tribute to Brown, July 16, 1977, reprinted in Gary Fishgall, *Pieces of Time: The Life of James Stewart* (New York: Scribner, 1997), 86.

5. *New York Times*, February 29, 1936, 11; *Los Angeles Times*, March 19, 1936, 11.

6. Schatz, *Genius of the System*, 174; Brown quoted in Lockhart, "Shepherd of the Stars," 7.

7. Kenneth Geist, *Pictures Will Talk: The Life and Films of Joseph L. Mankiewicz* (New York: Charles Scribner's Sons, 1978), 83; Walker, *Joan Crawford*, 110.

8. Breen notes on script of October 7, 1935, PCA files, Margaret Herrick Library, AMPAS; Breen to Mayer, March 10, 1935, ibid.; conference notes, March 14, 1936, MGM collection, USC.

9. Brown's accident reported in *Los Angeles Times*, June 11, 1936, 19; Bondi and Folsey quoted in Directors Guild of America tribute to Brown, July 16, 1977; Fred Lawrence Guiles, *Joan Crawford: The Last Word* (London: Pavilion Books, 1995), 109; Brown, interview with Brownlow and Knox, 1969; Thomas, *Joan Crawford*, 117; Julia Gwin, "The Inside 'Low Down,'" *Silver Screen*, May 7, 1936, 74; Lockhart, "Shepherd of the Stars," 7.

10. Melvyn Douglas with Tom Arthur, *See You at the Movies: The Autobiography of Melvyn Douglas* (New York: University Press of America, 1986), 90–91.

11. *Los Angeles Evening Herald Express*, May 2, 1936; *Hollywood Spectator*, September 12, 1936, 10–11.

12. *New York Times*, September 5, 1936, 7; *Washington Post*, August 28, 1936, X11; Elizabeth Yeaman, *Hollywood Citizens News*, September 3, 1936.

Notes

13. *New York Times*, September 5, 1936, 7.

14. Newquist, *Conversations with Joan Crawford*, 80; Haun, "UT Grad Who Engineered Dreams," 7.

15. Sidney Skolsky, *Hollywood Citizens News*, October 8, 1936; Brown, interview with Brownlow, 1966; Mankiewicz quoted in Geist, *Pictures Will Talk*, 84.

20. Conquest

1. Viertel, *Kindness of Strangers*, 199.

2. Behrman, *People in a Diary*, 162; Breen to Thalberg, December 10, 1935, PCA files, Margaret Herrick Library, AMPAS.

3. Viertel, *Kindness of Strangers*, 214; Sidney Skolsky, "Stories about the Pictures You're Seeing," *Los Angeles Examiner*, November 6, 1937.

4. Vieira, *Garbo*, 235; Cukor quoted in Vieira, *Hollywood Dreams Made Real*, 330; Swenson, *Greta Garbo*, 362n.

5. Viertel, *Kindness of Strangers*, 215–16; Skolsky, "Stories about the Pictures You're Seeing"; Brown, interview with Brownlow and Knox, 1969.

6. *Los Angeles Times*, August 15, 1937, C4; *Los Angeles Times*, April 27, 1937, 14; Swenson, *Greta Garbo*, 358; Brown, interview with Brownlow, 1966.

7. *Los Angeles Evening Herald Express*, March 7, 1937; Eyman, "Clarence Brown: Garbo and Beyond," 22; Swenson, *Greta Garbo*, 365.

8. Boyer quoted in *Picturegoer*, April 1938, reprinted in Haining, *Legend of Garbo*, 32.

9. Frank Nugent, *New York Times*, November 5, 1937, 19; Elizabeth Yeaman, *Hollywood Citizens News*, December 9, 1937; Louella Parsons, *Los Angeles Examiner*, December. 9, 1937.

10. Mosher quoted in Haining, *Legend of Garbo*, 237; Greene quoted in David Parkinson, *Mornings in the Dark: The Graham Greene Reader* (London: Carcanet, 2003), 247; *Motion Picture Herald*, January 1, 1938, 50.

11. Gene Reynolds, telephone interview with Young, January 3, 2011; *Los Angeles Examiner*, October 24, 1937.

12. Swenson, *Greta Garbo*, 435.

21. A Little Piece of Humanity

1. Lockhart, "Shepherd of the Stars," 6.

2. Gregory Squire, "Not Done with Mirrors," *Silver Screen*, March 1938, 51; *Los Angeles Times*, March 7, 1938, A4.

3. Breen to Considine, August 20, 1937, PCA files, Margaret Herrick Library, AMPAS.

4. Dewey, *James Stewart*, 155.

5. Gene Reynolds, interview with Young, January 3, 2011.

6. Squire, "Not Done with Mirrors," 51; *Hollywood Citizens News*, November 3, 1937.

7. Reynolds, interview with Young, 2011; Henry Colman, interview with

Gene Reynolds for the Archive of American Television, August 22, 2000, http://www.emmytvlegends.org/interviews/people/gene-reynolds; Reynolds, interview with Young.

8. Gene Reynolds, interview with Kevin Brownlow, 2004, Brownlow collection; Reynolds, interview with Young, 2011.

9. Leatrice Gilbert Fountain, email to Young, June 26, 2000; William Everson, "Clarence Brown: A Survey of His Work," *Films in Review* 24 (1973): 584; Leatrice Gilbert Fountain, interview with Kevin Brownlow, Brownlow collection; Fountain, email to Young, June 22, 2000.

10. *New York Times*, February 18, 1938, 23; *Washington Post*, February 12, 1938, 17; *Los Angeles Examiner*, March 31, 1938.

11. Unpublished notes for the article "Fifty Million Feet of Hollywood Romance," Brown Collection, University of Tennessee; Donald Lyons, "Fathers and Sons in American Cinema," *Film Comment*, July–August 1998, 57.

12. Squire, "Not Done with Mirrors," 51.

13. Baxter, *Hollywood in the Thirties*, 27, 23.

14. Ibid., 27; Jean Renoir, interview with Kevin Brownlow, April 18, 1962, Brownlow collection.

22. Foreign Affairs

1. *Los Angeles Times*, September 18, 1939, A4.

2. Vasey, *World According to Hollywood*, 187; Gregory D. Black, *Hollywood Censored: Morality Codes, Catholics and the Movies* (New York: Cambridge University Press, 1994), 283.

3. Black, *Hollywood Censored*, 283; Vasey, *World According to Hollywood*, 189, 190.

4. Brown, interview with Brownlow and Knox, 1969.

5. Newquist, *Conversations with Joan Crawford*, 48; Harrison Carroll, *Los Angeles Evening Herald Express*, November 19, 1938; Lambert, *Norma Shearer*, 271; Day, *This Was Hollywood*, 60–70.

6. Louella Parsons, *Los Angeles Examiner*, November 6, 1938; *Los Angeles Evening Herald Express*, December 24, 1938.

7. *Variety*, January 25, 1939, 11; Nelson Bell, *Washington Post*, February 10, 1939, 9A; Otis Ferguson quoted in Black, *Hollywood Censored*, 286; Graham Greene, *Spectator*, April 21, 1939, quoted in Parkinson, *Mornings in the Dark*, 283, 287.

8. Vasey, *World According to Hollywood*, 192; *London Evening News*, October 2, 1939.

9. *New York Times*, July 3, 1938, 99; *Los Angeles Times*, October 23, 1938, C4; *Los Angeles Times*, May 31, 1939, 37, 39.

10. Contract dated March 18, 1938, Fox legal files, UCLA. Fox used the source a second time: *The Rains of Ranchipur*, directed by Jean Negulesco in 1953.

11. Dunne and Josephson to Zanuck, Fox script collection, UCLA; Joy to Za-

nuck, May 13, 1938, ibid. For more on Hollywood's representation of India and Indians, see Prem Chowdhry, *India and the Making of Empire Cinema* (Manchester, UK: Manchester University Press, 2000), 194.

12. Philip Dunne quoted in Rudy Behlmer, *Memo from Darryl F. Zanuck* (New York: Grove Press, 1995), iv; Zanuck to Dunne and Josephson, October 11, 1938, Fox script collection, UCLA.

13. Zanuck memo, October 5, 1938, Fox legal files, UCLA. Robert Birchard, in his commentary for the DVD release of *The Rains Came,* mentions that Herbert Marshall, Rosalind Russell, Tallulah Bankhead, Basil Rathbone, and Ramon Novarro were also considered. See Gwenda Young, "George Brent," in *Ireland and the Americas: Culture, Politics and History,* ed. James Patrick Byrne, Philip Coleman, and Jason Francis King (Santa Barbara, CA: ABC-CLIO, 2008), 119–20; Ruth Barton, *Acting Irish: From Fitzgerald to Farrell* (Dublin: Irish Academic Press, 2006). For Joyce's "discovery," see *Life,* October 2, 1939, 38. It was Brown's idea to give her the stage name Brenda Joyce (in honor of his wife, Alice Joyce); her real name was Betty Leabo.

14. Patrick McGilligan, *Film Crazy* (New York: St. Martin's Press, 2000), 56–57; Loy, *Being and Becoming,* 157; contract dated April 6, 1939, Fox legal files, UCLA.

15. Patrick McGilligan, "Interview with Philip Dunne," in *Backstory,* 155; Philip Dunne, *Take Two: A Life in Movies and Politics* (New York: Limelight, 1992), 66; Philip Dunne quoted in Directors Guild of America tribute to Brown, July 16, 1977; *The Rains Came* script conference notes, April 10, 1939, Fox script collection, UCLA; Dunne, *Take Two,* 83.

16. Eyman, "Clarence Brown: Garbo and Beyond," 22; Brown quoted in McGilligan, *Film Crazy,* 57.

17. Arthur Miller quoted in Higham, *Hollywood Cameramen,* 143.

18. Arthur Miller with Fred Balshofer, *One Reel a Week* (Berkeley: University of California Press, 1967), 192.

19. Miller quoted in Higham, *Hollywood Cameramen,* 146–47.

20. Loy, *Being and Becoming,* 157.

21. Ibid., 158.

22. James Crow, *Hollywood Citizens News,* September 7, 1939; Frank Nugent, *New York Times,* September 9, 1939, 11; Mary Harris, *Washington Post,* November 3, 1939, 18; Graham Greene, "The Rains Came," *Spectator,* December 29, 1939, 16.

23. For more on the portrayal of India and its inhabitants, see Chowdhry, *India and the Making of Empire Cinema,* 228–31.

24. Daniel Eagan, *America's Film Legacy: The Authoritative Guide to the Landmark Movies in the National Film Registry* (New York: Bloomsbury, 2009), 309.

23. Inventions and Conventions

1. Dore Schary, *Heyday* (New York: Berkley Books, 1981), 106; Patrick McGilligan and Paul Buhle, *Tender Comrades: A Backstory of the Hollywood Blacklist* (London: St. Martin's Press, 1999), 161.

2. James Curtis, *Spencer Tracy: A Biography* (London: Arrow Books, 2012), 393, 403.

3. *Hollywood Reporter,* May 17, 1940, 3; *Los Angeles Times,* February 16, 1940, A9; transcript of a conversation between Brown and Kevin Brownlow, n.d., Brownlow collection; Reynolds, interview with Young, 2011; *Los Angeles Times,* February 26, 1940, 9.

4. *Variety,* May 17, 1940, 14; *New York Times,* June 7, 1940, 27; Curtis, *Spencer Tracy,* 403.

5. Letter from Julia C. Lieb to Clarence Brown, May 17, 1940, Brown Collection, University of Tennessee.

6. Dewey, *James Stewart,* 499.

7. *Los Angeles Times,* July 23, 1940, 12; Breen to MGM, October 4, 1940, PCA files, Margaret Herrick Library, AMPAS

8. *Film Daily,* October 29, 1940, 9; Polly Rittenberg, "Adeline de Walt Reynolds," https://thestuffthatdreamsaremadeofblog.com/blog/2016/7/9/spotlight-on-adeline-de-walt-reynolds.

9. For more on Lamarr as star and émigré, see Ruth Barton, *Hedy Lamarr: The Most Beautiful Woman in Film* (Lexington: University Press of Kentucky, 2010). The Bergere joke was remembered by cinematographer Arthur Miller, who recounted it to George Mitchell. He, in turn, related it to Kevin Brownlow in a letter dated May 17, 1967, Brownlow collection.

10. Theodore Strauss, *New York Times,* February 28, 1941, 17; *Film Daily,* February 6, 1941, 8.

11. Gary Carey, *Anita Loos: A Biography* (New York: Alfred Knopf, 1988), 196–97.

12. Brown, interview with Brownlow, 1966.

13. Hye Seung Chung, *Hollywood Asian: Philip Ahn and the Politics of Cross-Ethnic Performance* (Philadelphia: Temple University Press, 2006), 50.

14. Bernard F. Dick, *Forever Mame: The Life of Rosalind Russell* (Jackson: University Press of Mississippi, 2006), 67; Brown, interview with Brownlow, 1966; *New York Times,* July 6, 1941, X3; *Washington Post,* July 18, 1941, 6.

15. *Los Angeles Times,* January 8, 1942, 13; *Los Angeles Times,* March 12, 1942, A10; Martin F. Norden, *The Cinema of Isolation: A History of Physical Disability in the Movies* (New Brunswick NJ: Rutgers University Press, 1994), 180.

16. *Los Angeles Times,* July 13, 1941, J12.

17. *Los Angeles Examiner,* September 16, 1945. For more on Alice Joyce, see Greta de Groat, "The Madonna of the Screen," http://www.stanford.edu/~gdegroat/AJ/essay.htm.

24. Representing the War Front at Home and Away

1. Tully, "Clarence Brown: Estimate," 79, 106. For the films' box-office success, see http://www.ldsfilm.com/misc/lds_Top5_boxoffice.html.

2. Dickran Kouymjian, "Saroyan Shoots a Film," in *William Saroyan: The Man*

and the Writer Remembered, ed. Leo Hamalian (Rutherford, NJ: Fairleigh Dickinson University Press, 1987), 77.

3. Patrick McGilligan, "*The Human Comedy:* Mr. Saroyan's Thoroughly American Movie," in *The Modern American Novel and the Movies,* ed. Gerald Peary and Roger Shatzkin (New York: Frederick Ungar, 1978), 157. On the word count: the American Film Institute catalog notes that it was 240 pages, but screenwriter William Ludwig variously recalled that it was either 900 or 500 pages, as quoted in Server, *Screenwriter,* 122, and Ronald L. Davis, *Words into Images: Screenwriters on the Studio System* (Jackson: University Press of Mississippi, 2007), 175. Eyman, *Lion of Hollywood,* 347; Eyman, "Clarence Brown: Garbo and Beyond," 23; Diamond quoted in Lawrence Lee and Barry Gifford, *Saroyan: A Biography* (Berkeley: University of California Press, 1998), 86.

4. Eyman, *Lion of Hollywood,* 347; Messenger to Franklin, May 29, 1942, MGM collection, USC; Charles Higham, *Merchant of Dreams: Louis B. Mayer, M.G.M., and the Secret Hollywood* (London: Sidgwick & Jackson, 1993), 312; Michael Sragow, *Victor Fleming: An American Movie Master* (New York: Pantheon, 2008), 403.

5. Server, *Screenwriter,* 122.

6. *Screen Stars,* January 1943, clipping in Brown Collection, University of Tennessee.

7. *Los Angeles Times,* April 4, 1943, G17. Brown gave Marian credit for discovering Jenkins; see Eyman, "Clarence Brown: Garbo and Beyond," 22.

8. Marsha Hunt, email to Young, January 18, 2011.

9. Rooney, *Life Is Too Short,* 104–6.

10. Marian Brown quoted in Barbara Aston-Wash, "Behind the Scenes," *Knoxville-News Sentinel,* September 30, 1990, E1–2; Eyman, *Lion of Hollywood,* 347; Eyman, "Clarence Brown: Garbo and Beyond," 22; Rooney, *Life Is Too Short,* 197–98.

11. Rooney, *Life Is Too Short,* 76; Hickman quoted in Eyman, *Lion of Hollywood,* 347; Darryl Hickman, *The Unconscious Actor: The Art of Performance in Acting and in Life* (Montecito, CA: Small Mountain Press, 2007), 11–12.

12. Jesse Lasky Sr. to Jesse Lasky Jr., in Pat Silver Lasky, *Hollywood Royalty: A Life in Films* (Albany, GA: Bearmanor Media, 2017), 265; *New York Times,* March 3, 1943, 19; *Los Angeles Times,* March 7, 1943, C2.

13. Edgar Anstey, *Spectator,* June 24, 1943, 11; James Agee, *Nation,* March 20, 1943, 30, 31, 32.

14. James Agee, *Nation,* May 1943.

15. Larkin's obituary appeared in *Los Angeles Times,* March 12, 1942, A9.

16. Brown, interview with Brownlow and Knox, 1969; Lyons, "Fathers and Sons in American Cinema," 54–61.

17. Brown, interview with Brownlow and Knox, 1969.

18. Ludwig quoted in Server, *Screenwriter,* 122.

19. Rooney, *Life Is Too Short,* 196; Hunt, email to Young, January 18, 2011; *Washington Post,* May 25, 1943, 15; *Los Angeles Times,* May 12, 1943, A11.

20. *New York Times*, June 13, 1943, X3; Stanley Craig, *Coronet*, December 1944, 117; Brown, interview with Brownlow, 1966.

21. *Los Angeles Times*, July 14, 1941, 2; *New York Times*, June 27, 1942, 9.

22. Sidney Franklin, "We Laughed, We Cried" (unpublished memoirs), 331, Brownlow collection; notes on *The White Cliffs of Dover* script, January 23, 1943, MGM collection, USC.

23. Mark Glancy, *When Hollywood Loved Britain: The Hollywood 'British' Film, 1939–45* (Manchester, UK: Manchester University Press, 1999), 203; West to Froeschel and Lustig, March 31, 1943, MGM collection, USC.

24. *New York Times*, June 13, 1943, X3.

25. Brown, interview with Brownlow, 1966.

26. *Los Angeles Times*, June 11, 1942, 15. The cast also featured another "evacuee": Stefan Muller, a German-born Jew who came to America to escape the Nazis and played a Nazi in *The White Cliffs of Dover*. See Michael Lawrence, "Bombed into Stardom," *Journal of British Cinema and Television* 12, no. 1 (2015): 45–46. Roddy McDowall quoted in Directors Guild of America tribute to Brown, July 16, 1977.

27. "Hands across the Screen," *Lion's Roar*, July 1944.

28. Doris Arden, *Chicago Sun Times*, July 2, 1944; Bosley Crowther, *New York Times*, May 12, 1944, 15; James Agee, *Nation*, May 27, 1944; Brown, interview with Brownlow and Knox, 1969.

25. Velvet and the Pie

1. *Hollywood Reporter*, October 20, 1943; Enid Bagnold, *Enid Bagnold's Autobiography (from 1889)* (London: Heinemann, 1969), 171.

2. Bagnold, *Enid Bagnold's Autobiography*, 170; *Variety*, July 16, 1936, October 29, 1935, and September 8, 1936 (all online at Variety.com); Lipscomb script dated February 16, 1937, Harry Ransom Center, University of Texas, Austin.

3. *Variety*, May 1, 1935, and September 7, 1935; Parsons piece reprinted in *Pittsburgh Post-Gazette*, October 5, 1936, 14; H. P. Mooring, "Clarence Brown's *National Velvet*," *Picturegoer*, March 3, 1945, 8; Noel Langley (reader's report), March 9, 1937, MGM collection, USC; Gilbert quoted in Eyman, *Lion of Hollywood*, 337; Fountain, *Dark Star*, 3 (the author found no trace of publicity announcing Gilbert in the role).

4. *Picturegoer*, March 3, 1945, 8; Furthman script drafts for *National Velvet*, June 7 and July 28, 1939, MGM collection, USC; Deutsch and Reeves script drafts, ibid.

5. *Variety*, November 3, 1943; Angela Lansbury, interview with Kevin Brownlow, September 2002, Brownlow collection.

6. *Variety*, January 29, 1943; American Film Institute catalog, https://catalog.afi.com/; Alexander Walker, *Elizabeth: The Life of Elizabeth Taylor* (1990; reprint, New York: Grove Press, 2011), 42.

7. David C. Heymann, *Liz: An Intimate Biography* (New York: Atria Books,

2011), 44–45; "Taylor Made Role," *Lion's Roar,* March 1945, 30; Elizabeth Taylor, *Elizabeth Takes Off* (New York: Putnam, 1987), 54; Brenda Maddox, *Who's Afraid of Elizabeth Taylor?* (New York: M. Evans, 1977), 39.

8. *Variety,* November 18 and 19, 1943; "Wanted: One Piebald Horse," *Lion's Roar,* March 1, 1945, 33; Carey, *All the Stars in Heaven,* 224; Enid Bagnold, *National Velvet* (1935; reprint, New York: Avon Books, 1991), 56.

9. Mooring, "Clarence Brown's *National Velvet,*" 8; Lansbury, interview with Brownlow, 2002; Liz Hunt, "Laurian, Comtesse d'Harcourt—The Original National Velvet Girl Hunt," *Telegraph,* December 27, 2011, http://www.telegraph.co.uk/culture/film/8971261/Laurian-Comtesse-dHarcourt-the-original-National-Velvet-girl.html.

10. Rooney, *Life Is Too Short,* 206; Lansbury, interview with Brownlow, 2002.

11. Elizabeth Taylor telegram, Directors Guild of America tribute to Brown, 1977; Eyman, "Clarence Brown: Garbo and Beyond," 22.

12. Donald Spoto, *Elizabeth Taylor* (London: Warner Books, 1996), 55. See Susan Smith, *Elizabeth Taylor* (London: British Film Institute, 2012), for a fuller analysis of Taylor's technique and her association with animals.

13. Maddox, *Who's Afraid of Elizabeth Taylor?* 41–42; Randy Taraborrelli, *Elizabeth* (London: Sidgwick & Jackson, 2006), 50.

14. Bagnold, *National Velvet,* 22; Oscar Rimoldi, "Clarence Brown," *Films in Review* 41 (October 1990): 454; Manny Farber, "Crazy over Horses," *New Republic,* February 3, 1945, 175; Claude Jarman, personal interview with Young, May 2013.

15. Although Bagnold liked the film, she didn't approve of its portrayal of Mr. Brown as a comic character. Bagnold to MGM, April 7, 1945, Brown Collection, University of Tennessee.

16. Jackie "Butch" Jenkins quoted in http://www.mildredsfatburgers.com/the-blog/wednesdays-child-jackie-butch-jenkins.

17. *Variety,* December 6, 1944, 14; *New York Times,* December 15, 1944, 25. For more on Brown and Smith's aesthetic, see clippings of publicity material, *National Velvet* folder, Brown Collection, University of Tennessee; Mooring, "Clarence Brown's *National Velvet,*" 8.

18. *Nation,* December 23, 1944, 133, 132. For a more extensive consideration of Agee's response to Taylor and the issue of the actress as a child-woman, see Smith, *Elizabeth Taylor,* 1–16; Gaylyn Studlar, "Velvet's Cherry: Elizabeth Taylor and Virginal English Childhood," in *Virgin Territory,* ed. Tamar Jeffers McDonald (Detroit: Wayne State University Press, 2010), 15–33.

19. *Time,* December 25, 1944; Farber, "Crazy over Horses," 175; Parker Tyler, "The Horse: Totem Animal of American Films," *Sight and Sound* 16 (1947): 112; Edwin Schallert, *Los Angeles Times,* January 28, 1945, B1, B2; Smith, *Elizabeth Taylor.*

20. Pauline Kael, *Kiss Kiss, Bang Bang: Film Writings, 1965–1967* (London: Arena Books, 1970), 316; Estrin, *Hollywood Professionals,* 172.

26. A Year with *The Yearling*

1. Sidney Franklin, MGM publicity booklet for *The Yearling*, 8, Brown Collection, University of Tennessee.

2. Sragow, *Victor Fleming*, 375; *The Yearling* script (various copies), MGM collection, USC; Vidor quoted in John P. Marquand, "Hollywood," unpublished article, n.d., 19, John P. Marquand Collection, Beinecke Library, Yale University, New Haven, CT; King Vidor, *A Tree Is a Tree* (Hollywood: Samuel French, 1980), 246–50; *Variety*, June 12, 1941, 1, 10. For extensive accounts of the Fleming production, see Sragow, *Victor Fleming*; Day, *This Was Hollywood*, 142–43; and Sidney Franklin's unpublished memoirs, "We Laughed, We Cried."

3. Franklin, "We Laughed, We Cried," 373, 372; MGM publicity booklet for *The Yearling*, 8; "A Tree Is a Tree," *Hollywood Reporter*, October 31, 1949.

4. *Los Angeles Examiner*, March 10, 1945; Osborn drafts, February 1945, MGM collection, USC; Mahin quoted in McGilligan, *Backstory*, 287.

5. Marjorie Kinnan Rawlings, *The Yearling* (1938; reprint, New York: Aladdin, 1988), 17; *Los Angeles Examiner*, April 18, 1945; *St. Petersburg (FL) Times*, May 27, 1945, 36; Jacqueline White Anderson, email to Young, November 6, 2013.

6. *Hollywood Reporter*, October 30, 1950; *St. Petersburg Times*, May 27, 1945, 36; *Life*, February 17, 1947, 68; correspondence between Brown and Hopper, December 27, 1961, Margaret Herrick Library, AMPAS.

7. Claude Jarman Jr., email to Young, July 18, 2001.

8. *New York Times*, April 8, 1945, 39; *St. Petersburg Times*, May 27, 1945, 36; William Gober, "MGM in Florida Filming *The Yearling*," *Deseret News*, June 7, 1945, 11.

9. Amy Porter, "Growth of *The Yearling*," *Collier's*, September 29, 1945, 74, 77; John Maloney, "Those Hollywood Nuts," *Liberty*, November 16, 1946, 25.

10. George Bartlett, *St. Petersburg News*, May 17, 1945, 36.

11. Brown, interview with Brownlow and Knox, 1969; audio recording of Jarman, interview with Kevin Brownlow, August 5, 2011, Brownlow collection; Brown to Franklin, June 19, 1945, Brownlow collection; Glen Lovell, "Director's Cut," *San Jose Mercury News*, June 30, 1994, 5.

12. Brown, interview with Brownlow and Knox, 1969; Jarman, email to Young, July 18, 2001; Jarman quoted in letter from Scott Eyman to Kevin Brownlow, December 26, 1997, Brownlow collection; Jarman, personal interview with Young, May 3, 2013.

13. Sidney Franklin, interview with Kevin Brownlow, November 27, 1971, Brownlow collection; Jarman, interview with Young, 2013.

14. Chester Franklin to Sidney Franklin, July 1945, Brownlow collection; Charles Rosher, "A Year with *The Yearling*," *American Cinematographer* 28 (May 1947): 168–69.

15. Chester Franklin to Sidney Franklin, July 15, 1945, Brownlow collection; Jarman, email to Young, June 14, 2001; Jarman, interview with Young, 2013.

16. Wolf quoted in *St. Petersburg News*, May 27, 1945; Brown to Franklin, quoted in Franklin, "We Laughed, We Cried," 377; Rosher, "A Year with *The Yearling*."

17. Jarman, interview with Young, 2013; *Ocala Star-Banner* quoted in *Gainesville Sun*, June 14, 2003 (online); Gregory Peck, interview with Scott Eyman, January 12, 1998, Brownlow collection.

18. White Anderson, email to Young, November 6, 2013.

19. Correspondence between Franklin and Brown quoted in Franklin, "We Laughed, We Cried," 375.

20. Jarman, interview with Young, 2013; White Anderson, email to Young, November 6, 2013.

21. Joe Morella and Edward Epstein, *Jane Wyman: A Biography* (London: Robert Hare, 1985), 80.

22. Brown, interview with Brownlow and Knox, 1969; Morella and Epstein, *Jane Wyman*, 91.

23. Franklin, "We Laughed, We Cried," 378–79; Rosher, "A Year with *The Yearling*," 169.

24. Jarman, interview with Young, 2013; *Los Angeles Times*, July 2, 1948, 7; Jarman, email to Young, July 18, 2001. For more on Gift, see http://summersrun.wordpress.com/2011/03/31/the-yearlings-fodderwing-donn-gift.

25. Scott Eyman, "Cross Creek Was the Site of *The Yearling* with Gregory Peck and Jane Wyman," *Palm Beach Post*, June 8, 2008 (online).

26. Eyman, *Lion of Hollywood*, 375; Gillam, "Clarence Brown," 34.

27. *New York Times*, January 24, 1947, 18.

28. Eyman, "Clarence Brown: Garbo and Beyond," 23; Jarman, interview with Young, 2013.

29. Day, *This Was Hollywood*, 201; *New York Times*, February 9, 1947, X4; Eyman, *Lion of Hollywood*, 375.

30. *New York Times*, February 9, 1947, X4; *Variety*, December 31, 1946, 6; Lyons, "Fathers and Sons in American Cinema," 58; Estrin, *Hollywood Professionals*, 173; Gillam, "Clarence Brown," 34–35; *Los Angeles Mirror*, February 2, 1949.

27. Songs and the South

1. *Variety*, April 3, 1946.

2. John C. Tibbetts, *The Classical Style: Composers in the Studio Era* (New Haven, CT: Yale University Press, 2005), 58; *Song of Love*, September 4, 1946, PCA files, Margaret Herrick Library, AMPAS.

3. William Mann, *Kate: The Woman Who Was Katharine Hepburn* (New York: Faber & Faber, 2006), 350. Hepburn's views were relayed by Brown to Sheilah Graham, "Rebellious Director," undated, uncredited clipping, Brown Collection, University of Tennessee.

4. Paul Henreid with Julian Fast, *Ladies Man: An Autobiography* (New York: St. Martin's Press, 1984), 176, 178.

5. *New York Times*, October 10, 1947, 31.

6. Eyman, *Lion of Hollywood*, 321, 298; Mann, *Kate*, 360.

7. MGM publicity booklet for *The Yearling*, 8, Brown Collection, University of Tennessee; Brown, interview with Brownlow, 1966; Bernard Gordon quoted in Eyman, *Lion of Hollywood*, 392.

8. *Los Angeles Times*, November 9, 1954.

9. Aston-Wash, "Behind the Scenes," 1.

10. Eyman, *Lion of Hollywood*, 409–11.

11. Philip Scheuer, "Brown Champions Work on Location," *Los Angeles Times*, October 30, 1949, D1; Eyman, *Lion of Hollywood*, 431.

12. For more on race relations in Knoxville, see Wheeler, *Knoxville*.

13. Brown, interview with Brownlow, 1966.

14. See Charles Crowe, "Racial Violence and Social Reform: Origins of the Atlanta Race Riot of 1906," *Journal of Negro History* 53 (July 1968): 234–56; Walter White, *A Man Called White: The Autobiography of Walter White* (Atlanta: Brown Thrasher Books/University of Georgia Press, 1995), 9. For a lengthier account of the impact this event had on Brown, see Gwenda Young, "Exploring Racial Politics," *Alphaville* 6 (2013), http://www.alphavillejournal.com/Issue6/HTML/Article Young.html.

15. Charles Crowe, "Racial Massacre in Atlanta, September 22, 1906," *Journal of Negro History* 54 (April 1969): 164. Crowe cites the actions of one "very frail white woman [who saved] a black man from a hundred assailants merely by standing before her door and 'refusing' to allow anyone to cross her threshold until the police arrived." Eyman, "Clarence Brown: Garbo and Beyond," 23; Brown, interview with Brownlow, 1966.

16. Walter Bernstein, *Inside Out: A Memoir of the Blacklist* (New York: Da Capo Press, 2000), 9; Brown, interview with Brownlow, 1966; Scheuer, "Brown Champions Work on Location," D4; Brown, interview with Brownlow, 1966. For more on Maddow's career (including his uncredited work for Philip Yordan in the 1950s), see Bernstein, *Inside Out*, 243; Jim Burns, "Ben Maddow," http://www.pennilesspress.co.uk/prose/ben_maddow.htm.

17. Patrick McGilligan, "Ben Maddow," in *Backstory 2: Interviews with Screenwriters of the 1940s and 1950s* (Berkeley: University of California Press, 1991), 171, 178, 172.

18. *New York Times*, August 23, 1948, 14; Schary, *Heyday*, 210; White quoted in Thomas Cripps, *Making Movies Black: The Hollywood Message Movie from World War II to the Civil Rights Era* (New York: Oxford University Press, 1993), 240. See also Ellen Scott, *Cinema Civil Rights: Regulation, Repression, and Race in the Classical Hollywood Era* (New Brunswick, NJ: Rutgers University Press, 2014), 181; McGilligan, *Backstory 2*, 177. For more on the adaptation, see Dorothy B. Jones, "William Faulkner: Novel into Film," *Quarterly of Film, Radio and Television* 8 (Autumn 1953): 51–71; Pauline E. Degenfelder, "The Film Adaptation of Faulkner's Intruder in the Dust," *Literature/Film Quarterly*, April 1973, 138–48; Regina Fadiman, *Intruder in the Dust: Novel into Film* (Knoxville: University of Tennessee Press, 1978).

19. *Hollywood Reporter,* February 24, 1949; *Chicago Daily Tribune,* February 19, 1949, 11. Dishmon was a significant figure in her community, serving as both a schoolteacher and a state agent for a postwar initiative that set up girls' clubs (4-H clubs) for African Americans; see *Pittsburgh Courier,* March 21, 1959, 4. She was proud of her performance in *Intruder* and later wrote to Brown to express her appreciation. Fadiman, *Intruder in the Dust,* 42.

20. For more on Hernandez's background, see "Hollywood's 'Hottest' Negro Actor," *Ebony,* August 1950, 22–26. Claude Jarman confirmed that Hernandez stayed in a private home. Jarman, interview with Young, 2013. Elzie Emanuel also had to stay at private lodgings. *Ebony,* August 1949, 27, 28.

21. Faulkner to Jim Devine, quoted in Joseph Blotner, *Faulkner: A Biography* (Jackson: University Press of Mississippi, 2010), 502; *Ebony,* August 1949, 27; Brown quoted in Blotner, *Faulkner,* 502; Scheuer, "Brown Champions Work on Location," D4; *Ebony,* August 1949, 27. Faulkner had been inspired by the castration and lynching of a local black man, Nelse Patton, in 1908. See Joel Williamson, *William Faulkner and Southern History* (New York: Oxford University Press, 2005), 159.

22. Scheuer, "Brown Champions Work on Location," D4; Blotner, *Faulkner,* 502–4.

23. *Oxford Eagle,* October 6, 1949 (emphasis added).

24. Surtees quoted in Fadiman, *Intruder in the Dust,* 36.

25. Paul Rotha, "Dark Victory," in *The Film Till Now* (London: Spring Books, 1967), 149. Jarman maintains that Brown's intention was always to re-record the sound back at MGM. Jarman quoted in letter to Kevin Brownlow, December 5, 2010, Brownlow collection; Jarman, interview with Young, 2013.

26. Fadiman, *Intruder in the Dust,* 37; Brown, interview with Brownlow, 1966. For more on Mayer's attitude toward race (which was, in practice, reasonably tolerant and progressive), see Eyman, *Lion of Hollywood,* 320.

27. *Memphis Press Scimitar,* October 12, 1949, 17; Ben Parker, *Memphis Commercial Appeal,* October 12, 1949, 187; Emily Wister, *Charlotte News,* January 23, 1950.

28. *Variety,* October 12, 1949, 6; *New York Times,* November 23, 1949, 19.

29. *New York Post,* December 6, 1949, 37; *Chicago Defender,* November 26, 1949, 27; "Bronze," *Mound Bayou News-Digest,* May 13, 1950, 22.

30. Robert Ellis, *California Eagle,* November 17, 1949, 15, and December 5, 1949, 15; John M. Lee, *California Eagle,* November 24, 1949, 7.

31. Ralph Ellison, "The Shadow and the Act," *Reporter,* December 6, 1949, 19.

32. Jones, "William Faulkner," 55, 68. *Intruder* was included in a showcase of African American noir at San Francisco's Noir City Festival in 2013.

33. Jones, "William Faulkner." See also Fadiman *Intruder in the Dust.*

34. Kael, *Kiss Kiss, Bang Bang,* 284; Fadiman, *Intruder in the Dust.* For recent examinations of the film, see Gene D. Phillips, *Fiction, Film, and Faulkner: The Art of Adaptation* (Knoxville: University of Tennessee Press, 1988); Charles Hannon,

"Race Fantasies: The Filming of Intruder in the Dust," in *Faulkner in Cultural Context,* ed. Donald Kartiganer and Ann Abadie (Jackson: University Press of Mississippi, 1997), 263–83; Stephanie Li, "Intruder in the Dust from Novel to Movie: The Development of Chick Mallison," *Faulkner Journal* 16 (Fall/Spring 2001–2002): 105–18; Williamson, *Faulkner and Southern History.*

28. The Twilight of a Career

1. Brown, interview with Brownlow, 1966.

2. *New York Times,* June 20, 1949, 14; Scheuer, "Brown Champions Work on Location," D4; *Los Angeles Times,* September 24, 1949, 12.

3. Robert Matzen, *Fireball: Carole Lombard and the Mystery of Flight 3* (Pittsburgh: Good Knight Books, 2014).

4. *Washington Post,* November 11, 1950, 4.

5. For more on DeMille and the guild, see Scott Eyman, *Empire of Dreams: The Epic Life of Cecil B. DeMille* (New York: Simon & Schuster, 2013), 399–405; Scott Eyman, *Print the Legend: The Life and Times of John Ford* (New York: Simon & Schuster, 2015); Joseph McBride, *Frank Capra: The Catastrophe of Success* (New York: Touchstone, 1992); Joseph McBride, *Searching for John Ford* (New York: St. Martin's Press, 2001); James Ulmer, "A Guild Divided: How a Fractured Guild Battled over a Loyalty Oath 60 Years Ago—and Ultimately Came Together," *DGA Quarterly* (Spring2011), http://www.dga.org/Craft/DGAQ/All-Articles/1101-Spring-2011/Feature-Loyalty-Oath.aspx; transcript, minutes of Screen Directors Guild (SDG) meeting, October 22, 1950, L. Tom Perry Special Collections, Harold B. Lee Library, Brigham Young University, Provo, UT; Kevin Brianton, *Hollywood Divided: The 1950 Screen Directors Guild Meeting and the Impact of the Blacklist* (Lexington: University Press of Kentucky, 2016).

6. *Variety,* October 11, 1950; Geist, *Pictures Will Talk,* 181.

7. McBride, *Frank Capra,* 573, 597.

8. Ibid., 576.

9. Transcript, SDG minutes, October 22, 1950, 84; Eyman, *Empire of Dreams,* 410.

10. *Variety,* October 11, 1950.

11. *New York Times,* January 9, 1952, 25; *Los Angeles Examiner,* February 2, 1952; *Hollywood Reporter,* February 14, 1952.

12. *New York Times,* January 19, 1951; Janet Leigh, *There Really Was a Hollywood* (New York: Doubleday, 1984), 131.

13. Marvin Kaplan, telephone interview with Young, June 14, 2015.

14. Kingsley quoted in McGilligan, *Backstory 2,* 126–27; *Variety,* August 31, 1951.

15. *Variety,* August 8, 1951; *Los Angeles Times,* September 21, 1951; *Variety,* August 27, 1951, 3; Leonard Maltin, email to Young, April 20, 2009; Brown quoted in McGilligan, *Film Crazy,* 61.

16. Curtis, *Spencer Tracy,* 614.

17. *New York Times*, May 12, 1952; *Variety*, February 28, 1952.

18. For more on Ernest Gébler, see Carlo Gébler, *The Projectionist* (Dublin: New Island Books, 2015).

19. Curtis, *Spencer Tracy*, 624–25.

20. Callow quoted in ibid., 627; Gene Tierney with Mickey Herskowitz, *Self Portrait* (New York: Berkley Books, 1980), 158; letter from Tierney to Brown, n.d., Brown Collection, University of Tennessee.

21. Daniels quoted in Higham, *Hollywood Cameramen*, 73. For more on Brown's engineering background and its role in *The Plymouth Adventure*, see souvenir program, Brown Collection, University of Tennessee.

22. Schary, *Heyday*, 244; *Daily Variety*, October 20, 1952, 3; *Time*, November 24, 1952; Truffaut quoted in Wheeler Winston Dixon, *The Early Film Criticism of François Truffaut* (Bloomington: Indiana University Press, 1993), 147.

23. Gilmore published an account of his experiences titled *Me and My Russian Wife* (New York: Doubleday, 1954). For more on Soviet-US relations and the "Russian brides," see Susan Carruthers, *Cold War Captives: Imprisonment, Escape, and Brainwashing* (Berkeley: University of California Press, 2009), 42–45. Letter from Tierney to Brown, n.d., Brown Collection, University of Tennessee.

24. Tierney, *Self Portrait*, 159; Daves quoted in transcript, SDG minutes, October 22, 1950, 67.

25. Tierney, *Self Portrait*, 159; Michael Barrett, review of *Never Let Me Go*, January 24, 2014, http://www.popmatters.com/post/177869-never-let-me-go/.

26. *Variety*, March 25, 1953, 6; *New York Times*, June 11, 1953, 37.

29. Slow Fade-out

1. Franklin, interview with Brownlow, November 27, 1971, Brownlow collection.

2. Lou Capra to Brownlow, undated notes from a personal conversation, ca. 1973, Brownlow collection; Franklin, interview with Brownlow, November 27, 1971; Kevin Brownlow to Young, November 8, 2001.

3. Charles Brakebill, interview with Young, November 5, 2008, Knoxville, TN.

4. Brakebill and Johnson, conversation with Young, November 5, 2008, Knoxville, TN.

5. Sarris, *American Cinema*, 227; Everson, "Clarence Brown," 577.

6. Joseph McBride quoted in Tom Sweeten, *Knoxville Journal*, July 29, 1977.

7. *Hollywood Reporter*, August 21, 1987.

8. Brown quoted in Ted Thackeray, "Obituary for Clarence Brown," *Los Angeles Times*, August 19, 1987, http://articles.latimes.com/1987-08-19/news/mn-808_1_flight-instructor.

Index

Index

SCREEN CLASSICS

Screen Classics is a series of critical biographies, film histories, and analytical studies focusing on neglected filmmakers and important screen artists and subjects, from the era of silent cinema through the golden age of Hollywood to the international generation of today. Books in the Screen Classics series are intended for scholars and general readers alike. The contributing authors are established figures in their respective fields. This series also serves the purpose of advancing scholarship on film personalities and themes with ties to Kentucky.

SERIES EDITOR

Patrick McGilligan

BOOKS IN THE SERIES